PARENTAL PRIORITIES AND ECONOMIC INEQUALITY

CASEY B. MULLIGAN

Parental Priorities and Economic Inequality

THE UNIVERSITY OF CHICAGO PRESS / CHICAGO AND LONDON

Casey B. Mulligan is assistant professor of economics at the University of Chicago.

The University of Chicago Press, Chicago 60637
The University of Chicago Press, Ltd., London

Printed in the United States of America
06 05 04 03 02 01 00 99 98 97 1 2 3 4 5

ISBN 0-226-54839-2 (cloth)
0-226-54840-6 (paper)

Library of Congress Cataloging-in-Publication Data
Mulligan, Casey B.
Parental priorities and economic inequality / Casey B. Mulligan.
p. cm.
Includes bibliographical references and index.
ISBN 0-226-54839-2 (cloth : alk. paper).—ISBN 0-226-54840-6 (pbk. : alk. paper)
1. Family—Economic aspects—Mathematical models. 2. Parent and child—Economic aspects—Mathematical models. 3. Intergenerational relations—Economic aspects—Mathematical models. 4. Income—Mathematical models. 5. Consumption (Economics)—Mathematical models. 6. Resource allocation—Mathematical models. I. Title.
HQ728.M86 1997
339.2′2—dc21 97-21621
CIP

♾ The paper used in this publication meets the minimum requirements of the American National Standard for Information Sciences—Permanence of Paper for Printed Library Materials, ANSI Z39.48–1992.

In loving memory of Don and Sue Mulligan

CONTENTS

ILLUSTRATIONS

TABLES

ACKNOWLEDGMENTS

This book derives from my 1993 University of Chicago doctoral dissertation entitled "Intergenerational Altruism, Fertility, and the Persistence of Economic Status." I enjoyed guidance from an excellent dissertation committee during the preparation of that material. Nancy Stokey was the chairperson of that committee, which included Bob Lucas, Gary Becker, and—unofficially—Xavier Sala-i-Martin. I was fortunate enough to have the feeling that I was completely unconstrained by the committee while at the same time learning volumes from them.

An entire book might be dedicated to appropriately acknowledging my committee; I use this paragraph to mention only the largest intellectual debts. Nancy strongly encouraged the empirical work, which, although I only appreciated it with a lag, both bolsters my argument and is an important part of what *economists* can contribute to understanding the transmission of inequality across generations. Gary contributed to this book in both interactive and noninteractive modes. I struggled with the idea of endogenizing preferences, thinking long and hard about Gary's 1976 book and his 1977 paper with George Stigler. Perhaps Gary was struggling with the idea too, because our opinions and emphasis appeared to change during our conversations about my dissertation, our emails concerning various drafts of his 1996 book *Accounting for Tastes,* and our various drafts of a paper concerned with modeling patience. "On the Methodology of Endogenizing Preferences" in chapter 1 has changed from its counterpart in my dissertation as a consequence of these interactions with Gary. As a student is prone to do, I often got lost in the details of my dissertation. I was lucky to have Bob "remind" me of the crux of my argument, which he always did under the guise that *he* was the one who was trying to understand. I have also benefited from many hours of

Xavier's teaching and advice, which began with my first economics classes and have continued in quality and quantity until the final draft of this book. I must also thank Nancy and Bob for, in a single day in April 1991, convincing me to leave Harvard and study at Chicago. I suspect that I would not have written a book like this if I had studied elsewhere.

I should point out that my committee did not have to support this research. When I (perhaps unwisely) distributed drafts of my dissertation to major research universities in an effort to obtain a faculty position, I learned that mainstream reactions ranged from outrage and loud disapproval to polite indifference. While they may not agree with sections of this book or even with its methodology and main argument, the committee always gave my work careful consideration and offered highly constructive suggestions.

I also appreciate the advice of several others. Robert Barro and Patti Macellaio read and commented on drafts of my dissertation. Comments on drafts of the book by Tove Edstrand, Claudia Goldin, Song Han, Larry Kotlikoff, Michael Kremer, Bob Margo, Tom Mulligan, Derek Neal, Anna Sjögren, Margo Wilson, and Irina Zavina substantially improved the final product. The research assistance of Song Han and Irina Zavina also resulted in important contributions. Chapter 13 has improved with my learning about principal-agent problems from Tomas Philipson.

Financial and computing support from the Department of Economics, the Division of Social Sciences, and the Social Science and Public Policy Computing Center at the University of Chicago as well as a National Science Foundation Graduate Fellowship are appreciated. The support came at a time when the marginal product was quite high.

CHAPTER 1

The Argument for Parental Priorities

Although inequality appears to be linked with the economy, politics, crime, and other items of substantial interest, its origins are not well understood. This book is about a potentially important source of inequality, the transmission of economic status from one generation to the next. The intergenerational transmission of economic status affects the evolution of inequality over time and the way in which government policies might alter the degree of inequality. Will blacks ever be as rich as whites? If so, when? How long does it take for immigrants to enjoy the success of native-born citizens? How long will the Northeast be the richest region of the United States? How long will Northern Italy be richer than Southern Italy? How do estate and income taxes affect inequality? Can education policies help children from poor families catch up with those from rich families? A theory of the evolution of inequality is necessary to answer these questions. The most important part of such a theory is a model of the intergenerational transmission of inequality.

I present some of the more standard and influential economic models of "intergenerational mobility" or the transmission of inequality from one generation to the next. The standard models emphasize opportunities (or lack of them) for families to borrow, save, and provide schooling for their children. I show that the models are inaccurate and suggest that they are very misleading in regards to the important forces determining intergenerational mobility. My approach to the problem is to model parental priorities by "endogenizing altruism." I answer questions such as "Which parents care more about their children's success?" I use the tools of economics to show how income, wages, taxes, interest rates, and other prices determine which parents are deeply concerned about their children's success and which parents are less concerned. I show how parental priorities translate into economic outcomes for the children and contrast my predictions with the predictions of other economic and noneconomic models. Endogenizing altruism not only delivers a better understanding of the evolution of inequality over time, but it also delivers predictions for a variety of other behavior.

Chapters 2 through 10 are concerned with modeling parental priorities and their relationship with intergenerational mobility. Some of these chapters are theoretical while others analyze a wide variety of data sources that relate to the intergenerational transmission of inequality. Chapters 11 through 13 apply my model of parental priorities to other human interactions, including the distribution of resources among siblings, charitable giving, and the principal-agent problem.

This book takes an economic approach to the problem, and this chapter contrasts this with other reasonable approaches to the issue at hand. One might say, however, that my approach is the modeling of "preferences" rather than the modeling of "incentives" or "markets" that is common practice in economics. Although I think my methods are very standard, it is true that by studying preferences I tackle something that most economists have left to anthropologists, biologists, or psychologists. The novelty of this has met with opposition from many economists, therefore this chapter concludes by addressing some of the criticisms of the methodology that have been raised by my colleagues.

Altruistic Parental Priorities

Economics is about choice. In order to bring choice into the analysis, one has to say something about the objects of choice and the motivation of the people doing the choosing. I suppose that parents make some of the important choices that influence the economic success of their children. In particular, parents decide how to divide their resources between themselves and their children. Resources that are passed on to children—perhaps in the form of educational and health expenditures, financial gifts, or time spent teaching and nurturing them—are important contributors to their economic success. I suppose that, for the most part, parental choices are altruistically motivated. Parents devote some of their resources to children because they *want* their children to be happy and successful.

Parents do not devote all of their resources to their children because their children's success is not their only concern. This concern must be balanced with others, especially the desire of parents to spend on themselves. This study examines how parents balance their priorities and shows how the balancing, through its effects on the transfer of resources to children, affects the economic success of children.

Chapter 2 introduces "indifference curves" and uses them to graphically model parental priorities for readers who are not trained in economics so that they will be better able to follow my argument from an economics perspective.

Two Models of Opportunity and Intergenerational Mobility

Chapter 3 takes models of altruistic parental priorities and combines them with models of family opportunities, deriving implications for parental choices and ultimately the economic success of children. The first of the two models, the "intergenerational permanent income model," has received a great deal of attention in economics. It is, for example, the basis of Robert J. Barro's (1974) "Ricardian Equivalence Theorem," which states that because families rather than governments control the division of resources across generations, government deficits and other policies that attempt to redistribute resources from one generation to the next do not have an important effect on economic activity. Other implications are studied in detail by Gary S. Becker (1991, chapter 6), and by Becker and Nigel Tomes (1979, 1986). In addition to implications for the dynamics of earnings and for the relationship between educational attainment and parental income, the intergenerational permanent income model has strong predictions for the transmission of consumption inequality.

Second is an "imperfect capital markets" or "borrowing constraints" model. It assumes that parents cannot borrow against the earnings of their children and, under some conditions, produces a very different set of predictions than does the permanent income model. The borrowing constraints assumption is at the center of a large fraction of the economic models of intergenerational mobility, including those proposed by Becker and Tomes (1986), Roland Bénabou (1994), Steven Durlauf (1996), Gerhard Glomm and B. Ravikumar (1992), Glenn Loury (1981), and Robert Tamura (1991).

How Altruism Is Influenced by Economic Status

The intergenerational permanent income and borrowing constraint models make predictions for parental choices by modeling the budget sets of (that is, the opportunities available to) families. Chapter 4 instead models parental priorities and uses the model to make predictions for parental choices. I "endogenize altruism," supposing that human nature is basically selfish but that parents make efforts to overcome their selfishness. Parents spend time and goods—which I call "child-oriented resources"—in order to influence their concern for their children. Time spent interacting with children is the most important example of child-oriented resources. I show how macroeconomic variables affect the overall concern for children in the economy and how parental income and wages determine which parents are more or less concerned for their children. I believe that parental attitudes are an important determinant of the success of children, but "attitudes," "moral convictions," or "feelings" are irrelevant for understanding inequality unless they translate into *actions.* Attitudes cannot affect inequality directly, but only through the choices by parents and child, so a final step in my analysis works out how differential parental concerns can translate into parental actions that affect the economic success of children.

Although the modeling of "preferences" or "attitudes" seems unusual for an economist, the model of altruism is really an application of a very standard model in economics, the "complementarity" model. Child-oriented resources and the success of children are complements in my model. Chapter 4 introduces the complementarity model, using "ski trips" and "ski equipment" as everyday examples. Just as we expect income, the price of ski equipment, and the price of ski trips to affect purchases of ski trips, we expect income, the price of consumption, and the price of child-oriented resources to affect purchases of child-oriented resources and therefore parental concern for children.

The model of altruism is one of the main contributions of this book. Chapter 4 therefore emphasizes how the predictions of the "endogenous altruism" model of intergenerational mobility differ from those of the permanent income and borrowing constraints models. The model predicts that, for the bulk of the population, consumption "regresses to the mean" in percentage terms regardless of financial opportunities. Consumption has historically regressed to the mean among the very rich because of fertility decisions, but I predict a reversal of that trend as overall fertility declines. Interest and tax rates are important reasons why parental concern for children changes over time.

Chapter 5 extends the three models to understand the effects of government attempts to redistribute resources from rich to poor. The results there are interesting because they speak to policy questions such as "How does government redistribution affect inequality?" I argue that progressive estate and income taxes are likely to reduce consumption inequality and increase intergenerational consumption mobility, but actually increase earnings inequality. The results also suggest that some, but by no means all, observed intergenerational mobility in the United States can be attributed to the progressivity of estate and income tax codes in place there.

Evidence on the Dynamics of Economic Inequality

The "permanent income," "borrowing constraints," and "government redistribution" models are the main alternatives to my "endogenous altruism" model of intergenerational mobility. Chapters 6 through 8 review a wide variety of evidence on the evolution of inequality over time (evidence that is mainly, but not exclusively, from the United States). The evidence allows the reader to compare the predictions of my model with those of the three main alternatives. Even if a reader is not especially interested in the four models, the evidence presented in chapters 6 through 8 is the kind of evidence that ought to be explained by *any* useful model of intergenerational mobility.

Chapter 6 argues that citizens of the United States have become more equal in terms of wealth, income, or earnings since the Civil War. There has been a slight reversal of this trend in the last fifteen or twenty years. Chapter 7 presents both new and old evidence on the intergenerational transmission of consumption, earnings, and wealth inequality. The empirical work in chapter 8 is especially concerned with the relationship between financial bequests and intergenerational mobility.

The three empirical chapters provide a large body of evidence that can be compared with the predictions of the three economic models presented in chapters 3 through 5. All measures of economic status have, over the period from 1870 to 1990, become substantially more equal. Consumption, earnings, and wealth regress to the mean across generations. These findings are consistent with the endogenous altruism model but inconsistent with the permanent income model. Consumption and wealth are much more persistent than earnings, a finding that is inconsistent with a borrowing constraints model in which the borrowing constraint binds for a sizable majority of households. Consumption does not regress to the mean less rapidly among families making financial bequests while earnings inequality is unrelated to financial inheritance—two more findings that are inconsistent with the borrowing constraints model. Only the endogenous altruism model is consistent with all of the evidence reported in chapters 6 through 8.

Another contribution of this book is to view the distribution of economic status among families, among regions, and among countries as common problems that can and should be studied with common modeling and statistical tools. My view is a strong contrast to that of many macroeconomists who see the distribution of income across countries as a much different problem from the cross-family income distribution. The work by Robert J. Barro and Xavier Sala-i-Martin (1995) and by Paul Romer (1986, 1987) are some widely cited examples. They model specialization and innovation, phenomena which they clearly do not intend to apply at the family level. They report cross-country empirical results from specifications that are remarkably similar to those studied at the family level by Francis Galton (1889), but they do not argue that the cross-country and cross-family evidence are so different that different modeling approaches are necessary. Chapters 6, 7, and 8 argue instead that income mobility across countries, across regions, across ethnic groups, and across families is very similar, suggesting that the best explanation of these observations is a single explanation. Endogenous altruism can be an important part of that single explanation.

Arguments from Other Disciplines

Some of the predictions of the permanent income and borrowing constraints model are inaccurate. The tools of economics can be used to model an important type of preference—the willingness of parents to sacrifice for their children. Why is it desirable to model this preference? The potentially most convincing argument to me and many other economists is that a model of altruism can generate a variety of accurate predictions for intergenerational mobility and other forms of human behavior. But scholars are sometimes convinced by other kinds of arguments, two of which I present in chapters 9 and 10.

Biologists have attempted to model the existence of altruism. Chapter 9 shows that some of the biological models predict not only that altruism should exist, but that it should respond to circumstances. Not all parents should have the same degree of concern for their children.

Chapter 10 argues that the idea that parents differ substantially in their concern for children and that these differences are related to the economic success of children is much older than the relatively modern ideas of "permanent income" or "borrowing constraints." Perhaps the real question is not "why endogenize altruism?" but "why introduce borrowing constraints?"

Other Implications of Endogenous Altruism

The idea that a person can choose his or her degree of concern for others is the cornerstone of my theory of intergenerational mobility. This idea has implications for intergenerational mobility that fit empirical observations better than some commonly used economic models, and my model has some additional implications which are the subject of future work. The final chapters add to the list of empirical implications by applying the idea of endogenous altruism to other forms of human behavior.

Chapter 11 derives predictions for differential treatment of siblings by parents. The analysis shows that the endogenous altruism model can be very different from the standard exogenous altruism model, with the former predicting that parental transfers can aggravate inequality within the family and the latter predicting that parental transfers mitigate inequality. I use the results to reinterpret a variety of studies of family transfers.

Implications for the interactions between charitable organizations and their donors are derived in chapter 12. Using the example of government welfare programs, I show how the altruism of donors can affect the altruism of the beneficiaries of the donation. Chapter 12 also suggests that charitable organizations try to affect the formation of altruism in order to overcome a "free-rider" problem frequently emphasized by economists.

Chapter 13 considers the "principal-agent" problem. A "principal" hires an "agent" to perform some tasks for him. For example, a patient may hire a doctor to cure him, a manager may hire a worker to perform a task, an automobile owner may hire a mechanic to fix his car, or a pollster may "hire" a citizen to truthfully answer some questions. A problem arises because the principal cannot observe the efforts of the agent. If the task is not performed properly, the principal cannot determine whether the agent failed to put forth effort—in which case he might want to withhold payment—or whether it was just bad luck. Chapter 13 introduces endogenous altruism, pointing out that a principal might benefit by teaching his agent to "like" or "be loyal to" him. The more that the agent cares about the principal, the less the principal has to worry about the agent's withholding the necessary effort. For example, a profit-maximizing owner of a corporation may want to hire relatives or old friends as managers even though they are less qualified according to a more "objective" criteria.

Although siblings, charities, and corporations may initially seem to be quite unrelated, my analysis of them is a very straightforward application of the model of the formation of altruism introduced in chapter 4. I show that the everyday "ski trip" and "ski equipment" example introduced there can also be used to understand the models presented in the final three chapters.

Since this book is about the intergenerational transmission of economic status, why do I include some of these other applications of endogenous altruism? I include these other applications because they demonstrate the wide applicability of my basic idea that the degree of altruism is an object of choice. The broad applicability of my idea partially justifies my applying it to the problem of intergenerational mobility. That endogenous altruism can unify a broad range of human behavior increases its appeal as a tool for understanding any particular form of behavior, including the intergenerational transmission of economic status.

Choice and the Economic Approach

Because intergenerational mobility is interesting for so many people, books on this subject could be, and have been, written from a variety of points of view: that of a biologist, an anthropologist, an economist, a historian, a political scientist, a psychologist, or a sociologist. This book emphasizes one approach—an economic approach. I argue that an economic approach, although often unused even by economists, offers unique—and probably accurate—predictions for intergenerational mobility.

I emphasize the uniqueness and the power of an economic approach to the problem. Economics, in my view, is concerned with the implications of *choice* for human behavior. Although other disciplines may at times be concerned with choice and human behavior, choice is the center of economics. Economists' main tools explicitly take choice into account. These tools include maximization in complicated dynamic and stochastic environments, such as those outlined by Gerard Debreu (1959) or Nancy Stokey and Robert E. Lucas, Jr. (1989). They also include statistical methods, such as those outlined by Lars Hansen (1982), James Heckman (1976), and Daniel McFadden (1982), that explicitly incorporate the idea that the human subjects of study are choosing. Consistent with my emphasis on the economic approach, I rely heavily on these kinds of maximization and statistical tools.

As Becker (1976) emphasizes, economics is not solely concerned with money, profits, and the marketplace. I am concerned with parental priorities, something which might seem to be from the realm of psychology or sociology. My departure from other disciplines is to almost exclusively use the tools of economics to study parental priorities and to show how the results are of broader interest.

Nor is the economic approach necessarily mathematical. I heavily employ the maximization and econometric tools, but my analysis is deliberately nonmathematical. My arguments are exposed through a series of simple charts and diagrams in addition to a very few equations. On average, there is about one equation and five illustrations per chapter, with mathematical versions of the analysis relegated to appendices. Although I initially eliminated the technical material in order to broaden the audience, I now believe that my arguments are more informative in this nonmathematical version.

Because mechanical, as opposed to choice-based, models of intergenerational mobility appear so often in economics and other literatures, it appears that the usefulness of an economic approach to intergenerational mobility is not widely accepted. Francis Galton's (1889) classical analysis of characteristics of parents and children, which does not rely on a choice-based theory, is the prototype of many modern empirical studies of intergenerational mobility. These studies include work by Anthony Atkinson (1980), Jere Behrman and Paul Taubman (1990), Arthur Goldberger (1979), C. D. Harbury and D. M. W. N. Hitchens (1979), Paul Menchik

(1979), and Gary Solon (1992).[1] There are few empirical studies that attempt to distinguish economic approaches to intergenerational mobility from mechanical approaches. Basically mechanical theoretical studies by economists include studies by John Conlisk (1974) and Michael Kremer (1996). My theoretical and statistical analyses, in contrast, emphasize the unique implications of the economic approach and utilize the statistical tools appropriate for the study of choice-based behavior.

On the Methodology of Endogenizing Preferences

I take an economic approach to the problem of intergenerational mobility, but an approach that is different from very many other economic approaches.[2] One could view this book as an attempt to endogenize preferences—and I acquiesce to this viewpoint for the purposes of exposition. However, I prefer a different perspective. My so-called endogenizing preferences is hardly different from the household production function analysis of Becker (1965) and K. J. Lancaster (1966).[3] In that analysis, agents take market goods and their time and, using a "household production function," produce consumption services. I might add that the production function is often unobservable to the econometrician (that is, it cannot be estimated from data on inputs *and* outputs because of missing data). I do the same as Becker and Lancaster, supposing that parents combine a particular good—their children's consumption—with their own time and perhaps other market goods to produce "child-oriented services."

The potential danger of my approach is not that it is fundamentally wrong to endogenize preferences, but that I introduce a variable—child-oriented resources—that is potentially unobservable. In this sense, my approach is not much different from, say, human capital theory. The potentially unobservable variable is "child-oriented resources" in my analysis and "human capital" in human capital theory. Anytime a theory appeals to an unobservable, it sacrifices some predictive power. However, like human capital theory, I believe that the approach more than compensates for this because it offers predictions for a wide variety of human behavior. The bulk of this book—chapters 2 through 4 and 11 through 13—is therefore concerned with developing implications of the idea that altruism responds to circumstances and of alternative models of intergenerational

1. See Goldberger (1989) for a comparison of mechanical and economic approaches to intergenerational mobility. Also see chapter 7 or Becker and Tomes (1986) for a survey of many empirical studies of intergenerational mobility.

2. A few economists have studied changing preferences, including Richard Easterlin (1995), Eileen Crimmins et al. (1991), Herbert Gintis (1974), and Robert Pollak (1970), but use a substantially different methodology and address very different problems.

3. See Becker (1996, chapter 1) for more discussion of related methodological issues.

mobility. The remaining chapters are devoted to evaluating the accuracy of some of the predictions of my approach and of alternative approaches. It turns out that my models of the formation of altruism have a large number of empirical implications, too many for all of them to be tested in this book. I therefore focus on a few implications of my approach to intergenerational mobility which contrast with those of some other economic models. Testing of the other implications are left to future research.

I also suggest that my theory does not rely on unobservables as much as it may first appear. In both my analysis and the human capital analysis, the "capital" accumulation may be observed. In the case of human capital theory, we often observe proxies for the human capital investment such as time spent in formal schooling. In the case of child-oriented resources, I argue that time spent by parents with children is an important input—a variable which is measured in some surveys. In the case of loyalty in the principal-agent problem, nepotism, "hiring from within" the firm, and "fair" employee relations can be interpreted as observable investments in loyalty. I also point out that theory often comes before measurement. As human capital theory gained popularity in the 1950s and 1960s, we saw more and more surveys include questions such as "How many years have you spent in school?" or "How much time do you spend learning how to be more productive in your job?" I hope that the surveys of the future include more questions about the time that parents and children spend together and about other activities that produce or encourage altruistic behavior among individuals.

PART 1
Modeling Altruism and Intergenerational Mobility

CHAPTER 2

Indifference Curve Diagrams as Models of Parental Priorities

In order to begin a theory of parental priorities and their effects on economic inequality, this chapter presents a very standard economic model of parental priorities. This graphical presentation will provide obvious information to readers familiar with the basic Fisherian (1930) intertemporal model of consumption.

Three main ideas are presented in the economic model of parental priorities and defined: (1) intergenerational altruism; (2) preference for moderation; and (3) homothetic preferences. The idea of intergenerational altruism is introduced, followed by a two-period intergenerational model and a discussion of how it is related to a "more realistic" multiperiod model. The three intermediate sections introduce the "indifference curve" diagrams and show how they display the basic ideas of intergenerational altruism and parental preferences for moderation. Homothetic preferences are defined in a final section.

A model of parental priorities is only one part of a full economic model of intergenerational mobility. A model of parental priorities is not enough to predict parental choices unless we say something about the *opportunities* available to a family. Chapter 3 introduces two models of opportunity and combines them with the model of parental priorities from this chapter to say something about the transmission of inequality across generations. The first model is the "permanent income model," which emphasizes the participation of families in a capital market in order to transfer resources across generations. The second model of opportunities assumes that capital market transactions are less typical.

A very standard economic model of parental priorities is presented here. Chapter 4 replaces that model with a newer, richer, and more realistic model. I show that, together with the permanent income model of opportunities, the newer model has more accurate predictions for intergenerational mobility, charitable giving, principal-agent relationships, and other human behavior.

Altruism

All of the models in this book—and many in the economics literature—begin with the idea of altruism, especially intergenerational altruism—altruism of parents for children. By assumption, parents are concerned about their own economic status as well as that of their children. Economic status, which I refer to as "consumption," includes material purchases such as food, clothing, cars, houses, and vacations. To the extent that economic resources determine their purchases, items such as prestige and respect might also be included as consumption.

Timing of Parental and Child Consumption

Parents, of course, are older than their children. Some parental consumption therefore occurs earlier in time than does consumption by children. The time line in figure 2.1 is a fairly realistic model of the birth and death of generations. Beginning with the early adulthood of the parents, the first main event is the birth of children. Next children become adults and have their own children. Parents die and the cycle goes on for future generations. I mark to the left of the time line how these life-cycle events relate to the timing of consumption by parents, children, and grandchildren.

For the derivation of the main implications developed here, it is reasonable to collapse lifetimes into a single period.[1] I therefore simplify figure 2.1 and think about a world with a sequence of periods: 1, 2, 3, 4, . . . , where parents consume in period one, children consume in period two, grandchildren consume in period three, etc. In fact, it is even easier—and not misleading—to discuss many issues in the context of a two-period world.[2] parents consume in period 1, children consume in period 2, and then the world ends. To emphasize that the analysis applies to any parent-child pair rather than to only one patriarch and his child, I generically refer to periods t and $(t + 1)$ rather than a particular pair of adjacent periods, such as periods 1 and 2.

1. See Nigel Tomes (1979) for an opposing view.

2. Appendix H of Gary Becker's work (1991, chapter 7) shows that the main implications for this two-period world carry over to a multiperiod world with a long sequence of generations as suggested in figure 2.1. Grandparents do not give directly to children in the two-period model. As an empirical matter, grandparents do give directly to children, but a large fraction of the giving may be on behalf of parents for tax reasons. If so, the two-period model is basically consistent with observed grandparental transfers even though they are not modeled explicitly.

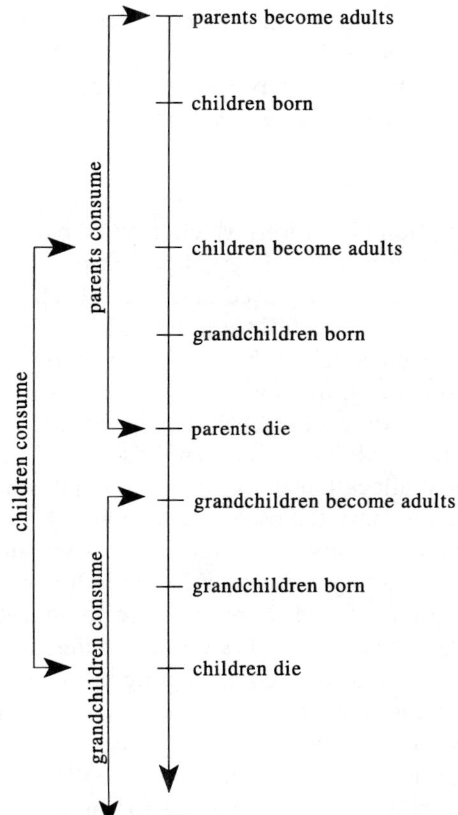

2.1 Intergenerational Time Line

For the sake of exposition, I assume for the time being that parents have only one child. Chapters 4 and 11 expand the analysis to include multiple children. I show that many of the implications developed with this single-child model of parental priorities carry over to some multiple child models.

I use the term *consumption allocation* to refer to a particular quantity of consumption for the parents and a particular quantity of consumption for the child. For example, ($1,000, $2,000) is a consumption allocation—the parents consume $1,000 and the child consumes $2,000. ($10,000, $5,000) is another consumption allocation.

Basic Properties of Parental Preferences

Parental preferences are assumed to have a few basic properties. First, more is assumed to be better. If a child were to have more consumption without sacrificing the consumption of the parent, the parent would be happier. Second, although they are not necessarily assumed to desire a equal division of consumption between parents and children, parents are assumed to prefer some kind of moderation.

Indifference Curve Diagrams

The set of consumption allocations which leaves a parent indifferent—or equally happy—is drawn in the $[c_t, c_{t+1}]$ plane as an indifference curve.[3] Two indifference curves are displayed in figure 2.2. The child consumes a lot and the parent consumes a little at point or allocation *A*. By comparison, the parent consumes relatively more at allocation *B*. At allocation *C*, the child consumes slightly more than at allocation *B*, but the parent consumes a lot less. Allocations *A* and *B* lie on the same indifference curve, so the parent is indifferent between those two allocations. The parent consumes less at allocation *A*, but the additional consumption by the child is just enough to leave the parent equally happy.

Since more is better, points to the northeast of any allocation must be preferred to that allocation. According to the indifference curves drawn in figure 2.2, allocations *A* and *B* are preferred to allocation *C*. This follows from the drawing because *C* lies on an indifference curve that is to the southwest of the indifference curve passing through allocations *A* and *B*. Notice that, for allocation *C*, the parent consumes slightly more than at point *A*. The parent still prefers allocation *A* because the child enjoys a substantially higher level of consumption—more than enough (according to the preferences shown in the diagram) to compensate for the lesser consumption by parents. But this result depends on the particular way that the indifference curves are drawn in figure 2.2. Consider figure 2.3. The same three allocations *A*, *B*, and *C* are displayed as in figure 2.2, but two indifference curves are drawn in figure 2.3 which represent a different set of parental priorities than are displayed in figure 2. 2. Now allocation *C* is preferred to allocations *A* and *B*. The large increase in the child's consumption as one moves from allocation *C* to allocation *A* is not enough to compensate this parent for the slight decrease in parental consumption.

Figures 2.2 and 2.3 both suggest that "moderation" is preferred, but to different degrees. *C* is a more moderate allocation than allocations *A* and *B* because, relatively speaking, consumption is less skewed toward either of the parties. At a skewed allocation such as *A*, parents are very willing to substitute away from the child's consumption and toward their own

3. A consumption allocation is displayed as a point in the $[c_t, c_{t+1}]$ plane. Horizontal distance from the origin represents the quantity of consumption by parents (c_t) and the vertical distance represents the quantity of consumption by the child (c_{t+1}).

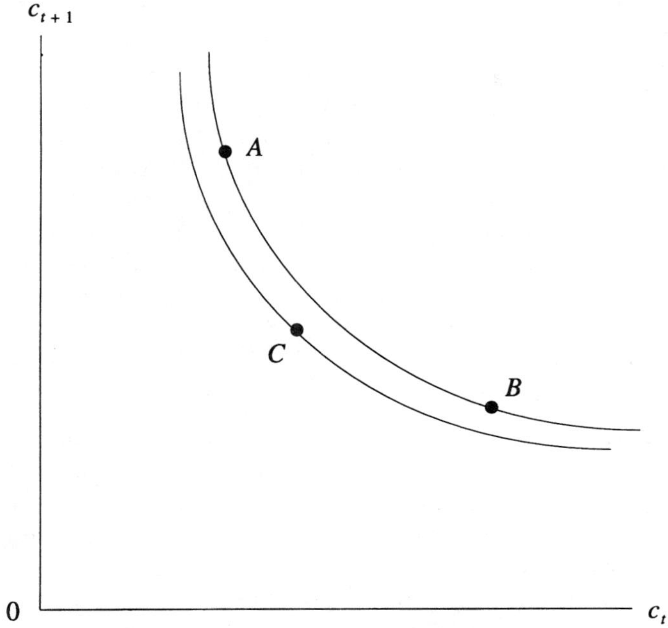

2.2 Parental Priorities Displayed as "Indifference Curves"

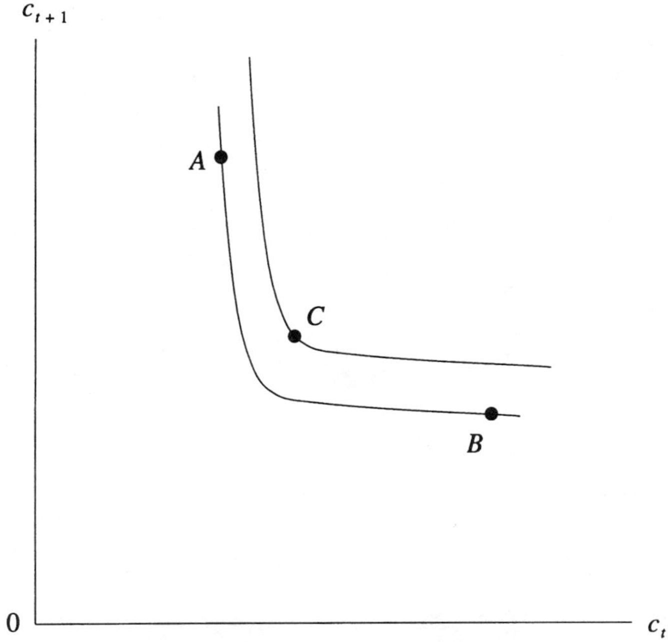

2.3 A Different Set of Parental Priorities

consumption. This can be seen in both figures from the relatively vertical orientation of the indifference curve at allocation *A* as compared with allocation *B* or *C*. A vertical indifference curve, by definition, means that parents will give up a lot of the child's consumption for a little of their own. At point *B* the indifference curve is relatively horizontal, so parents will give up some of their child's consumption only if they are compensated by a large increase in their own consumption. Notice that a stronger preference for moderation appears in an indifference diagram as more sharply curved indifference curves, as in figure 2.3. More gently curved indifference curves, such as those shown in figure 2.2, indicate a weaker preference for moderation.

Intergenerational Altruism

In addition to the degree of preference for moderation, parental preferences can also be characterized according to their degree of intergenerational altruism. More altruistic parents are relatively more concerned about their child's consumption than are less altruistic parents. Figure 2.4 uses the indifference curve diagrams to compare the priorities of more altruistic and less altruistic parents. Indifference curves of more altruistic

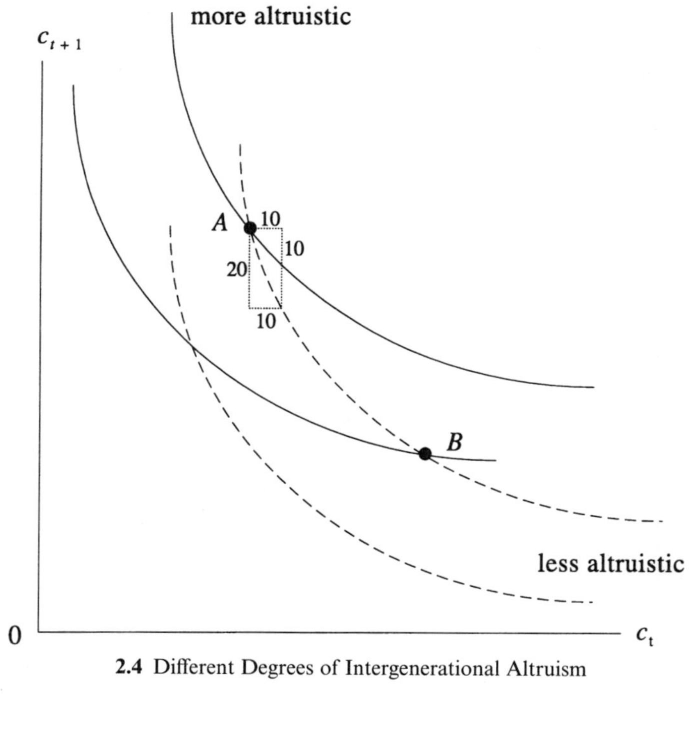

2.4 Different Degrees of Intergenerational Altruism

parents are shown as solid curves; those of less altruistic parents are shown as dashed curves.

Consider the allocation *A*. The more altruistic parents have the flatter indifference curve—they require less of an increment to their child's consumption (for example, the $10 shown in small print in the figure) in order to justify a given sacrifice of their own consumption (the $10 shown in the figure) then are the less altruistic parents (who, in the figure, need $20 more consumption for their children to justify the same parental sacrifice). Equivalently, a flatter indifference curve means that parents are willing to give up more of their own consumption for a given increment to their child's consumption. The same is true at allocation *B*—the less altruistic parents will give up less of their own consumption in order to increase that of their children. Roughly speaking, figure 2.4 suggests that more altruism has the effect of shifting indifference curves to the northwest.

Altruism and Economic Status

Indifference curve diagrams can also model the effect of economic status on parental priorities. Consider figure 2.5. As in the previous figures, parental priorities are displayed as indifference curves. Also shown in the

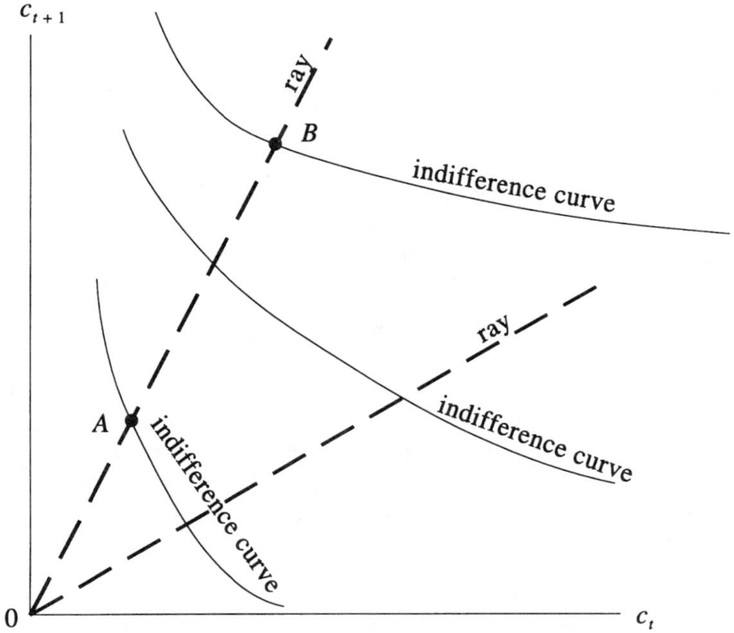

2.5 Altruism and Economic Status

figure as dashed lines are rays emanating from the origin. Notice that, as one follows a ray from the origin, consumption of both the parents and child increase, but their *ratio* c_{t+1}/c_t does not.[4] For example, c_{t+1}/c_t is the same for both allocations *A* and *B* because both are on the same ray. Higher rays correspond to higher c_{t+1}/c_t ratios.

We can imagine that richer families will be on indifference curves to the northeast because they can afford more of both parental and child consumption. Poorer families can afford less, so they are on indifference curves that are nearer the origin of the diagram. So as one moves along a ray, say from allocation *A* to allocation *B*, there is, effectively, an increase in wealth.[5] That is because any parents that can afford both *A* and *B* would never choose *A*. A family that chooses *A* must not be able to afford *B*.

Now let's study the slope of the indifference curves as one moves along a ray from *A* to *B*. The indifference curve at *B* is flatter than is the indifference curve at *A*. This means that parents are more willing to give up their consumption at allocation *B* than they are at allocation *A*. So, as the indifference curves are drawn in figure 2.5, richer parents tend to prefer higher rays than do poorer parents. In other words, richer parents tend to allocate a larger *share* of their resources to the consumption of their children.

Of course, the indifference curves could be drawn in a different way so that poor parents prefer a higher ratio c_{t+1}/c_t. Which way *should* they be drawn? It's hard to say without a *theory* of how economic status and parental priorities interact. The standard economic models presented in the next chapter are theories of economic opportunities, not parental priorities, so they make the neutral assumption that intergenerational altruism is unrelated to economic status. In terms of our indifference diagrams, this means that all indifference curves have the same slope along a given ray. This is the case for the indifference curves shown in figure 2.6. For example, the slope of the indifference curve at *A* is the same as at *B*. Preferences that are "neutral" in this way—slopes of all indifference curves are the same along a fixed ray—are said to be *homothetic.*

Although the standard economic model of parental priorities is neutral on the relationship between intergenerational altruism and economic status, the object of this book is to build a model of the formation of altruism and derive the implications of that model for economic inequality. Chapter 4 presents such a model, which has a lot more to say about parental priorities than the standard economic model displayed in figure 2.6.

4. This result follows from the definition of a ray: a ray in the $[c_t, c_{t+1}]$ plane is a set of points for which c_{t+1}/c_t is always the same.

5. Wealth, income, and other economic variables are more carefully defined in the models of economic opportunity presented in chapter 3.

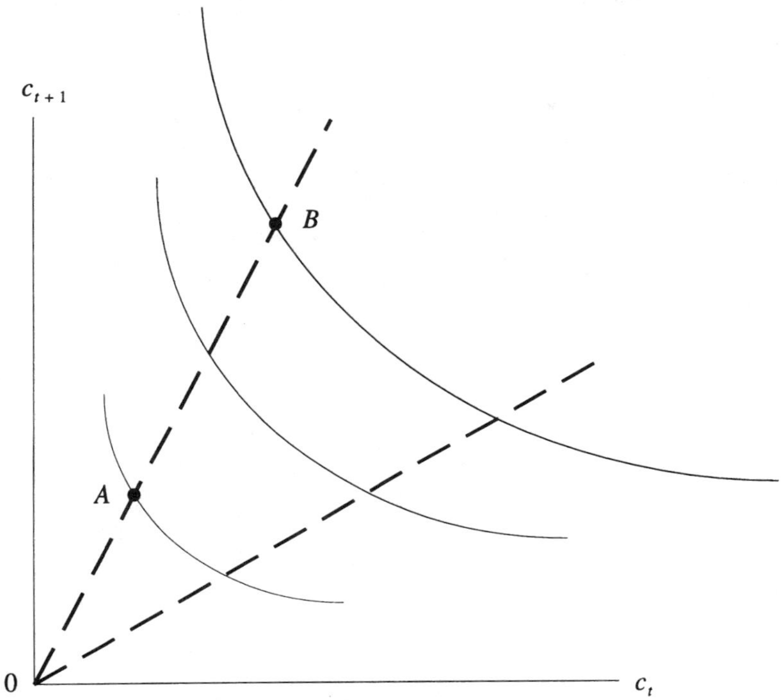

2.6 Homothetic Parental Preferences

Summary

Parents are concerned about their consumption and about consumption by their children. Although parents care about consumption by children, the model does not rule out the possibility that parents may be much more concerned about their own consumption. Such a case is modeled as a very low degree of intergenerational altruism.

In a two-period intergenerational model, parental preferences can be displayed as indifference curves. Those indifference curves model three properties of parental preferences: intergenerational altruism, preference for moderation, and homotheticity. High intergenerational altruism is modeled with indifference curves that are skewed toward the northwest in the $[c_t, c_{t+1}]$ plane. With low altruism, indifference curves are skewed to the southeast. Preference for moderation is modeled with the curvature of indifference curves. Parents who strongly (weakly) prefer moderation have very (slightly) curved indifference curves. Homotheticity is the idea that parental willingness to sacrifice their consumption for that of their children is independent of economic status and is graphically modeled with indifference curves whose slope does not change as one moves away from the origin along a ray.

A model of parental priorities is only part of a full economic model of intergenerational mobility. Chapter 3 introduces the "permanent income" and "imperfect capital markets" models of opportunity and combines them with the model of parental priorities from this chapter to say something about the transmission of inequality across generations.

A very standard economic model of parental priorities is presented here; chapter 4 replaces that model with a newer, richer, and more realistic model.

CHAPTER 3
Two Models of Opportunity and Intergenerational Mobility

Introduction

Chapter 2 shows how economists often model parental concern for children. However, a model of parental priorities is not enough to predict parental choices unless we say something about the *opportunities* available to a family. This chapter presents two models of family opportunities: the "intergenerational permanent income" model and the "imperfect capital markets" model. I show how those models, together with a model of parental priorities, have predictions for parental choices and the intergenerational transmission of inequality. The validity of these predictions are the focus of the three empirical chapters that constitute Part 2.

The models of opportunity here and the model of parental priorities from chapter 2 have appeared in previous economic research. This book builds on that previous research in four ways. First, I derive an extensive list of empirical implications of those models—that is the goal of this and the previous chapter. Second, chapters 6, 7, and 8 thoroughly review the available evidence on those predictions, showing that much observed behavior remains unexplained. Third, I propose in chapter 4 an alternative model of parental priorities and derive its predictions for intergenerational mobility. Fourth, I show in the chapters in Part 4 how the same model of altruism has predictions for a variety of other human behavior.

The graphical analysis of dynamic consumption problems outlined in this chapter is due to Irving Fisher (1930), although he applied the analysis to life-cycle consumption and savings and did not pursue implications for the dynamics of inequality. Milton Friedman (1976) and others have used these diagrams to analyze the dynamics of inequality. The important idea that parents transfer human capital to children until diminishing returns set in and then transfer financial assets appears in a large economics literature, including work by Gary Becker (1975), Alan S. Blinder (1974), and Becker and Nigel Tomes (1979).

Becker (1991) and Becker and Tomes (1986) algebraically derive many of the implications of the permanent income and imperfect capital markets models. My presentation differs in four ways. First, its graphical rendering displays the fundamental assumptions and logical steps of the argument more prominently and is more accessible to noneconomists. Second, my presentation emphasizes the role played by parental priorities in the derivation of the main implications. Third, implications for the inequality of consumption and wealth are treated as primary. Implications for earnings are seen as secondary, a departure from Becker and Tomes that follows from my argument that the consumption implications are those that are especially unique to an economic analysis. Fourth, my presentation provides the economic justification for the statistical procedures—especially instrumental variables and maximum likelihood techniques—that I use in Part 2.

Before presenting the two models of opportunities and intergenerational mobility, allow me to define "intergenerational persistence" and "intergenerational mobility." The *intergenerational persistence* of income, earnings, wealth, or other variable is the fraction of differences among parents that is typically observed among their adult children. I measure intergenerational persistence in *logarithmic* or percentage terms. Consider two sets of parents whose incomes differ by 50 percent. If, on average, the incomes of their children differ by 20 percent, then the intergenerational persistence of income is said to be 0.4 or 40 percent. An equivalent way of thinking about the intergenerational persistence of a variable Y is in terms of a regression equation.

$$\ln Y^i_{t+1} = \alpha + \beta \ln Y^i_t + \varepsilon^i_{t+1} \tag{3.1}$$

α and β are constants. I refer to Y as "income," but it could refer to earnings, years of schooling, wealth, or another variable. Equation 3.1 can be thought of as generating the income of family i's children (Y^i_{t+1}) according to two influences: family i parental income (Y^i_t) and other influences (ε^i_{t+1}). "Other influences" are, by definition, unrelated to parental income. Luck, intelligence, or a willingness to work are candidate other influences to the extent that they are unrelated to parental income. According to equation 3.1, a 1 percent difference in parental incomes is associated, on average, with a β percent difference in the incomes of children. In the 20 percent/50 percent example above, $\beta = .4$.

In principle, β could be zero. $\beta = 0$ means that parental income differences are not associated with income differences among children. If relatively high parental income were associated with relatively *low* incomes of children, then β would be negative. β can also be larger than one if parental income differences (in percentage terms) are associated with even larger income differences among children.[1] Although β could conceivably be any real number, the vast majority of empirical estimates of β are between 0 and 1. I therefore refer to the quantity $(1 - \beta)$ as the *degree of intergenerational mobility* or *the degree of regression to the mean.* More mobility therefore means less persistence and more persistence means less mobility. $\beta = 0$, for example, implies no intergenerational persistence and a degree of intergenerational mobility of 1 (or "perfect" mobility). $\beta = 1$ implies "perfect" persistence and no mobility. β between zero and one means that there is both mobility and persistence. Incomes are said to "regress away from the mean" when $\beta > 1$.

The perfect mobility case—$\beta = 0$—is often referred to as perfect "equality of opportunity" because the income of a child is unrelated to the income of his or her parents. The degree of intergenerational mobility is therefore an index of the degree of "equality of opportunity." Equality of opportunity is often seen as desirable because, with little correlation between the incomes of parents and children, children from rich families do not enjoy much of a "head start" on children from poor families. Equality of opportunity is often distinguished from "equality of outcome" because the former only implies $\beta = 0$, while the latter implies that all children have identical incomes: $\beta = 0$ *and* ε^i_{t+1} the same for all families.

Throughout the book, I refer to "regression to the mean" in *logarithmic* or percentage terms. Because of economic growth, regression to the mean in percentage terms is more interesting than, say, regression to the mean in absolute terms. Economic growth alone tends to multiply everyone's income, which produces regression away from the mean in absolute terms but not in percentage terms.[2] Measuring mobility in percentage terms is also consistent with several measures of inequality used in the economics literature, especially the standard deviation of log income.

1. β is closely related to the correlation ρ between the log income of parents and the log income of children:

$$\beta = \rho \frac{sd(\ln Y_{t+1})}{sd(\ln Y_t)}$$

where $sd(x)$ denotes the standard deviation of the variable x. Since $sd(\ln Y)$ is a commonly used index of inequality, it can be said the β is the intergenerational correlation of log income when inequality is not changing over time. However, I show in the text how changes in inequality over time depend on the magnitude of β.

2. Suppose, for example, that *A*'s father earned $1,000 per year and *B*'s father earned $10,000 per year back in the days when $10,000 was more than enough to buy a house. Now *A* earns $100,000 and *B* earns $109,000. This is not regression to the mean in absolute terms, but it is strong regression to the mean in percentage terms.

The Permanent Income View of Intergenerational Mobility

This section outlines the permanent income view of intergenerational mobility. The first part presents the simplest version of the intergenerational permanent income model where earnings of parent and child are exogenous, while the second part derives the main implications of the permanent income model for intergenerational mobility. Earnings of children are—more realistically—assumed in the third part to depend on parental investments. I show that endogenizing children's earnings does not change the main implications of the permanent income model, although some additional predictions are obtained. The main assumptions and implications are reviewed in the conclusion of this section. Readers familiar with a Fisherian (1930) analysis of consumption and savings and its application to the dynamics of inequality will find the first three parts to be a review of this analysis.

Economic Opportunities with Exogenous Earnings

Given the notation of chapter 2, I use c_t to denote consumption by parents and c_{t+1} to denote consumption by a child. Suppose that the parent will earn e_t during his lifetime and the child will earn e_{t+1}. "Earnings" can include any "unearned" income that results from savings that accumulate during either the parents' or the child's lifetime but should exclude unearned income of the child that derives from transfers from the parents. The earnings e_t and e_{t+1} are plotted as a square dot in the $[c_t, c_{t+1}]$ plane, labeled "earnings endowment" in figure 3.1.[3] The purpose here is to derive "budget constraints"—the set of affordable consumption allocations—and show that all families have budget constraints with the same slope. What follows shows that this "same slope" result has implications for intergenerational mobility.

Clearly it is feasible for the parent to consume e_t and for the child to consume e_{t+1}.[4] If the parents were to save some of their earnings rather than consuming it all, then the savings could be accumulated and passed on to the child and the child could consume this amount over and above his own earnings.[5] For example, suppose the parent saves $\$x_{t+1}$ and that

3. In a model with more than two generations, parents may receive assets from grandparents. If so, the grandparental inheritance can be included with parental earnings for the purpose of locating the endowment point in the $[c_t, c_{t+1}]$ plane.

4. If there are taxes or other "nonconsumption" items that must be purchased, then e can be defined to be earnings net of any of these nonconsumption purchases. Income, estate, and gift taxes are studied carefully in chapter 5.

5. The parental savings might accumulate in a bank account, a portfolio of stocks and bonds, a family business, or a home.

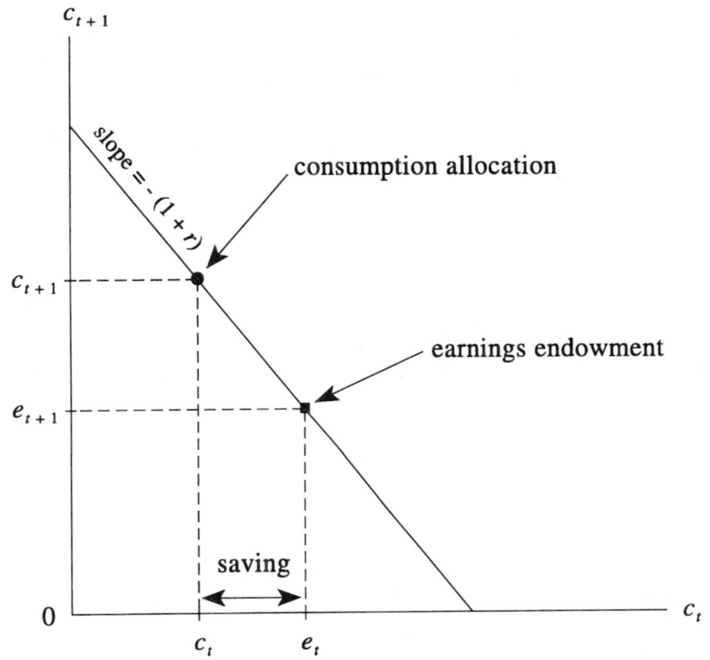

3.1 Parents Save for Children

the savings accumulate interest by the time the child receives them. The child receives the amount $\$x_{t+1}(1 + r)$ from his parents—$\$x_{t+1}$ is the initial savings of the parents and $\$rx_{t+1}$ is the accumulated interest—so he can consume $e_{t+1} + x_{t+1}(1 + r)$. Such a consumption allocation is displayed as a round dot in figure 3.1.

The round and square dots can be used to graphically compute parental savings x_{t+1}. x_{t+1} is simply the difference between parental earnings e_t and parental consumption c_t. x_{t+1} is displayed graphically as the horizontal distance between the earnings endowment and the consumption allocation and is shown as "saving" in figure 3.1. The more the parent saves, the larger is x_{t+1}, and the farther to the northwest of the earnings point we move in the figure. The rate at which parental savings turns into additional consumption for the child depends on the interest rate r. For example, an interest rate of $r = 1$ means that $1,000 saved by the parent accumulates $1,000 in interest so that the child can consume an additional *two* thousand dollars. If instead the interest rate were zero, the child would only consume an additional $1,000. The interest rate manifests itself in figure 3.1 as the slope of the line between the consumption allocation and the earnings endowment. A high interest rate means that parents can give up

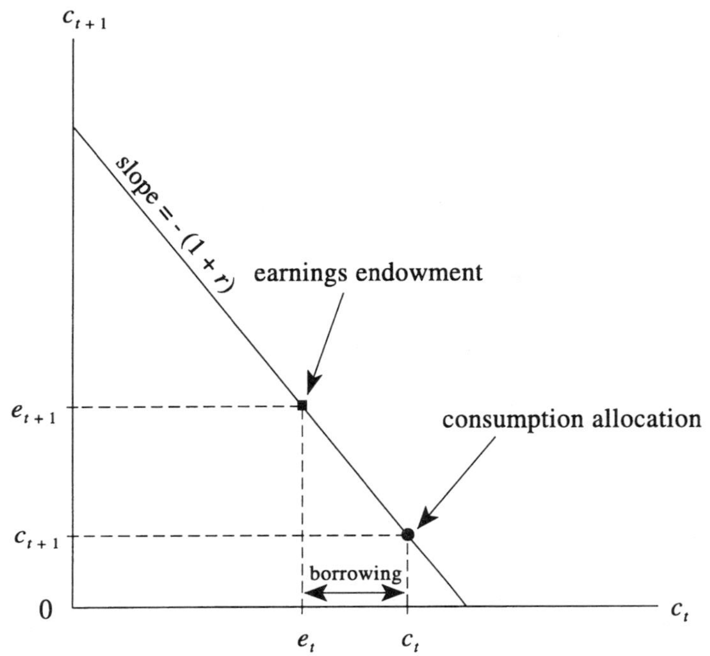

3.2 Parents Borrow from Children

a little consumption and obtain a lot of additional consumption for their child so that savings would result in a consumption allocation that would be above and only slightly to the left of the earnings endowment in figure 3.1. By contrast, the consumption allocation would be almost as much to the left as it is above the earnings endowment if the interest rate were close to zero.

Similarly, imagine that a parent might consume more than his earnings, go into debt, and pass the debt on to his children. This may not be possible in the "real world" because no bank would lend to such a parent or because the government does not allow such behavior, but let's consider the possibility for the sake of argument. Borrowing corresponds to a *negative* amount for x_{t+1} and movements to the southeast in figure 3.2. We assume that the rate of interest charged to borrowers is the same as the rate of interest r paid to lenders. If, for example, parents borrow \$1,000 during their lifetime, they are able to consume \$1,000 more than their earnings e_t. Their child has to pay back the amount $1{,}000(1 + r)$, so he must consume this amount less than his earnings.

What might be the form of borrowing in the "real world?" Families might borrow from a bank to finance schooling for a child and that loan be paid back to the bank later by the adult child when he or she has a job. Another possibility is for middle-aged parents to sacrifice assets that they would otherwise save for retirement to finance investments in the human capital of a child. Years later, the child enjoys a higher level of earnings as a result of the human capital investments and some of those earnings are given to retired parents to repay them for their sacrifice of retirement assets. Even when parents do not finance the schooling of a child, he or she may (perhaps with a little convincing) provide resources for elderly parents.

Parents have a range of choices for the consumption allocation. They can save zero so that $c_t = e_t$ and $c_{t+1} = e_{t+1}$. They can choose some allocations to the northwest of their earnings endowment by saving the appropriate amount or they can choose some allocations to the southeast by borrowing the appropriate amount. The interest rate dictates exactly how they can do this. A single interest rate therefore presents a whole *line* of choices in the figure—a line that includes (e_t, e_{t+1}) and has slope $-(1 + r)$. Actually, a whole triangle of choices are available: those on the line and those to the southwest of the line. I refer to the line as the *intergenerational budget constraint* and to the triangle as the *intergenerational budget set.* I do not emphasize the distinction between the budget constraint and the budget set because the interesting part of the budget set is its northeast border, the budget constraint. The northeast border is most interesting because "more is better." No parent would choose any point in the budget set that was not on the northeast border.

Now let's consider the economic opportunities of two different families: one with rich parents and one with poor parents. For the time being, assume that the child earns the same in each family (the following section on "Opportunities and Inequality with Parental Investments in Children" allows the earnings of children to be related to the earnings of parents). Rich parents have higher earnings than do poor parents: $e_t^{\text{rich}} > e_t^{\text{poor}}$. As illustrated, feasible consumption choices lie on a line passing through the earnings endowment with slope $-(1 + r)$. The rich endowment is to the right of the poor endowment, so the rich budget constraint is to the northeast of the poor budget constraint. *Because both families face the same interest rate, their budget constraints are parallel.*

Figures 3.1, 3.2, and 3.3 also show that the distribution of earnings between parents and child does not affect the opportunities facing the family. If, for example, one were to reduce parental earnings by $1,000 and increase earnings of the child by $1,000*(1 + r), this would appear as a movement to the northwest by the square dot in figures 3.1 and 3.2. However, because the square dot would remain on the same line with slope $-(1 + r)$, the budget constraint is unchanged. It is the discounted sum

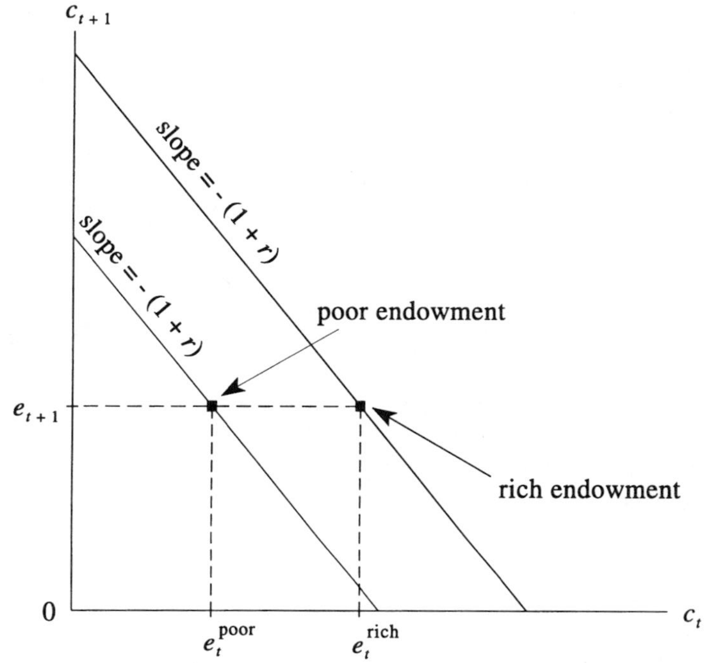

3.3 Budget Sets of Rich and Poor Families Compared

$[e_t + e_{t+1}/(1 + r)]$ that determines the position of the budget constraint. Any reallocation of earnings from parents to children that does not change this sum—such as a parental reduction of \$1,000 and a child increase of \$1,000*(1 + r)—does not change the budget constraint. Because the position of the intergenerational budget constraint is determined by $[e_t + e_{t+1}/(1 + r)]$, a kind of average across generations of earnings, this model is referred to as a "intergenerational permanent income model" or a "dynastic wealth model."[6]

The Transmission of Inequality with Exogenous Earnings

Now that both parental priorities and parental opportunities have been modeled, parental choices can be derived—parents choose their favorite feasible allocation. To derive the choice graphically, indifference curves are placed in the same diagram as the budget set. I show how the result from the previous section—that all families have parallel budget constraints—has implications for intergenerational consumption mobility.

Three indifference curves are displayed and labeled as U_1, U_2, U_3 in

6. The term "permanent income" was used by Milton Friedman (1957) in reference to a very similar model that he used to study life-cycle consumption and savings.

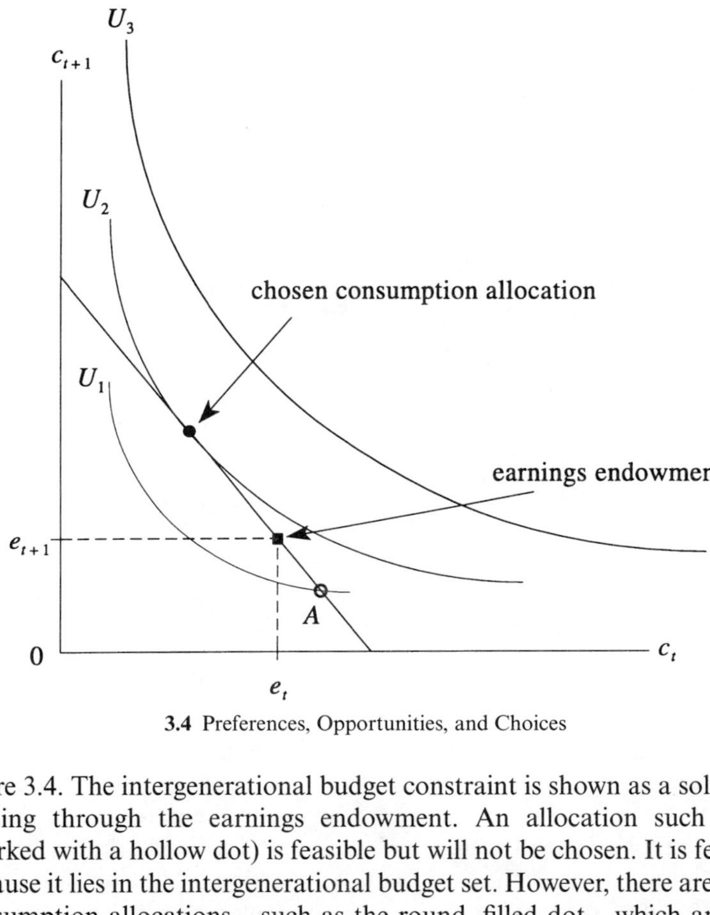

3.4 Preferences, Opportunities, and Choices

figure 3.4. The intergenerational budget constraint is shown as a solid line passing through the earnings endowment. An allocation such as *A* (marked with a hollow dot) is feasible but will not be chosen. It is feasible because it lies in the intergenerational budget set. However, there are other consumption allocations—such as the round, filled dot—which are also feasible and are preferred. Figure 3.4 shows that the round, filled dot is preferred to the hollow dot because the former lies on an indifference curve U_2 that is higher than the indifference curve U_1 passing through *A*. The chosen allocation must lie on the edge of the intergenerational budget set at a point where the corresponding indifference curve is tangent. Tangency, of course, means that the two have the same slope at the chosen allocation. We have derived that the slope of the budget constraint is $-(1 + r)$, so it follows that the indifference curve has slope $-(1 + r)$ at the chosen allocation.

Now consider changing the earnings endowment in a such a way that the intergenerational budget constraint shifts. This could be achieved, for example, by increasing earnings of the parent while holding child earnings constant. Because there is a new budget set, there will be a new choice. Such an earnings endowment is shown in figure 3.5 with the correspond-

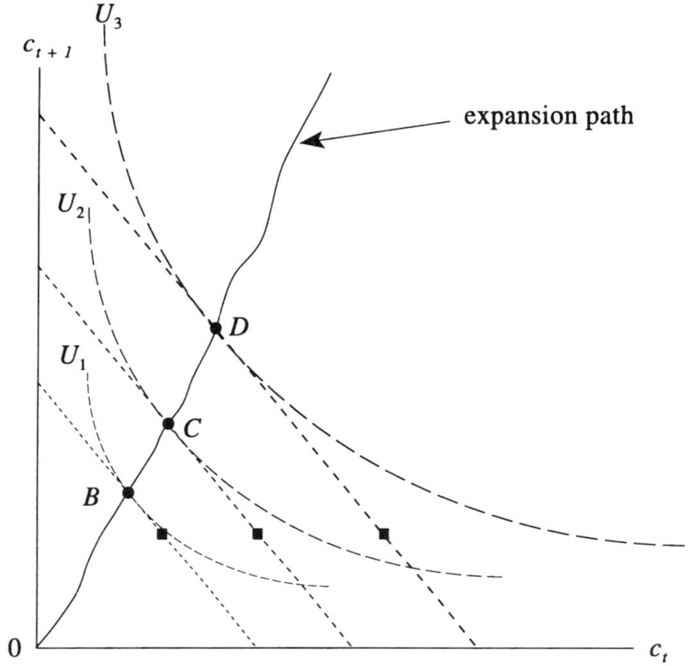

3.5 Derivation of the "Expansion Path"

ing choice shown as allocation *D*. The new budget constraint is parallel and to the northeast of the old constraint. The new choice *D*, according to the preferences drawn in figure 3.5, is also to the northeast of the old choice *C*. If one, instead, were to reduce parental earnings, the new budget constraint would be to the southwest. A reduction is also shown in figure 3.5, with the corresponding choice labeled as allocation *B*.

Holding fixed the rate of interest, one could consider all of the different choices that could occur for different parallel movements of the intergenerational budget constraint. The *expansion path* is the curve displaying all of the choices, including the choices *B, C,* and *D*.

There is a different expansion path for every rate of interest. A higher rate of interest, for example, means that the intergenerational budget constraints are steeper. The top panel of figure 3.6 displays the intergenerational budget constraints associated with a higher interest rate as dashed lines. Those associated with lower interest rates appear as dotted lines in the top panel. Curvature of indifference curves implies that the tangency of the indifference curves and high interest rate budget constraints occurs at allocations to the northwest. A higher interest rate therefore shifts the expansion path to the northwest.

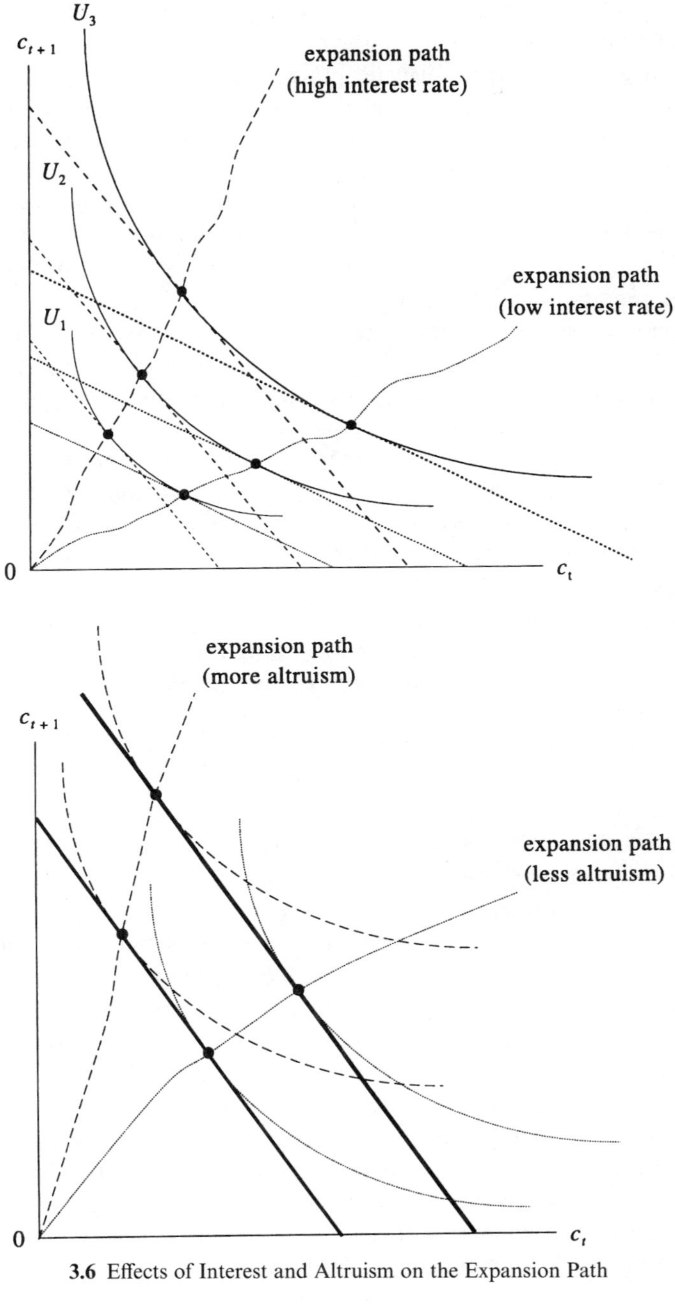

3.6 Effects of Interest and Altruism on the Expansion Path

Each set of preferences also has its own expansion path. More altruistic parental preferences are shown in the bottom panel of figure 3.6 as dashed indifference curves. Less altruistic preferences are shown as dotted indifference curves. The lower panel shows that more altruistic preferences mean that chosen allocations are more to the northwest. More altruism therefore shifts the expansion path to the northwest.

The expansion path does not depend on the earnings or income of parents or children. Instead it shows—for a single interest rate and a single set of preferences—all possible choices that could occur for different values of parental and child earnings.

Because an increase in either altruism or interest rates shifts the expansion path to the northwest, one expects altruism and interest rates to be positively correlated with savings and long-run economic growth. To see this, notice that the ratio c_{t+1}/c_t—which is higher on an expansion path that is to the northwest—is a measure of long-run economic growth; a higher ratio means that children do well relative to their parents. Also notice in figure 3.1 that a consumption allocation further to the northwest is associated with a larger quantity of savings.

The permanent income model predicts that all families in the economy, regardless of wealth, have intergenerational budget constraints with the same slope. If all families in the economy have the same preferences, then *all families choose consumption allocations on a single expansion path.* Figure 3.5 illustrates the prediction. Under the assumption that all families have the same preferences, allocations *B, C,* and *D* could represent the choices of three different families in the permanent income model. Family *B*'s allocation is closest to the origin because it is poorest. The richest family, *D*, is able to choose an allocation furthest from the origin. All three allocations are on the same expansion path, however, because all families have the same preferences and face the same interest rate.

When all families choose allocations on a single expansion path, the expansion path reveals everything about the intergenerational mobility of consumption in the economy. A linear expansion path, for example, is shown as a solid line in the top panel of figure 3.7 (the dashed curves and the dotted lines are indifference curves and budget constraints, respectively). The ratio c_{t+1}/c_t is the same everywhere on this expansion path; all families in the economy choose c_{t+1}/c_t in the same ratio. Richer families enjoy more consumption for both generations than do poor families, but the ratio c_{t+1}/c_t is the same for all. If we compare two families *B* and *D*, and the *D* parents consume 150 percent more than the *B* parents, then it must be that the *D* child consumes 150 percent more than the *B* child. In other words, an expansion path represented by a ray from the origin means that consumption does not regress to the mean across generations in percentage terms when preferences are the same for all families.

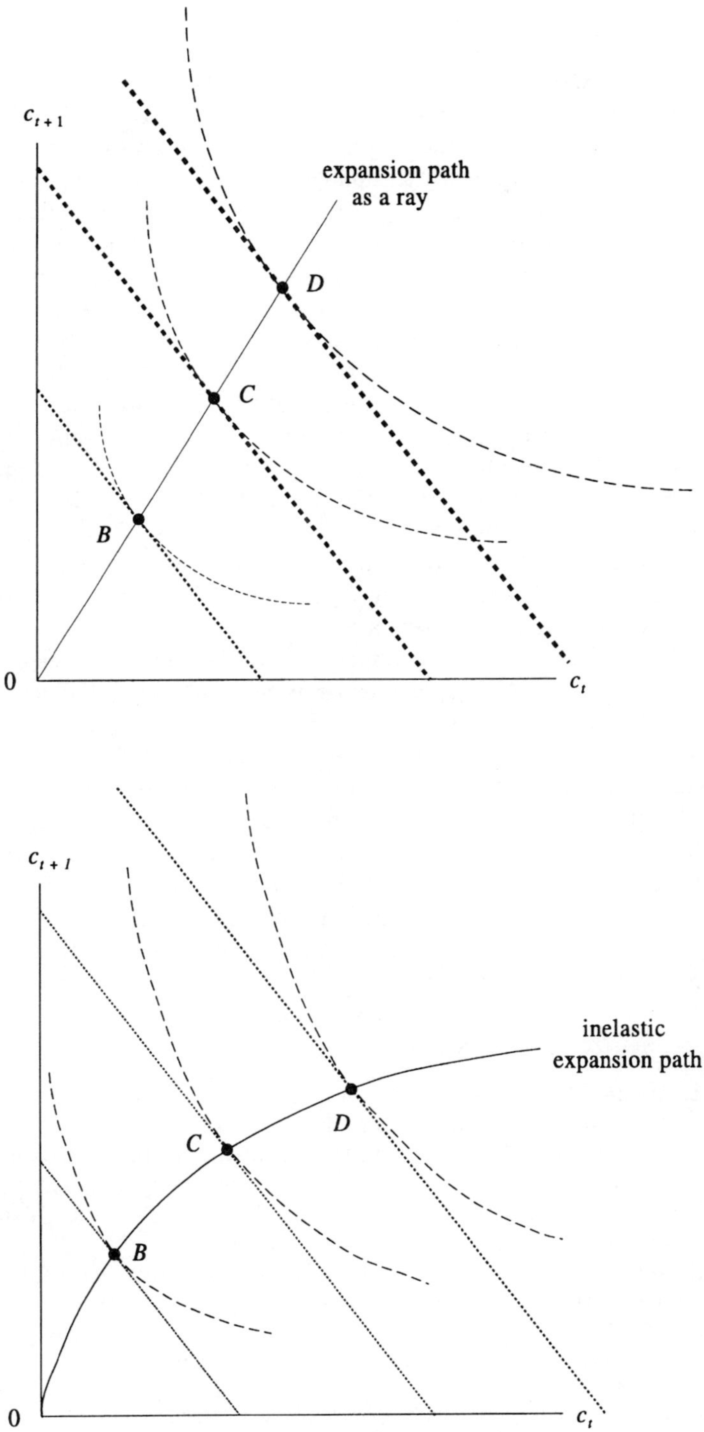

3.7 Linear and Inelastic Expansion Paths

The expansion path shown in the lower panel of figure 3.7 (a solid curve) does not follow a ray from the origin, but is flatter than such rays. Richer families choose allocations with a smaller ratio c_{t+1}/c_t than do poorer families. If we observe that *D* parents consume 150 percent more than the *B* parents, then the *D* child consumes more than the *B* child, but the difference is less than 150 percent. An expansion path that is *inelastic* or flatter than rays to the origin means that consumption does regress to the mean across generations in percentage terms when preferences are the same for all families.[7] Inelastic expansion paths are said to be "flatter than rays to the origin" because, at any point on the expansion path, the ray to the origin has a steeper slope than the expansion path at that point.[8]

What if preferences differ across families? The implications of the permanent income model are most easily seen in the case when there are two types of preferences in the economy. One set of families is more altruistic than the other, so chosen allocations lie on two expansion paths, such as the two shown in the bottom panel of figure 3.6. When one compares allocations across families, there are two reasons why allocations differ. First, families have different incomes. Because income movements produce movements along a single expansion path, income differences affect chosen consumption allocations according to *movements along a single expansion path.* Second, families have different degrees of intergenerational altruism. The degree of altruism shifts the expansion path so preference differences affect chosen consumption allocations according to *shifts from one expansion path to another* along a single budget constraint. The shape of any single expansion path no longer tells the whole story of the transmission of inequality across generations. The shape of a single expansion path summarizes how consumption inequality *produced by income inequality* is transmitted across generations but not how consumption inequality *produced by taste differences* is transmitted.

To summarize the results so far:

1. When all families have the same preferences, the shape of the expansion path summarizes the implications of the model for the intergenerational dynamics of consumption. There is no regression to the mean in percentage terms when expansion paths are rays emanating from the origin. Regression to the mean occurs when expansion paths are inelastic.
2. When preferences differ across families, the first result is qualified slightly. The expansion path summarizes the transmission of

7. Note that, throughout the book, I measure intergenerational mobility in logarithmic or percentage terms.

8. Along an inelastic expansion path—one that is "flatter than rays to the origin"—the elasticity of c_{t+1} with respect to c_t is less than one. The path drawn in the lower panel of figure 3.7 is concave, but an expansion path need not be concave to be inelastic.

> any consumption inequality that arises from income inequality. Consumption inequality that arises from preference differences is not transmitted to the next generation in a way that is related to the shape of the expansion path.

So one final question remains: what is the shape of an expansion path in the permanent income model?

If preferences are homothetic, then the expansion path must be a ray emanating from the origin. This result follows in three logical steps. First, because indifference curves are tangent to a budget constraint with slope $-(1 + r)$ along the expansion path, the slope of all indifference curves must be $-(1 + r)$ along the expansion path. Second, homothetic preferences means that indifference curves have the same slope along a ray emanating from the origin. The first and second statements imply the final result that the expansion path is a ray emanating from the origin.

Now consider a group of families with identical homothetic preferences but with different incomes. According to the permanent income model, all families face the same interest rate r. This means that their choices all lie on the same expansion path. If their preferences are homothetic, the expansion path must be a ray emanating from the origin so the ratio c_{t+1}/c_t must be the same for all families. In other words, *consumption does not regress to the mean across generations in percentage terms* when all families have the same homothetic preferences.

If preferences are homothetic but the degree of altruism varies across families in a way that is uncorrelated with parental income, one qualifies this result only slightly. Any consumption inequality in the parental generation that is the result of income inequality persists in the child's generation. Regression to the mean of consumption in percentage terms can occur only to the extent that preference differences produce consumption inequality in the parental generation. This slightly modified result can be seen in an example. Suppose there are two groups of families. Parental income is A in the first group and B in the second. Altruism varies within groups but, because altruism is assumed to be uncorrelated with parental income, not across groups. Families with different tastes are on different expansion paths (each of which is a ray), but the average A family is on the same expansion path as the average B family, so consumption does not regress to the mean *across parental income categories.*[9]

9. More precisely, a regression of ln c_{t+1} on ln c_t yields a coefficient of one when (log) parental income is used as a instrument for ln c_t. An important statistical assumption is that log parental income is uncorrelated with tastes. A precise derivation of the required statistical assumptions is available from the author upon request.

Opportunities and Inequality with Parental Investments in Children

The analysis above takes the earnings of parents and children as given. Here I use the permanent income model to analyze parental investments in the earning capacity of their children. The previous result that consumption does not regress to the mean in percentage terms still holds, and the result is still proven by demonstrating that all families still have budget constraints with slope $1 + r$ so that expansion paths are linear. The additional result that earnings do regress to the mean across generations is obtained from the permanent income model.

As a fairly realistic approximation, I suppose that, without parental assistance, children can earn nothing. Parents can choose how much to assist their children with more assistance resulting in more earning power for children. I follow the economics literature and refer to these attempts by parents to enhance the earning power of their children as *human capital investments.* Figure 3.8 shows two possible relationships between human capital investments (h_{t+1}) and the earnings of a child (e_{t+1}). Notice two features of each graph. First, more human capital investments result in more earnings for the child. Second, human capital investments produce additional earnings for the child at a decreasing rate. The initial investments in children, which I think of as basic health expenditures and the provision of some kind of literacy for the child, make a big impact on the earnings of the child. This can be seen in the figure as the steep slope of the earnings functions near the origin. Additional investments increase earnings at a slower rate.

Of course, parental investment is not the sole determinant of a child's earnings. Luck, discrimination, intelligence, and peer influences are some of the other factors that might affect a child's earnings. I will group all of these "other" factors together and call them "ability" or "endowments." A high-ability child, by definition, will earn more from a given parental investment than a low-ability child. This is shown in figure 3.8 as the dashed "high-ability" earnings function drawn above the solid "low-ability" earnings function. The important conceptual distinction between "ability" or "endowments" and "human capital" in the model is that the latter is determined by parental choice while the former is not.[10]

As any parent can attest, investments in the earnings capacity of children are not free. Investments in the earnings capacity of children are resources that parents cannot consume or cannot pass on to their children as the financial transfer that was denoted as x_{t+1} previously. When decid-

10. I apologize to readers for whom the words "ability" and "human capital" suggest other distinctions. Parental control of "human capital" is the only key idea in my models.

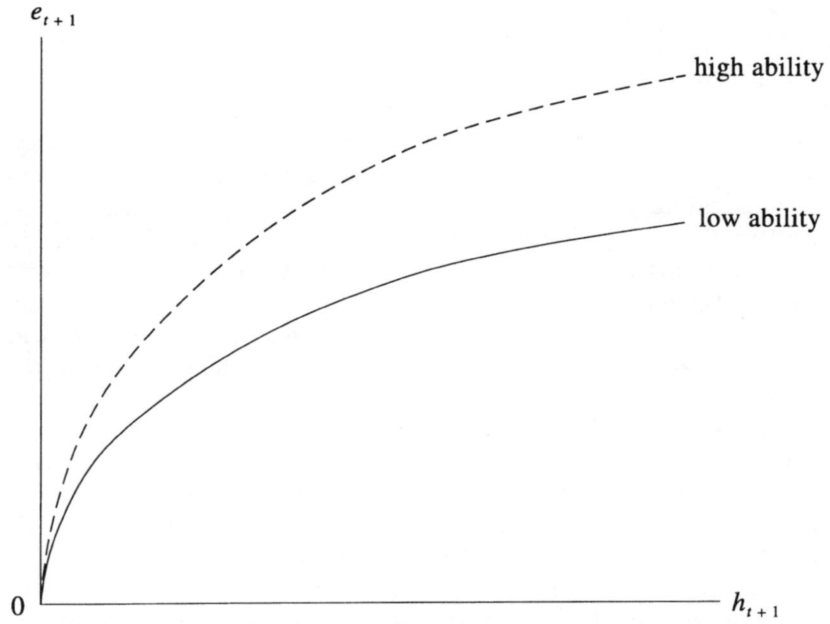

3.8 Earnings Functions: Human Capital Investments versus Child's Earnings

ing whether to make additional human capital investments, parents have to weigh the additional earnings against the lost consumption or the decreased financial transfer. The intergenerational permanent income model offers some strong predictions for how parents will handle these tradeoffs.

Remember that there are two things that matter to parents in the intergenerational permanent income model: consumption by the parents and consumption by the child. The only purpose for human capital and financial transfers in the model is for parents to provide the child with resources for consumption. This means that parents will choose human capital investments and financial transfers in such a way that both earn the same rate of return. To see this, suppose that an additional $1,000 investment in a child's human capital produced $1,100 in additional earnings (and therefore consumption) for the child. Suppose further that the rate of return on financial investments is 20 percent—an additional $1,000 transfer will allow the child to consume $1,200 more. This means that parents are not investing properly. By merely reducing human capital investments and using the proceeds as a financial transfer for the child, parents would not affect their consumption but would increase consumption by the child. If, for example, the parents reallocated $1,000, the child would lose $1,100 in earnings but would gain $1,200 in financial income for a net gain of $100.

Therefore, according to the permanent income model, parents will invest in the human capital of children up to the point were the rate of return is equal to the interest rate.

I refer to the human capital investment that produces a marginal return of $(1 + r)$ as the *efficient human capital investment,* where r is the interest rate earned on financial assets. Each level of ability has its own earnings function and therefore its own efficient human capital investment. Investments in high-ability children yield higher returns, so more is invested in them.[11] The efficient investments for two ability levels, h^*_{t+1} and $h^{*\prime}_{t+1}$, and their corresponding earnings, e^*_{t+1} and $e^{*\prime}_{t+1}$, are shown in figure 3.9. Ability and the interest rate are the only factors that influence the efficient human capital investment because ability is the only thing that affects the earnings function.

All families make the efficient human capital investment in the intergenerational permanent income model. For very poor parents or for parents of a very able child, this can mean human capital investments that are very large in comparison with their income. Nevertheless, the efficient human capital investment is made by obtaining a loan in the financial market. Parents pass on the loan to their child, who pays it off with the additional earnings he enjoys from his parents' human capital investment. Because all families make the efficient human capital investment in the intergenerational permanent income model and the efficient human capital investment depends only on ability, ability is the only thing that ultimately determines the earnings of children in that model. The intergenerational dynamics of earnings therefore depends only on the intergenerational dynamics of ability.[12] It is hardly controversial that there is regression to the mean across generations in earnings ability, so the intergenerational permanent income model predicts that earnings regress to the mean.

Consumption, on the other hand, does not regress to the mean in percentage terms in the intergenerational permanent income model even when the model is enhanced to allow for human capital investments. The proof of this result is much the same as in the simpler version of the model:

11. It is conceivable that "ability" affects the level of the earnings function, but not its slope. The efficient human capital investment is the same for all families (although the associated level of earnings is not) in this case. I show later in the chapter that this other case generates a few different—and simpler—results.

12. Suppose $e_t = B_t^v$ for each generation, where B_t is the "ability" or "endowment" of generation t and v is a constant. Suppose the intergenerational dynamics of ability are $\ln B_{t+1} = \beta \ln B_t + \varepsilon_{t+1}$; ability regresses to the mean at rate $(1 - \beta)$ in percentage terms. Then the dynamics of earnings are $\ln e_{t+1} = \beta \ln e_t + v\varepsilon_{t+1}$ and earnings regress to the mean at rate $(1 - \beta)$ in percentage terms.

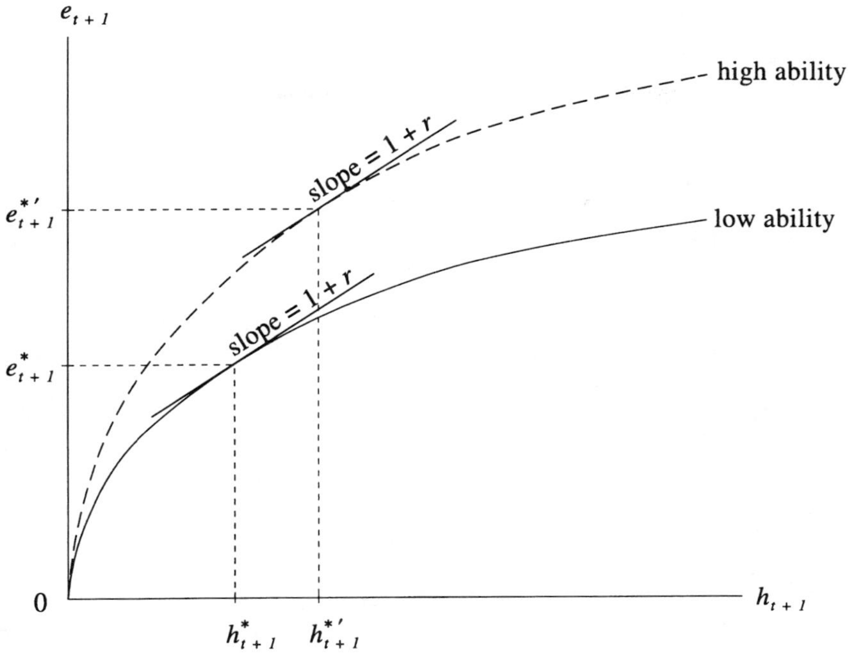

3.9 Efficient Human Capital Investments

it shows that the expansion path is a ray emanating from the origin. To begin the proof, one needs to derive the intergenerational budget constraint for the model with human capital investments. Consider three families: "poor," "middle," and "rich." Suppose for the moment that financial transfers are not possible. Each family clearly can afford the allocation $(I_t, 0)$: parents consume their entire income I_t, invest nothing in the human capital of children, and children consume and earn nothing. Less consumption by parents allows some income to be diverted to human capital investment, which produces earnings and consumption for the child according to an earnings function such as those shown in figure 3.8. Because one is moving to the left in figure 3.10 as human capital investment increases, the mirror image of an earnings function from figure 3.8 is traced out in figure 3.10 for each of the three families beginning at the point $(I_t, 0)$.

Now let's allow both human capital and financial transfers to children. Suppose for the moment that the children in all three families have the same ability. This means that the efficient human capital investment is the same for all three families. Remember that the slope of the earnings function is $(1 + r)$ at the efficient human capital investment, which means that

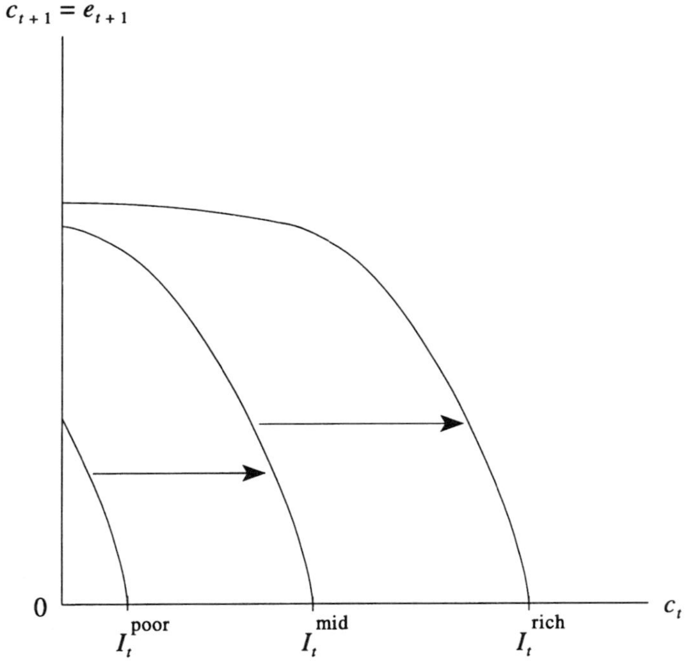

3.10 Consumption Possibilities with Human Capital Investment Only

the corresponding slope of the curved budget constraints in figure 3.10 is $-(1 + r)$. The curved budget constraints from figure 3.10 are redrawn as dashed curves in figure 3.11 together with solid lines indicating the point where slopes are $-(1 + r)$. The horizontal gap between the efficient human capital investment and the zero investment point $(I_t^{\text{rich}}, 0)$ is therefore marked as h^*_{t+1}. The same human capital investment could be graphically computed for the poor and middle families (but is not to avoid cluttering the figure). Because ability is assumed to be the same for all three families, the same earnings function and the same e^*_{t+1} apply to all three families. For "poor," the efficient human capital investment h^*_{t+1} is more than parental income I_t^{poor}. The efficient investment is less than parental income I_t^{mid} for "middle," but it is still a substantial fraction of I_t^{mid}. h^*_{t+1} is a relatively trivial fraction of parental income I_t^{rich} for "rich."

For the "middle" and "rich" families, the allocation $(I_t - h^*_{t+1}, e^*_{t+1})$ is feasible when $x_{t+1} = 0$. This can be thought of as the "earnings endowment" shown in figures 3.1 and 3.2. To emphasize this, I display the allocation $(I_t - h^*_{t+1}, e^*_{t+1})$ as a square dot for the poor, middle, and rich families. Because families can borrow and lend in the financial market at interest

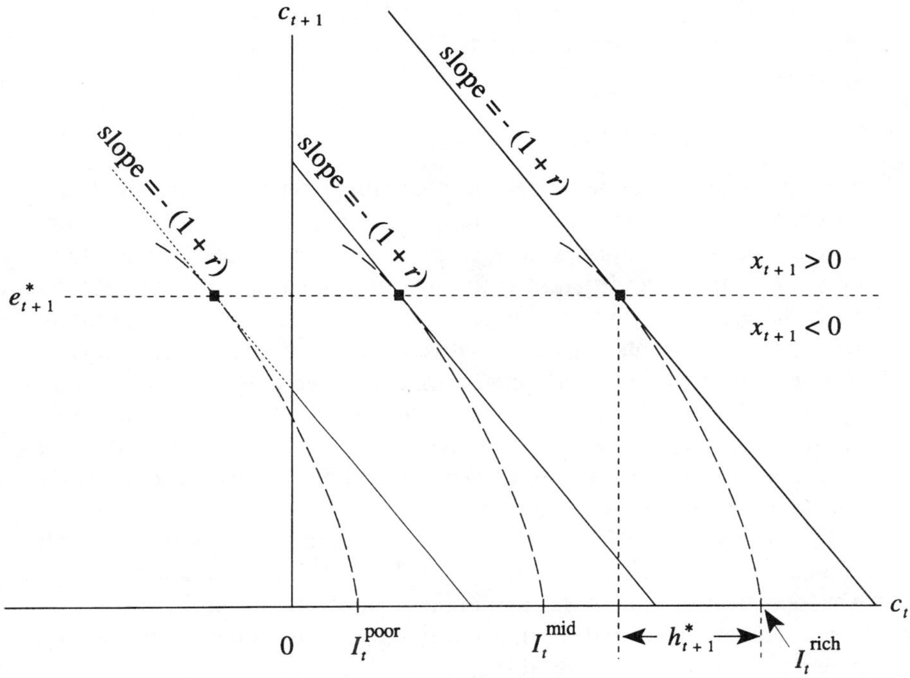

3.11 IG Budget Set with Human Capital and Financial Investment

rate r, points to the northwest and southeast of the square dot along a line with slope $-(1 + r)$ are also feasible. Lending in the financial market ($x_{t+1} > 0$) delivers a consumption allocation above the dashed line. Borrowing ($x_{t+1} < 0$) delivers an allocation below the horizontal dashed line. Therefore, the intergenerational budget set is a straight line with slope $-(1 + r)$ and passing through the point ($I_t - h^*_{t+1}, e^*_{t+1}$), at least for the "middle" and "rich" families. The same turns out to be true for poor families for whom the efficient human capital investment exceeds parental income. Intergenerational budget constraints are shown as solid lines in figure 3.11 in order to distinguish them from the dashed, curved mirror images of the earnings functions.

If one increases ability, this will raise the dashed earnings functions, raise e^*_{t+1}, and raise the dashed horizontal line. The intergenerational budget constraint is still a straight line with slope $-(1 + r)$. Thus *all families in the intergenerational permanent income model—regardless of wealth, earnings or ability—face an intergenerational budget constraint with the same slope,* $-(1 + r)$. As in the exogenous earnings case, it can be shown that expansion paths are rays emanating from the origin. It then follows that consumption does not regress to the mean in percentage terms across generations.

Review of the Main Points

The intergenerational permanent income model assumes that parents are concerned about their own consumption and that of their children. More is better, but resources are scarce, so parents face a tradeoff between their own consumption and that of their children. Relatively altruistic parents consume less of their income, passing more resources on to their children. Less altruistic parents consume relatively more and give less to their offspring. Without a theory of preferences, there is no reason to assume that richer parents are either more or less willing to give to their children than are poor parents. We therefore expect that, for parents facing the same incentives, the *fraction* of resources consumed by parents will not be systematically related to the wealth of the family.

The ability to transfer resources across generations is the same for all families because all families interact in the same capital market. That is why incentives are similar for all families regardless of wealth; the permanent income model predicts that the fraction of resources consumed by parents is independent of wealth.

Another way of thinking about this implication of the permanent income model is in terms of the dynamics of inequality. With all economic classes passing similar fractions of their wealth on to their children, there is no tendency for consumption to "regress to the mean" in percentage terms. If, for instance, your parents consume twice as much as my parents and their preferences are similar, then you will consume twice as much as I do. If surprises about family opportunities occur as new generations are born, there will be a spreading out of the cross-sectional distribution of consumption as generations pass. By chance, some dynasties will enjoy repeated good luck while others will suffer from repeated misfortune.

The dynamics of earnings are much different than the dynamics of consumption in the permanent income model. A person's earning capacity is partly determined by luck, implying that parents with high earnings have no guarantee that their children will earn a lot. Earnings regress to the mean across generations, and the distribution of earnings within a generation can be stable.[13]

The main results of this chapter are quite general. Consider one possible

13. A more careful derivation of the relationships between "regression to the mean" and the evolution of inequality appears in chapter 6.

generalization: time as an input into the production of human capital. If the time is mainly that of children and the value of that time depends only on ability, then even the details of our analysis go through. Remember that the earnings function maps foregone parental consumption into earnings for children and that the earnings function is allowed to vary with ability of children, so family-specific costs of human capital accumulation according to ability is entirely consistent with this analysis. If parental time is also an important factor in the production of human capital and the parental time is valued differently across families, then one would have to allow the shape of earnings functions to depend on two factors: ability of children and the value of parental time. However, the main result here—that intergenerational budget constraints are linear with slope $(1 + r)$—would be unmodified.[14]

The imperfect capital markets view is discussed in the next section. There it is assumed that poor parents are less able to participate in capital markets and, as a consequence, face very high returns to investments in their children. It is then argued that poor parents respond to these high rates of return by devoting a higher fraction of resources to their children—a force that helps the children of poor parents to catch up with those of rich parents.

The Imperfect Capital Markets View

According to the intergenerational permanent income model, all families are able to invest the efficient amount of human capital for their children, even if this means borrowing against the adult earnings of their children. Parents with low income borrow in the financial market to finance the human capital investment and their own consumption, passing the debt on to their child. The child pays off the debt with the additional earnings that he or she enjoys as the result of the parents' human capital investments.

It may be unrealistic to suppose that parents are able to pass substantial amounts of debt on to their children. The "imperfect capital markets" or "borrowing constraints" model therefore modifies the intergenerational permanent income model by ruling out the ability of parents to borrow against their child's adult earnings. The prohibition of intergenerational borrowing in the model might be justified because markets cannot force children to pay back debts accumulated by their parents (thus the phrase

14. Earnings might be negatively correlated across generations if parental time were an especially important input into the production of a child's human capital. The main results are also robust to certain forms of uncertainty. See Appendix A at the end of this chapter for some examples.

"imperfect capital markets") or because societies prohibit parental borrowing to avoid abuse by selfish parents.[15]

As in the enhanced version of the intergenerational permanent income model, parents have two ways to transfer consumption across generations: human capital investments and financial transfers. The important distinction between the two is that financial transfers are purchased in a market where market forces tend to equalize the return on financial investment for all families. In contrast, human capital investments do not earn the same marginal return for all families in the borrowing constrained model. Some families would financially gain very little by increasing their human capital investments while others would gain a great deal. It is assumed in the borrowing constrained model that market forces cannot equalize these human capital returns by allowing families with low marginal returns to invest in the human capital of *other* families that face higher marginal returns. My purpose here is not to justify or refute this assumption but to derive implications for the degree of intergenerational mobility. These implications are compared with empirical observations in chapter 8.

A large fraction of the economic models of intergenerational mobility are based on the imperfect capital markets model. Related economic models of intergenerational mobility at the family level include Becker and Tomes (1986), Roland Bénabou (1994), Steven Durlauf (1996), Gerhard Glomm and B. Ravikumar (1992), Glenn C. Loury (1981), John Laitner (1992), and Robert Tamura (1991). Jere R. Behrman, Robert Pollak, and Paul Taubman (1995) extend the imperfect capital markets model to consider the allocation of resources within a family with heterogenous children (see also my chapter 11 for some analysis of this problem). There is also a very closely related macroeconomic literature concerned with intergenerational mobility across regions and countries, including Robert Barro and Xavier Sala-i-Martin (1992), N. Gregory Mankiw, David Romer, David Weil (1992), Barro, Mankiw, Sala-i-Martin (1995), and Tamura (1991). Like the family-level analyses, the macroeconomics literature relies on a version of the imperfect capital markets model and works with Galton-style empirical specifications but, with the exception of Tamura (1991), does not appear to be aware of its strong theoretical and empirical links with the family-level literature. I treat the family-and macro-level analyses as different versions of the same problem and pursue the links between the two more extensively in chapters 6 and 7.

"Opportunities with an Intergenerational Borrowing Constraint" introduces the borrowing constraint and graphically derives the intergenera-

15. An observation that intergenerational borrowing does not occur may indicate something about the preferences and opportunities of families. I discuss this point later in the chapter.

tional budget constraint. As in the permanent income model, the expansion path displays the model's main implications for the transmission of consumption inequality. The shape of the expansion path is derived in the following part. It is shown that there are a subset of families (which I call "Group 1" families) who do not wish to borrow and are therefore able to behave like permanent income families. The remainder of the families ("Group 2") do wish to borrow but are unable. As compared with Group 1, consumption regresses to the mean more rapidly for Group 2 while earnings regress to the mean less rapidly. For Group 2, there is not an important difference between the transmission of consumption inequality and the transmission of earnings inequality.

Becker and Tomes (1986) show that a borrowing constraint creates two groups of families and that the intergenerational mobility of consumption and earnings differs across the two groups. They show, but do not emphasize, that consumption and earnings are quite similar for Group 2 families while the two behave quite differently for Group 1 families.

The Becker and Tomes presentation is mainly algebraic, while mine is graphical. A graphical analysis of consumption in the imperfect capital markets model can be found in Tomes (1980), although he does not derive the expansion path and the implications of its shape for the dynamics of consumption inequality. I also use the diagrammatic analysis to show which statistical tools might be appropriate for an empirical analysis.

The analysis of the imperfect capital markets model is conceptually the most demanding in the book. Because I ultimately conclude that—despite its popularity in the economics literature—the imperfect capital markets model is not a useful model of intergenerational mobility, some readers may prefer to skip this section.

Opportunities with an Intergenerational Borrowing Constraint

Suppose parents were allowed to make positive financial transfers to their child and/or to make investments in the human capital of the child. As in the permanent income model, it does not make sense for parents to invest in so much human capital that the rate of return is below the financial rate of return r. If they did, they could increase the consumption of the child without sacrificing their own consumption merely by reducing their human capital investment and using the proceeds to make a financial investment. In terms of figure 3.9, the possibility of making financial investments with rate of return r ensures that no family will choose human capital (h_{t+1}) to the right of its efficient level (h^*_{t+1}). To see how this affects the intergenerational budget constraint, consider first those families for whom parental income I_t is greater than h^*_{t+1} so that the efficient human capital investment is feasible (although perhaps not desirable) without borrowing. For example, h^*_{t+1} is feasible without borrowing for the "mid" and "rich" families in figure 3.11. These families could invest h^*_{t+1} in human capital, invest zero in the financial asset, consume the positive amount $(I_t - h^*_{t+1})$, and have their children consume the corresponding level of earnings (e^*_{t+1}). The "poor" family cannot afford the efficient human capital investment without borrowing. The most the "poor" family can invest in human capital without borrowing is $I_t^{\text{poor}} < h^*_{t+1}$, which would require them to consume zero and to invest zero in the financial asset.

The point $(I_t - h^*_{t+1}, e^*_{t+1})$ is feasible for the "mid" and "rich" families and is achieved by setting financial transfers (x_{t+1}) equal to zero. These families can also choose points to the northwest of $(I_t - h^*_{t+1}, e^*_{t+1})$ by increasing their investments in the financial asset. Their budget constraints extend to the northwest in figure 3.11 along the solid line with slope $-(1 + r)$. However, they cannot choose points to the southeast by decreasing x_{t+1} because x_{t+1} can be no smaller than zero in the borrowing constraints model. Consumption allocations to the southeast must be achieved in the borrowing constraints model by decreasing human capital investments below their efficient level. So the intergenerational budget constraint extends to the southeast along the dashed *curve*—according to the shape of the earnings function. The intergenerational budget constraint is partly a straight line (to the northwest of the square dot) and partly a curve (to the southeast of the square dot). Notice that points on the dashed curve to the southeast of the square dot correspond to human capital investments less than h^*_{t+1} where the marginal earnings produced by human capital investments is greater than $(1 + r)$. This can be seen in the earnings function diagram shown in figure 3.9, where the slope of an earnings function is greater than $(1 + r)$ for investments to the left of h^*_{t+1}.

At the bottom end of the dashed curve in figure 3.11, children consume 0 and parents consume I_t. The allocation $(I_t, 0)$ is also feasible for the "poor" family in figure 3.11. From $(I_t, 0)$, the poor family could increase the consumption of children by either investing in human capital or by making a financial transfer, but the human capital investment is more profitable because, at first, it earns a return greater than $(1 + r)$. The "poor" intergenerational budget constraint therefore consists entirely of the dashed curve.

Transmission of Consumption Inequality

As in the permanent income model, the intergenerational transmission of consumption inequality is summarized by the expansion path. Consumption regresses to the mean when paths are inelastic ("flatter than rays to the origin") and away from the mean when they are elastic ("steeper than rays to the origin").

The poorest families, of course, choose consumption allocations that are nearest to the origin. The previous part shows that the intergenerational budget constraint is curved for the poorest families. Holding constant the ability of the child (which determines e^*_{t+1}), an increase in their income I_t^{poor} shifts their budget constraint to the right, in the direction of the arrow shown in the upper panel of figure 3.12. The family shown in the top panel does not make financial transfers to children ($x_{t+1} = 0$). It is especially important to notice that, because a change in parental income does not change the earnings function, the shift to the right is a parallel horizontal shift. For any allocation on the curve, the horizontal position is determined by parental income minus the human capital investment (this is what parents have left over to consume) and the vertical position is determined by the earnings of the child. Since the earnings of the child are determined by the human capital investment, more parental income shifts the curve horizontally to the right.

Consider the choice *A* corresponding to the initial position of the budget constraint. Because *A* is a choice, the indifference curve and the budget constraint have the same slope at *A* (indifference curves are drawn as long-dashed curves; budget constraints are drawn as short-dashed curves). Let's call the slope at *A* $-s$. A dotted ray is drawn through the origin and through the allocation *A*. That ray intersects the new budget constraint at the allocation *B*, denoted by a hollow dot. Because *A* and *B* lie on the same ray and because preferences are assumed to be homothetic, the indifference curves at *A* and *B* have the same slope $-s$, which is also equal to the slope of the old budget constraint at *A*. However, $-s$ is not the slope of the budget constraint at allocation *B*. The budget constraint is flatter than $-s$ at *B* because the new budget constraint was produced by a horizontal shift of the old budget constraint. The new budget constraint has slope $-s$ at allocation *C*, an allocation to the southeast of *B*. It follows from the curvature of the budget constraint that the budget constraint is flatter than $-s$ at *B*.

Since the indifference curve and the budget constraint do not have the same slope at allocation *B*, that allocation cannot be the new choice and the expansion path cannot be a ray. The new choice *D* must be to the southeast of *B* because of the curvature of the indifference curves. For those families on the curved portion of the intergenerational budget constraint, the expansion path must therefore be inelastic. The expansion path is shown as a solid curve in the upper panel of figure 3.12.

Notice that the above proof of the shape of the expansion path requires the curvature of both the earnings function and the indifference curves.

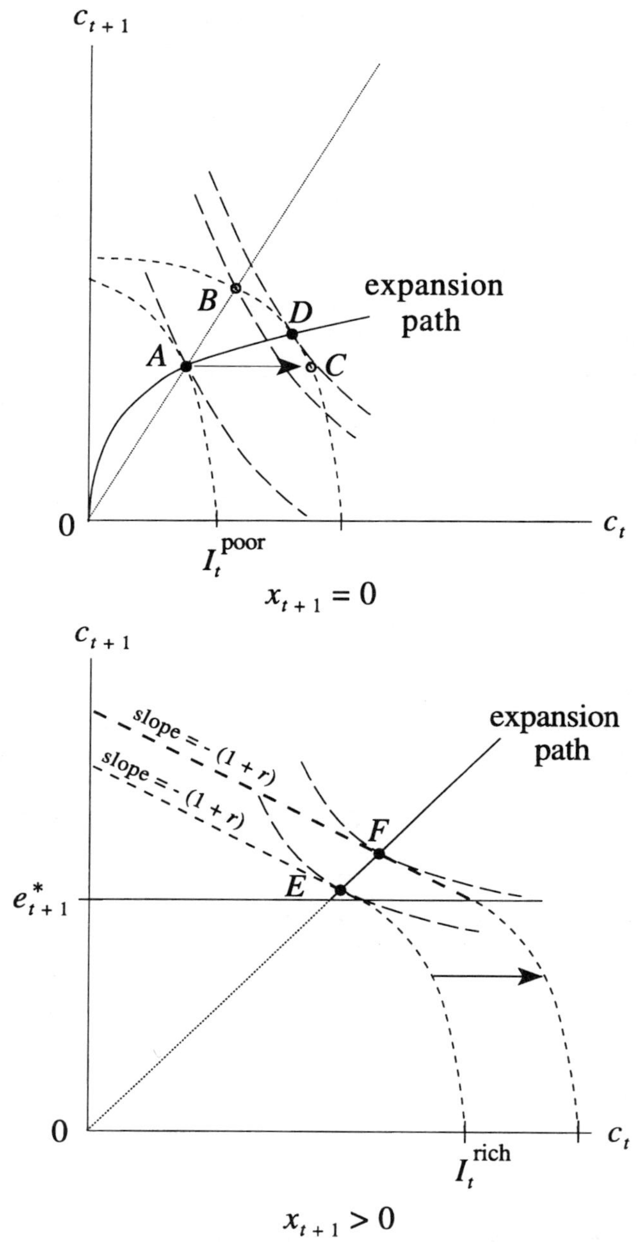

3.12 Derivation of the Expansion Path with and without a Binding Borrowing Constraint

The part on "Are the Permanent Income and Imperfect Capital Market Models Different?" returns to these curvature assumptions and suggests that perhaps the borrowing constraints and permanent income models do not have very different predictions for the intergenerational transmission of consumption inequality.

Richer families, making positive financial transfers to children ($x_{t+1} > 0$), are on the linear portion of their intergenerational budget constraint, which has slope $-(1 + r)$. Consider a family with income I_t^{rich} and choice E such as that shown in the lower panel of figure 3.12. E is on the linear portion of the budget constraint, which begins at vertical position e^*_{t+1} (see figure 3.11 and the corresponding discussion for a proof). Because E is a choice, the indifference curve at E must have slope equal to the slope of the budget constraint at E, which is $-(1 + r)$. An increase in I_t^{rich} will shift the intergenerational budget constraint to the right in a parallel fashion, which will generate a new choice F. F is also on the linear portion of the budget constraint. The same argument made for choice E implies that the indifference curve has slope $-(1 + r)$ at choice F. Since the indifference curves at E and F have the same slope and preferences are homothetic, E and F must lie on the same ray through the origin. The expansion path, shown as a solid line in the bottom panel of the figure, therefore follows a ray.

Combining the top and bottom panels of figure 3.12, the expansion path is inelastic near the origin where families are too poor to afford the efficient human capital investment. Human capital investments grow with income as one moves away from the origin along the curved expansion path. When the human capital investment reaches the efficient level, further income increases are passed on to children via financial transfers. These richer families are on the linear portion of their intergenerational budget constraint, where the expansion path follows a ray. Two expansion paths of this shape, one corresponding to more altruistic parents and one to less altruistic parents, are shown in figure 3.13. A horizontal dashed line provides the demarcation of the ray and inelastic portions of the expansion paths. The same horizontal line applies to both expansion paths because both families are assumed to have children of the same ability. Remember that ability is the only reason why efficient human capital investments and their corresponding earnings might differ across families.

How does ability affect the expansion path? Remember that indifference curves have slope $-(1 + r)$ along the portion of the expansion path that follows a ray from the origin. This means that portion of the expansion path must follow the same ray regardless of ability. Ability does affect the earnings function, the efficient human capital investment, and the earnings of the child, so ability affects the vertical position of the inelastic

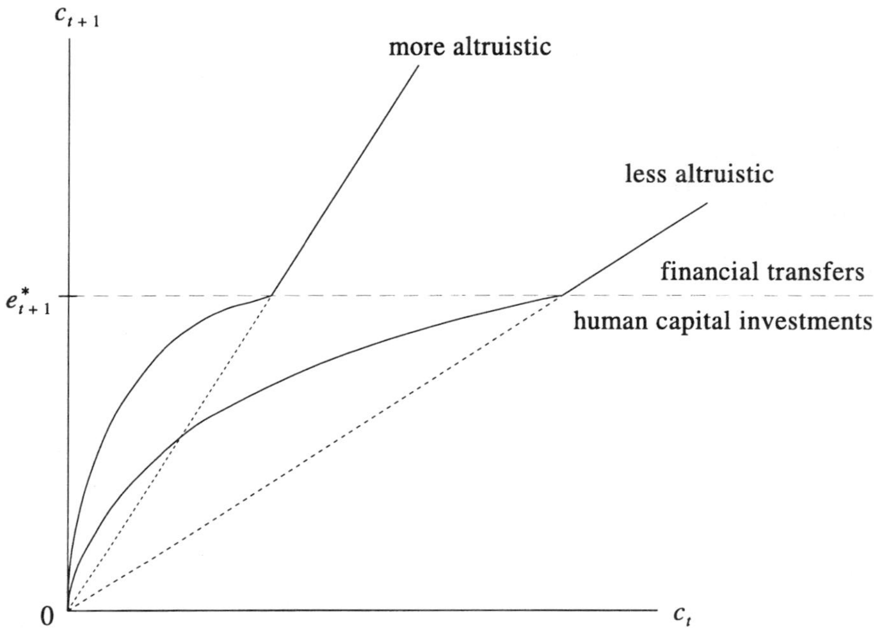

3.13 Expansion Paths in the Presence of Borrowing Constraints

portion of the expansion path. For earnings functions such as those shown in figure 3.8—where ability affects the slope of the earnings function—families with higher-ability children will lie on expansion paths that are above those of families with low-ability children. The inelastic portions of both the high-and low-ability expansions paths will intersect the same ray, but the inelastic portion of the high-ability expansion path will do so further from the origin.

For lower levels of parental income, expansion paths are inelastic. This means that the ratio of the adult child's consumption to that of his parents (c_{t+1}/c_t) is smaller for larger incomes. If one were to consider a group of families with children of the same ability who were all on the inelastic part of the same expansion path, the poor families would have the largest ratio (c_{t+1}/c_t). In other words, one would see consumption regressing to the mean in percentage terms across generations. The higher (c_{t+1}/c_t) ratios among the poor are explained by the high rates of return to human capital investment which, by the assumption of diminishing returns to human capital investments, arise from the low levels of human capital investment by the poor. The high rate of return tempts the poor parents to sacrifice a bigger share of their resources for their children.

For higher levels of parental income, families are on the linear portion of the expansion path, which follows a ray that emanates from the origin. All families on the linear portion of their expansion path with the same tastes choose allocations on the same ray and therefore choose c_{t+1} and c_t in the same ratio. If one observes a group of families who are all on the linear portion of the same expansion path, there would be no regression to the mean of consumption in percentage terms across generations. This result holds even when ability varies across families because ability does not affect the linear part of the expansion path.

It cannot be expected that all families can be on the same expansion path because not all families have the same tastes. However, without a theory of those tastes, one cannot assume that tastes are systematically correlated with parental income in one particular direction or another.[16] The assumption here is that, for each possible taste configuration, all income classes are equally represented. For example, one might suppose that 25 percent of families are on the higher expansion path and 75 percent are on the lower expansion path, but a rich family is just as likely to be on the lower path as on the upper. If all families happened to be on the inelastic portion of their expansion path, then one would see that, on average, poor families have the higher (c_{t+1}/c_t) ratios. This will not be true family by family because some of the poor families have very selfish parents—those selfish families are located on very low expansion paths. But the average poor family will have a high (c_{t+1}/c_t) ratio so, on average, one will see consumption regressing to the mean in percentage terms. If, instead, all families happened to be on the portion of their expansion path that follows a ray from the origin, then one would see, on average, poor families with about the same ratio (c_{t+1}/c_t) as rich families.

In general, some families will be on the portion of their expansion path that follows a ray from the origin and some families on the inelastic portion. Imagine dividing our sample of families into two groups:

Group 1: Parents making financial transfers to children
Group 2: Parents not making financial transfers to children

Families in Group 1 would be on the portion of their expansion path that follows a ray from the origin while those in Group 2 would be on the inelastic portion. Suppose, for the sake of argument, that all tastes are equally represented in the two groups. Then the imperfect capital markets

16. In a model with more than two generations, one might expect altruistic grandparents to be related to altruistic parents. Because of the greater grandparental altruism, more altruistic parents would tend to be richer. Thus, a many-generation model can produce a *positive* correlation between altruism and parental income. However, this positive correlation may (counterfactually) imply that consumption regresses *away* from the mean across generations. See Friedman (1976, p. 64) for more analysis of this effect in a life cycle context.

model predicts that consumption will regress to the mean across parental income categories in Group 2, but not in Group 1. I will show some evidence in chapter 8 suggesting that consumption regresses to the mean at similar rates in both groups.

To the extent that there is heterogeneity across families in tastes, it will not be true that all tastes are equally represented in the two groups. More altruistic parents, by definition, want to transfer more resources to their children and therefore are more likely to engage in financial transfers. Chapter 8 considers some empirical strategies for dealing with heterogeneity in tastes.

For those families with identical tastes who are in Group 1, consumption inequality is greater among children than among parents. Regression to the mean in consumption among Group 2 families means that consumption inequality need not grow for that group, but the Group 1 families look very much like permanent income families. Remember that consumption inequality grows among permanent income families because a very few families enjoy strings of good luck while a very few others enjoy strings of bad luck (with luck shared equally among all remaining generations). The same is true in the borrowing constraints model. Although consumption inequality grows for families that begin in Group 1, overall consumption inequality need not grow because inequality may be falling for families that begin in Group 2.[17] Moreover, consumption inequality might be stable if one were to repeat our two-generation model for children and grandchildren because some families that began in Group 1 join Group 2 while some Group 2 families join Group 1.[18]

Transmission of Earnings Inequality

All Group 1 families make the efficient human capital investment. The efficient investment and the associated level of earnings depend on the ability of the child. Human capital investments are therefore insensitive to parental income, although they may be correlated with parental income if it is correlated with ability. Earnings regress to the mean according to the intergenerational correlation of ability.

Group 2 families make less than the efficient human capital investment. Their investment is sensitive to parental income. The borrowing constraint

17. If there is enough heterogeneity in tastes across families, consumption inequality may not grow among Group 1 families because of a "selection bias." See chapter 8 for a detailed analysis of the selection bias.

18. See Appendix A of this chapter, John Laitner (1992), or Jesus Navarro-Zermeno (1993) for a more detailed discussion of the dynamics of consumption inequality in a many-generation borrowing constraints model.

thereby introduces an additional link between the earnings of parents and the earnings of children so that earnings regress to the mean more slowly in Group 2 than in Group 1. A proof that parental income affects the human capital investment of Group 2 families can be seen in the lower panel of figure 3.12. More income moves the consumption allocation along the expansion path away from the origin, which increases the consumption allocation's vertical position. Because the curved budget constraint is derived from the earnings function, a higher vertical position of the consumption allocation corresponds to a higher vertical position on the earnings function, which corresponds to more human capital and earnings.

Many of the results for the borrowing constraints model assume that the ability of children is the same for all families. It is easy to show that all results which do not involve separating Groups 1 and 2 still obtain when ability differs across families but in a way that is uncorrelated with parental income.[19] Results also obtain if ability varies across families—perhaps in a way that is correlated with parental income—but the efficient human capital investment does not.[20] If ability varies a lot across families and is highly correlated with parental income, then it is no longer clear that the borrowing constraints model has predictions that differ from those of the permanent income model. I discuss similarities between the two models later.

Human Capital, Ability, and Family Background

Remember that "ability" is the sole determinant of earnings in my version of the intergenerational permanent income model. This result is somewhat special because I assume that ability has only one dimension: the same ability that shifts the earnings function (for each level of human capital investment) also determines the efficient human capital investment. In a more general model, one dimension of ability might shift the earnings function while another determines the efficient human capital investment.[21] Denote these two dimensions B_{t+1} and B^*_{t+1} respectively. Now

19. See Appendix A for a proof. Heterogeneity in the efficient human capital investment creates a "selection bias" when either Group 1 or Group 2 is analyzed separately (Han and Mulligan 1997).

20. Ability can vary across families while the efficient human capital investment is the same for all when ability affects the position of the earnings function but not its slope.

21. In one example of such a two-dimensional ability model, one dimension of ability would shift the earnings function in an additive way (leaving the slope of the earnings function—and therefore the efficient human capital investment—unchanged) while a second would affect the slope of the earnings function. To the extent that men earn more than women but schooling and other human capital investments do not *increase* earnings at

consider a group of adult children whose parents made the same human capital investments. How are earnings related to parental income among this group of adult children? In the permanent income model, actual human capital investments are identical to efficient human capital investments, so every adult child in the group has the same efficient human capital investment and therefore the same ability along the dimension of ability that determines the efficient human capital investment (B^*_{t+1}). If this is the only dimension of earnings ability, then every adult child in the same group has the same earnings; earnings are therefore unrelated to parental income within the group.[22] If instead earnings are determined by two dimensions of ability, the dimension B_{t+1} (and therefore earnings) would not necessarily be the same for all adult children in the group. If B_{t+1} were correlated with B^*_t and B_t (the two dimensions of parental ability), then B_{t+1} and earnings of adult children would be correlated with parental income within the group. Because so many intergenerational correlations are positive, one expects intergenerational ability correlations to be positive as well so, in the perfect capital markets model, one expects earnings of adult children to be positively related to parental income within a group of adult children whose parents made the same human capital investments.

Now consider the imperfect capital markets model. Actual human capital investments are often less than efficient human capital investments, with the gap determined by parental income. Among a group of adult children whose parents made the same human capital investments, the efficient human capital investment and its corresponding dimension of earnings ability B^*_{t+1} are highest for children of poor parents and lowest for children of rich parents. If B^*_{t+1} is the only dimension of earnings ability, earnings of adult children are *negatively* related to parental income within a group of adult children whose parents made the same human capital investments. Families with very low parental income appear in the group only because human capital investments in children have relatively high returns (that is, highly able children) while families with very high parental income appear in the group because human capital investments in children have relatively low returns (in this case, less able children).

With two dimensions of ability, this unique implication of the imperfect capital markets model is weakened because the second dimension of abil-

---

different rates for the two genders, gender may be an example of the first dimension ability. IQ, "learning ability," or "scholastic aptitude" are examples of the second dimension of ability because these abilities are often associated with more effective schooling investments.

22. If observed earnings were determined by ability plus measurement and forecast errors, earnings would not necessarily be identical for each child. If the measurement and forecast errors were uncorrelated with parental income, it would still be true that observed earnings are unrelated to parental income within the group.

ity B_{t+1} is associated with high earnings of adult children and may be positively correlated with B_t^* and B_t (and therefore with parental earnings and income). In the two-dimensional ability model, are earnings positively or negatively related to parental income among this group of adult children? Four factors determine the answer: (1) the importance of the borrowing constraint and therefore the link between parental income and human capital investments, (2) the correlation of the two dimensions of ability B_{t+1}^* and B_{t+1}, (3) the importance of the second dimension of ability B_{t+1} in determining earnings, and (4) the magnitude of intergenerational ability correlations. Earnings and parental income are likely to be negatively correlated within the group if the first two factors are especially important and positively correlated within the group if the final two factors are especially important. See Mulligan (1996b) for a more extensive derivation of these results, a review of relevant empirical studies, and an analysis of associated measurement issues.[23]

Are the Permanent Income and Imperfect Capital Markets Models Different?

I argue in chapter 8 that some of the unique implications of the imperfect capital markets model are refuted. The unique implications rely on some auxiliary assumptions in addition to the presence of a borrowing constraint. This section explores the auxiliary assumptions in more detail. My analysis suggests that a rejection of the implications of the imperfect capital markets model may be a rejection of the auxiliary assumptions rather than the assumption of a borrowing constraint. In this case, however, the imperfect capital markets model is not very interesting from a positive point of view because its predictions are very similar to those of the permanent income model.

The auxiliary assumptions are of two types. First, certain types of curvature of indifference curves and budget constraints are required. Second, ability cannot be the primary determinant of human capital investments.

Curvature in the Imperfect Capital Markets Model

Remember that the curvature of the intergenerational budget constraint and the curvature of the indifference curves provide two key steps in the proof of the inelasticity of the expansion path in the imperfect capital markets model. The lower part of the intergenerational budget constraint is curved because it is the mirror image of a curved earnings function. The

23. Mulligan (1996b) studies regressions of log wages on log parental income and measures of parental human capital investments, including years of schooling and schooling quality as well as related empirical studies of education, income, and ability.

curvature of the earning function is justified on the grounds that human capital investments are subject to diminishing returns, perhaps because the finiteness of life or because of limited human intellectual capacities. This intuition, however, says little about the degree of curvature. If the earnings function is only slightly curved, then the imperfect capital markets budget constraint is only slightly curved. If the imperfect capital markets budget constraint is only slightly curved, then it is very similar to the linear permanent income budget constraint. The expansion paths for the imperfect capital markets would then be very similar to the linear paths of the permanent income model—only slightly inelastic. A very slightly inelastic expansion path means that consumption regresses to the mean, but only very slightly.

How curved are earnings functions? This is a difficult question to answer, but I do point out that the cost of a borrowing constraint depends on the curvature of the earnings function. Consider figure 3.11 again. With perfect capital markets, families enjoy the entire triangle to the southwest of the solid lines. When the borrowing constraint is introduced, families lose a portion of their budget set—that portion between the dashed curve and the solid line to the southeast of the square dot. The less curved the earnings function, the smaller this area is and therefore the smaller the loss from imperfect capital markets. If one observes that it is not possible to borrow against children's earnings, one conclusion is that the market for borrowing has not been created because the earnings function is not curved and the gains to creating the market are small. In this case, the prediction would be that consumption regresses to the mean, but only very slowly; the borrowing constraints model is not very different from the permanent income model. In order to generate predictions that are different from the permanent income model, the borrowing constraint model must assume that borrowing constraints exist regardless of the cost of those constraints.

The curvature of the indifference curve provides another important step in the proof of the inelasticity of the expansion path. The assumption of curved indifference curves is justified on the grounds that parents prefer moderate allocations rather than allocations that are substantially skewed toward parents or children. But *how* curved are the indifference curves? It is conceivable that parents have a very strong preference for moderation, so the indifference curves are sharply curved, such as those shown in figure 2.3, rather than being gently curved, such as those shown in figure 2.2. Maintaining the assumption of homothetic preferences, I draw in figure 3.14 preferences that show such a strong preference for moderation that indifference curves are practically shaped like an "L." The family is assumed to be on the curved portion of their intergenerational budget constraints as in the upper panel of figure 3.12. The graphical proof presented

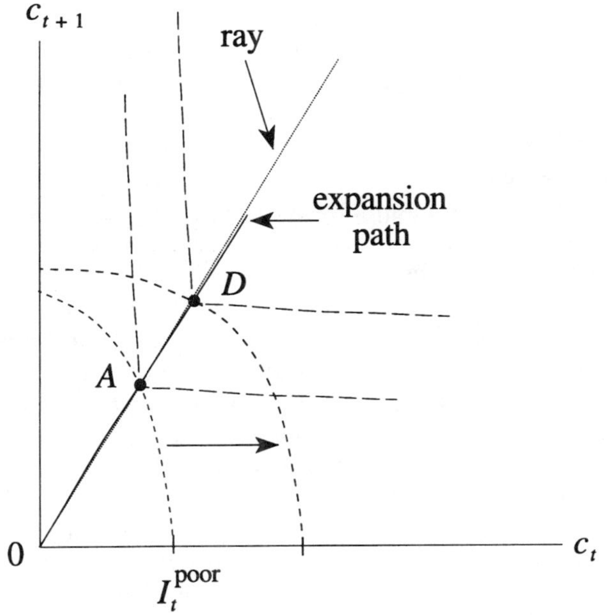

3.14 Curved Expansion Paths When the Preference for Moderation Is Strong

in the top panel of figure 3.12 still applies—an increase in income generates a new choice *D* that lies below the ray passing through the old choice *A*. The only difference between figure 3.14 and the upper panel of figure 3.12 is that the preference for moderation is so strong in the former that the expansion path—although different from a ray—is extremely similar to a ray. Consumption regresses to the mean in percentage terms for families along this expansion path, but only very slowly.

Figure 3.14 shows that imperfect capital markets need not produce much intergenerational consumption mobility. It can even be the case that the earnings function is very concave so that the losses from "imperfect" capital markets are large but there will be very little intergenerational mobility. All that is required is a strong preference for moderation.

Several implications of the borrowing constraints model for human capital investment and the transmission of earnings inequality are not robust to quantitative assumptions about curvature.[24] The borrowing constraints model is unique in predicting that earnings regress to the mean more rap-

24. There is one robust implication: as long as there is some curvature in the earnings function—even if it is very slight—parents will make positive financial transfers only after they have invested in human capital up to the point that the returns on both human and financial investments are equalized. This prediction is not, however, unique to the borrowing constraints model.

idly among families making financial transfers, but that prediction depends on curvature assumptions. Suppose that parental preferences for moderation are only very slight so that indifference curves are only slightly curved. The upper panel of figure 3.12 shows that, for a broad range of incomes, the inelastic portion of the expansion path is nearly horizontal in this case. The nearly linear indifference curves have slopes that are very similar for nearly all consumption allocations, so the new choice *D* is at a point where the budget constraint is sloped similarly to the old choice *A*. This means that *D* must be close to the allocation *C* where the slope of the budget constraint is exactly equal to the slope at the old choice *A*. Human capital investments are identical at *A* and *C* (remember that the human capital investment can be computed from the figure by taking the horizontal distance between the consumption allocation and the point $(I_t, 0)$) so human capital investments are very similar at *A* and *D* when the expansion path is nearly horizontal. A horizontal expansion path means that human capital investments are insensitive to parental income, just as they are in the permanent income model.[25] When indifference curves are nearly linear, the borrowing constraints and permanent income models have very similar predictions for the sensitivity of human capital investments to parental income and therefore for the intergenerational transmission of earnings inequality.

A similar argument applies when the earnings function is very curved. Rapidly diminishing returns means that all families make very similar human capital investments and that the expansion path is nearly horizontal.

Regardless of the curvature assumptions, both the borrowing constraints and permanent income models have very similar predictions for "Group 1" families making positive financial transfers. Table 3.1 summarizes the curvature results for Group 2 families, with asterisks denoting implications that are different from those of the permanent income model. Notice a tension between uniqueness of the earnings and consumption implications. Very curved indifference curves deliver unique implications of the borrowing constraints model for the sensitivity of human capital investments to parental income and for the intergenerational transmission of earnings inequality but not for the transmission of consumption inequality. Removing curvature from the indifference curves produces regression to the mean of consumption among Group 2 families—an impli-

25. The efficient human capital investment is a function of ability. Because ability may be positively correlated with parental income, a correlation between human capital investments and parental income could arise regardless of the presence of borrowing constraints. It is still true that, when indifference curves are nearly linear, the borrowing constraints model has predictions for human capital investments and the dynamics of earnings that are very similar to those of the permanent income model.

Table 3.1 Sensitivity of the Borrowing Constraint Model to Curvature Assumptions

	Curvature of Indifference Curves		Curvature of Earnings Function	
Implication for Group 2	very curved	slightly curved	very curved	slightly curved
sensitivity of h_{t+1} to I_t	strong*	weak	weak	strong*
persistence of earnings	strong*	weak	weak	strong*
persistence of consumption	strong	weak*	weak*	strong

* Implication is unique to the borrowing constraints model.

cation which is unique to the borrowing constraints model—but produces human capital investments that are insensitive to parental income and earnings that rapidly regress to the mean across generations—implications which are common to the two models. The final two columns of table 3.1 show that the same tension is present if one varies the degree of curvature of the earnings function.

Ability and Parental Income as Determinants of Human Capital

The main results derived for the borrowing constraints model are obtained under the assumption that either the efficient human capital investment does not vary a lot across families relative to parental income or that ability is not highly correlated with parental income. Results that rely on the assumption include the greater intergenerational persistence of earnings among borrowing constrained families and a negative relationship between earnings and parental income within a group of children whose parents made the same human capital investments. Is the assumption valid? An interesting result obtains when the assumption is violated and ability is a more important determinant of the human capital investment than is parental income: children with low earnings are more likely to receive a financial transfer from parents. To see this, consider the extreme case that all parental incomes are equal and only the ability of children varies. Parents with high-ability children enjoy a high rate of return to human capital investments so they may not choose to make a financial transfer or, if they make a financial transfer, it will be relatively small. Parents with low-ability children do not enjoy very high returns to human capital investments and are therefore more likely to use the financial transfer to provide consumption for children. Chapter 8 shows that this result is counterfactual: high-income adults are more likely to receive an inheritance from their parents. The evidence suggests that parental income rather than the ability of children is the main determinant of financial transfers so that the results derived above and proved in Appendix A (under the assumption that parental income is more important than ability) are in fact of empirical interest.

Consumption Inequality in the Two Models

Overall consumption inequality must grow in the permanent income model but not in the borrowing constraints model. However, a variety of auxiliary assumptions—including the curvature assumptions mentioned above—are required to prevent growing consumption inequality in the borrowing constraints model. Appendix A discusses some of those additional auxiliary assumptions.

Review of the Main Points

Summary of Assumptions and Results

The borrowing constraints model rules out negative financial transfers from parents to children. This additional restriction transforms the linear intergenerational budget constraint of the permanent income model into a two-part intergenerational budget constraint. The northwest portion, like the intergenerational budget constraint of the permanent income model, is linear with slope $-(1 + r)$, where r is the interest rate earned on financial transfers. The southeast portion is curved according to the earnings function. The two parts are joined at the consumption allocation $(I_t - h^*_{t+1}, e^*_{t+1})$, where I_t is parental income, h^*_{t+1} is the efficient human capital investment, and e^*_{t+1} is the corresponding level of child earnings. The expansion path is inelastic for allocations below the vertical position e^*_{t+1} in the $[c_t, c_{t+1}]$ plane. It is linear, following a ray emanating from the origin, for allocations above the vertical position e^*_{t+1}.

Poor parents or the parents of able children face an efficient human capital investment that is a large fraction of their income, so they are unwilling to make that investment when they cannot borrow to finance it. Parental income is an important determinant of human capital investment for these families. None of these parents make financial transfers because the marginal return to human capital investments is superior. Their chosen consumption allocation is on the inelastic portion of the expansion path so that parental consumption differences that are associated with parental income differences among these families are only partially transmitted to children.

Rich parents or the parents of unable children do not face an efficient human capital investment that is a large fraction of their income, so they are willing to make that investment without borrowing to obtain the funds. These families also make a financial transfer to their children. Because they all make the efficient human capital investment, parental income does not affect (although it may be correlated with) the earnings of children for these families. Earnings regress to the mean according to the regression to the mean of ability, which is more rapid than the regression to the mean of earnings among poor families.

The chosen consumption allocation of the richer families (or of families with less able children) is on the portion of the expansion path that follows a ray from the origin. This means that parental consumption differences across parental income categories are fully transmitted in percentage terms to the next generation. With no heterogeneity in tastes, this simply means that consumption does not regress to the mean in percentage terms across generations.

Becker and Tomes (1986) show that the borrowing constraints model has a somewhat surprising prediction for the relationship between the income or earnings of children and grandparents. In a regression of the income or earnings of a child on the earnings of parents and grandparents, the coefficient on the grandparental variable should be negative! This grandparental prediction has been tested by Behrman and Taubman (1985), Jenny Bourne Wahl (1985), Mulligan (1993), and others. However, Arthur Goldberger (1989) correctly argues that the grandparental prediction is not related to the economics of the borrowing constraints model but depends instead on the mathematical assumption that *two* separate variables matter for income and earnings (parental income and ability are the two variables in the Becker-Tomes case). The grandparental results should therefore obtain in almost any model where two variables—such as two dimensions to "ability"—matter for income and earnings. I therefore neglect the grandparental prediction in my theoretical and empirical analysis. See Mulligan (1993, chapter 6) for a discussion and some evidence on the grandparental effect.

Group 1 and Group 2

The analysis of the borrowing constraints model and a comparison of that model with the intergenerational permanent income model suggests a separate empirical analysis of the dynamics of consumption and earnings for each of two groups:

Group 1: Parents making financial transfers to children
Group 2: Parents not making financial transfers to children

According to the borrowing constraints model, earnings should regress to the mean more rapidly in Group 1, but consumption should regress to the mean more slowly. In fact, *all* parental consumption differences among Group 1 families that are associated with parental income differences should be transmitted to the next generation.

The implications of the borrowing constraints model that are distinct from those of the permanent income model depend on auxiliary assumptions. Under some assumptions about the curvature of the earnings function and indifference curves, expansion paths are nearly linear and consumption regresses to the mean only very slowly. Under other curvature assumptions, human capital investments are quite insensitive to parental income and earnings regress to the mean according to the intergenerational transmission of ability. I discuss in the text how these curvature assumptions are related to the idea that borrowing constraints exist because they are not very costly. An assumption about the relative importance of ability and parental income inequality is also required to derive some of the results. However, I show that without the auxiliary assumptions the imperfect capital markets model is extremely similar to the permanent income model and therefore not a very useful model.[26]

Appendix A: A Two-Period Mathematical Model of Intergenerational Mobility

The implications of the Becker-Tomes approach are proved for a mathematical model of intergenerational mobility. My mathematical model incorporates the important assumptions of the Becker-Tomes model as well as explicitly modeling uncertainty. Several results are proven analytically. The appendix concludes with a discussion of some computer simulations of the mathematical model.

Parents begin with resources I_t, which is a combination of earnings and financial transfers that they received from their parents. Parents spend I_t on three items: their own consumption, c_t, financial transfers to their child, x_{t+1}, and investments in the human capital of their child, h_{t+1}. The parental budget constraint is therefore:

$$I_t = (1 + r_t)x_t + e_t = c_t + x_{t+1} + h_{t+1} \tag{A.1}$$

26. Arthur Goldberger (1989) also criticizes some standard economic models of intergenerational mobility on the grounds that they offer few clear predictions. He argues, from a positive point of view, that the permanent income model is not very different from Galton's (1889) very simple and mechanical model, whereas I argue that, without some auxiliary assumptions, the imperfect capital markets model is not very different from the permanent income model.

A child may also enjoy income from two sources: earnings and financial transfers from his parents. He spends this income on his own consumption. Equation A.2 displays the child's budget constraint.

$$I_{t+1} = (1 + r_{t+1})x_{t+1} + e_{t+1} = c_{t+1} \tag{A.2}$$

Earnings have three determinants: human capital investments, h, anticipated ability, B, and unanticipated luck, λ. I use the function $e(h, B, \lambda)$ to denote the relationship between ability, human capital, and earnings.

$$e_{t+1} = e(h_{t+1}, B_{t+1}, \lambda_{t+1}) \tag{A.3}$$

The function $e(h, B, \lambda)$ is assumed to be increasing and concave in h.

The rate of return on financial assets has an anticipated component $(1 + r)$ and an unanticipated component χ_{t+1}:

$$(1 + r_{t+1}) = (1 + r)\chi_{t+1} \tag{A.4}$$

The shocks λ and χ are assumed to be uncorrelated with B_t, I_t. B_{t+1} and I_t may be correlated.

Equations A.1, A.2, A.3, and A.4 can be combined to form a permanent income intergenerational budget constraint like those shown in figures 3.1 and 3.2:

$$c_{t+1} = [e^*_{t+1} + (1 + r_{t+1})(I_t - h^*_{t+1})] - (1 + r_{t+1})c_t \tag{A.5}$$

where h^*_{t+1} is the efficient human capital investment and e^*_{t+1} is the corresponding level of earnings for the child. The efficient level of human capital investment equates the risk adjusted expected return on human capital and financial investments.[27] The efficient level of human capital investment depends mainly on the interest rate and on the ability of the child, although this result depends somewhat on the risks facing the family and their attitudes toward them. e^*_{t+1} is defined below:

$$e^*_{t+1} \equiv e(h^*_{t+1}, B_{t+1}, \lambda_{t+1}) \tag{A.6}$$

h^*_{t+1} is the human capital investment which equates marginal risk-adjusted expected returns on human and financial investments (an equation defining h^*_{t+1} appears below for a special case of the model). h^*_{t+1} and e^*_{t+1} therefore depend on the ability of the child, the interest rate, the shock λ, and risk factors.

Like the intergenerational budget constraints shown in figures 3.1 and

27. In general, the risk adjustment depends on parental attitudes toward risk. The equations below display the mathematics of this claim.

3.2, the slope of the constraint in equation A.5 is $-(1 + r_{t+1})$. However, the constraints in figures 3.1 and 3.2 were derived under the assumption that parents faced no uncertainty. Equation A.5 actually represents a whole series of constraints, one for each realization of the shocks λ and χ. The shocks affect both the intercept of the constraint (the term in square brackets) through their effect on earnings and financial asset income and the slope of the constraint through their effect on the interest rate.

The permanent income version of the model allows x_{t+1} to take on any value. The borrowing constraint version rules out negative financial transfers:

$$x_{t+1} \geq 0 \tag{A.7}$$

If the borrowing constraint $x_{t+1} \geq 0$ is imposed, the intergenerational budget constraint shown in equation A.5 only applies for $c_{t+1} \geq e^*_{t+1}$. For $c_{t+1} < e^*_{t+1}$, the earnings technology $e(h, B, \lambda)$ dictates the possibilities for a family to transfer consumption between parents and child:

$$c_{t+1} = e(I_t - c_t, B_{t+1}, \lambda_{t+1}) \tag{A.8}$$

Unlike the permanent income intergenerational budget constraint, this segment of the budget constraint is not linear because the slope of the earnings function with respect to h is not the same for all levels of h. Combining the constraint A.5 for $c_{t+1} \geq e^*_{t+1}$ and the constraint A.8 for $c_{t+1} < e^*_{t+1}$, we have a single intergenerational budget constraint such as that shown in the right panel of figure 3.12, with a linear segment above e^*_{t+1} and a curved segment below e^*_{t+1}. The difference between the constraint shown in figure 3.12 and those that apply in this stochastic model is that equations A.5 and A.8 represent an intergenerational budget constraint for each possible realization of the shocks λ and χ.

According to the discussion in the text, parents are concerned with two things: their consumption and the consumption of their child. In the stochastic model of this appendix, parents are concerned about their consumption and the consumption of their child for every possible realization of the shocks λ and χ. I use the utility function below:

$$\frac{\sigma}{\sigma - 1} c_t^{(\sigma - 1)/\sigma} + \alpha \frac{\sigma}{\sigma - 1} E\left[c_{t+1}^{(\sigma - 1)/\sigma}\right] \tag{A.9}$$

where the expectations operator represents the integral over all possible realizations of the shocks (λ, χ), weighting by the density.

λ and χ are unknown when parents choose c_t, h_{t+1}, and x_{t+1} so c_t, h_{t+1}, and x_{t+1} cannot vary according to the realizations of λ and χ. c_{t+1}, on the other hand, is determined after the shocks are realized so it can take on a different value for each possible realization for λ and χ. In the permanent income model, c_t, h_{t+1}, x_{t+1}, and one value of c_{t+1} for each possible (λ, χ) are chosen so as to maximize A.9 subject to the constraints A.1, A.2, A.3, and A.4. The borrowing constraint model adds the constraint $x_{t+1} \geq 0$.

Assume (i) $\lambda = \chi$

(ii) $\ln \lambda \sim N(\mu_\lambda, \sigma_\lambda^2)$

(iii) $e(h, B, \lambda) = B\lambda h^\nu$

These assumptions allow me to obtain some clear analytical results, although the qualitative results can be found in many other versions of the model.

First consider some results relating to the chosen human capital investment. In the intergenerational permanent income model—and in the borrowing constraints model in families for whom the borrowing constraint does not bind—parents make the efficient human capital investment h^*_{t+1}. h^*_{t+1} equates the risk-adjusted expected returns on human capital and financial investments:

$$E(\lambda_{t+1}\, c_{t+1}^{-1/\sigma})\frac{\partial e(h^*_{t+1}, B_{t+1})}{\partial h} = E(\chi_{t+1} c_{t+1}^{-1/\sigma})(1 + r)$$

$$\frac{\partial e(h^*_{t+1}, B_{t+1})}{\partial h} = (1 + r) \tag{A.10}$$

The first equality shows the risk adjustments explicitly. Because $\chi = \lambda$, the risk adjustments for human and financial investment are the same and we can derive the second equality from the first. This means that the efficient human capital investment depends *only* on r and the child's ability B_{t+1}; it does not depend on parental income. If B_{t+1} is correlated with parental income, this result still holds but we would observe a correlation between e_{t+1} and I_t. When the borrowing constraint binds, actual human capital investments are less than h^*_{t+1} and will be related to parental income.

Assumptions (i)–(iii) deliver a special case of the mathematical models displayed above. Analytical solutions are available for the expansion path:

Permanent Income Model

$$\ln c_{t+1} = \left[\sigma \ln \alpha + \sigma \ln(1 + r) + \sigma\mu_\lambda + \frac{\sigma}{2}\left(\frac{\sigma - 1}{\sigma}\right)^2 \sigma_\lambda^2\right] + \ln c_t + \varepsilon_{t+1}$$

Imperfect Capital Markets Model

$$\ln c_{t+1} = \begin{cases} \left[\sigma \ln \alpha + \sigma \ln(1+r) + \sigma\mu_\lambda + \frac{\sigma}{2}\left(\frac{\sigma-1}{\sigma}\right)^2 \sigma_\lambda^2\right] & \\ + \ln c_t + \varepsilon_{t+1} & \textit{if } \ln c_{t+1} \geq \ln e^*_{t+1} \\ \beta\left[\sigma \ln \alpha + \sigma \ln(1+r) + \sigma\mu_\lambda + \frac{\sigma}{2}\left(\frac{\sigma-1}{\sigma}\right)^2 \sigma_\lambda^2\right] & \\ + (1-\beta)\ln e^*_{t+1} + \beta \ln c_t + \beta\, \varepsilon_{t+1} & \textit{if } \ln c_{t+1} < \ln e^*_{t+1} \end{cases}$$

$$\beta \equiv \frac{\nu}{\nu + \sigma(1-\nu)}$$

$$\varepsilon_{t+1} \equiv \ln \lambda_{t+1} - E[\ln \lambda_{t+1}]$$

$$\ln e^*_{t+1} \equiv -\frac{\nu}{1-\nu} \ln(1+r) + \frac{1}{1-\nu} \ln B_{t+1} + \frac{\nu}{1-\nu} \ln \nu + \mu_\lambda + \varepsilon_{t+1}$$

$c_{t+1} > e^*_{t+1}$ if and only if $x_{t+1} > 0$. Assumptions (i)–(iii) imply that e^*_{t+1} depends only on B_{t+1}, λ_{t+1}, ν, and r. Because r, ν, and μ_λ are assumed to be the same across families, B_{t+1} and λ_{t+1} are the only source of cross-family differences in e^*_{t+1}. Notice that β depends on ν and σ. If there are only very slight diminishing returns to human capital investments (ν is close to 1) *or* parents have a very strong preference for moderation (σ close to 0), then β is close to 1 and the slope of the expansion path in the imperfect capital markets model is very similar for Groups 1 and 2. In order to generate implications that are very different from those of the permanent income model, Becker and Tomes (1986) require that there be a borrowing constraint *and* that σ and ν are sufficiently different from 0 and 1, respectively.

In order to prevent the growth of overall consumption inequality, the term in large square brackets must be negative or—if the efficient level of earnings tends to grow over time—be less than the intergenerational growth rate of e^*. See Laitner (1992) or Jesus Navarro-Zermeno (1993) for further discussion. Consider the case that e^* grows over time at rate g and notice that it is feasible for the consumption of the typical family to grow at the same rate. Consumption of Group 1 families grows less rapidly than e^* (because the term in square brackets is less than g), but Group 2 families have more rapid consumption growth because of the concavity of the expansion path. One can imagine that there might be enough Group 2 families with consumption growth more rapid than g that the consumption growth of an average family is exactly g. However, the result relies on a difference between the consumption growth of Group 1 and Group 2 families—it depends on a β that is different from 1. Without the curvature assumptions, β may be very close to one so that it is not likely to have both (*a*) stable overall consumption inequality and (*b*) average consumption growth equal to g.

Proposition A-1: Parental consumption differences that are associated with parental income differences (rather than parental differences in α and r), do not regress to the mean in percentage terms across families in the permanent income model. The proof of this proposition follows from the expression for $\ln c_{t+1}$ above.

Proposition A-2: If α and r are the same for all families, consumption does not regress to the mean in percentage terms across families in the borrowing constrained model with $c_{t+1} > e^*_{t+1}$. If there is heterogeneity in α or r, consumption does regress to the mean across Group 1 families in both models because of a "selection bias." The proof of this proposition follows from the expression for $\ln c_{t+1}$ above.

A closed form solution for e_{t+1} is not available for the borrowing constraints model. However, one can be derived in terms of an implicit function $H(I_t, B_{t+1})$ whose derivatives can be computed analytically:

Imperfect Capital Markets Model

$$\ln e_{t+1} = \begin{cases} -\dfrac{\nu}{1-\nu}\ln(1+r) + \dfrac{1}{1-\nu}\ln B_{t+1} + \dfrac{\nu}{1-\nu}\ln \nu + \mu_\lambda + \varepsilon_{t+1} & \textit{if } \ln c_{t+1} \geq \ln e^*_{t+1} \\ \ln H(I_t, B_{t+1}) + \mu_\lambda + \varepsilon_{t+1} & \textit{if } \ln c_{t+1} < \ln e^*_{t+1} \end{cases}$$

$$\frac{\partial \ln H}{\partial \ln B_{t+1}} < \frac{1}{1-\nu}$$

$$\frac{\partial \ln H}{\partial \ln I_t} = \frac{I_t}{I_t - \left(\dfrac{H(I_t, B_{t+1})}{B_{t+1}}\right)^{1/\nu}}\beta > 0$$

Proposition A-3: In the permanent income model, the intergenerational dynamics of earnings are the same for Groups 1 and 2. The proof follows from the implication that all families have $e_{t+1} = e^*_{t+1}$ and e^*_{t+1} varies across families only according to exogenous factors (B_{t+1} and λ).

Proposition A-4: If a child's ability is uncorrelated with his parent's earnings and Group 1 is sufficiently large, then earnings in the borrowing constrained model are more persistent in Group 2.

Proof: From the equation for e_{t+1}, there are three reasons for an intergenerational earnings correlation: (*a*) a correlation between B_{t+1} and e_t, (*b*) a correlation between I_t and e_t, and (*c*) an upward selection bias. The first reason is assumed away by the proposition. When Group 1 is sufficiently large, the upward selection bias is as large or larger for Group 2. Finally, reason (*b*) generates a larger correlation for Group 2.

Proposition A-5: If the efficient human capital investment is not too variable across families, earnings are more unequal among the adult children of borrowing constrained families.

Proof: From the expression for $\ln e_{t+1}$, the variance of log earnings is approximately:

$$v(\ln e_{t+1}) \approx \begin{cases} \dfrac{1}{(1-\nu)^2} v(\ln B_{t+1}) + v(\varepsilon_{t+1}) & \text{if } \ln c_{t+1} \geq \ln e^*_{t+1} \\[2ex] \left(\dfrac{\partial \ln H}{\partial \ln B_{t+1}}\right)^2 v(\ln B_{t+1}) + v(\varepsilon_{t+1}) + & \\ \left(\dfrac{\partial \ln H}{\partial \ln I_t}\right)^2 v(\ln I_t) + & \text{if } \ln c_{t+1} < \ln e^*_{t+1} \\ 2\left(\dfrac{\partial \ln H}{\partial \ln I_t}\dfrac{\partial \ln H}{\partial \ln B_{t+1}}\right) c(\ln I_t, \ln B_{t+1}) & \end{cases}$$

$$\frac{\partial \ln H}{\partial \ln B_{t+1}} < \frac{1}{1-\nu}, \quad \frac{\partial \ln H}{\partial \ln I_t} = \frac{I_t}{I_t - \left(\dfrac{H(I_t, B_{t+1})}{B_{t+1}}\right)^{1/\nu}} \beta > 0$$

If parental income does not vary among the Group 2 families, then earnings are more equal among the adult children of that group. The gap between Group 1 and Group 2 inequality depends on the B_{t+1} inequality (that is, inequality in the efficient human capital investment). However, parental income inequality contributes to earnings inequality among Group 2 families but not among Group 1. As parental income inequality becomes important relative to inequality in the efficient human capital investment, Group 2 earnings equality becomes relatively greater.

Proposition A-5 seems somewhat ambiguous because efficient human capital investments are not always observed in the borrowing constrained model. What if efficient human capital investments are highly variable across families? Proposition A-6 shows that this possibility has some empirical implications.

Proposition A-6: If the efficient human capital investment is highly variable across families relative to parental income, then poorer children are more likely to receive a financial transfer. If the efficient human capital investment is not too variable across families, earnings are more unequal among the adult children of borrowing constrained families.

Proof: A child receives a positive financial transfer if and only if $c_{t+1} > e^*_{t+1}$. Very low ability decreases e^*_{t+1} and, holding constant c_{t+1}, therefore makes it likely that the inequality holds. By reducing the earnings of children, very low ability also reduces family resources and therefore consumption by children c_{t+1}, but, assuming that parental income is relatively unchanged, this effect is less than dollar-for-dollar because parental consumption also depends on family resources.

Suppose we observe that richer children are more likely to receive a financial transfer. Proposition A-6 suggests that efficient human capital investments are not too variable across families so that we might safely ignore the conditional clause in Proposition A-5.

Results from Computer Simulations

Using assumptions (i)–(iii), $\sigma \leq 1$, and an autoregressive process for ability, I have explored computer simulations of the mathematical model when ability is both variable and correlated across generations (Han and Mulligan 1997). Simulations results show that consumption does not regress to the mean in either Group 1 or Group 2 or, if it does, it does so only very slowly (that is, a persistence of 0.95 or higher). The plausibility of the result can be seen in the mathematical formulas above. For Group 2 families, the equation for $\ln c_{t+1}$ includes both $\ln c_t$ and $\ln e^*_{t+1}$. When $\ln e^*_{t+1}$ is sufficiently correlated with $\ln c_t$ (for example, because parental income is highly correlated with the child's ability), it can appear that consumption does not regress to the mean.

I state in the text that earnings in Group 1 regress to the mean "according to the intergenerational persistence of ability," but the simulations suggest that log earnings may be more or less correlated across generations than is ability—depending on how the model is parameterized.

I also explored heterogeneity of altruism across families. I state in the text that taste heterogeneity can produce regression to the mean of consumption even in Group 1, an effect which can be quantitatively important for moderate degrees of heterogeneity.

CHAPTER 4

How Altruism Is Influenced by Economic Status

The permanent income and borrowing constraints models make the neutral assumption that intergenerational altruism is not related to parental income. Deviations from this assumption change the predictions of those models for the dynamics of inequality. Consider, for example, the permanent income model. If one supposes that richer parents are less altruistic, then, as shown in figure 3.7, expansion paths are inelastic and consumption regresses to the mean across generations. If, instead, richer parents are more altruistic, expansion paths are elastic and consumption regresses away from the mean. Which of these assumptions is correct? This chapter writes down two models of the *formation* of altruism. Rather than *assuming* that altruism is related in one way or another to income and other variables, the models *predict* these relationships and therefore have implications for the dynamics of inequality. The first model maintains the assumption from previous chapters that all parents have one child, focusing on the incentives to accumulate altruism. The simple graphical model is new to the economics literature and is used throughout the book to generate predictions for a variety of human behavior, including intergenerational mobility, inequality within the family, charitable giving, and loyalty within firms.

I also present an alternative model of the effect of economic status on intergenerational altruism. The model, due to Gary Becker and Robert Barro (1988), abstracts from the purposeful accumulation of altruism but allows parents to choose the number of children. I present a simple graphical exposition of the Becker-Barro model and show that—at least for modern economies—their model counterfactually predicts regression away from the mean of consumption. A final subsection incorporates both the purposeful accumulation of altruism from my model and the fertility choice from the Becker-Barro model into a single model.

The models in this chapter can be interpreted as "models of preferences." I argue that parental actions affect their willingness to sacrifice their own consumption for consumption by their child. Parents are aware of the effects of their actions on their "preferences" and take those effects into account when determining what actions to take. These two assumptions allow me to predict how income, prices, and other variables affect parental priorities and the transmission of inequality across generations. As a mathematical model of variable intergenerational preferences, my model addresses an issue that has been addressed in a few other economics papers, including Larry Epstein (1987), Robert Lucas and Nancy Stokey (1984), Tjalling Koopmans (1960), and H. Uzawa (1968). However, these other economics papers basically assume a particular relationship between income and altruism rather than deriving the result from other considerations that also have implications for behavior other than intergenerational mobility.

This chapter begins with a discussion of intergenerational substitution effects. I argue that the usual source of intergenerational substitution—gentle curvature of the indifference curves in the $[c_t, c_{t+1}]$ plane—is unnecessary. Indifference curves in the $[c_t, c_{t+1}]$ plane are always L-shaped in this chapter, and the first section develops some of the implications of the L-shape. The next section introduces the purposeful accumulation of altruism by parents, showing how budget sets, preferences, and ultimately inequality are affected by this activity. The Becker-Barro model of fertility and altruism is analyzed in "The Quantity and Quality of Intergenerational Altruism," and the final section reviews the main results of the chapter and discusses the methodology of "endogenizing preferences."

Implications for the intergenerational transmission of inequality are the focus of this chapter, but my model of the formation of altruism also has several other predictions. These other predictions, derived in chapters 11, 12, and 13, include the distribution of resources among siblings, optimal advertising for charitable organizations, the effects of divorce on the concern and giving of fathers, and the compensation of agents.

Intergenerational Substitution Effects in the Theory of Altruism

Chapter 3 shows that standard analyses of consumption choices require that parental preferences for moderation are not too strong (that is, indifference curves are only mildly curved). Mild curvature allows the permanent income and borrowing constraint models to predict "intergenerational substitution"—that the ratio c_{t+1}/c_t responds to changes in the slope of the intergenerational budget constraint.[1] However, I show in this

1. Remember from chapter 3 that c_t is consumption by parents and c_{t+1} is consumption by children. The intergenerational budget constraint is the line in the $[c_t, c_{t+1}]$, which denotes

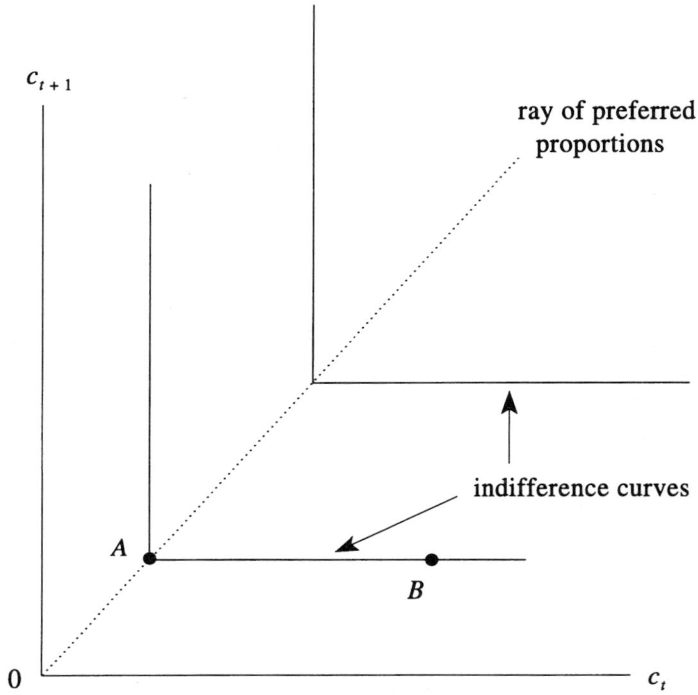

4.1 Strong Preference for Moderation

chapter that, with a model of the determination of altruism, we can predict substitution of c_{t+1} for c_t even when the parental preference for moderation is strong. I therefore simplify the analysis by drawing L-shaped indifference curves in the $[c_t, c_{t+1}]$ plane as in figure 4.1. Appendix C presents results for weaker parental preferences for moderation.

I maintain the other assumptions about preferences: homotheticity and "more is better." The homotheticity of preferences for $[c_t, c_{t+1}]$ is shown in figure 4.1 by the corner of each of the L's lying on a single ray. Along the ray shown in the figure—which I call the ray of *preferred proportions*—the slope of the indifference curve is undefined, but the slope along any other ray is either $-\infty$ or 0, depending on whether the ray lies above or below that shown in figure 4.1. "More is better" can also be seen in figure 4.1, although it might be more accurate to say "more is better in moderation." Beginning from an allocation such as A or B, a movement to the northeast represents an increase of both c_t and c_{t+1} and is associated with a movement to a new and higher indifference curve.

---

the feasible allocations available for a family. The constraint is determined by the interest rate and earnings opportunities for parents and children.

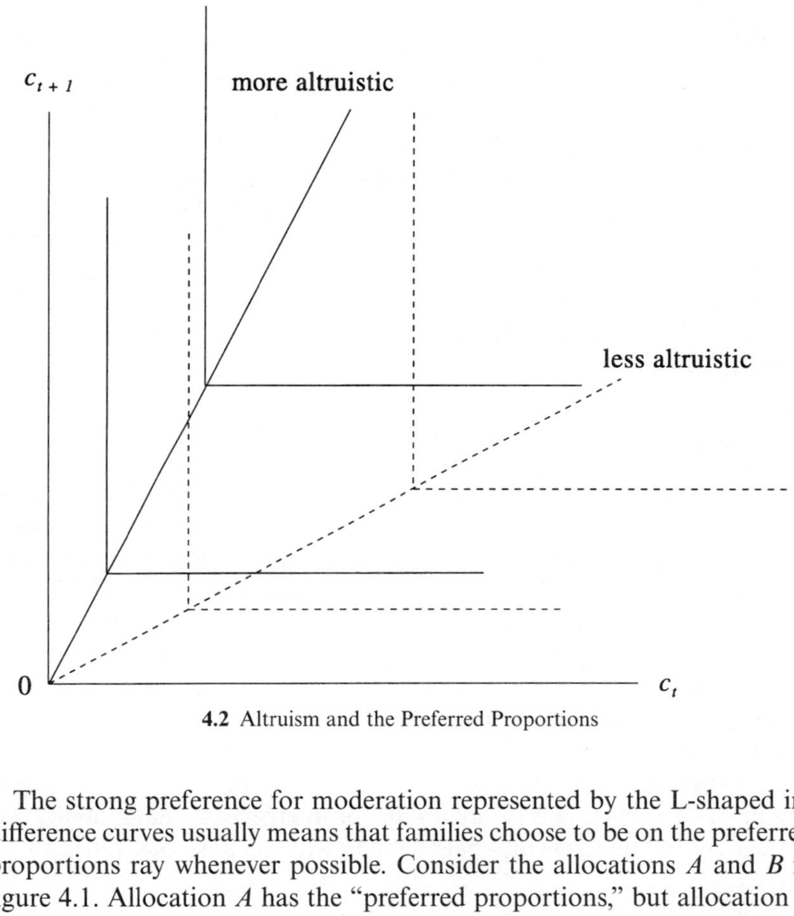

4.2 Altruism and the Preferred Proportions

The strong preference for moderation represented by the L-shaped indifference curves usually means that families choose to be on the preferred proportions ray whenever possible. Consider the allocations *A* and *B* in figure 4.1. Allocation *A* has the "preferred proportions," but allocation *B* does not. Both are on the same indifference curve, so neither is preferred to the other. *A* and *B* involve the same level of c_{t+1} but, because *B* has more c_t, allocation *B* is probably more expensive.[2] Therefore, without knowing much about budget sets, one can predict that families with L-shaped indifference curves choose allocations somewhere on the preferred proportions ray. "More is better" means that families will choose a point on their preferred proportions ray that is as far away from the origin as their budget set allows.

Consider indifference curves in the $[c_t, c_{t+1}]$ plane that lie on a flatter ray, such as the dashed curves displayed in figure 4.2. "More is better"

2. I write "probably" because the cost of any allocation depends on the budget set. But, for most budget sets worth thinking about (including those in this book), all goods are costly in the sense that more consumption of one good requires less consumption of some other good.

for parents with these preferences, but they prefer not to have their child consume more than they do. Such parents are labeled as "less altruistic" in the figure. More altruistic parents have a stronger concern for their child's success; their indifference curves lie on a steeper ray, such as the solid curves in figure 4.2. The point of my analysis is to allow adults to affect the kind of parents they will be. Do they want to be altruistic parents who place a lot of weight on their child's success or do they want to be less altruistic parents whose personal consumption is their main priority? In other words, parents in my model take actions that affect their degree of altruism, actions that affect their ray of preferred proportions in the $[c_t, c_{t+1}]$ plane. What follows explains exactly how parents in my model "affect their degree of altruism."

The Formation of Altruism

This section uses the tools of economic analysis to predict which families choose to be more altruistic. The first part describes the "child-oriented resources," which I claim affect intergenerational altruism. "The Effect of Altruism on Preferences" and "'Total Resource' and 'Substitution' Effects in the Permanent Income Model" describe how the chosen degree of altruism is determined by family opportunities when opportunities are as in the permanent income model. The "Complementarity between Child-Oriented Resources and a Child's Consumption" is then examined. The theory of altruism is extended to the imperfect capital markets model in "Parental Income and Substitution Effects in the Borrowing Constraints Model." The implications of my results for intergenerational mobility are worked out in "Intergenerational Mobility with Endogenous Altruism."

Definition of Child-Oriented Resources

I argue that child-oriented resources are time-intensive and show how they fit into a permanent income budget constraint. I conclude here by defining the cost of accumulating altruism. This cost function is used later in the chapter to prove some of the main results.

Child-Oriented Resources Are Time-Intensive

People are born selfish. Concern for the welfare of others only comes with *effort.* Adam Smith explains in his *Theory of Moral Sentiments,*[3]

3. See chapter 10 or David Sally (1995) for further discussion of Smith's views on sympathy.

> As we have no immediate experience of what other men feel, we can form no idea of the manner in which they are affected, but by conceiving what we ourselves should feel like in the situation. . . . [our senses] never did, and never can, carry us beyond our own person, and it is by the imagination only that we can form any conception of what are [our brother's] sensations (1982 [1790], I.i.I.2).

I apply this idea to intergenerational altruism. A parent's concern for a child's consumption or welfare is assumed to depend on the quantity of resources—mainly time and effort—directed toward the accumulation of concern. If parents do little to accumulate altruism, they will not be very concerned for their child's welfare. In terms of an indifference curve diagram, few resources spent on altruism means that indifference curves in the $[c_t, c_{t+1}]$ plane are more like the dashed indifference curves shown in figure 4.2. Substantial efforts, on the other hand, can help parents appreciate their children's happiness, shifting their indifference curves in the $[c_t, c_{t+1}]$ plane to the solid curves shown in figure 4.2. I refer to the resources spent accumulating altruism as *child-oriented resources.*

The important properties of child-oriented resources are: (*a*) they increase parental willingness to make sacrifices for their children, (*b*) they are costly, and (*c*) the cost is mainly a cost of time and effort. Time spent interacting with children is the most important example of the accumulation of child-oriented resources by parents. Child-oriented resources also include other time and mental effort spent by parents anticipating and appreciating the success that children will someday enjoy as a result of parental transfers of money, schooling, and other resources. People may naturally tend to be selfish, but parents may also spend time and effort in self-reflection in order to overcome such a natural bias, making sure that they are choosing a "proper" or "fair" allocation of resources between themselves and children.

A Graphical Derivation of the Budget Constraint

Nobody enjoys access to unlimited resources, especially time and effort. Even a billionaire has twenty-four hours in his day and a limited number of days in his lifetime. Time, effort, or goods devoted to accumulating altruism are therefore resources that cannot be devoted to work, leisure, and other activities. These constraints can be displayed in a diagram similar to figures 3.1 and 3.2, with one important difference. In the discussion of the previous chapters, there are only two goods: the consumption of parents and children. The intergenerational budget constraint from previous chapters can therefore be shown in the $[c_t, c_{t+1}]$ plane. However, there are now *three* goods: consumption by parents, consumption by children, and resources devoted to the accumulation of altruism. The budget constraint must therefore be shown in the three-dimensional space $[c_t, c_{t+1}, q_t]$, where q_t is child-oriented resources.

Figure 4.3 uses a two-dimensional diagram to illustrate the three-dimensional permanent income budget constraint in the $[c_t, c_{t+1}, q_t]$ space.[4] The figure displays the intergenerational permanent income budget constraint when families purchase child-oriented resources in addition to consumption for parents and child. Now the diagram has three axes rather than two—an axis for c_t, an axis for c_{t+1}, and an axis for q_t. Consider first the earnings endowment, which is plotted before as a square dot in the $[c_t, c_{t+1}]$ quadrant (to the northeast of "0"). If parents were to purchase *zero* child-oriented resources, then all of the endowment could be spend on c_t and c_{t+1}. As before, feasible choices lie on a straight line of slope $-(1 + r)$ passing through the earnings endowment (shown as a long-dashed line in the figure). However, if resources are spent on child-oriented resources, then less can be spent on c_t and c_{t+1}. Purchases of q_t therefore reduce the feasible set of choices for c_t and c_{t+1}. This is shown in figure 4.3 as a parallel shift from the long-dashed line to the solid line in the $[c_t, c_{t+1}]$ quadrant.

Exactly how many resources are used by purchases of q_t can be determined geometrically in figure 4.3 in three steps. First, choose an amount for q_t and locate it on the q_t axis. Second, move horizontally toward the budget constraint—the upward-sloping solid line—shown in the $[c_t, q_t]$ quadrant (see, for example, the horizontal portion of the dotted line). Third, move upwards from the point of intersection with the upward-sloping solid line (again the dotted line provides an example). The point of intersection with the c_t axis, labeled *C*, provides the starting point for the intergenerational budget constraint in the $[c_t, c_{t+1}]$ quadrant.

Notice three properties of figure 4.3. First, $q_t = 0$ produces an intergenerational budget constraint in the $[c_t, c_{t+1}]$ quadrant that has slope $-(1 + r)$ and passes through the earnings endowment. It can be derived by moving horizontally from the point $q_t = 0$—and therefore along the c_t axis—to the point of intersection with the $[c_t, q_t]$ budget constraint. This point of intersection, labeled *A*, is exactly the point of intersection of the long-dashed line, so the intergenerational budget constraint in the $[c_t, c_{t+1}]$ quadrant coincides with the long-dashed line. Second, the $[c_t, q_t]$ budget constraint has slope $1/p$, where p is the price of child-oriented resources. If p is very high, the $[c_t, q_t]$ budget constraint has a very flat slope. A flat

4. An intergenerational borrowing constraint is introduced in "Parental Income and Substitution Effects in the Borrowing Constraints Model."

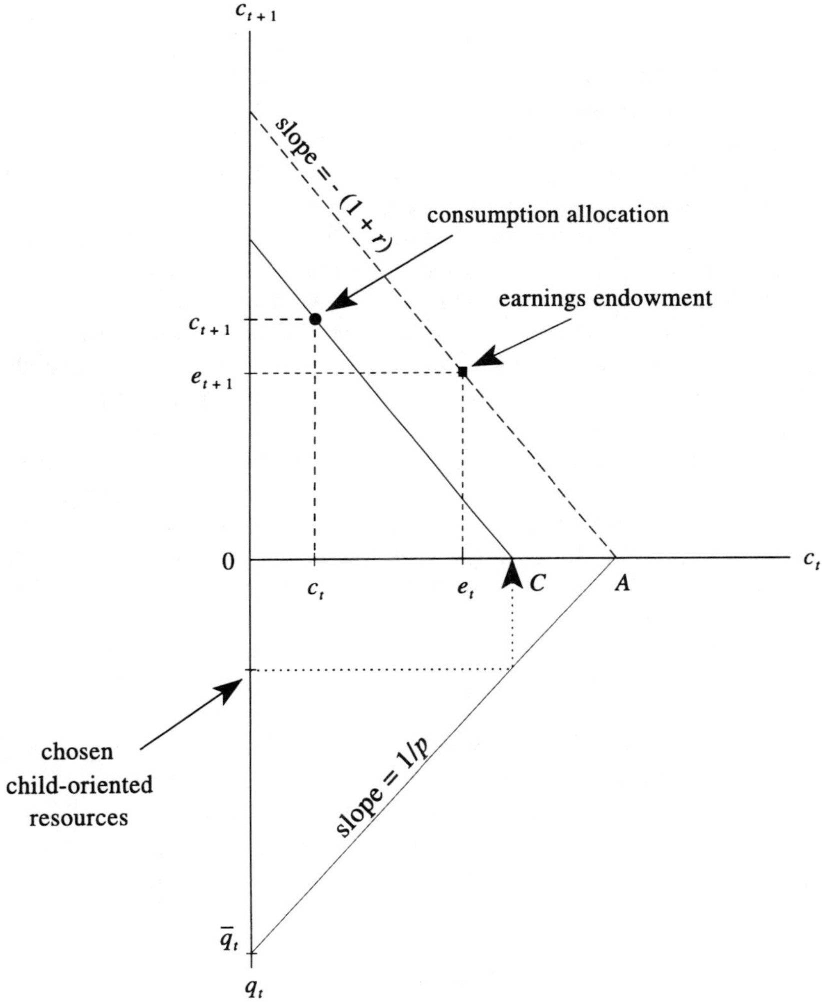

4.3 Intergenerational Budget Constraint with Child-oriented Resources

slope means that purchases of q_t—vertical movements along the q_t axis—translate into large horizontal movements of the intergenerational budget constraint in the $[c_t, c_{t+1}]$ quadrant. The reason, of course, is that expensive q_t uses up a lot of the family's resources. Third, the maximum amount of q_t that the family can afford is $\overline{q}$. If parents were to purchase $q_t = \overline{q}$, the diagram shows that the intergenerational budget constraint in the $[c_t, c_{t+1}]$ quadrant must intersect the c_t axis at the origin—the family has no resources left to purchase c_t or c_{t+1}. A lower price would steepen the $[c_t, q_t]$

budget constraint and increase the maximum affordable amount $\bar{q}$. More earnings for the parents or for the child would shift the long-dashed line—and therefore the $[c_t, q_t]$ budget constraint—outward, increasing $\bar{q}$.

Consider the special case when parental time is the only child-oriented resource. Normalize the total endowment of parental time to one. Parents spend q_t of their time learning to enjoy their children and spend the other $(1 - q_t)$ of their time working. In this special case, one can use a diagram much like figure 4.3, except that one has to be careful about the use of the word "earnings." One interpretation of earnings in this special case is as the product of time spent working $(1 - q_t)$ and a wage rate per unit time w_t.[5] Under this interpretation, it is appropriate to think about a "full earnings endowment" (w_t, w_{t+1}) which could be attained if parents and child spend all of their one unit of time working. A full earnings endowment, shown as a solid square dot in the $[c_t, c_{t+1}]$ quadrant of figure 4.4, replaces the earnings endowment of figure 4.3. If parents choose $q_t > 0$, then actual parental earnings $(1 - q_t)w_t$ is less than full parental earnings w_t. This difference is shown in figure 4.4 as the horizontal distance between the solid square dot and the hollow square dot. The price of q_t is the parental wage rate w_t in this special case. The $[c_t, q_t]$ budget constraint therefore has a slope of $1/w_t$.

Under the time interpretation of q_t, a diagram of the budget constraint must also reflect the restriction that q_t cannot be less than 1, the total time endowment. This restriction is shown in figure 4.4 by a $[c_t, q_t]$ budget constraint that stops at the vertical position $q_t = 1$. When $q_t = 1$, parental earnings are zero and the only resources available for the purchase of c_t or c_{t+1} is the earnings of the child w_{t+1}. Figure 4.4 therefore shows with a long dashed-line that $q_t = 1$ produces an intergenerational budget constraint in the $[c_t, c_{t+1}]$ quadrant that intersects the c_{t+1} axis at the point $(0, w_{t+1})$.

The Cost of Accumulating Altruism

Consider a given expenditure on child-oriented resources q and its corresponding level of altruism a. Let $\theta(a)$ be that expenditure, expressed as a function of a, when the price of child-oriented resources (p) is equal to 1. $\theta(a)$ must be an increasing function because additional altruism must be accumulated by purchasing additional child-oriented resources. Moreover, if child-oriented resources have a diminishing effect on intergenera-

5. There is another interpretation of the previous models which might be carried over to this one: "consumption" includes both purchases of material goods *and* the enjoyment of leisure. Under this interpretation, the solid square boxes in all of the previous figures would be interpreted as "full earnings" endowments.

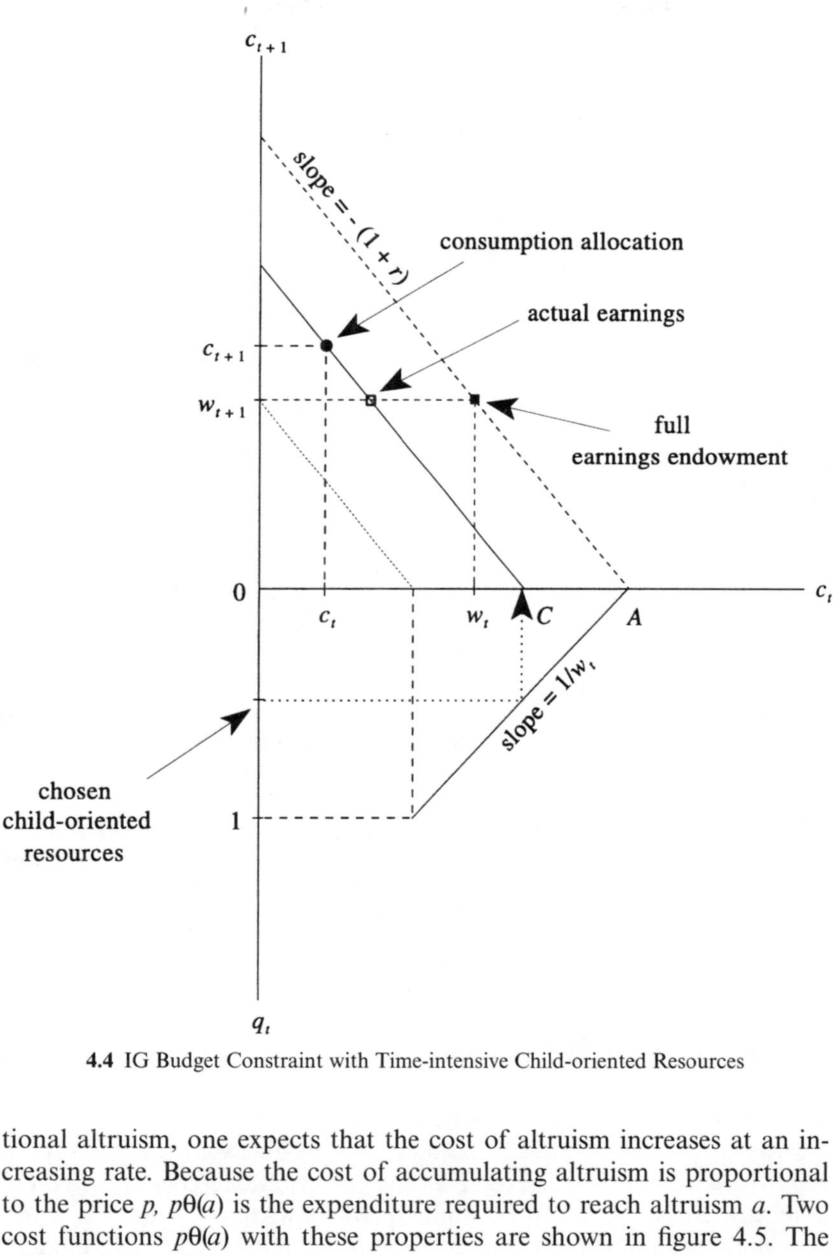

4.4 IG Budget Constraint with Time-intensive Child-oriented Resources

tional altruism, one expects that the cost of altruism increases at an increasing rate. Because the cost of accumulating altruism is proportional to the price *p*, $p\theta(a)$ is the expenditure required to reach altruism *a*. Two cost functions $p\theta(a)$ with these properties are shown in figure 4.5. The slope of the cost function is the *marginal cost of accumulating altruism;* it indicates the expenditures on child-oriented resources required to obtain more altruism.

The resources in the permanent income model that are available for

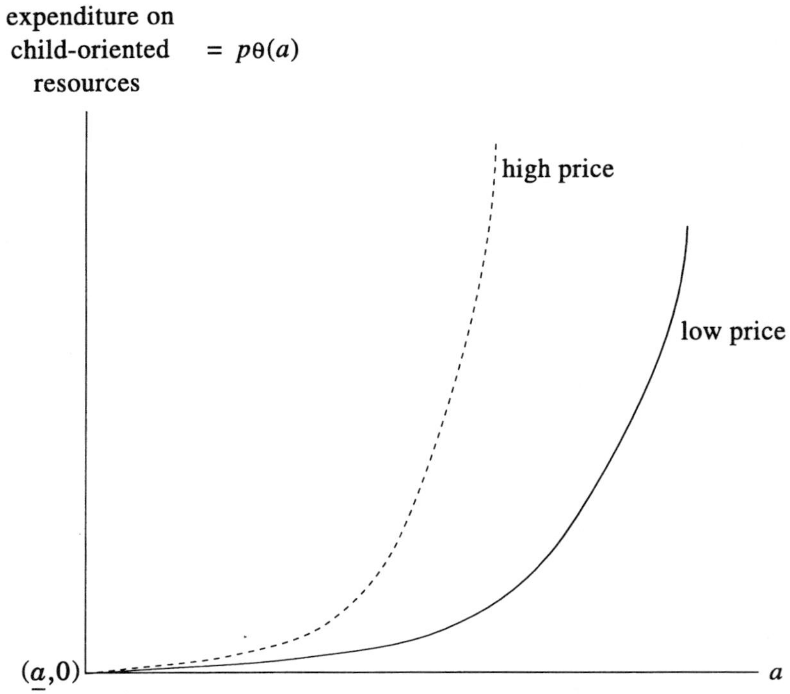

4.5 The Cost of Accumulating Altruism

parent and child consumption purchases, which I call *consumption resources* (C), are equal to total family resources (A) minus expenditures on child-oriented resources ($p\theta(a)$).[6] Families like additional consumption resources because they like consumption, but they also like child-oriented resources because it gives them additional altruism. A family's limited resources therefore confronts it with a tradeoff between consumption resources and child-oriented resources. The combinations of altruism a and consumption resources C that make a family equally happy can be displayed as indifference curves in the $[a, C]$ plane—see figure 4.6. The indifference curves slope down because both a and C are goods—an increase of either a or C must be accompanied by a decrease in the other to leave the family equally happy. The slope of the indifference curve at any point is the willingness of the family to pay for additional altruism; families with steep indifference curves are very willing to pay, while families

6. Consumption resources (C) and total family resources (A) are displayed in figures 4.3 and 4.4.

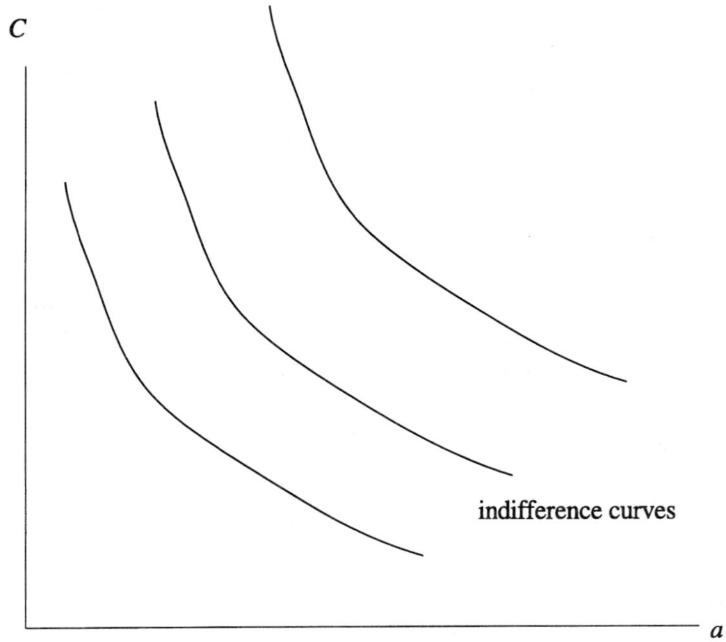

4.6 Indifference Curves in the [a, C] Plane

with flat indifference curves are less willing. A family's preference for moderation between a and C can be seen in the curvature of the indifference curve.

The cost function $p\theta(a)$ shown in figure 4.5 allows one to graph feasible choices in the [a,C] plane. Families can spend all of their resources on consumption and none on child-oriented resources and have some minimum level of altruism $\underline{a}$—a feasible allocation shown as ($\underline{a}$, A) in figure 4.7. More altruism decreases resources available for consumption according to the cost function $p\theta(a)$. Feasible allocations in the [a,C] plane are therefore constrained by the curve $A - p\theta(a)$.

Families will accumulate altruism up to the point where the willingness to pay equals the marginal cost of altruism $p\theta'(a)$, where $p\theta'(a)$ denotes the (absolute value of the) slope of the cost function $p\theta(a)$:

$$\text{willingness to pay for altruism} = p\theta'(a) \tag{4.1}$$

Such a choice is seen in figure 4.7 as the point on the set of feasible allocations where there is a tangent indifference curve.

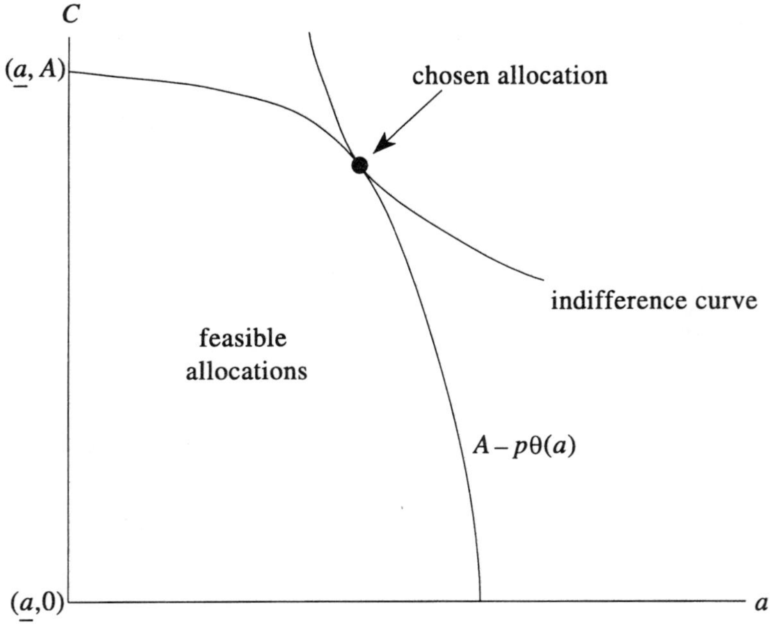

4.7 Feasible Altruism

The Effect of Altruism on Preferences

The section on the "Intergenerational Substitution Effects in the Theory of Altruism" shows that a strong preference for moderation means families will choose c_t and c_{t+1} on a ray of preferred proportions, but which ray will they choose? Parents enjoy their child's success more on higher rays, but it is costly to accumulate altruism and move to a higher ray. Before deriving some predictions, I introduce some basic assumptions about altruism and its accumulation:

(1) more altruism raises the desired proportion c_{t+1}/c_t;
(2) all parents prefer to accumulate at least a small amount of altruism and would accumulate more if it were costless to do so;
(3) at a given level of altruism, the willingness to pay for altruism is proportional to child consumption c_{t+1};
(4) holding constant c_{t+1}, the willingness to pay for altruism is less when altruism is greater.

Assumption (1) is consistent with the discussion of figure 4.2; more altruism means that families choose on a higher ray. Assumption (2) states that altruism is a "good."[7] Assumption (3) requires that parents gain from altruism according to the consumption of their child; the willingness to pay for intergenerational altruism is 50 percent greater in a family where the child consumes 50 percent more. Assumption (3) is only a statement about the effect of c_{t+1} on the willingness to pay for altruism—it is consistent with assumption (4) that the willingness to pay falls as altruism is accumulated.

For a given level of a, the desired proportion c_{t+1}/c_t is fixed. Changes in consumption resources C, for a given level of a, move the consumption allocation along a single ray of preferred proportions, changing c_{t+1} and c_t proportionally. With the result that c_{t+1} is proportional to C and the result above that the willingness to pay for altruism is proportional to c_{t+1}, there is yet another result that the willingness to pay for altruism is proportional to C. In terms of figure 4.6, this means that—for a given a—the slope of the indifference curve is proportional to consumption resources C.

"Total Resource" and "Substitution" Effects in the Permanent Income Model

In the two-dimensional case of the previous chapters, the chosen consumption allocation depends on the position of the budget constraint, which in turn depends on two factors: the earnings endowment (e_t, e_{t+1}) and the interest rate r. The interest rate determines the slope of the intergenerational budget constraint and the earnings endowment pins down its final position.[8] A similar result obtains in the three-dimensional case. The chosen allocation (c_t, c_{t+1}, q_t) depends on the position of the intergenerational budget constraint, which depends on *three* factors: the earnings endowment (e_t, e_{t+1}), the interest rate r, and the price of child-oriented resources p. The model of altruism outlined so far allows one to make some predictions about exactly how these three factors affect the degree of intergenerational altruism and the distribution of consumption across generations. First I show that more total resources increases altruism. I then prove that the effect of the price of child-oriented resources is closely re-

7. To the extent that the accumulation of altruism involves time that parents spend with children, there is obviously a point where time spent with children—and therefore altruism—is no longer a "good." Because time is costly, parents in my model would not go beyond this point. What is crucial for my analysis is that there exist some families for whom altruism is a good at the margin.

8. For the borrowing constraint model, the slope of the budget constraint also depends on the shape of the earnings function and the ability of the child.

lated to the effect of total resources. The proof of the third result—that a higher interest rate increases altruism—is deferred until "Complementarity between Child-oriented Resources and a Child's Consumption."

The Total Resource Effect

How does a change in a family's endowment with no corresponding change in the interest rate or the price of child-oriented resources—which I refer to as a change in "total family resources" A—affect their accumulation of altruism? If one did not have the assumptions (1)–(3) and the L-shaped indifference curves in the $[c_t, c_{t+1}]$ plane, it would be possible that child-oriented resources were inferior goods—more family resources decreases the accumulation of altruism. Another possibility would be that child-oriented resources are normal goods—more family resources increases the accumulation of altruism. The *total resource effect* for child-oriented resources could either be positive or negative. However, the model outlined so far delivers less ambiguous results—one of which is the normality of child-oriented resources.

Consider an increase in total family resources from A to A'. Total resources *vertically* shift the boundary of the feasible set in the $[a, C]$ plane as shown figure 4.8. Let the chosen allocation corresponding to the original level of total resources be labeled B as in the figure. If altruism a is held constant, more total resources means more consumption for both generations. From assumption (3), more c_{t+1} means more willingness to pay for altruism. However, for a unchanged, the marginal cost of altruism is unchanged while the willingness to pay has increased—a result which can be seen in the figure at allocation D, where the indifference curve is steeper than the boundary of the feasible set. It cannot be optimal for a family to leave its altruism unchanged in response to more total resources. More total resources increases the willingness to accumulate altruism without changing the marginal cost, so it must increase the chosen level of altruism.

What is the total resource effect on consumption resources? One expects that a family with more total resources would consume more, a result which is easily proven in my model. Consider the allocation F shown in figure 4.8, where altruism increases in response to more total resources, but consumption resources are unchanged. The feasible set is steeper at F than at B because altruism, and therefore its marginal cost, is higher. If the optimal choice is at F, it must be that the indifference curve is steeper at F than at B—something which violates assumption (4). Assumption (4) requires that rightward horizontal movements in the graph be associated with *less* willingness to pay and therefore flatter indifference curves. With

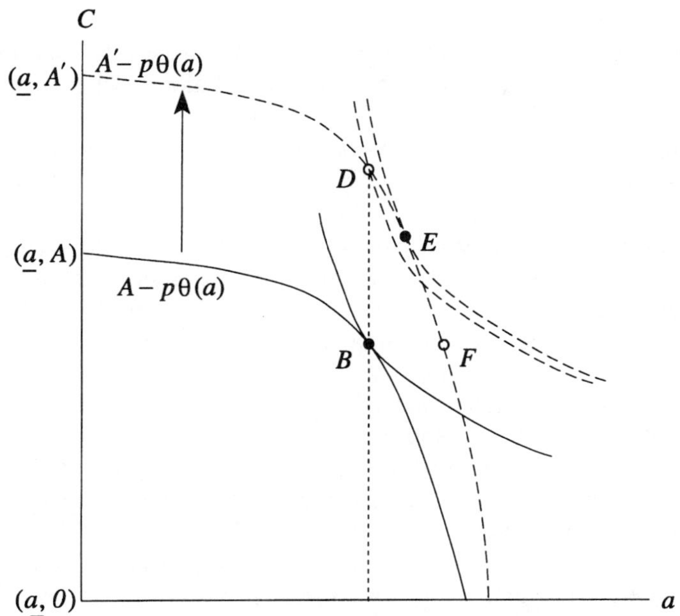

4.8 The Effect of Total Resources on Altruism

an indifference curve that is flatter at *F* than at *B*, the chosen allocation must be above *F*. More total resources therefore increase both *a* and *C*, as shown in figure 4.8 as a movement from allocation *B* to allocation *E*.

The Substitution Effect Is of the Same Magnitude as the Total Resource Effect

The total resource effect has to do with changes in the family's endowment that are not associated with changes in the interest rate or the price of child-oriented resources. A total resource effect is a useful conceptual experiment for thinking about the predictions of the model, but it may not directly generate empirical predictions because families often differ in dimensions other than their total resources. For example, parents of richer families may tend to have a greater value of time which makes time-intensive child-oriented resources more expensive for them. One therefore has to consider the effect of the price of child-oriented resources on the quantity demanded—the *substitution effect*—in order to determine the model's predictions for comparisons of families who have different values of time. In general, one would expect a higher price of child-oriented resources to discourage their use.

Do rich families accumulate more altruism than do poor families? Because rich and poor families differ in two ways—their endowment and the value of their time—one must consider both the total resource and substitution effects. From the substitution effect alone, richer families can be expected to accumulate less altruism because their time tends to be more valuable and child-oriented resources are time-intensive. If child-oriented resources were an inferior good, then the total resource effect would reinforce this prediction. On the other hand, the total resource effect generates the opposite prediction when child-oriented resources are a normal good—as in my setup; the final prediction depends on the relative magnitudes of the total resource and substitution effects. It can be shown that my model predicts that the total resource and substitution effects are of equal magnitudes.

Consider a proportional increase of total family resources A and the price p of child-oriented resources. A doubling, for example, of A and p doubles consumption resources C because $C = A - p\theta(a)$. This doubles the willingness to pay for altruism—the left-hand side of equation 4.1—because the willingness to pay is proportional to C. A doubling of p also doubles the marginal cost of altruism, the right-hand side of equation 4.1. Equation 4.1 is repeated below for convenience.

$$\text{willingness to pay for altruism} = p\theta'(a) \qquad (4.1)$$

Family choices in the permanent income model depend on A, p, and r, but it has just been shown that the chosen altruism depends on A and p only according to their *ratio* A/p. Why? Suppose one begins with values for A, p, and r and considers the corresponding choice for a. Equation 4.1 holds. I show above that a proportional change of A and p—which leaves the ratio A/p unchanged—leaves the equation 4.1 unchanged without any change in a. So if a is the choice for a family with total resources A, price p, and interest rate r, then the *same* choice a is optimal for a family with $2A$, $2p$, and r. A family's choice of a (and therefore child-oriented resources q) is insensitive to proportional changes in A and p—only disproportional changes (that is, changes in the ratio A/p) affect the accumulation of altruism.

Altruism Across Families

It is interesting to compare two sets of parents who did not inherit any financial wealth from their parents but who enjoy different wage rates. There is again a total resource and a substitution effect to be considered. However, the percentage difference in the total resources of the two families is less than the percentage difference in their wage rates because each family's resources is a weighted sum of the earnings of parents and children.[9] The wage difference generates a relatively small total resource effect and a large substitution effect so that the net effect is for the poorer family to accumulate more altruism.

Pay-as-you-go Social Security

Consider the introduction of a pay-as-you-go social security program. Such a program taxes the young and gives the proceeds to the old. Barro (1974) has shown that, when the young cannot take actions to avoid the social security taxes, the social security program has no affect on the consumption allocation chosen by families in the permanent income model. He obtains this result because the program fails to have a "total resource effect"—it fails to shift the intergenerational budget constraint in the $[c_t, c_{t+1}]$ plane. However, pay-as-you-go social security is financed with labor income taxes in the vast majority of countries (Sala-i-Martin [1996]), which means that the young can take actions to avoid some of the taxes. In particular, the young can reduce their social security tax liability by working less. Social security effectively reduces the value of time (of the young as well as the old—see Sala-i-Martin [1996]), which means that, when the accumulation of altruism is time-intensive, social security has a substitution effect encouraging the accumulation of altruism. Since the analysis of Barro (1974) suggests that the "total resource effect" of social security is minimal, the model of the accumulation of altruism in this chapter suggests that the introduction of pay-as-you-go social security increases intergenerational altruism, savings, and long-run economic growth.[10] This prediction is contrary to the theoretical analysis of Martin Feldstein (1974) and consistent with the cross-country empirical findings of Paul Cashin (1995) and Xavier Sala-i-Martin (1996). The cross-country studies find that—controlling for GDP per capita, the fraction of elderly in the population, and other variables—a country's economic growth over the last few decades is positively correlated with the size of its social security program.

9. I assume that wages regress to the mean across families—a result which obtains in the permanent income model with human capital investment.

10. One potential force in the other direction is that social security seems to be associated with less time that parents and children spend together later in life (Michael, Fuchs, and Scott 1980).

Any wage-financed transfer program increases altruism, savings, and economic growth in the model unless transfers are concentrated on families with low altruism.

Complementarity between Child-oriented Resources and a Child's Consumption

Child-oriented resources, by definition, increase parental appreciation of a child's consumption. As the previous section discusses, I assume that the willingness to pay for altruism increases with the quantity of consumption by children. These two properties—that q_t increases the desire for c_{t+1} and c_{t+1} increases the desire for q_t—means that I model child-oriented resources and child consumption as *complements.*[11]

I begin the analysis of complements by presenting a more familiar example of complementarity—ski trips and ski equipment. I then use the complementarity property to show that interest encourages the accumulation of altruism. Later chapters use complementarity to analyze the effect of taxes, divorce, and other variables on altruism.

An Example of Complements

A complementarity between two goods allows us to make some predictions in addition to the total resource and substitution effects. Before I derive those implications, consider an everyday example of complements—ski trips and ski equipment. A person who takes more ski trips is more willing to purchase expensive ski equipment because he can utilize that ski equipment on several different occasions, thus, "getting his money's worth." Another person who only takes one ski trip every few years is less willing to buy expensive ski equipment—and may not purchase ski equipment at all—because the equipment would rarely be used. Ski trips increase the desire to buy ski equipment, but the converse is also true: ski equipment increases the desire to take ski trips. Skiing is often more enjoyable with nicer equipment; nice equipment decreases the chance of injury, keeps the skier from getting too hot or too cold or from getting a sunburn.

The fact that ski equipment and ski trips are complements generates some predictions about consumer purchases of ski trips and ski equipment. For example, suppose the price of a ski trip falls, perhaps because airfare or condominium rentals become cheaper. Suppose that the price of ski equipment is unchanged. The complementarity model predicts that purchases of *both* ski trips and ski equipment increase. There are three reasons for this result:[12]

11. Child-oriented resources and child consumption need not be modeled as complements in order for the former to shift parental indifference curves as in figure 2. 4. See Mulligan (1993, chapter 2) for further discussion.

12. There are three goods in this example: ski trips, ski equipment, and non-ski items.

(a) cheaper trips encourage the "substitution" or replacement of some non-ski purchases with ski trips;
(b) cheaper trips increase real income;
(c) cheaper trips make skiing cheaper.

The effects (*a*), (*b*), and (*c*) are shown as the left, middle, and right arrows in figure 4.9, respectively.

More ski trips and fewer non-ski items might be purchased because ski trips are cheaper. This effect is shown on the left-hand side of figure 4.9 as "substitution of trips for non-ski items." From the definition of complements, more ski trips increase the desire to purchase ski equipment. With no change in the price of ski equipment, more desire to purchase the equipment means more actual purchases, which is shown in figure 4.9 as the rightward arrow at the bottom of the diagram.

Even if cheaper ski trips don't directly encourage "substitution of trips for non-ski items," there is an indirect effect. To derive the indirect effect, notice that purchases of ski equipment have two effects on the resources available to purchase non-ski items. First, more equipment takes away from non-ski purchases according to the price of equipment. Second, more equipment encourages trips, which take away from non-ski resources according to the price of *trips.* A cheaper price of trips effectively reduces the cost of skiing, thereby encouraging purchases of equipment. This "substitution of ski items for non-ski items" is shown on the right-hand side of figure 4.9. From the definition of complements, more ski trips increases the desire to purchase ski equipment, which is shown in figure 4.9 as the leftward arrow at the bottom of the diagram.

A very similar argument can be used to show that more purchases of *both* ski trips and ski equipment are also the result of a lower price of equipment even when the price of trips is unchanged.

Holding constant skiers' incomes, a fall in the price of either ski trips or ski equipment also has a wealth effect. The wealth effect is represented by the middle three arrows in figure 4.9. A lower price of some good increases the purchasing power of income so that skiers are effectively more wealthy. More real income is likely to increase purchases of both ski trips and ski equipment, but the wealth effect is often unimportant. Notice that a wealth effect is the result of any falling price (not just ski trips and ski equipment) and the magnitude of the effect depends on the share of ski purchases in the skiers' budgets. If skiers spend most of their income on non-ski items such as rent or food when they're not skiing, a change in the price of ski items has only a small effect on their real income.

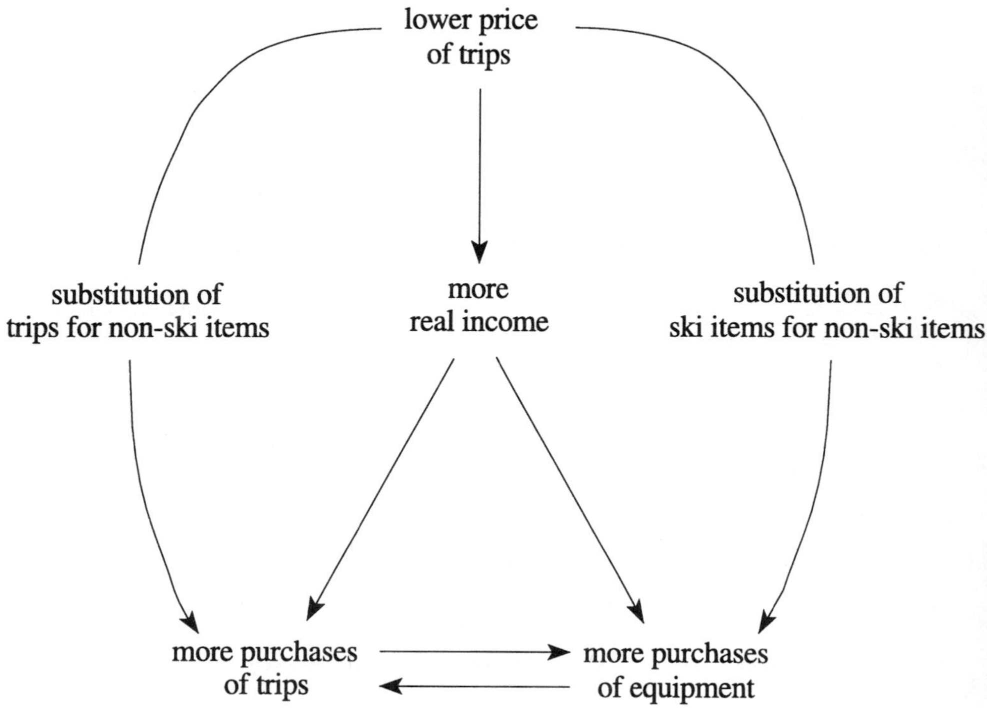

4.9 Complementarity and the Effects of Price—Ski Example

Interest Encourages Altruism

The complementarity between q_t and c_{t+1} in the intergenerational model means that a fall in the price of one increases purchases of both items. Suppose that p_t falls while total resources A and the interest rate r are held constant. There is a wealth effect, but it is small if child-oriented resources are a small share of family expenditures. Cheaper q_t increases purchases of q_t, which increases altruism and shifts the ray of preferred proportions. More c_{t+1} is purchased.

The converse is also true. Suppose p_t is held constant. A higher interest rate means that consumption by children is cheaper. To see this, consider two interest rates—0 percent and 100 percent. At an interest rate of 0 percent, parents must give up $1,000 of their own consumption to increase c_{t+1} by $1,000. At an interest rate of 100 percent, only $500 of parental consumption must be sacrificed by parents to achieve the same $1,000 increase for the child because the $500 sacrifice earns another $500 in interest. Higher interest makes it easier to provide for a child's consumption. If parental preferences for moderation were not too strong (as in figure 3.6), then one would expect a higher interest rate to encourage parents to sacrifice their own consumption to increase their child's consumption. However, indifference curves are L-shaped in our model, so parents do not deviate from their ray of preferred proportions. Even with the L-shaped indifference curves, one can show that the ray of preferred proportions will change in response to a different interest rate so that higher interest encourages altruism and, ultimately, consumption by children.

To see that interest encourages altruism, remember that the willingness to pay for altruism is proportional to c_{t+1}. Consider a low degree of altruism, represented by a dashed ray of preferred proportions and dashed indifference curves in figure 4.10, and a high degree of altruism represented by a solid ray and solid indifference curves. For a given amount of consumption resources C, the feasible (c_t, c_{t+1}) choices available with a high and low interest rate are shown in figure 4.10. The chosen allocations for the four possible combinations of high and low altruism and high and low interest are *F, E, D* and *B*. Notice that, at a low interest rate, a change from the low degree of altruism to the high degree makes a small increase in c_{t+1} (the vertical distance between allocations *B* and *D*) and a fairly large decrease in c_t (the horizontal distance between allocations *B* and *D*) while more altruism produces a proportionally larger increase in c_{t+1} and a proportionally smaller decrease in c_t (compare allocations *E* and *F*). Because more altruism has a proportionally larger impact on c_{t+1} at high rather than low interest rates, more altruism tends to increase the willingness to pay for altruism (which is proportional to c_{t+1}) at a high interest rate.[13] Even if there were not a wealth effect of higher interest, one could therefore expect more altruism at higher interest rates.

A wealth effect is not necessary to argue that more interest encourages altruism, but families are effectively wealthier when the interest rate rises and total family resources *A* are held constant. The wealth effect of a higher interest rate works in much the same way as the "total resource effect," with purchases of all three goods increasing. Is the wealth effect important? It may be important because expenditures on c_{t+1} can be an important fraction of the household's budget. At the same time, one also has to think about whether it makes sense to hold *A* constant when considering a higher interest rate. Notice that *A*—the intersection of the intergenerational budget constraint with the c_t axis when $q_t = 0$[14]—must change in response to a higher interest rate *if the earnings endowment* (e_t, e_{t+1}) is fixed. A higher interest rate twists the intergenerational budget

13. This force works against the lower willingness to pay, which, according to assumption (4), comes with more altruism.

14. See the dashed line in figure 4.3.

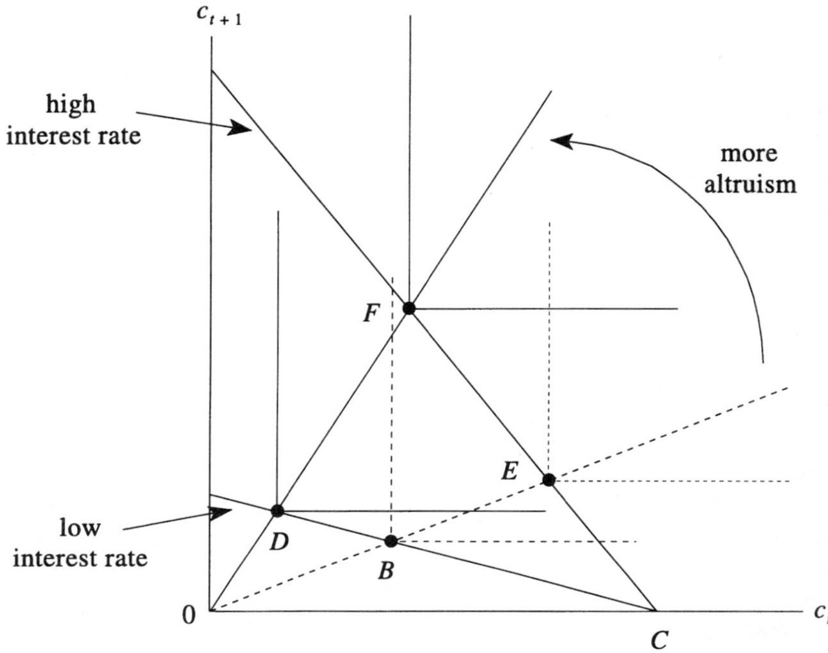

4.10 Interest Increases the Effectiveness of Altruism

constraint clockwise around the earnings endowment. This hurts families who are consuming below the earnings endowment and helps families who consume above it. Notice that the families consuming below the earnings endowment are borrowers and those who consume above are lenders, so it is no surprise that higher interest makes lenders more wealthy and borrowers less wealthy. Moreover, the magnitude of the wealth effect depends on the magnitude of borrowing and lending. There is no wealth effect for a family that neither borrows nor lends.

A higher interest rate potentially has three effects. One effect is ruled out with L-shaped indifference curves. The wealth effect depends on whether a family borrows or lends. The same three effects of interest on altruism can also be derived from the analogy to ski trips and equipment. Since we are considering a lower price of c_{t+1}, c_{t+1} is the analogue to trips. Altruism complements c_{t+1}, so equipment is the analogue to altruism. c_t is the analogue to "non-ski items." L-shaped indifference curves rule out substitution of c_{t+1} for c_t when altruism is held fixed. The analogy in the ski example is the elimination of the left-hand arrow from figure 4.9. But even without the left-hand arrow and without wealth effects (the middle arrows), the ski example shows that more interest (that is, cheaper c_{t+1}) encourages purchases of altruism and c_{t+1}.

This chapter begins with a proposal to rule out the "usual" substitution effect by introducing L-shaped indifference curves in the $[c_t, c_{t+1}]$ plane. If altruism were given, the L-shaped indifference curves imply that only the wealth effect of a higher interest rate could increase c_{t+1}. This implication has led economists to refrain from using L-shaped indifference curves in their modeling. I have shown here that endogenizing altruism allows me to predict that interest encourages c_{t+1}—even with L-shaped indifference curves and without a wealth effect. From a positive point of view, my ability to predict such an effect with L-shaped indifference curves eliminates a justification for assuming that indifference curves fail to be L-shaped.

Other Implications of Complementarity

The complementarity between q_t and c_{t+1} also produces several other results that are reported in later chapters. For example, I show that higher estate tax rates look like lower rates of interest; they therefore serve to lower intergenerational altruism. Higher income tax rates have a similar effect, although income taxes also lower the value of time and make altruism cheaper to accumulate. Chapter 12 shows that divorce can increase the cost of transferring resources from parents to children, which, from the complementarity result, means less intergenerational altruism. A related result is shown to apply to charitable giving.

Altruism and Economic Growth

Many countries have experienced and will experience economic growth—increases in incomes and wages over time. Should altruism grow over time? To study the effects of economic growth consider the total resource, substitution, and interest rate effect again. As incomes grow, the total resource effect increases the accumulation of altruism but—because the accumulation of altruism is time-intensive—growing wages discourage altruism. Since the "total resource" and "substitution" effects are equal, the income and substitution effects should cancel when economic growth exhibits roughly proportional growth of wages and incomes.

Interest rates may increase or decline with economic growth which, according to the "interest rate effect," would affect altruism. Tax rates have historically increased with economic growth.[15] Increasing tax rates is very similar to a declining interest rate (see chapter 5 for a proof) and therefore reduces altruism. Divorce may increase with economic growth, and chapter 11 suggests that divorce decreases altruism. Without changes in inter-

15. See Dennis Mueller (1989) for some evidence on this.

est or tax rates or divorce, however, the model predicts that economic growth will not affect altruism.

Parental Income and Substitution Effects in the Borrowing Constraints Model

How does the theory of the formation of altruism modify the implications of the imperfect capital markets model? Some predictions are unchanged while others are different in important ways. As before, the borrowing constraint produces two groups of families—one that makes financial transfers to children and another that wishes to borrow but cannot. It is still true that consumption regresses to the mean across generations among the borrowing-constrained families, but the theory of altruism predicts that consumption also regresses to the mean among the "unconstrained" families. Consumption may not regress to the mean at different rates in the two groups. These results are proven here. First I derive the intergenerational budget constraint for (c_t, c_{t+1}, q_t) in the presence of a borrowing constraint. Second, I show that some families behave like families in the permanent income model analyzed previously—which means that the only new results to be derived are for the families that do not make financial transfers to children. For these families, I discuss the effect of parental income on intergenerational altruism. I also analyze the effects of the value of parental time and display some of the implications of the complementarity between q_t and c_{t+1}.

Budget Constraints in the Imperfect Capital Markets Model

There are three goods (c_t, c_{t+1}, q_t). As in figures 4.3 and 4.4, the intergenerational budget constraint can be drawn in two dimensions by assigning one axis to each of the three goods. I first draw the intergenerational budget constraint on these three axes in the special case $q_t = 0$. I then show how q_t different from zero fits into the intergenerational budget constraint.

With $q_t = 0$, the imperfect capital markets budget constraint is the same as in chapter 3. The intergenerational budget constraint intersects the c_t axis at the point $(I_t, 0)$ where I_t is parental income. At first, parents transfer consumption to their children by making additional human capital investments so that the intergenerational budget constraint follows the curvature of the earnings function. At a high enough level of consumption by the child, human capital investments are large enough that their marginal return is less than or equal to the payoff from financial transfers, $1 + r$. As shown in chapter 3, the corresponding level of consumption and earnings for the child is e^*_{t+1}, the "efficient" earnings for the child. If parents want to achieve higher consumption for their child, they switch to financial transfers and the intergenerational budget constraint is a straight line with slope $-(1 + r)$ in the $[c_t, c_{t+1}]$ plane. The intergenerational budget constraint corresponding to $q_t = 0$ is shown in figure 4.11 as a long-dashed curve. Notice the curvature along the portion where parents make no financial transfers (below the vertical position e^*_{t+1} in figure 4.11) and the linearity along the portion where parents make positive financial transfers (above the vertical position e^*_{t+1}).

With $q_t > 0$, parents have less resources to spend on consumption for either generation, which appears in figure 4.11 as a horizontal shift of the budget constraint in the $[c_t, c_{t+1}]$ plane. Consider the chosen amount of child-oriented resources shown in figure 4.11. Following the dotted line horizontally to the solid budget constraint in the $[c_t, q_t]$ plane and then vertically to the c_t axis determines the amount of parental income that remains for parents to consume or to pass on to children. I refer to the remaining income as "consumption resources," which is labeled as C_t in the figure. Because the amount of child-oriented resources q_t costs p_t per unit, total expenditures on child-oriented resources are $p_t q_t$ and the remaining income is $C_t = I_t - p_t q_t$. Notice that "consumption resources" are defined slightly differently in the imperfect capital markets model than in the permanent income model.[16] Regardless of the parental income remaining for consumption purposes, there is only one point on the earning function where the slope is $(1 + r)$ and therefore only one vertical position e^*_{t+1} in figure 4.11 where intergenerational budget constraint changes from being curved to linear. A solid curve displays the budget constraint in the $[c_t, c_{t+1}]$ plane corresponding to the chosen amount of child-oriented resources shown in figure 4.11.

Group 1 and Group 2

Choices for (c_t, c_{t+1}, q_t) in the imperfect capital markets model depend on parental income I_t, the price of altruism p_t, the interest rate r, and the efficient level of earnings e^*_{t+1}. For some values of these four variables, families will choose their consumption allocation above the vertical position e^*_{t+1} in the $[c_t, c_{t+1}]$ plane—as is the case for the consumption allocation shown in figure 4.11. Families that choose above the vertical position e^*_{t+1} are "Group 1" families and are on the linear portion of their budget constraint in the $[c_t, c_{t+1}]$ plane. Because they are on the linear portion, Group 1 families behave like the permanent income families analyzed earlier in this section.

Many different results are obtained for "Group 2" families—families

16. The definitions of consumption resources in the permanent income and borrowing constraint models are $C = A - p_t q_t$ and $C_t = I_t - p_t q_t$, respectively.

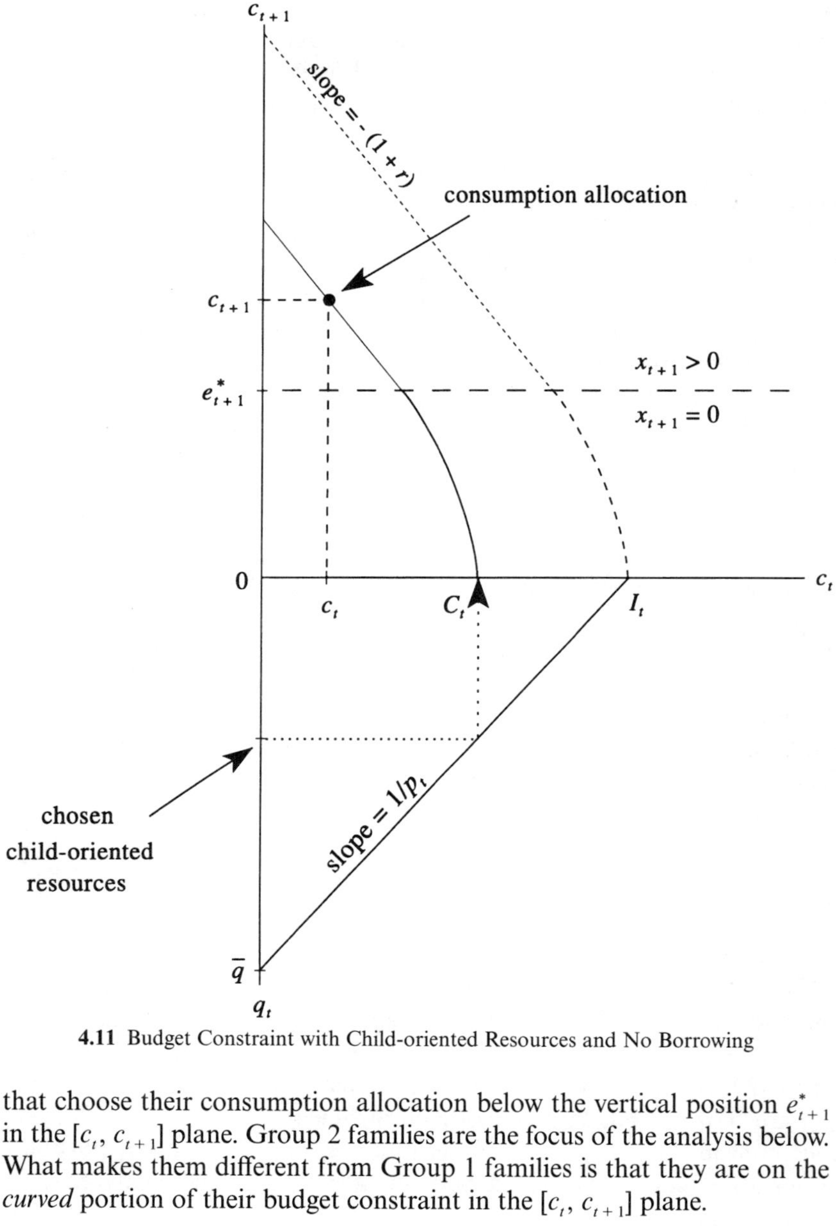

4.11 Budget Constraint with Child-oriented Resources and No Borrowing

that choose their consumption allocation below the vertical position e^*_{t+1} in the $[c_t, c_{t+1}]$ plane. Group 2 families are the focus of the analysis below. What makes them different from Group 1 families is that they are on the *curved* portion of their budget constraint in the $[c_t, c_{t+1}]$ plane.

Parental Income Effects

Parental income has three effects on altruism in the imperfect capital markets model. The three effects are analogous to the "total resource," "substitution," and "interest rate" effects derived previously for the permanent income model.

Indifference curves in the $[c_t, c_{t+1}]$ plane are still assumed to be L-shaped, following a ray of preferred proportions which depends on the degree of intergenerational altruism. For a degree of intergenerational altruism a, choices in the $[c_t, c_{t+1}]$ plane therefore follow the ray of preferred proportions.

Consider an increase of parental income I_t, holding constant the interest rate r and the price of child-oriented resources p_t. Holding constant altruism, more parental income therefore means more c_{t+1}, which, according to assumption (3), increases the willingness to pay for altruism. The marginal cost of intergenerational altruism is (as shown earlier in the chapter) $p_t\theta'(a)$, which is independent of parental income. With more willingness to pay and no change in the marginal cost of altruism, the chosen degree of altruism must increase in response to more parental income. This result is analogous to the total resource effect in the permanent income model.

A change in the parental wage rate increases parental income but also affects the value of time and, because child-oriented resources are time-intensive, the price of child-oriented resources. A higher parental wage can thereby discourage the accumulation of altruism, an effect analogous to the "substitution effect" derived for the permanent income model.

Notice that parental income also has something like an interest rate effect in the imperfect capital markets model, an effect that is not present in the permanent model. In the permanent income model, a change in total family resources does not change the *slope* of the intergenerational budget constraint in the $[c_t, c_{t+1}]$ plane; the slope depends only on the interest rate. In the imperfect capital markets model, parental income does effect the slope of the budget constraint in the $[c_t, c_{t+1}]$ plane. Consider figure 4.12, where budget constraints are shown as dashed curves. An increase in parental income increases consumption resources from C_t to C_t'. With no change in the degree of altruism, the corresponding change in the consumption allocation is from B to D. Notice that the slope of the budget constraint is different at B and D and, because of the complementarity between q_t and c_{t+1}, the incentives to accumulate altruism are different.[17] With the flatter slope at higher parental incomes, more parental income is associated with a lesser incentive to accumulate altruism.

Another way to see the "interest rate" effect of parental income in the

17. Remember from the discussion of complementarity that there is an "interest rate effect" on altruism—the slope of the budget constraint determines the effectiveness of altruism.

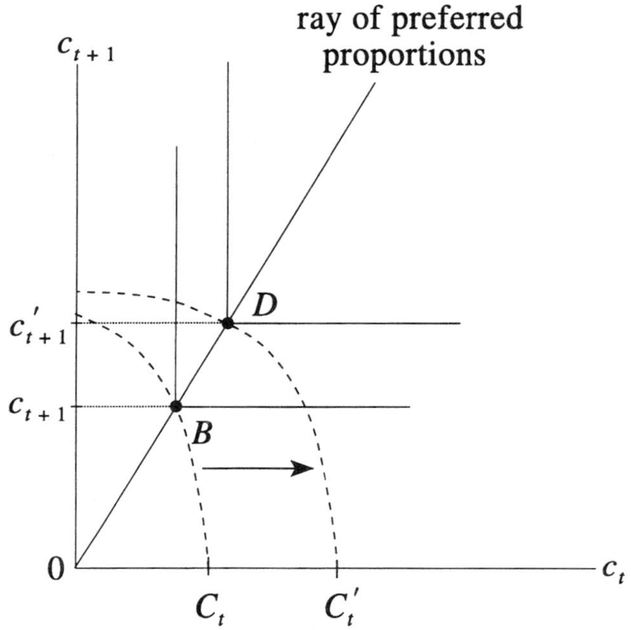

4.12 The "Interest Rate Effect" of Parental Income

imperfect capital markets model in figure 4.12 is to notice that a change in consumption resources is associated with a less than proportional change in consumption by the child, which, according to assumption (3), means a less than proportional change in the willingness to pay for altruism. Contrast this result with a result from the permanent income model: proportional changes in consumption resources produce an exactly proportional change in the willingness to pay for intergenerational altruism.

There can be another "interest rate" effect of parental income in the imperfect capital markets model. If more parental income is associated with higher earnings ability for children, the curved portion of the intergenerational budget constraint can be steeper for high-income families. This "interest rate effect" of parental income works in the opposite direction as the interest rate effect discussed above, with higher-income families having a greater incentive to accumulate altruism.

In summary, parental income can be associated with four effects on the chosen degree of intergenerational altruism in the model with borrowing constraints:

(a) More parental income has a "total resource" effect which increases altruism.

(b) If associated with a higher parental wage rate, more parental income has a substitution effect when child-oriented resources are time intensive. This effect decreases altruism.
(c) More parental income has an "interest rate" effect as higher-income parents choose to be on flatter portions of the earnings function. This effect decreases altruism.
(d) If associated with a higher earnings ability for children, more parental income has another "interest rate" effect as higher-income parents tend to face a steeper earnings function for their children. This effect increases altruism.

More parental income only has the first two effects in the permanent income model or among Group 1 families of the imperfect capital markets model. Moreover, parental income has a smaller total resource effect in the permanent income model because parental income is only a fraction of total family resources. With effect (*d*) and a larger total resource effect in the imperfect capital markets model, one might expect to see a positive association between parental income and altruism among borrowing constrained families. On the other hand, effects (*b*) and (*c*) tend to produce a negative association. It is therefore unclear whether the association between parental income and altruism is stronger or weaker among borrowing constrained (Group 2) or the unconstrained (Group 1).

Intergenerational Mobility with Endogenous Altruism

With an analysis of total resource, substitution, and interest rate effects, I show above how altruism is influenced by economic status. What are the implications of my model for intergenerational mobility? These implications are derived separately below for the permanent income and imperfect capital markets models.

Even if altruism were not influenced by economic status, the claim that altruism merely *differs* across families has implications for intergenerational consumption mobility.[18] Suppose, for example, that all families had the same budget set and they only differed according to their ray of preferred proportions. Some families would have relatively high c_{t+1} and relatively low c_t while others would have relatively low c_{t+1} and relatively high c_t. Consumption therefore regresses to the mean across generations. In fact, the children of low-consumption parents enjoy the most consumption. Allowing both incomes and altruism to vary across families would relax this result, but it would still be true that consumption regresses to the mean across generations in both the permanent income and borrowing

18. Altruism that differs across families in a way that is uncorrelated with parental income or wages does not affect the degree of earnings mobility.

constraints models. If one looks at only those parental consumption differences associated with parental income differences, then consumption does not regress to the mean in percentage terms even when altruism varies across families.[19]

The Permanent Income Model of Opportunities

When child-oriented resources are time-intensive, three results for the permanent income model allow me to make some sharp predictions for the degree of intergenerational consumption mobility. The first result is the total resource effect—more total family resources increases altruism (holding constant w_t and r). Second, there is a substitution effect on altruism—a higher parental wage decreases altruism (holding constant A and r). The third result is the equal magnitude of the resource and substitution effects; a proportional increase of the parental wage w_t and total family resources A leaves altruism unchanged. A higher ratio A/w_t raises altruism while a lower ratio lowers it.

Suppose all families are identical except for the parental wage. In other words, all families inherit the same amount from grandparents (x_t) and all children have the same earnings (w_{t+1}). How do the different parental wages affect altruism? The parental wage has both a total resource and a substitution effect. Because total family resources is a weighted sum of the wage of parents, earnings of children, and grandparental inheritances, total family resources must vary across families. However, total family resources are likely to vary less than parental wages so that high-wage families have a low ratio A/w_t.[20] A lower ratio for high-wage families means less altruism for those families. The richer families have a lower ratio c_{t+1}/c_t and consumption regresses to the mean across generations in percentage terms. This is not just a result of the heterogeneity of altruism across families but also of the correlation of altruism with economic status. Consumption regresses to the mean in percentage terms even if one looks at parental consumption differences across parental income categories.

Suppose all families are identical except for the grandparental inheritance. In other words, all families have the same parental wage (w_t) and all children have the same earnings (w_{t+1}). How do the different grandparental inheritances affect altruism? Assuming that the wage is related to the value of time, the grandparental inheritance has a total resource but not a substitution effect. Richer families therefore accumulate more altru-

19. See the "Transmission of Consumption Inequality" in chapter 3 for a discussion of these results.

20. The only exception to this result is when grandparental inheritances x_t are very negative so that the parental wage exceeds total family resources.

ism and consumption regresses *away* from the mean across generations. This is not just a result of the heterogeneity of altruism across families, but also of the correlation of altruism with economic status. Consumption regresses away from the mean in percentage terms even if one looks at parental consumption differences associated with parental income differences (although not parental wage differences).

It is possible that parents who enjoy a substantial grandparental inheritance choose not to work. If so, their wage does not measure their value of time. A larger grandparental inheritance is, in this case, likely to have both a total resource and a substitution effect on altruism because of the effect of the inheritance on the parental value of time. If the parental value of time is sufficiently sensitive to the inheritance, it is possible that the substitution effect dominates, that is, richer "inherited income" parents are less altruistic, and consumption regresses to the mean.

In reality, both grandparental inheritances and parental wages differ across families. Whether or not consumption regresses to the mean across generations depends on which differences are more important across families and whether "inherited income" parents choose to work. With the exception of some of the very rich, it is fairly realistic to expect that parental wage differences are the important reason why parental income varies across families. My model therefore predicts that consumption regresses to the mean across generations in percentage terms for the bulk of the population. For some of the very rich for whom grandparental inheritance is the important determinant of parental income and who choose to work, consumption regresses away from the mean in percentage terms.

My model of altruism does not change the results for intergenerational earnings mobility in the permanent income model. Regardless of the degree of intergenerational altruism, all families make the efficient human capital investment in children so that earnings is determined only by ability. Earnings regress to the mean according to the regression of the mean of ability.

An interesting application of the model is to immigrants. Immigrants to the United States, for example, may often face relatively low wages when they reach the United States because they are unfamiliar with the language or other peculiarities of working in this country. Despite the low wage, immigrants may expect very good prospects for their children's earnings as adults. With a low value of time but higher "total family resources," both the "substitution" and "total resource" effects require that immigrants in our model of altruism be very altruistic. This not only means that earnings should grow more rapidly across generations for immigrants than for native Americans—a result which follows from a variety of models—but that immigrating parents should "consume less" or "sacrifice more for the sake of their children" than do American-born residents with similar wages. "Consumption" here can also be a broad measure of "economic success" that includes leisure. It is consistent with the model of altruism, for example, for immigrating parents to actually make a financial transfer to their child that is large relative to the parents' lifetime incomes. Positive financial transfers by poor immigrant parents are inconsistent with either the permanent income or borrowing constraints models with a fixed degree of altruism.

A closely related result also applies to families that suffer from discrimination in the workplace but who expect less discrimination to prevail against their children. The parental wage is low because of discrimination but, like the immigrants in my example above, wages are expected to be better for children. Not only should earnings increase more rapidly for these families, but parents should sacrifice a larger fraction of their resources for their children than do otherwise similar parents.

The Imperfect Capital Markets Model of Opportunities

The parental income, substitution, and "interest rate" effects allow me to derive the predictions of the imperfect capital markets model of opportunities and my model of parental priorities for the intergenerational mobility of consumption and earnings. Group 1 families are on the linear portion of their intergenerational budget constraint in the $[c_t, c_{t+1}]$ plane so that they behave like permanent income families. Consumption regresses to the mean in percentage terms if parental wage differences are most important or away from the mean if grandparental inheritances are most important. Earnings regress to the mean according to the intergenerational dynamics of ability.

Suppose all Group 2 families are identical except for parental income. Parental income has both a "total resource" and an "interest rate" effect in this case. The effects work in the opposite direction but, because more parental income must increase c_{t+1} to some degree and the willingness to pay for altruism is proportional to c_{t+1}, richer families must be more altruistic. Consumption may or may not regress to the mean, depending on the relative importance of the curvature of the intergenerational budget constraint (which produces regression to the mean in the model with fixed altruism) and the parental income effect on altruism (which produces regression away from the mean).

To the extent that parental wages vary across families, there is a substitution effect and an additional total resource effect to consider. If x_t is the same for all Group 2 families, parental wages must vary at least as much across families as parental income. Since we know that total resource and substitution effects are equal in the permanent income model and the total resource effect is mitigated by an interest rate effect in the imperfect capital markets model, the substitution effect of a higher parental wage in the imperfect capital markets model must dominate. Different parental wages therefore produce regression to the mean of consumption among Group 2 families. If both parental wages and grandparental inheritances vary across families, one must consider all of the effects, but I expect the substitution effect to dominate and consumption to regress to the mean among Group 2 families.[21]

If one deviates from this example and allows ability to differ across families and assumes that higher-income families have children with higher ability, there is an additional interest rate effect that tends to produce regression away from the mean. Higher-ability children for high-income families means that the intergenerational budget constraints are steeper for these families. The "interest rate" effect requires that a steeper budget constraint encourages the accumulation of altruism. From this effect alone, higher-income families tend to be more altruistic.

There are several effects of income on altruism for Group 2 families in the imperfect capital markets model, so it is difficult to determine exactly how altruism is related to parental income. If the relationship is positive, I predict that consumption may or may not regress away from the mean. If it is negative, consumption unambiguously regresses to the mean. We know that consumption regresses to the mean among the Group 1 families, so the ambiguity for Group 2 means that we cannot predict whether consumption regresses to the mean more rapidly in Group 1 or Group 2.

If there is no relationship between altruism and parental income, the L-shaped indifference curves in the $[c_t, c_{t+1}]$ plane imply that earnings regress to the mean faster among Group 1 families than among Group 2.[22] A positive correlation between altruism and parental income strengthens this result while a negative correlation weakens it (but not entirely).

Intergenerational Mobility in Six Models

According to the economic approach, intergenerational mobility depends on two factors: parental priorities and family opportunities. Chapter 3 presents two models of opportunities: the permanent income and borrowing constrained models. Three models of parental priorities are introduced in chapters 2 through 4. One assumes that all parents are equally altruistic, while a second assumes that altruism varies across families but

21. Remember that Group 2 families make no financial transfer to children ($x_{t+1} = 0$), so it is likely that x_t is small or zero for most Group 2 families.

22. See page 60 for a proof.

in a way that is unrelated to parental income.[23] The third model explored in the first half of this chapter is a model of the formation of intergenerational altruism, which has predictions for the relationship between altruism and parental income.

With two models of opportunities and three models of parental priorities, there are a total of six models of intergenerational mobility. Table 4.1 summarizes the predictions of these models. The first column lists each of the three models of parental priorities. The second column indicates the model of opportunities. There are a total of six models, the implications of which are displayed in the final column of table 4.1.

The Mulligan model changes slightly if one allows parents to choose the number of children in addition to transfers per child and the quantity of child-oriented resources. The following section uses the results above to derive predictions for a model of fertility. The fertility model is then integrated with the model of child-oriented resources.

The Quantity and Quality of Intergenerational Altruism

Because the previous section models parental concerns for the happiness or consumption of a particular child, one might say that the model is concerned with the "intensity" of intergenerational altruism. This section is concerned with another dimension, the *number* of recipients of intergenerational altruism. In other words, I model the number of children as the object of choice and allow the fertility choice to affect the degree of intergenerational altruism per child.

Some of the modeling here is due to Becker and Barro (1988). I extend their analysis in several important ways. First, Becker and Barro think of their model as one of aggregate economic growth—predicting relationships between wages, interest, fertility, and per capita income, while I use their model to think about inequality within an economy. Second, I show that, for the bulk of the U.S. population, their model cannot explain intergenerational mobility without counterfactual assumptions about the relationship between fertility and family income. Third, I argue that their model is an appropriate model of inequality only for the small fraction of the U.S. population for whom income is primarily "unearned." Fourth, I present a very simple graphical derivation of their results. Fifth, I suggest how to integrate both the purposeful accumulation of altruism from my model and the fertility choice from the Becker-Barro model into a single model.

23. It is assumed that, to the extent that parental altruism is uncorrelated with observed variables such as income or schooling, parental altruism is unobserved. If parental altruism can be completely observed, then the second model of parental priorities is very similar to the first, with the added qualifying statement that parental altruism is held constant.

Table 4.1 Intergenerational Mobility in Six Models

Model of Parental Priorities	Model of Opportunities	Predictions for Intergenerational Mobility
identical for all families	permanent income	• Consumption does not regress to the mean • Consumption does not regress to the mean across parental income categories • Consumption inequality grows over time • Earnings regress to the mean • Among families that make identical human capital investments, earnings of children are positively related (or unrelated) to parental income
	borrowing constrained	• Consumption does not regress to the mean among Group 1 families • Consumption regresses to the mean among Group 2 families • Consumption does not regress to the mean across parental income categories among Group 1 families • Consumption regresses to the mean across parental income categories among Group 2 families • Consumption inequality grows in Group 1 and falls in Group 2 • Earnings regress to the mean • Earnings regress to the mean more rapidly among Group 1 families • Earnings inequality is greater among the children of Group 2 families than among the children of Group 1 families • Among Group 2 families that make identical human capital investments, earnings of children are negatively related to parental income
altruism unrelated to parental income	permanent income	• Consumption regresses to the mean • Consumption does not regress to the mean across parental income categories • Consumption inequality grows over time • Earnings regress to the mean • Among families that make identical human capital investments, earnings of children are positively related (or unrelated) to parental income
	borrowing constrained	• Consumption regresses to the mean • Consumption regresses to the mean more rapidly among Group 2 families • Consumption does not regress to the mean across parental income categories among Group 1 families • Consumption regresses to the mean across parental income categories among Group 2 families • Earnings regress to the mean • Earnings regress to the mean more rapidly among Group 1 families • Earnings inequality is greater among the children of Group 2 families than among the children of Group 1 families • Among Group 2 families that make identical human capital investments, earnings of children are negatively related to parental income

continued

Table 4.1—*Continued*

Model of Parental Priorities	Model of Opportunities	Predictions for Intergenerational Mobility
Mulligan model	permanent income	• Consumption regresses to the mean among "wage-income" families • Consumption does not regress to the mean among "inherited-income" families with working parents • Consumption regresses to the mean across parental income categories among "wage-income" families • Consumption inequality does not grow over time among "wage-income" families • Consumption inequality grows over time among "inherited-income" families with working parents • Consumption and earnings should grow more rapidly across generations for immigrant families • Earnings regress to the mean • Among families that make identical human capital investments, earnings of children are positively related (or unrelated) to parental income
	borrowing constrained	• Consumption regresses to the mean • Consumption regresses to the mean across parental income categories among Group 1 "wage-income" families • Consumption does not regress to the mean across parental income categories among Group 1 "inherited-income" families with working parents • Consumption regresses to the mean across parental income categories among Group 2 families • Consumption inequality grows over time among Group 1 "inherited-income" families with working parents • Consumption and earnings should grow more rapidly across generations for immigrant families • Earnings regress to the mean • Earnings regress to the mean more rapidly among Group 1 families • Earnings inequality is greater among the children of Group 2 families than among the children of Group 1 families • Among Group 2 families that make identical capital investments, earnings of children are negatively related to parental income

Notes:

1. "Regression to the mean" is always in logarithmic or percentage terms.
2. $x_{t+1} > 0$ for Group 1 families, $x_{t+1} \leq 0$ for Group 2 families.
3. "Wage-income families" are families for whom parental earnings is the primary determinant of parental income.
4. "Inherited-income families" are families for whom the grandparental inheritance is the primary determinant of parental income.
5. The "auxiliary assumptions" discussed in the text are required for deriving some of these predictions.
6. Additional predictions of the Mulligan model are derived in the section on fertility in this chapter.

Intergenerational Mobility and Preferences for Per Capita Consumption

The model of the previous section features three goods: consumption by parents c_t, consumption by a child c_{t+1}, and child-oriented resources q_t. More child-oriented resources produce more altruism (per child) in that model. The Becker-Barro model (hereafter referred to as "the BB model") is very similar in this regard. There are three goods: consumption by parents c_t, consumption *per* child c_{t+1}, and the number of children n_t. n_t affects altruism per child, although Becker and Barro assume that higher fertility *lowers* altruism *per child.* Figure 4.13 displays the indifference curves for the BB model in the $[c_t, c_{t+1}]$ plane. With fewer children (n), parents care more about the consumption of each child so that the ray of preferred proportions is higher, as shown by the solid curves in figure 4.13. More children (n') shifts the ray of preferred proportions downward as shown by the dashed curves in figure 4.13.

Although I have not yet described enough of the BB model to make predictions about which families have more altruism per child, figure 4.13 is enough to derive an important result concerning the degree of intergen-

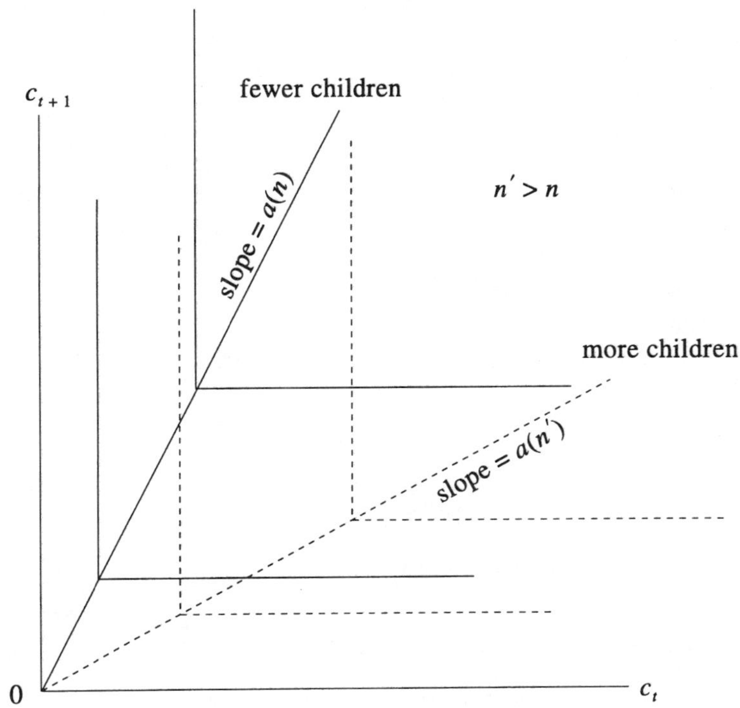

4.13 Fertility Affects Altruism per Child

erational mobility. Remember that there is regression to the mean in percentage terms when richer families are on lower rays of preferred proportions in the $[c_t, c_{t+1}]$ plane and regression away from the mean when richer families are on higher rays. In the BB model, higher rays in the $[c_t, c_{t+1}]$ plane are associated with lower fertility and lower rays with higher fertility. This gives us the most important result of the section: *consumption (per capita) regresses to the mean in percentage terms across generations if richer families have more children and away from the mean if richer families have fewer children.* This is a conditional statement and the condition—whether or not the rich have more children—is a prediction of the model, but the conditional statement says a lot about the empirical validity of the BB model as a model of intergenerational mobility.

How Is Fertility Related to Family Income?[24]

The BB model can be used to make predictions about the types of parents that will choose to have many children—and I do so later in this section—but I introduce some facts about family income and family size for the United States. Figure 4.14 displays four series that compare number of children to family income.[25] The solid triangle series is from the 1990 U.S. Census of Illinois and compares household income to the number of children born to the household head for household heads that were between the ages of forty-one and eighty-four in 1990. The figure shows that these Illinoisans typically had between two and three children. Fertility declines slightly with income for family incomes between $5,000 and $30,000. Fertility is fairly constant for family incomes up to $250,000. Since the vast majority of American families have annual incomes less than $250,000, it appears from the Census data displayed in figure 4.14 that there is not a strong positive relationship between fertility and family income for the bulk of the U.S. population.

To maintain the confidentiality of U.S. citizens, the Census does not publicize very high incomes. To study the fertility of families with annual incomes that are in the millions of dollars per year, I look at some data from the 1989 Survey of Consumer Finances. The solid box series counts the number of children of household heads between the ages of forty-one

24. This section presents some rough indicators of the relationship between family income and fertility. A thorough analysis is beyond the scope of this book, but can be found in Julian Simon's works (1974; 1977).

25. All four series in the figure are computed by fitting a fifth-order polynomial in log (family income) to the number of children. Results for fourth-and sixth-order polynomials are similar except at very high incomes (near $250,000) in the Census.

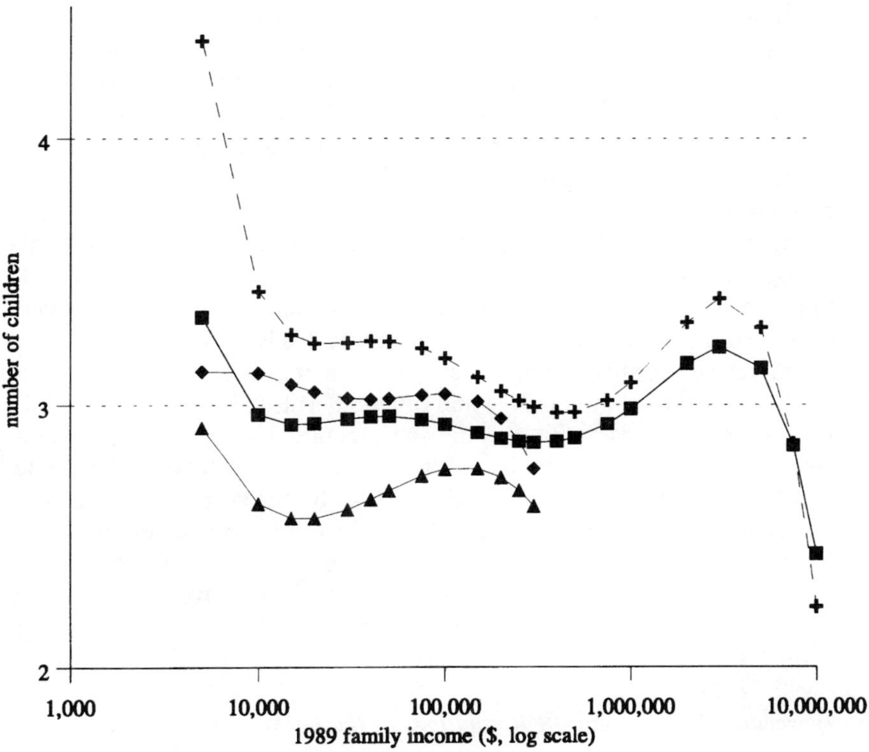

4.14 U.S. Family Size versus Family Income
—■— 1989 SCF —▲— 1990 Census --✚-- 1989 SCF (without childless)
--◆-- 1990 Census (without childless)

and eighty-four and compares that with family income.[26] Fertility appears to rise with income for incomes between $300,000 and $3,000,0000. Fertility appears to fall with income after $3,000,000, although this is based on only thirty-three observations.[27]

The negative fertility-income relationship displayed in figure 4.14 is consistent with other results for the United States reported in the economics literature. For example, Julian Simon (1977) finds a negative relationship between the fertility of married women and the income of their respective husbands in the 1960 Census. However, the relationships displayed in the

26. There is a slightly different definition of "children" in the Survey of Consumer Finances. Step-children and children of spouses who live with the household head are not distinguished from biological children.

27. There were 282 SCF families with annual incomes between $300,000 and $3,000,000.

two solid lines in figure 4.14 are not directly relevant to the issue of intergenerational mobility in the BB model because they include adults with *zero* children. Obviously, childless adults cannot affect the degree of intergenerational mobility! The two dashed lines therefore display the fertility-family income relationship among families with at least one child. The relationship is more negative in both data sets for families with annual incomes up to $250,000.

The gap between the solid (all families) and dashed (only families with children) lines is a measure of the likelihood of an adult to have *any* children as a function of family income. The gap is larger for poorer families. Poorer adults in the two data sets are more likely to have no children and therefore not affect intergenerational mobility, a result consistent with those reported by Simon (1977) and others. Fertility of families with children appears to rise with income for incomes between $300,000 and $3,000,0000. Fertility of families with children appears to fall with income after $3,000,000, although this is based on only thirty-three observations.

Judging from figure 4.14, the BB model cannot explain regression to the mean of consumption per capita for the bulk of the United States population because income and fertility fail to be positively related. The model may do well for very rich families where there is some evidence that income and fertility are positively related among the very rich.

Aggregate and Per Capita Formulations of the Becker-Barro Model

Here I show that, although the per capita formulation of the BB model displayed in figure 4.13 is somewhat different than my model of altruism, there is a reformulation of the BB model that is analytically very similar to my model so that we can apply the total resource, substitution, and interest rate effects that I derive earlier in the chapter to prove some results for the BB model.

The Per Capita Formulation

Figure 4.13 displays indifference curves for the BB model in the $[c_t, c_{t+1}]$ plane, where c_{t+1} is consumption *per* child. These curves are somewhat different than in my model because child-oriented resources increase altruism per child in my model, while fertility decreases altruism per child in the BB model. Moreover, the per capita budget constraints are different in the two models. In my model, total family resources are spent on the three goods c_t, c_{t+1}, and q_t, where expenditure is determined by a weighted *sum* of these three items (the weights are the prices). In the BB model, total family resources are spent on the three goods c_t, c_{t+1}, and n_t, but expenditures are not simply determined by the *sum*. To see this, let d_t be a "fixed" cost of having each child, which includes food, some basic health and housing expenditures, and a minimum amount of parental time. I refer to d_t as a "fixed" cost because it is independent of the amount of consumption or human capital that parents provide for each child. Even if children consume zero, parents are required to pay d_t for each child.

Because children also contribute to family resources by earning income as an adult (or even as a child), d_t overstates the cost of having children. The *net* cost of having an additional child is $\delta_t = d_t - w_{t+1}/(1 + r)$. If children earned more in present value terms ($w_{t+1}/(1 + r)$) than they cost (d_t), then the net cost of children would be negative and parents would have children merely to expand family resources. Becker and Barro assume that $d_t > w_{t+1}/(1 + r)$, so that the net cost of having children is positive.

Family expenditures are then the weighted sum of consumption by parents c_t, *total* consumption by children $n_t c_{t+1}$, and the net costs of having children $\delta_t n_t$. Notice that two goods, n_t and c_{t+1}, appear *multiplicatively* in the BB budget constraint. The multiplication is necessary because increasing consumption per child is obviously more costly in a larger family than in a small family. Conversely, it is more costly to increase family size for parents who are determined to provide a higher level of consumption for *each* child than for parents who will give few resources to children. Such multiplication does not occur in my model. The cost of child-oriented resources is independent of c_{t+1} and the cost of c_{t+1} is independent of child-oriented resources.

Total family resources A in my model, the sum of parental earnings, child earnings, and a grandparental inheritance, were beyond the control of the family. I therefore analyzed the model by thinking of parental choices subject to the *constraint* of total family resources. Total family resources are not beyond the control of parents in the BB model because A includes earnings of children and parents control the number of children. Parental income is beyond the control of parents in the BB model.

To see an algebraic display of the interaction between fertility and consumption per child in the BB model, consider the intergenerational budget constraints below.

Per Capita Budget Constraint in the Mulligan Model

$$A = c_t + \frac{c_{t+1}}{1 + r} + p_t q_t \tag{4.2}$$

Per Capita Budget Constraint in the Becker-Barro Model

$$I_t = c_t + \frac{n_t c_{t+1}}{1 + r} + \delta_t n_t \tag{4.3}$$

In the Mulligan model, total family resources are spent on the three goods c_t, c_{t+1}, and q_t. The interest rate determines the cost of providing consumption for children, with a higher interest rate making c_{t+1} cheaper. p_t is the price of child-oriented resources. In the BB model, n_t multiplies c_{t+1} in the budget constraint because, by definition, c_{t+1} is consumption *per child.* Total family resources A is the constraint in the Mulligan model, while parental income I_t is the constraint in the BB model.

The Aggregate Formulation

We could analyze the per capita budget constraint directly as Becker and Barro do, but there is a reformulation of the problem that allows us to apply many of the results from the Mulligan model. Define $C_{t+1} \equiv n_t c_{t+1}$ to be *aggregate* consumption by children in the family. Without changing the problem, we can disregard c_{t+1} and think of the three goods c_t, C_{t+1}, and n_t. Per capita consumption can always be computed from these three variables as $c_{t+1} = C_{t+1}/n_t$. The aggregate version of the budget constraint in the BB model is:

Aggregate Budget Constraint in the Becker-Barro Model

$$I_t = c_t + \frac{C_{t+1}}{1+r} + \delta_t n_t \tag{4.4}$$

Notice the similarity of the BB budget constraint in its aggregate form with the Mulligan budget constraint. The BB budget constraint in its aggregate form is drawn graphically in figure 4.15. The figure displays the intergenerational permanent income budget constraint when families determine the number of children in addition to consumption for parents and children. The diagram has three axes—an axis for c_t, an axis for C_{t+1}, and an axis for n_t. Consider the case when parents choose to have very few children.[28] Parents do not have to spend many resources producing children ($\delta_t n_t$ is low), so nearly all parental income can be allocated for consumption. The budget constraint for this case is shown as a dashed line in figure 4.15. The dashed line begins at the position $(I_t, 0)$ where all parental income is spent on parental consumption and none is spent on consumption for children. The slope of $-(1 + r)$ means that foregone parental consumption allows for consumption by children with interest. However, if more resources are spent producing children, then less can be spent on c_t and C_{t+1}. "Purchases" of n_t therefore reduce the feasible set of

28. In reality, "very few children" means one, but I am thinking about $n_t \doteq 0$. I defer any discussion of the integer constraints (that is, that the number of children must be 1, 2, 3, . . . rather than 0.2 or 1.6) until later in the chapter.

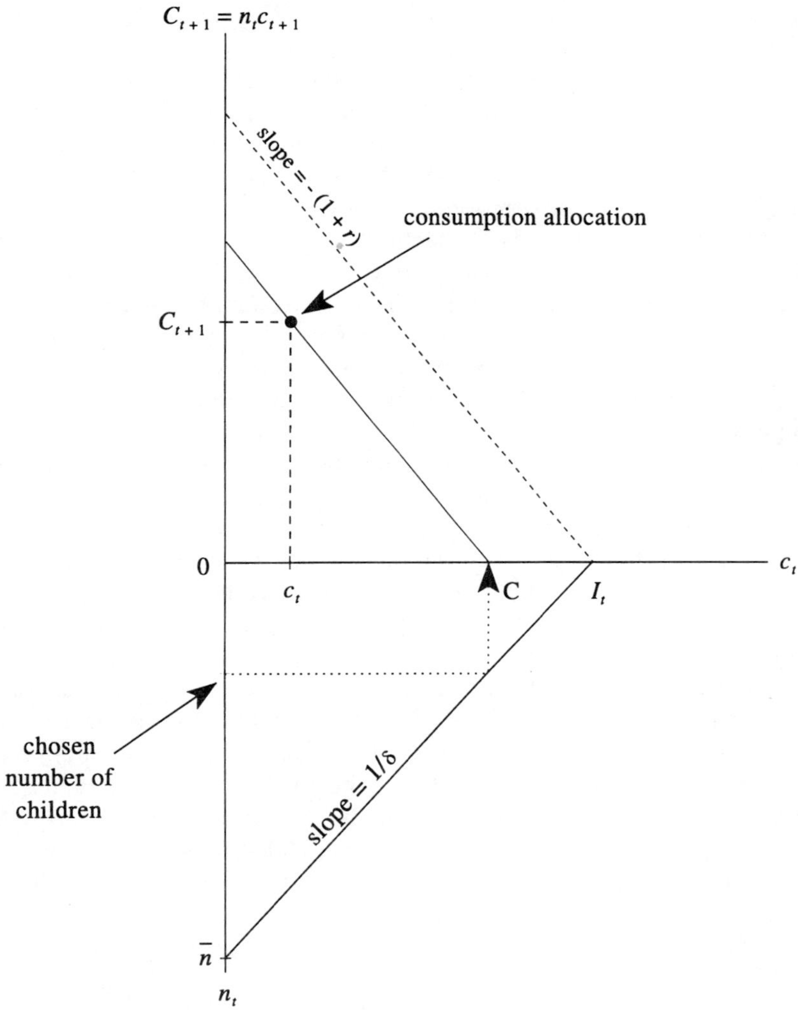

4.15 Aggregate Version of the Becker-Barro Budget Constraint

choices for c_t and C_{t+1}. This is shown in figure 4.15 as a parallel shift from the long-dashed line to the solid line in the $[c_t, C_{t+1}]$ quadrant.

Exactly how many resources are used by purchases of n_t can be determined geometrically in figure 4.15 in three steps. First, choose an amount for n_t and locate it on the n_t axis. Second, move horizontally toward the budget constraint—the upward-sloping solid line—shown in the $[c_t, n_t]$ quadrant (see, for example, the horizontal portion of the dotted line). Third, move upwards from the point of intersection with the upward-sloping solid line (again the dotted line provides an example). The point of intersection with the c_t axis, labeled C, provides the starting point for the intergenerational budget constraint in the $[c_t, C_{t+1}]$ quadrant.

Notice two properties of figure 4.15. First, the $[c_t, n_t]$ budget constraint has slope $1/\delta$, where δ is the net price of children. If δ is very high, the $[c_t, n_t]$ budget constraint has a very flat slope. A flat slope means that purchases of n_t—vertical movements along the n_t axis—translate into large horizontal movements of the intergenerational budget constraint in the $[c_t, C_{t+1}]$ quadrant. The reason, of course, is that expensive n_t uses up a lot of the family's resources. Second, the maximum number of children that the family can afford is $\bar{n}$. If parents were to purchase $n_t = \bar{n}$, the diagram shows that the intergenerational budget constraint in the $[c_t, C_{t+1}]$ quadrant must intersect the c_t axis at the origin—the family has no resources left to purchase c_t or C_{t+1}. A lower price would steepen the $[c_t, n_t]$ budget constraint and increase the maximum affordable amount $\bar{n}$. More income for the parents would shift the long-dashed line—and therefore the $[c_t, q_t]$ budget constraint—outward, increasing $\bar{n}$.[29]

Figure 4.15 shows that when the three goods are taken to be c_t, C_{t+1}, and n_t, the budget constraint in the BB model is geometrically very similar to the budget constraint in the Mulligan model. It also can be shown that indifference curves for the BB model in the $[c_t, C_{t+1}]$ plane are similar to the indifference curves for the Mulligan model in the $[c_t, c_{t+1}]$ plane. Consider figure 4.16, which displays parental preferences for aggregate consumption, and compare it with figure 4.13, which displays parental preferences for per capita consumption. The ray of per capita preferred proportions shown in figure 4.13 depends on the degree of altruism per child $a(n)$, which depends on the number of children. More children decreases altruism per child and lowers the ray of per capita preferred proportions. Because aggregate consumption is per capita consumption times the number of children, the corresponding ray of aggregate preferred proportions depends on the *aggregate degree of altruism* $na(n)$, which is the product of the number of children and altruism per child. More children increases aggregate altruism, even though it decreases altruism per child. More children therefore raises the ray of aggregate preferred proportions shown in figure 4.16.

29. I assume that there are "constant returns to scale" in the production of children. In other words, each additional child has a net cost of δ_t regardless of the number of children. If this assumption were relaxed to allow for economies or diseconomies of scale, the budget constraint in the $[c_t, n_t]$ plane would be curved. My results would still obtain as long as any economies of scale were not too strong (see Mulligan [1993] for a proof).

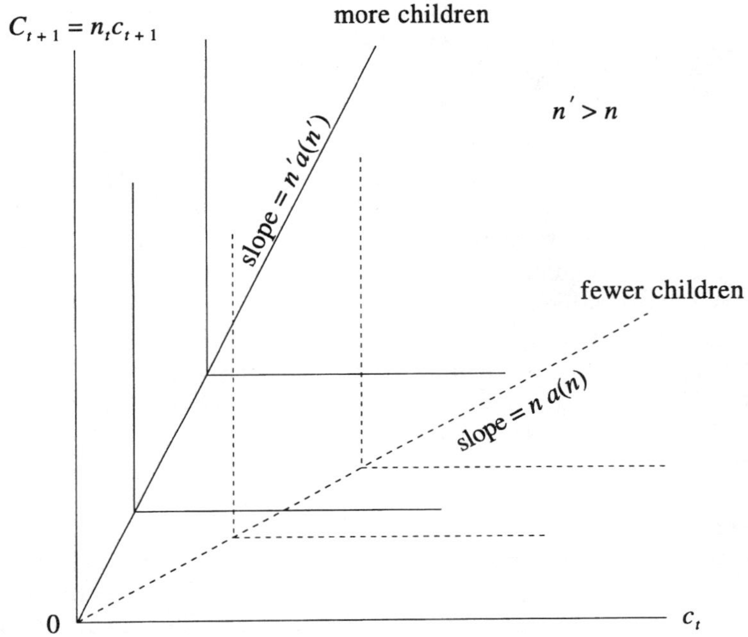

4.16 Preferences for Aggregate Consumption

Aggregate and Per Capita Results

Graphically, the aggregate formulation of the BB model is quite similar to the formulation of the Mulligan model. Both models have three goods with a linear budget constraint such as those shown in figures 4.3 and 4.15. Indifference curves are L-shaped for two of the goods (c_t and c_{t+1} in the case of the Mulligan model and c_t and C_{t+1} in the case of the BB model) and more of the third good shifts the ray of preferred proportions upward. Because of the mathematical similarity of the two models, there is no need to carefully prove the results of the BB model. Instead, I derive them from the results obtained for the Mulligan model: total resources, substitution, and interest rate effects. Before I do so, I state the four assumptions about preferences, which are the analogues to assumptions (1)–(4) made in the Mulligan model:

(1)′ More fertility lowers altruism *per child* and therefore the desired proportion c_{t+1}/c_t; more fertility raises aggregate altruism and therefore the desired proportion C_{t+1}/c_t.

(2)′ If the accumulation of children were costless, all parents would prefer more.

(3)′ At a given level of fertility, the willingness to pay for fertility is proportional to per capita child consumption c_{t+1}.
(4)′ Holding constant C_{t+1}, the willingness to pay for fertility is less when fertility is greater.

The total resource effect in the Mulligan model means that additional total family resources increases purchases of all three goods. In the case of the BB model, the analogue is that more parental income (holding constant r and δ_t) increases parental consumption, aggregate consumption by children, and the number of children.[30] Because the number of children increases, more parental income must decrease altruism per child and increase aggregate altruism.

When child-oriented resources are time-intensive, a substitution effect in the Mulligan model predicts that purchases of child-oriented resources fall in response to a higher parental wage. When the cost of children is time-intensive, the analogue in the BB model is that the number of children falls in response to a higher parental wage. With fewer children, altruism and consumption per child increase.

Because aggregate consumption by children and the number of children are complements, there is also an interest rate effect in the BB model. Holding constant the net cost of raising children, a higher interest rate makes C_{t+1} cheaper so both C_{t+1} and n_t increase. However, a higher interest rate also increases the net cost of raising children because it devalues the earnings of children. A higher net cost of raising children decreases n_t. Which effect dominates? It depends on altruism per child and parental income. If parents are rich enough or altruistic enough that they plan to make sizable financial transfers to children, a higher interest rate encourages fertility. This result is most easily seen in the case when the discounted earnings of children are very low relative to the fixed cost of children d_t and parental income. Higher interest devalues earnings of children, but the magnitude of this effect on the net price of "raising" children is small because most of the net cost is the fixed cost d_t.

Earnings of children may be large relative to parental income, so parents may borrow against the earnings of children or make positive but small financial transfers. In this case, higher interest can discourage fertility because interest is an important determinant of the net cost of raising children.[31]

When grandparental inheritances are the main determinant of parental

30. In general, the effect of parental income on consumption per child is ambiguous. A key factor in determining the effect is the precise way in which fertility n shifts the ray of preferred proportions. The mathematical appendix provides an example where consumption per child is a normal good and another example where it is independent of parental income.

31. The same effect is present in Becker and Barro's (1988) formulation of the model. They report an unambiguous interest rate effect because they hold the net cost of raising children constant.

income, the parental income effect produces a positive relationship between fertility and parental income, therefore a negative relationship between altruism per child and family income, and therefore regression to the mean of consumption in percentage terms across generations. However, when parental wages are the main determinant of parental income, the substitution effect produces a negative relationship between fertility and parental income, therefore a positive relationship between altruism per child and family income, and therefore regression away from the mean of consumption in percentage terms across generations.

Earnings depend only on ability in the BB model with a permanent income budget constraint because, regardless of the number of children, parents invest in the human capital of each child up to the point where the rate of return equals $1 + r$. If efficient human capital investments exhaust parental income, funds are obtained by borrowing in the financial market. With earnings determined only by ability, intergenerational earnings mobility is no different than in the other versions of the permanent income model.

Additional Results

The BB model might be a useful model of intergenerational consumption mobility when fertility varies across families, but it is much less useful when zero or one child is the choice for many couples. Its usefulness diminishes because couples can only have *integer* numbers of children—0.067 children is not a feasible choice. At low levels of fertility, most couples may choose zero or one child. Those couples with no children cannot affect intergenerational mobility. Those with one child all have the same number of children and therefore the same altruism per child in the BB model. The BB model is an uninteresting model of altruism—and therefore intergenerational consumption mobility—when one or even two children is the most popular fertility choice.

One might want to interpret the "children" in the BB model more generally to include other people's children. I do so in my analysis of charitable giving in chapter 12. The Mulligan and BB models of altruism can be used to make predictions about the "type" of altruism that is encouraged by charitable organizations, governments, and employers.

My exposition of the BB model utilizes the permanent income model of family opportunities, but the borrowing constrained model could be used as well. Using parental income, substitution, and "interest rate" effects, results could be derived as they were in the Mulligan model.

A Model of Fertility and Child-Oriented Resources

The BB model studies fertility and abstracts from child-oriented resources while the Mulligan model studies child-oriented resources and abstracts from fertility. It is straightforward to combine the two models. In the combined model, child-oriented resources shift upward the ray of preferred proportions in the $[c_t, c_{t+1}]$ plane for a given level of fertility. Fertility shifts the ray downward for a given amount of child-oriented resources.

All of the results reported in table 4.1 for the Mulligan model still obtain if one adds the qualifying statement "among families with the same number of children." For example, "consumption regresses to the mean among wage-income families with the same number of children" and "consumption regresses away from the mean among inherited-income families with working parents and with the same number of children."

If fertility and income were positively related among wage-income families, then altruism per child must be lower among families with more wage income, both because fertility is higher and because child-oriented resources are lower. However, the model suggests that fertility and income might be negatively related—and actual data suggests that they are—because high wage-income parents have a high value of time and bearing and raising children is time-intensive. So the child-oriented resources part of the model predicts regression to the mean of consumption among wage-income families (because child-oriented resources are negatively related to income) while the fertility side of the model predicts regression away from the mean of consumption among wage-income families (because fertility is negatively related to income). The net result depends on the particular magnitudes of the costs of children and child-oriented resources as well as the effect of those variables on the ray of preferred proportions.[32] However, given that the number of children must be an integer (for example, 1.5 children is not feasible), and as fertility falls over time for technological, social, and other reasons, 0 and 1 child will be popular choices of parents so that fertility varies very little among families with children and therefore cannot be an important force producing regression away from the mean of consumption.

If fertility and income were negatively related among inherited-income families with working parents, then altruism per child must be higher among families with more inherited income both because fertility is lower and because child-oriented resources are higher. However, the model suggests that fertility and income might be positively related—and actual data suggests that they are—because inherited-income families with working parents do not have a particularly high value of time. So the child-oriented resources part of the model predicts regression away from the mean of consumption among inherited-income families (because child-

32. Mulligan (1993) shows that there exist versions of the combined model for which consumption regresses to the mean both among wage- and inherited-income families.

oriented resources are positively related to income) while the fertility side of the model predicts regression to the mean of consumption among inherited-income families (because fertility is positively related to income). The net result depends on the particular magnitudes of the costs of children and child-oriented resources as well as the effect of those variables on the ray of preferred proportions. Given that the number of children must be an integer (for example, 1.5 children is not feasible), and as fertility falls over time for technological, social, and other reasons, 0 and 1 child will be popular choices of parents so that fertility varies very little among families with children and therefore cannot be an important force producing regression to the mean of consumption. The combined model therefore predicts that, as average fertility falls over time, consumption inequality will grow among inherited-income families with parents that work.

Review of the Main Points

A simple graphical model of the formation of intergenerational altruism is proposed and developed in this chapter. The model has a variety of predictions for intergenerational mobility which are reviewed here. The methodology and extensions of the analysis are also briefly discussed.

Predictions of the Models

Parents are assumed to be predisposed toward selfishness. However, they can and do take steps to overcome their selfishness. These steps are costly but, when taken, cause parents to happily sacrifice some of their own consumption for their children. Eleven implications are derived:

(1) Savings, estate, and inheritance taxes discourage the formation of altruism.
(2) Parents with high wage rates choose to have less altruism.
(3) In the permanent income model, consumption regresses to the mean across generations among families for whom income is mainly earned if fertility is unrelated to parental income.
(4) If fertility is unrelated to parental income, consumption regresses away from the mean among families for whom most income is "unearned" but the parents work.
(5) Consumption regresses to the mean if fertility is positively correlated with parental income.
(6) Consumption does not necessarily regress to the mean more rapidly among Group 2 families in the borrowing constraints model.
(7) Earnings regress to the mean more rapidly among Group 2 families in the borrowing constraints model.

(8) Intergenerational consumption mobility falls among the very rich when their fertility approaches one child per couple.
(9) Low-wage immigrants in the United States sacrifice more consumption for children than do American-born citizens with similar wages, perhaps even to the point of making a sizable financial transfer.
(10) Without changes in interest rates, tax rates, or divorce, economic growth does not affect altruism.
(11) Wage-tax financed pay-as-you-go social security increases altruism, savings, and long-run economic growth.

Result (1) follows from the fact that altruism complements the consumption of future generations. Because savings, estate, and inheritance taxes discourage the transfer of resources to children, they must also discourage the formation of intergenerational altruism.[33] The assumption that the costs of forming altruism are primarily time costs delivers results (2) and (3). Result (4) derives from the positive total resource effect (holding constant the value of time) on the formation of altruism. The assumption of diminishing marginal utility of children delivers result (5).

Result (6) obtains because there are potentially four opposing effects of parental income on altruism for Group 2 families in Mulligan's model. Result (7), on the other hand, is a prediction that is unaffected by the theory of the formation of altruism. I proved result (9) by showing that the substitution effect on altruism is relatively important for low-wage immigrants. Result (10) follows from the fact that the economic growth increases wages and incomes roughly proportionally and that proportional changes in wages and total family resources have no effect on altruism in the model. The reduction of the value of time and the relatively small total resource effect of pay-as-you-go social security in the permanent income model delivers result (11).

The fertility choice produces intergenerational consumption mobility among families for whom parental income is primarily determined by a grandparental inheritance. However, the fertility choice can vary less across families as fertility falls over time and the integer constraint becomes important.[34] This result is marked as (8) in the list above.

Results (4) and (5) are conditional on a particular correlation between fertility and parental income. In fact, fertility is positively correlated with income among families for whom most income is "unearned" and negatively correlated with income among families for whom most income is "earned." By combining the two models of this chapter, I derived these

33. The next chapter carefully shows how taxes have an "interest rate" effect on altruism.
34. Fertility may fall over time for social, religious, and other reasons.

two correlations as predictions, with the additional implication that consumption regresses to the mean among families for whom income is mainly "earned" and among families for whom income is mainly "unearned."

The complementarity between q_t and c_{t+1} also produces several other results that are reported in later chapters. For example, I show that higher estate tax rates look like lower rates of interest, so they serve to lower intergenerational altruism. Higher income tax rates have a similar effect, although income taxes also lower the value of time and make altruism cheaper to accumulate. Chapter 12 shows that divorce can increase the cost of transferring resources from parents to children which, from the complementarity result, means less intergenerational altruism. A related result is shown to apply to charitable giving.

A Theory of Preference Formation?

Parental actions—namely the purchase of child-oriented resources—affect their willingness to sacrifice consumption for their children in the Mulligan model. Because parents anticipate the effects of their actions on their intergenerational altruism, they take these effects into account when determining the quantity of child-oriented resources to purchase. This purposeful accumulation of altruism allows me to use the usual tools of economics to predict which parents are likely to be more altruistic than others.

It is a departure from most economic analyses to emphasize the role of preferences in explaining important behavior, but my ski example reveals that my method of modeling preferences is not a dramatic departure from more traditional economic modeling. The idea of complements is not a new one in economics. What is new is to apply the complementarity model to the formation of preferences, as has been done recently by Gary Becker (1996), Becker and Mulligan (1997), Becker and Murphy (1993), and Mulligan (1993). My simple graphical model is used throughout the book to generate predictions for a variety of other human behavior, including inequality within the family, charitable giving, and loyalty within firms.

The effect of child-oriented resources is mechanical and well understood by parents in my model, but a precise understanding by parents is not necessary for parents to willingly purchase child-oriented resources and for my results to obtain. Advertising is an example where the effect of something on preferences is modeled as well-known, but those models clearly provide insights into the "real world" where advertising has effects that are not always predictable.[35] Investments in schooling for children

35. See, for example, Becker and Murphy (1993).

is another example where parents cannot predict results with complete accuracy, but they undertake the investments anyway.

Appendix B: Two Mathematical Models of the Formation of Intergenerational Altruism

Mathematical versions of the Mulligan and Becker-Barro (1988) models are displayed. The first section derives the preferences and permanent income constraints for the Mulligan model. The following section derives the total resource, substitution, and interest rate effects on altruism. The next section introduces an intergenerational borrowing constraint into the Mulligan model. Results for the Becker-Barro model are derived in the final section.

Preferences and Permanent Income Constraints

The results derived in "The Formation of Altruism" are proved for a mathematical model. As in figures 4.3 and 4.4, there are three goods (c_t, c_{t+1}, q_t). Total family resources, the sum of parental full earnings w_t, parental inheritances $(1 + r)x_t$, and the discounted full income of children $w_{t+1}/(1 + r)$, can be spent on the three goods:

$$(1 + r)x_t + w_t + \frac{w_{t+1}}{1 + r} \equiv A_t = c_t + \frac{c_{t+1}}{1 + r} + p_t q_t \qquad \text{(B.1)}$$

Equation B.1 is the intergenerational budget constraint. The expenditures for the purpose of accumulating altruism, $p_t q_t$, can be written equivalently as $p_t\theta(a)$, where a is the degree of intergenerational altruism:

$$(1 + r)x_t + w_t + \frac{w_{t+1}}{1 + r} \equiv A = c_t + \frac{c_{t+1}}{1 + r} + p_t\theta(a) \qquad \text{(B.2)}$$

If child-oriented resources have a positive but diminishing effect on altruism, we must have $\theta' > 0$ and $\theta'' > 0$.

The overall parental objective V depends on consumption by parents (c_t) and children (c_{t+1}) according to the degree of intergenerational altruism a:

$$V(c_t, c_{t+1}, a) \equiv \min\{f(a)c_t, g(a)c_{t+1}\} \qquad \text{(B.3)}$$

For a given degree of intergenerational altruism, indifference curves in the $[c_t, c_{t+1}]$ plane are L-shaped, as in figure 4.1. The ray of preferred proportions is $c_{t+1} = f(a)c_t/g(a)$.

Characterization of the Optimal Choices

Parental decisions are those that maximize B.3, subject to the intergenerational budget constraint B.2. The chosen degree of intergenerational altruism a depends on the three factors $(A, p_t, 1/(1 + r))$.

Consumption resources C are $c_t + c_{t+1}/(1 + r)$. Using the utility function V and the fact that c_{t+1} and c_t are chosen in a fixed proportion that depends on a, we can derive an equivalent reduced form utility function in terms of a and C:

$$v(a, C) \equiv \frac{f(a)}{1 + \frac{1}{1+r}\frac{f(a)}{g(a)}} C \tag{B.4}$$

The indifference curves of this reduced form utility function are displayed in the $[a,C]$ plane in figures 4.6 and 4.7. The utility maximizing altruism also maximizes this reduced form utility function subject to the constraint $C = A - p\theta(a)$; figure 4.7 displays a solution to this maximization problem. The equation of the slope of the indifference curve to the slope of the boundary of the feasible set is expressed algebraically below:[36]

$$\frac{C}{a}\left(\varepsilon_f(a) - [\varepsilon_f(a) - \varepsilon_g(a)]\frac{1}{1+r}\frac{c_{t+1}}{C}\right) = p\theta'(a) \tag{B.5}$$

Four assumptions about the effect of altruism on preferences are made in the text. Those assumptions are repeated below:

(1) More altruism raises the desired proportion c_{t+1}/c_t.
(2) All parents prefer to accumulate at least a small amount of altruism and would accumulate more if it were costless to do so.
(3) At a given level of altruism, the willingness to pay for altruism is proportional to child consumption c_{t+1}.
(4) Holding constant c_{t+1}, the willingness to pay for altruism is less when altruism is greater.

The "willingness to pay for altruism" is the MRS of the reduced form utility function. The assumptions can be expressed mathematically as follows:

$$(1)\quad \frac{d}{da}\left(\frac{f(a)}{g(a)}\right) > 0$$

$$(2)\quad f, g, f' > 0, \quad \frac{g'(0)}{g(0)} + \frac{1}{1 + \frac{1}{1+r}\frac{f(0)}{g(0)}}\left[\frac{f'(0)}{f(0)} - \frac{g'(0)}{g(0)}\right] > \frac{p\theta'(0)}{A - p\theta(0)}$$

36. $\varepsilon_f(a)$ and $\varepsilon_g(a)$ denote the elasticities of the functions f and g.

(3) the function $g(a)$ multiplying c_{t+1} in the utility function V

$$(4)\quad g \geq 0, \quad \frac{d^2}{da^2}\left(\ln \frac{f(a)}{g(a)}\right) \leq 0 \tag{B.6}$$

Mathematical assumption (3) is actually stronger than necessary; c_t and c_{t+1} could each be raised to a power $\varepsilon > 0$ in the utility function V without changing any results. The additional assumption $d^2[\ln g(a)]/da^2 \leq 0$ is sufficient to guarantee that second-order conditions hold.[37]

Proposition 1. Child-oriented resources are a normal good.

Proof: The Leontief utility function means that, given q and r, the ratio c_{t+1}/C is independent of A. Begin at an optimum for the consumer (that is, equation B.5 holds) and suppose q is not a normal good. Then, from the intergenerational budget constraint, C must be normal. An increase in A must increase C and, in order to maintain equation B.5, increase a. More a in response to more A contradicts the assumption that q is not normal, so q must be normal.

Proposition 2. Child-oriented resources are insensitive to proportional changes of A and p.

Proof: It suffices to show that, for fixed a, the equality in equation B.5 remains unchanged in response to a proportional change of A and p. Consider an initial position $(A, p, 1/(1 + r), a)$ that satisfies the equality B.5. Because a and r are fixed, c_{t+1}/C is fixed and therefore all of the terms inside the round brackets on the left-hand side of equation B.5 are fixed. Multiplying A and p by the same factor and holding a fixed therefore multiplies both sides of equation B.5 by that factor, leaving the equality unchanged.

Proposition 3. A higher interest rate encourages the purchase of child-oriented resources.

Proof: Holding fixed a, a higher interest rate decreases the fraction of consumption resources spent on children $(c_{t+1}/[C(1 + r)])$ and therefore increases the willingness to pay for altruism. With a and p fixed, the marginal cost of altruism $(p\theta')$ is unchanged, so more altruism must be the response to a higher interest rate.

Accumulation of Altruism with an Intergenerational Borrowing Constraint

Under the borrowing constrained model, there are two groups of families—those for whom the borrowing constraint is binding and those for

37. Some functional forms that satisfy conditions (1)–(4) and the second-order conditions are $f(a) = e^{\phi a}$, $g(a) = e^{-\gamma a}$, with $\phi > \gamma > 0$ and $\theta'(0) = 0$. $f(a) = a^{\phi}$, $g(a) = a^{-\gamma}$, with $1 > \phi, \gamma > 0$ and $\theta'(0) = 0$ also satisfy conditions (1)–(4) and the second-order conditions, even though $d^2[\ln g(a)]/da^2 > 0$.

whom it is not. Families who do not face a binding borrowing constraint behave like permanent income families, which are analyzed above. This section of the appendix therefore focuses on families for whom the borrowing constraint is binding ($x_{t+1} = 0$).[38] Uncertainty is not considered in this appendix.

For a borrowing constrained family, children consume their earnings w_{t+1}, which depend on their ability B_{t+1} and human capital h_{t+1}:

$$c_{t+1} = w_{t+1} = B_{t+1} h_{t+1}^{\nu} \tag{B.7}$$

Parents have income I_t, which consists of their own full earnings w_t and inheritance x_t (if any). Parental income is spent on parental consumption c_t, human capital for children h_{t+1}, and accumulating altruism $p_t\theta(a)$:

$$(1 + r)x_t + w_t \equiv I_t = c_t + h_{t+1} + p_t\theta(a) \tag{B.8}$$

Parents choose c_t, h_{t+1}, and a so as to maximize their objective B.3, subject to the constraints B.7 and B.8.

The optimal degree of intergenerational altruism a equates the family's willingness to pay for intergenerational altruism to the marginal cost:

$$\frac{C_t}{a}\left(\frac{1}{\alpha + (1-\alpha)\nu}\varepsilon_g(a) + [\varepsilon_f(a) - \varepsilon_g(a)]\frac{c_t}{C_t}\right) = p\theta'(a)$$

$$C_t \equiv I_t - p\theta(a)$$

$$\alpha \equiv \frac{1}{1 + \frac{1}{\nu}\left(\frac{f(a)/g(a)}{B_{t+1}}\right)^{1/\nu} c_t^{(1-\nu)/\nu}} \tag{B.9}$$

As in the permanent income model, I refer to C_t as "consumption resources," although it is defined here as parental income net of expenditures on child-oriented resources (as opposed to total family resources net of expenditures on child-oriented resources). α can be thought of as an index of the distribution of consumption across generations; more alpha means that parents consume more relative to children.

Notice that the willingness to pay for altruism is very similar with a borrowing constraint, as shown in equation B.9, as it is without, shown in equation B.10.[39] Holding constant the distribution of consumption across generations (α in equation B.9 and c_t/C in equation B.10) and the degree

38. See Appendix A for more analysis of the borrowing constraint and a proof of how the unconstrained families behave like permanent-income families.

39. Equation B.10 is the same as equation B. 5. The latter can be derived from the former with a substitution from the definition of consumption resources.

of altruism a, the willingness to pay for altruism is proportional to consumption resources C_t in both equations B.9 and B.10. However, the magnitude of the term in large round parentheses differs in the two models. Consider the willingness to pay for altruism in the permanent income model:

Willingness to Pay for Altruism in the Permanent Income Model

$$\frac{C}{a}\left(\varepsilon_g(a) + \left[[\varepsilon_f(a) - \varepsilon_g(a)]\,\frac{c_t}{C}\right]\right) = p\theta'(a) \tag{B.10}$$

The first term in large round parentheses is ε_g. ε_g is a measure of the desire to purchase child-oriented resources for given c_{t+1} and can be either positive or negative. The second term involves $\varepsilon_f - \varepsilon_g$, which is the rate at which altruism changes the preferred proportion. The analogues to these two terms appear in the borrowing constraints expression for the willingness to pay (equation B.9), but the first is multiplied by a factor greater than one. The factor is $1/[\alpha + (1 - \alpha)\nu]$. The second term appears in the expression for the willingness to pay of both models, but the factor depends only on altruism and interest in the permanent income model while it also depends on parental income in the borrowing constraints model. Whether the willingness to pay for altruism is larger or smaller in the borrowing constraints model depends on c_t/C and on the magnitude of the factor $1/[\alpha + (1 - \alpha)\nu]$.

Proposition 4. Holding fixed p_t and B_{t+1}, more parental income I_t increases the chosen degree of altruism if ε_g is not too negative.

Proof: Without a change in altruism, parental income cannot change the marginal cost of altruism. It only remains to be shown that the willingness to pay for altruism increases when parental income rises. Holding constant p and a, more parental income increases consumption resources C_t. The elasticity of the willingness to pay for altruism with respect to C_t is:

$$1 - (1 - \alpha)(1 - \nu)\frac{\alpha\varepsilon_\lambda - \dfrac{1 - \nu}{\nu}\varepsilon_g}{\alpha\varepsilon_\lambda + \varepsilon_g} > 0 \tag{B.11}$$

The inequality follows from $\alpha \leq 1$, $\nu < 1$, $\varepsilon_\lambda \equiv \varepsilon_f - \varepsilon_g > 0$, and $\varepsilon_g \geq 0$ (or ε_g sufficiently close to zero).

Proposition 5. Holding fixed B_{t+1}, a higher parental wage w_t decreases the chosen degree of altruism when child-oriented resources are time-intensive.

Proof: If there is no grandparental inheritance and altruism is fixed, then a higher parental wage w_t increases p and C_t proportionally. However, more C_t must decrease the term in parenthesis on the lefthand side of equation B.9, so the entire expression for the willingness to pay for altruism increases less than proportionally. With the marginal cost of altruism increasing more than the willingness to pay, altruism must fall. If there is a grandparental inheritance, C_t increases less than proportionally with w_t, and the result is only stronger.

The Quantity and Quality of Intergenerational Altruism

The overall parental objective $\tilde{V}$ depends on consumption by parents (c_t) and children (c_{t+1}) according to the number of children n:

$$\tilde{V}(c_t, c_{t+1}, n_t) \equiv \min\{f(n_t)c_t, \tilde{g}(n_t)c_{t+1}\} \tag{B.12}$$

For a given number of children, indifference curves in the $[c_t, c_{t+1}]$ plane are L-shaped as in figure 4.3. The ray of preferred proportions is $c_{t+1} = f(n)c_t/\tilde{g}(n)$.

A family has total resources A, which can be spent on parental consumption c_t, the fixed cost of children $d_t n_t$, and consumption by the n_t children $n_t c_{t+1}$. c_{t+1} is consumption *per* child. The intergenerational budget constraint is:

$$(1+r)x_t + w_t + n_t \frac{w_{t+1}}{1+r} \equiv A = c_t + n_t \frac{c_{t+1}}{1+r} + d_t n_t \tag{B.13}$$

One can maximize $\tilde{V}$ subject to the intertemporal budget constraint above, but there is a reformulation of that problem that is perfectly analogous to the problem presented in the first section of this appendix. To do so, define aggregate consumption by children $C_{t+1} \equiv n_t c_{t+1}$, parental income $I_t \equiv (1+r)x_t + w_t$, the net price of children $\delta_t \equiv [d_t - w_{t+1}/(1+r)]$, and a different g function $g(n_t) \equiv \tilde{g}(n_t)/n_t$. The equivalent problem is:

$$V(c_t, C_{t+1}, n_t) \equiv \min\{f(n_t)c_t, g(n_t)C_{t+1}\}$$

$$\text{s.t.} \tag{B.14}$$

$$I_t = c_t + \frac{C_{t+1}}{1+r} + \delta_t n_t \tag{B.15}$$

Consumption resources C are $c_t + C_{t+1}/(1+r)$. Using the utility function V and the fact that C_{t+1} and c_t are chosen as fixed proportions that depend on n, we can derive an equivalent reduced form utility function in terms of n and C:[40]

40. Compare this reduced form utility function to the earlier reduced form utility function in equation B.4.

$$v(n_t, C) \equiv \frac{f(n_t)}{1 + \frac{1}{1+r}\frac{f(n_t)}{g(n_t)}}C \qquad \text{(B.16)}$$

Consider four assumptions about the effect of fertility on preferences:

(1)′ More fertility lowers altruism *per child* and therefore the desired proportion c_{t+1}/c_t; more fertility raises aggregate altruism and therefore the desired proportion C_{t+1}/c_t.
(2)′ If the accumulation of children were costless, all parents would prefer more.
(3)′ At a given level of fertility, the willingness to pay for fertility is proportional to per capita child consumption c_{t+1}.
(4)′ Holding constant c_{t+1}, the willingness to pay for fertility is less when fertility is greater.

The "willingness to pay for fertility" is the MRS of the reduced form utility function. The assumptions can be expressed mathematically as follows:

$$(1)' \quad \frac{d}{dn}\left(\frac{f(n)}{\tilde{g}(n)}\right) < 0, \; \frac{d}{dn}\left(\frac{f(n)}{g(n)}\right) > 0$$

$$(2)' \quad f, g, f' > 0, \; \frac{g'(0)}{g(0)} + \frac{1}{1 + \frac{1}{1+r}\frac{f(0)}{g(0)}}\left[\frac{f'(0)}{f(0)} - \frac{g'(0)}{g(0)}\right] > \frac{p\theta'(0)}{A - p\theta(0)}$$

(3)′ the function $g(n)$ multiplying C_{t+1} in the utility function $\tilde{V}$

$$(4)' \quad g \geq 0, \; \frac{d^2}{dn^2}\left(\ln \frac{f(n)}{g(n)}\right) \leq 0 \qquad \text{(B.17)}$$

The additional assumption $d^2[\ln g(n)]/dn^2 \leq 0$ is sufficient to guarantee that second-order conditions hold.[41]

Not surprisingly, the willingness to pay for additional children is similar to the willingness to pay for altruism from the previous models:

Willingness to Pay for Additional Children

$$\frac{I_t - \delta_t n_t}{n_t}\left(\varepsilon_g(n_t) + \frac{\varepsilon_f(n_t) - \varepsilon_g(n_t)}{1 + \frac{1}{1+r}\frac{f(n_t)}{g(n_t)}}\right) = \delta_t \qquad \text{(B.18)}$$

where ε_f and ε_g are the elasticities of the functions $f(n)$ and $g(n)$, respectively.

41. The functional forms $f(n) = n^{\phi}$, $g(n) = n^{-\gamma}$, with $1 > \phi, \gamma > 0$ and $\theta'(0) = 0$ satisfy conditions (1)′–(4)′ and the second-order conditions, even though $d^2[\ln g(n)]/dn^2 > 0$.

Proposition 6. The number of children n_t is a normal good, where normal is defined with respect to I_t.

Proof: The Leontief utility function means that the ratio C_{t+1}/C is independent of I_t. Begin at an optimum for the consumer (that is, equation B.18 holds) and suppose n_t is not a normal good. Then, from the intergenerational budget constraint, C must be normal. An increase in I_t must increase C and, in order to maintain equation B.18, increase n_t. More n_t in response to more I_t contradicts the assumption that n_t is not normal, so n_t must be normal. The mathematical expression for the effect of income on fertility is:

$$\frac{dn_t}{dI_t} = \frac{1}{-(\text{SOC})}\frac{\delta_t}{I_t - \delta_t n_t} \tag{B.19}$$

The expression is positive because the second-order condition of the problem requires (SOC) < 0.

Proposition 7. Aggregate consumption by children is a normal good.

Proof: From the fact that families choose a consumption allocation on their ray of preferred proportions, we have:

$$C_{t+1} = \frac{\dfrac{f(n_t)}{g(n_t)}}{1 + \dfrac{1}{1+r}\dfrac{f(n_t)}{g(n_t)}}[I_t - \delta_t n_t] \tag{B.20}$$

Totally differentiating the RHS with respect to I_t, using the expression for dn_t/dI_t from Proposition 6, and using (SOC) < 0 delivers the result that $dC_{t+1}/dI_t > 0$.

Proposition 8. If $f(n)$ and $g(n)$ are Cobb-Douglas functions, then per capita consumption by children is a normal good.

Proof: (1) From the fact that families choose a consumption allocation on their ray of preferred proportions, we have:

$$C_{t+1} = n_t c_{t+1} = \frac{\dfrac{f(n_t)}{g(n_t)}}{1 + \dfrac{1}{1+r}\dfrac{f(n_t)}{g(n_t)}}[I_t - \delta_t n_t] \tag{B.21}$$

(2) Substituting from equation B.18,

$$c_{t+1} = \frac{\delta_t}{\varepsilon_f(n_t)\dfrac{g(n_t)}{f(n_t)} + \dfrac{1}{1+r}\varepsilon_g(n_t)} \tag{B.22}$$

(3) With Cobb-Douglas $f(n)$ and $g(n)$, $\varepsilon_f(n)$ and $\varepsilon_g(n)$ are constants. From Proposition 6, parental income increases fertility, which decreases $g(n)/f(n)$ and increases c_{t+1}.

Proposition 9. If $g(n) = 1$ and $f(n) = \alpha/(\beta - \ln n)$, $\alpha > 0$, $\beta > [\ln (I/\delta) + 1]$, then—holding constant δ and R—per capita consumption is independent of parental income.

Proof: (1) Because of the assumed functional forms, $\varepsilon_g(n) = 0$ and $\varepsilon_f(n) = 1/(\beta - \ln n)$. (2) Substitution of the assumed functional forms for $\varepsilon_g(n)$ and $\varepsilon_f(n)$ into the expression for c_{t+1} shown in Proposition 8, shows that $c_{t+1} = \alpha\delta_t$, which is independent of parental income.

Propositions 8 and 9 are related to a very strong result obtained by Becker and Barro (1988). For a particular functional form for their altruism function (Cobb-Douglas), they find the per capita consumption by children to be independent of parental income. I do not obtain this result for Cobb-Douglas $f(n)$ and $g(n)$, but Proposition 9 does prove the result for another functional form.

Proposition 10. Fertility is insensitive to proportional changes of I_t and δ_t.

Proof: It suffices to show that, for fixed *a*, the equality in equation B.18 remains unchanged in response to a proportional change of I_t and δ_t. Consider an initial position (I_t, δ_t, $1/(1 + r)$, n_t) that satisfies the equality in equation B.18. Because n_t and r are fixed, all of the terms inside the round brackets on the left-hand side of B.18 are fixed. Multiplying I_t and δ_t by the same factor and holding a fixed therefore multiplies both sides of equation B.18 by that factor, leaving the equality unchanged.

Proposition 11. If the earnings of a child is small enough, higher interest encourages fertility.

Proof: If w_{t+1} is small, then the effect of a higher interest rate on the net cost of children is small. An interest rate effect holding constant δ_t can be derived as in the Mulligan model. Algebraically, the effect of the interest factor $R \equiv 1/(1 + r)$ on fertility n is:

$$\frac{\partial n_t}{\partial R} = \frac{1}{-\text{SOC}}\left[\frac{w_{t+1}I_t}{(I_t - \delta_t n_t)^2} - \frac{\dfrac{d}{dn_t}\left(\dfrac{f(n_t)}{g(n_t)}\right)}{\left(1 + R\dfrac{f(n_t)}{g(n_t)}\right)^2}\right] \tag{B.23}$$

SOC is an expression that must be negative when the second-order conditions of the problem are satisfied. Clearly $\partial n/\partial R$ is negative when w_{t+1} is very small. Since R is inversely related to the interest rate r, we have $\partial n/\partial r$ positive.

Proposition 12. If parents leave no financial transfers to children and $\varepsilon_g(n) \geq 0$, higher interest discourages fertility.

Proof: (1) From equation B.18,

$$\varepsilon_f - \frac{\delta_t n_t}{I_t - \delta_t n_t} - \frac{\frac{1}{1+r}\frac{f(n_t)}{g(n_t)}}{1 + \frac{1}{1+r}\frac{f(n_t)}{g(n_t)}}[\varepsilon_f - \varepsilon_g] = 0 \qquad \text{(B.24)}$$

Rearranging, we get:

$$\varepsilon_f \leq \left[1 + \frac{1}{1+r}\frac{f(n_t)}{g(n_t)}\right]\frac{\delta_t n_t}{I_t - \delta_t n_t} < \frac{1}{1+r}\frac{f(n_t)}{g(n_t)}\frac{I_t}{I_t - \delta_t n_t} + \frac{\delta_t n_t}{I_t - \delta_t n_t} \qquad \text{(B.25)}$$

The first inequality follows from $\varepsilon_g \geq 0$ and the second from $I_t > \delta_t n_t$. (2) Because parents do not make a financial transfer, $w_{t+1} = c_{t+1}$. Using the fact that the consumption allocation lies on the ray of preferred proportions, we have:

$$w_{t+1}\frac{I_t}{(I_t - \delta_t n_t)^2} = \frac{1+r}{n_t}\frac{1}{1 + \frac{1}{1+r}\frac{f(n_t)}{g(n_t)}} \times \left[\frac{1}{1+r}\frac{f(n_t)}{g(n_t)}\frac{I_t}{I_t - \delta_t n_t} + \frac{\delta_t n_t}{I_t - \delta_t n_t} - \frac{\delta_t n_t}{I_t - \delta_t n_t}\right] \qquad \text{(B.26)}$$

The result (1) above is sufficient to show that the first term in brackets in equation B.23 is larger than the second term, so $dn_t/dR > 0$. A higher interest rate lowers fertility.

Appendix C: More on "Total Resource" and "Substitution" Effects

This appendix generalizes the results reported in the text in "The Formation of Altruism" and proved in the previous appendix by relaxing the assumption of L-shaped indifference curves in the $[c_t, c_{t+1}]$ plane. When the elasticity of substitution of consumption across generations is a constant, it is shown that the three main results reported in the text still obtain. Those results are:

(1) Child-oriented resources are a normal good.
(2) Child-oriented resources are insensitive to proportional changes of A and p.
(3) A higher interest rate encourages the purchase of child-oriented resources.

Results are not derived for the imperfect capital markets model, although the text indicates how the results (1)–(3) for the permanent income model can be used to derive results for the borrowing constraints model.

Preferences and Permanent Income Constraints

In this more general setup, parents and children are assumed to derive happiness from their own consumption according to the utility function $u(c)$. Parents weight the happiness of a child in their decisions according to the altruism parameter a. a is a function of child-oriented resources q_t.

$$V = u(c_t) + a(q_t)u(c_{t+1}) \tag{C.1}$$

The overall parental objective V is the weighted sum of parental and child utilities. The functions $u(c)$ and $a(q)$ are assumed to be positive, increasing and concave.

The intergenerational permanent income budget constraint (equation B.1) is the same and is reprinted below for the reader's convenience:

$$(1 + r)x_t + w_t + \frac{w_{t+1}}{1 + r} \equiv A_t = c_t + \frac{c_{t+1}}{1 + r} + p_t q_t \tag{B.1}$$

Characterization of the Optimal Choices

Parental decisions are those that maximize equation C.1 subject to the intergenerational budget constraint shown in equation B.1 and the constraint $q_t \in [0, \overline{q}]$. The demand for child-oriented resources takes the form $q_t = D(A_t, p_t, 1/(1 + r))$. Locally, the elasticities of this demand function with respect to A and p are (for interior allocations):

$$\frac{\partial \ln D}{\partial \ln A} = J(c_t, c_{t+1}, q_t, A_t, p_t, R)$$

$$\frac{\partial \ln D}{\partial \ln p} = -J(c_t, c_{t+1}, q_t, A_t, p_t, R)$$

$$\times\left(1 + \frac{c_t}{A_t}\frac{\varepsilon_u(c_t) - \varepsilon_u(c_{t+1}) + \eta_u(c_t)[1 - \varepsilon_u(c_t) - \eta_u(c_{t+1})]}{[1 - \varepsilon_u(c_t) - \eta_u(c_t)][1 - \eta_u(c_{t+1})]}\right.$$

$$\left. + \frac{R\,c_{t+1}}{A_t}\frac{\eta_u(c_{t+1})}{1 - \eta_u(c_{t+1})}\right)$$

$$J(c_t, c_{t+1}, q_t, A_t, p_t, R) \equiv \left[\left(\frac{c_t}{A_t}\frac{1 - \varepsilon_u(c_{t+1}) - \eta_u(c_{t+1})}{1 - \varepsilon_u(c_t) - \eta_u(c_t)} + \frac{Rc_{t+1}}{A_t}\right)\right.$$

$$\times \frac{1-\eta_a(q_t)}{1-\eta_u(c_{t+1})} + \frac{pq_t}{A_t} - \frac{c_t}{A_t}\frac{\varepsilon_a(q_t)}{1-\varepsilon_u(c_t)-\eta_u(c_t)}\Bigg]^{-1}$$

$$R \equiv \frac{1}{1+r}$$

$$\text{for a function } f(x): \varepsilon_f(x) \equiv \frac{f'(x)x}{f(x)},\ \eta_f(x) \equiv \frac{\varepsilon'_f(x)x}{\varepsilon_f(x)} \tag{C.2}$$

We assume that a second-order condition, $\sigma\varepsilon_a < 1$, is satisfied.

Lemma 1. When the elasticity of substitution of parental consumption for child consumption is a constant σ, $\varepsilon_u(c) = (\sigma - 1)/\sigma$ and $\eta_u(c) = 0$.

Proof: From the definitions of elasticity of substitution, $\varepsilon_u(c)$, and $\eta_u(c)$.

Proposition 1. When the elasticity of substitution of parental consumption for child consumption is a constant σ, child-oriented resources are a normal good.

Proof: From Lemma 1, $\varepsilon_u(c_t) = \varepsilon_u(c_{t+1}) = (\sigma - 1)/\sigma$ and $\eta_u(c_t) = \eta_u(c_{t+1}) = 0$. Plugging these equations into equation C.2 proves the proposition.

Proposition 2. When the elasticity of substitution of parental consumption for child consumption is a constant σ, the magnitudes of the total resource and price elasticities of the demand for child-oriented resources are equal.

Proof: From Lemma 1, $\varepsilon_u(c_t) = \varepsilon_u(c_{t+1}) = (\sigma - 1)/\sigma$ and $\eta_u(c_t) = \eta_u(c_{t+1}) = 0$. Plugging these equations into equation C.2 and using $\sigma\varepsilon_a < 1$ proves the proposition.

Proposition 3. When the elasticity of substitution of parental consumption for child consumption is a constant σ, a higher interest rate encourages the purchase of child-oriented resources.

Proof: The proof follows from differentiating the first-order conditions of the maximization problem with respect to the interest rate.

Proposition 2 generates sharper results when child-oriented resources are time-intensive because it compares the magnitudes of the total resource and substitution effects. Suppose time comprises a share ω of the cost of q. A k percentage change in the value of time creates a ωk percentage change in p. This effect alone decreases the demand for q according to the price elasticity shown in equation C.2. However, a change in the wage also has a total resource effect. A k percentage change in the wage produces a $(w_t/A_t)k$ percentage change in total family resources. Proposition 4 and its corollary summarize:

Proposition 4. When the elasticity of substitution of parental consumption for child consumption is a constant σ and ω is greater (less) than

(w_t/A_t), a higher wage decreases (increases) the demand for child-oriented resources.

Proof: Follows directly from Proposition 2.

Corollary: Assume that parental inheritances x_t are nonnegative. When the elasticity of substitution of parental consumption for child consumption is a constant σ and child-oriented resources are totally time-intensive, a higher wage decreases the demand for child-oriented resources.

Proof: It is assumed that $\omega = 1$. Because $w_t/A_t < 1$, the result follows from Proposition 2.

CHAPTER 5

Taxation and Intergenerational Mobility in the Three Models

The analysis in previous chapters does not explicitly incorporate the taxation of income and financial intergenerational transfers. This chapter shows, however, that the results obtained previously still hold when there is a single rate of income taxation and a single rate of estate taxation. Graduated-rate income and estate taxes do modify the implications of the models for intergenerational mobility.

Previous chapters offer two explanations of intergenerational consumption mobility: borrowing constraints and endogenous altruism. The graduated-rate models of this chapter offer a third explanation: government tax policies encourage intergenerational mobility. The empirical analyses in chapters 6 through 8 provide evidence on the validity of the three competing explanations.

The first two sections of this chapter derive the implications of the three models for intergenerational mobility in the presence of income and estate taxation. To do so, I follow the same logical steps that appear in chapter 3. First, I outline a hypothetical tax system. Second, I show how that tax system affects the shape of the intergenerational budget constraint. Third, I show how the shape of the budget constraint determines the shape of the expansion path which, as shown in chapter 3, delivers the main predictions for intergenerational consumption mobility. For this third step, I recall from chapter 3 that, holding constant intergenerational altruism, consumption does not regress to the mean in percentage terms among families whose choices lie on the same linear portion of the budget constraint.[1]

1. As shown in chapter 3, a related result obtains when intergenerational altruism varies in a way that is unrelated to parental income. Those parental consumption differences associated with parental income differences do not regress to the mean in percentage terms among families on the same linear portion of their budget constraint.

Among families on a curved portion of the budget constraint, consumption does regress to the mean in percentage terms with the rate of regression depending on the curvature of the budget constraint.

The section on the "Overview of the United States Estate, Gift, and Income Taxation" outlines the relevant features of the U.S. federal income, estate, and gift tax rules. The final section reviews the main results discussed in this chapter.

Estate and Gift Taxation

This section introduces estate and gift taxes into the economic models. I show that a flat-rate tax does not modify the implications of any of the three models for the transmission of inequality across generations but that a graduated-rate tax does.

Flat-Rate Taxes

Suppose that parents who make \$$x$ in financial transfers to their children must pay \$$\tau x$ in estate and gift taxes, where τ is a constant.[2] Then \$$x$ of consumption sacrificed by parents leaves \$$(1 - \tau)x$ after taxes, which earns \$$r(1 - \tau)x$ in interest, thereby producing \$$(1 - \tau)(1 + r)x$ of additional consumption for a child.[3] Parents therefore move away from their earnings endowment along a line with slope $-(1 - \tau)(1 + r)$ rather than along a line with a slope $-(1 + r)$ as in figures 3.1 and 3.2. *The intergenerational budget constraint is still linear* with a single estate tax rate, but it has a different slope than it does in the absence of estate taxation. A linear intergenerational budget constraint means that the implications of the permanent income model are unchanged when a flat-rate estate tax is introduced:

(1) Consumption does not regress to the mean in percentage terms, and consumption inequality grows over time when altruism is the same for all families.
(2) When altruism varies across families in a way that is uncorrelated with parental income, consumption does not regress to

2. Notice that, under this hypothetical estate tax system, parents who leave a negative financial transfer *receive* funds from the tax authorities.

An estate tax usually refers to taxes paid by a donor on funds transferred at his death. A gift tax is the tax on funds transferred before death. These two taxes are the same in one period/two generation models. The two are also treated very similarly by the U.S. tax code (McNulty 1994).

3. I suggest that taxes are paid on the financial transfer before the interest accrues. One could assume instead that interest accrues first—\$$x$ sacrificed by parents becomes \$$(1 + r)x$ before taxes—and then taxes of \$$\tau(1 + r)x$ are levied on the estate. In either scenario, \$$x$ sacrificed by parents leaves a child with \$$(1 - \tau)(1 + r)x$ additional consumption.

the mean in percentage terms across parental income categories. Consumption inequality grows over time.

(3) When poorer parents are more altruistic, consumption regresses to the mean in percentage terms.

The efficient human capital investment is higher with the flat-rate estate tax—it occurs at the point where the earnings function has slope $(1 - \tau)(1 + r)$—but is still the same for all families with children of the same ability.[4] Earnings still regress to the mean according to the intergenerational mobility of ability.

The shape of the intergenerational budget constraint for the imperfect capital markets model is also qualitatively unchanged when a flat-rate estate tax is introduced. With or without the tax, the intergenerational budget constraint consists of a straight-line portion and a curved portion. The straight-line portion applies to consumption allocations in which children consume more than the efficient level of earnings. The curved portion applies to small consumption levels for children. The similarity of the budget constraint with and without the tax means that the implications of the imperfect capital markets model are also qualitatively robust to the introduction of a flat-rate estate tax.

In the Mulligan model of altruism with either permanent income or borrowing constraints, predictions for intergenerational consumption and earnings mobility are unchanged by the introduction of a flat-rate estate tax. A flat-rate tax reduces the slope of the intergenerational budget constraint in the $[c_t, c_{t+1}]$ plane, which, because of the "interest rate effect," reduces altruism. However, the relationship between altruism and parental income—and therefore intergenerational mobility—is unchanged by the introduction of a flat-rate estate tax.

Graduated-Rate Taxes

A flat-rate estate tax does not affect the intergenerational transmission of consumption and earnings inequality in any of the three models of chapters 3 and 4. However, a graduated-rate estate tax—where the tax rate depends on the amount being taxed—does affect the degree of intergenerational mobility. The derivation of some additional results for the three models with graduated-rate tax systems follows three steps. First, it is shown how a graduated-rate tax affects the shape of the intergenerational budget constraint. Second, the shape of the expansion path—which summarizes the main implications for intergenerational consumption mobility—is derived. Third, effects of the graduated-rate system on the efficient

4. If human capital investments were also taxed at rate τ, the efficient human capital investment would be the same as it is in the absence of estate taxation.

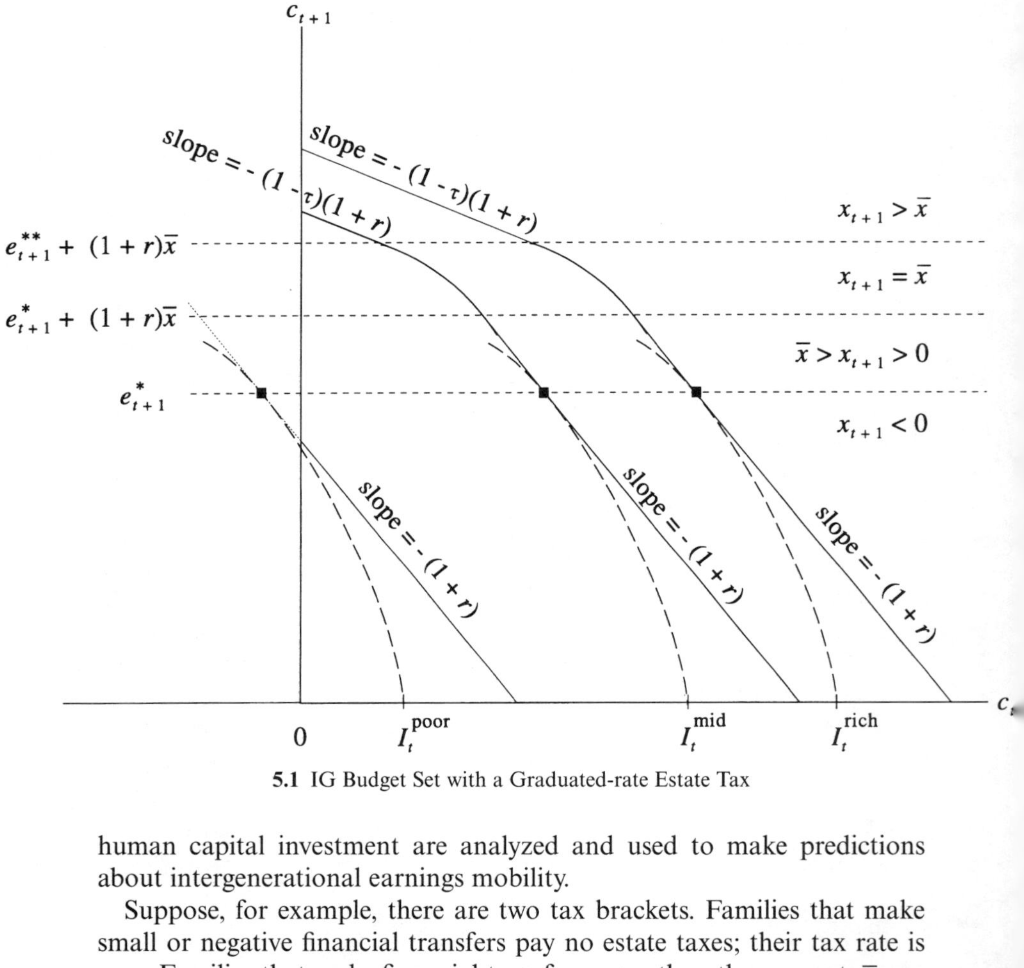

5.1 IG Budget Set with a Graduated-rate Estate Tax

human capital investment are analyzed and used to make predictions about intergenerational earnings mobility.

Suppose, for example, there are two tax brackets. Families that make small or negative financial transfers pay no estate taxes; their tax rate is zero. Families that make financial transfers more than the amount $\overline{x}$ pay taxes at rate τ on the amount above $\overline{x}$. Figure 5.1 displays the intergenerational budget constraint. If families choose $c_{t+1} < e^*_{t+1}$, then they borrow against the earnings of children at rate r with no estate tax consequences; the budget constraint is linear below the square dot with slope $-(1 + r)$. As long as financial transfers are less than $\overline{x}$, families can choose $c_{t+1} > e^*_{t+1}$ without estate tax consequences; the budget constraint in the region between the bottom two horizontal dashed lines also has slope $-(1 + r)$. The intergenerational budget constraint below the middle dashed horizontal line ($c_{t+1} < e^*_{t+1} + (1 + r)\overline{x}$) is the same as in the permanent income model without taxes derived in chapter 3. The graduated-rate estate tax has its effects on the shape of the intergenerational budget constraint above the middle dashed horizontal line. Notice that the allocation exactly on the horizontal line $c_{t+1} = e^*_{t+1} + (1 + r)\overline{x}$ is achieved by making the "efficient" human capital investment (where the slope of the earnings function is $(1 + r)$) in addition to a financial transfer of exactly $\overline{x}$. Suppose parents wanted to choose an allocation slightly above that line, with c_{t+1} slightly larger than $e^*_{t+1} + (1 + r)\overline{x}$. Parents could achieve the allocation by increasing the financial transfer above $\overline{x}$ but, because of the estate tax, a dollar sacrificed by parents would increase the consumption of the child by only $(1 - \tau)(1 + r)$ dollars. If, instead, parents held the financial transfer fixed at $\overline{x}$ and increased the human capital investment above the "efficient" level h^*_{t+1}, a dollar sacrificed by parents would increase the consumption of the child by $e'(h^*_{t+1})$ dollars, which, according to the definition of the "efficient" human capital investment, is equal to $(1 + r)$ dollars. Since $(1 + r)$ dollars is more than $(1 - \tau)(1 + r)$ dollars, parents choose to increase the human capital investment beyond the "efficient" level; parents who desire these higher levels of consumption for their child invest in his human capital even when the rate of return is low because estate taxes are avoided. The intergenerational budget constraint is therefore curved, following the shape of the earnings function as shown in figure 5.1 between the middle and top horizontal dashed lines.

Since human capital investments are subject to diminishing returns, very large investments will drive the rate of return below $(1 - \tau)(1 + r)$. At the human capital investment h^{**}_{t+1} where the slope of the earnings function $e'(h^{**}_{t+1})$ is equal to $(1 - \tau)(1 + r)$, it no longer makes sense for parents to continue human capital investments. Parents who want to allocate consumption to their child above the amount $e^{**}_{t+1} + (1 + r)\overline{x}$ (where $e^{**}_{t+1} = e(h^{**}_{t+1})$ is the level of earnings associated with human capital investment yielding marginal return of $(1 - \tau)(1 + r)$) make financial transfers beyond the amount $\overline{x}$. Because financial transfers beyond the amount $\overline{x}$ earn a constant after-tax rate of return of $(1 - \tau)(1 + r)$, the intergenerational budget constraint above the top horizontal dashed line is linear with slope $-(1 - \tau)(1 + r)$.

The implications of the graduated-rate tax system derive from its effects on the shape of the intergenerational budget constraint. The graduated-rates produce intergenerational budget constraints with several linear and curved portions. With a "progressive" rate structure—where the tax rate is higher on larger estates—each portion of the budget constraint becomes less steeply sloped as one moves vertically in a diagram such as figure 5.1.

The intergenerational budget constraint for the two-bracket estate tax shown in figure 5.1 consists of two linear pieces and a curved piece. If one considers a group of families with homothetic preferences, the same degree of intergenerational altruism, and who are all choosing on the

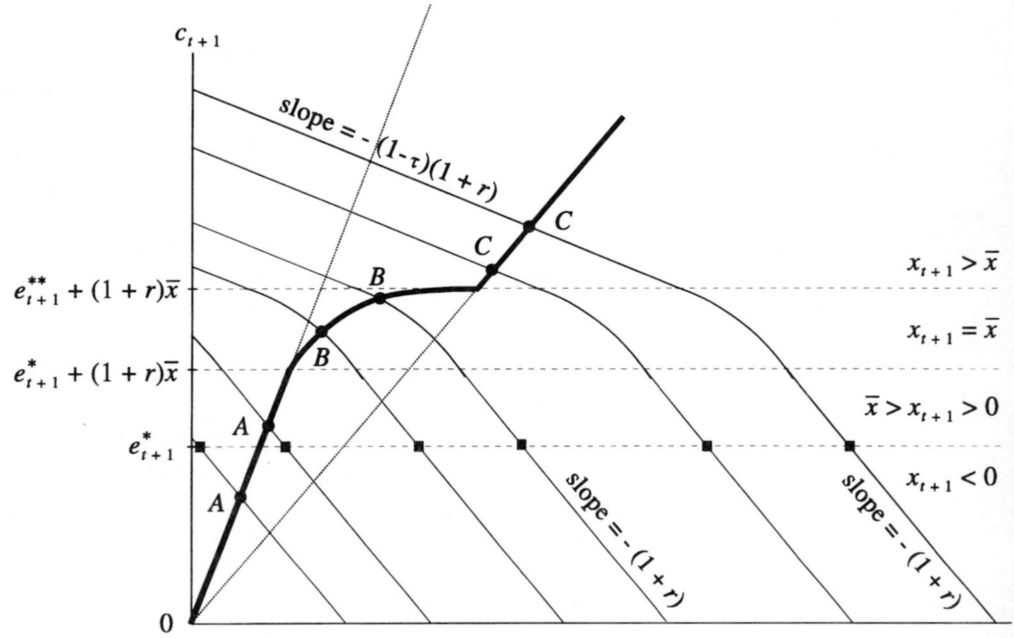

5.2 Expansion Path with a Graduated-rate Estate Tax

$-(1 + r)$ sloped linear portion of the budget constraint, their choices lie along a ray emanating from the origin (see chapter 3 for a proof). All families in this group, two of which are labeled *A* in figure 5.2, make financial transfers less than $\overline{x}$. Choices by families on the $-(1 - \tau)(1 + r)$ sloped linear segment of the budget constraint also lie on a ray, but on a different, flatter ray. Two such families are labeled *C* in figure 5.2. All of this second set of families are making financial transfers greater than $\overline{x}$ and therefore are subject to estate tax. A third set of families, labeled as *B* in figure 5.2, are at the curved portion of the intergenerational budget set. This set of families is exactly between the two estate tax brackets, so decreasing financial transfers decreases consumption of children at rate $(1 + r)$, but increasing financial transfers only increases consumption of children at rate $(1 - \tau)(1 + r)$. The marginal transfer to children for the *B* families is therefore a human capital investment rather than a financial transfer because the former earns a return of less than $(1 + r)$ but more than $(1 - \tau)(1 + r)$. The use of human capital investments at the margin by the *B* families means that they are on a portion of the intergenerational budget constraint that is curved according to the shape of the earnings function. If one considers a group of families with homothetic preferences, the same degree of intergenerational altruism, and who are all choosing on the curved portion of the budget constraint, their choices lie along an inelastic expansion path—a path that is "flatter than rays to the origin" (see the imperfect capital markets section of chapter 3 for a proof).

As shown in figure 5.2, financial transfers are less than $\overline{x}$ for the poorest family. As parental income increases, the chosen consumption allocation increases along the more steeply sloped ray. When parental income is high enough that financial transfers equal $\overline{x}$, additional parental income is no longer allocated to children in the form of a financial transfer but instead as a human capital investment above the "efficient" level. The expansion path—shown as a thick solid line in figure 5.2—is inelastic or "flatter than rays to the origin" for this middle parental income range. When parental income is even higher, parents are so willing to make transfers to their children and human capital investments earn such low returns that they are willing to incur the estate tax. The expansion path follows the flatter ray for these very high incomes. The overall expansion path therefore has three segments—a steeply sloped linear segment following a ray from the origin for low incomes, an inelastic portion for intermediate incomes, and a linear segment following another flatter ray from the origin for the highest incomes.[5]

The slopes of the rays delineating the expansion path are independent of ability or the earnings function. Only parental preferences, the interest rate, and the estate tax rates determine the slopes of the rays. The position and shape of the inelastic portion—which is the point where financial transfers reach $\overline{x}$—depend on the ability of the child. More human capital investment is efficient for more able children, so the use of financial transfers to allocate consumption to the child occurs only at higher incomes.

It is easy to generalize figure 5.2 to the case of three progressive tax brackets. In the progressive three-bracket system, the smallest financial transfers are taxed at the lowest rate. Intermediate financial transfers are taxed at a moderate rate and the largest transfers are taxed at the highest rate. The expansion path in the three-bracket system would have *five* sections: a steeply sloped linear segment, an inelastic portion, a moderately sloped linear segment, another inelastic portion, and a flatter sloped linear segment. Each of the three upward sloping linear segments correspond to one of the three tax rates. A progressive four-bracket system would have seven sections, a five-bracket system would have nine, etc.

Regardless of the number of tax brackets, a progressive graduated-rate structure means that richer families who are subject to a higher tax rate choose consumption allocations that are on a flatter ray than those chosen

5. The inelastic portion of the expansion path is drawn as concave in figure 5.2, but it can be linear or even convex. The important property is that it is flatter than rays to the origin.

by poorer families. This means that the ratio c_{t+1}/c_t falls as one moves from a low tax bracket to a high one. If one studies groups of families—some of whom are in high tax brackets and some of whom are in low brackets—the ratio c_{t+1}/c_t (according to the permanent income model) tends to be higher for poorer families. In other words, consumption regresses to the mean in percentage terms in samples that include families from different estate tax brackets. On the other hand, a sample that includes families from the *same* tax bracket (and who have the same degree of intergenerational altruism and who are not on the "kink" between two tax brackets) are on the same portion of the expansion path and therefore on the same ray. The ratio c_{t+1}/c_t is the same for all; consumption does not regress to the mean in percentage terms in samples that include only families from the interior of a single estate tax bracket.

With a graduated-rate estate tax, it is no longer true that all families with children of the same ability make the same human capital investments in the permanent income model. Poorer families are not subject to the estate tax and therefore invest in human capital up to the point where the slope of the earnings function is $(1 + r)$. Richer families invest beyond that point because the estate tax discourages them from making financial transfers. Human capital investments in the permanent income model depend only on ability in the absence of estate taxation or with flat-rate estate taxation but depend on *both* ability and the parental estate tax bracket when there are several tax rates. A graduated-rate estate tax tends to increase the intergenerational persistence of earnings because richer families make larger human capital investments to avoid the high rates of estate taxation tax that apply to them.

Consumption regresses to the mean across tax brackets in the permanent income model when all families have the same degree of intergenerational altruism but not *within* tax brackets. The prediction that consumption does not regress to the mean within tax brackets also means that consumption inequality must grow over time if there is a substantial fraction of people in either the highest or the lowest tax bracket.

If poorer families are more altruistic, then consumption also regresses to the mean both within and across tax brackets. However, consumption is more persistent within tax brackets than across brackets because both altruism and the progressivity of the tax system are forces promoting regression to the mean across tax brackets while only altruism operates within tax brackets. High estate tax rates also have an "interest rate" effect on the accumulation of altruism by rich families; the "interest rate effect" is another force promoting regression to the mean of consumption across estate tax brackets.

Chapter 3 shows that the expansion path has two sections in the imperfect capital markets model without estate taxes. The section nearest the origin is curved and applies to families that do not make financial transfers to their children. The section furthest from the origin is linear, following a ray. The introduction of a graduated-rate estate tax breaks the linear section into several linear segments and inelastic portions. With a two-bracket system, for example, the expansion path is inelastic nearest the origin and below the point where $c_{t+1} = e^{*}_{t+1}$. Moving away from the origin, the expansion path follows a ray until $c_{t+1} = e^{*}_{t+1} + (1 + r)\overline{x}$. The expansion path is inelastic again until parents are rich enough to justify paying estate taxes at the higher rate ($c_{t+1} = e^{**}_{t+1} + (1 + r)\overline{x}$). The last portion of the expansion path follows a ray. The last three of these four portions correspond to the three linear portions shown in figure 5.2.

As in the permanent income model, a graduated-rate estate tax tends to increase the intergenerational persistence of earnings in the imperfect capital markets model because richer families make larger human capital investments to avoid the high rates of estate taxation that apply to them.

Summary of Theoretical Results

A flat-rate estate tax does not change any of the implications of the three models for intergenerational consumption and earnings mobility. A graduated-rate estate tax, on the other hand, increases intergenerational consumption mobility and decreases earnings mobility. It is likely that neither tax system changes the prediction from chapters 3 and 4 that, without a theory of intergenerational altruism, consumption inequality must grow over time in the permanent income model.

Income Taxation

Income taxes are introduced into the three models and are shown to have very similar effects on altruism and intergenerational mobility as estate taxes. A flat-rate income tax does not change any of the implications of the three models for intergenerational consumption and earnings mobility. A graduated-rate system does affect intergenerational mobility, and those effects depend on the tax treatment of human capital investments by parents.

Flat-Rate Taxes

Suppose that children have to pay income taxes τI_{t+1}, where their income I_{t+1} consists of earnings plus interest earned on the family's financial assets. \$$x$ of consumption sacrificed by parents for the sake of financial transfers therefore produces $\$[1 + r(1 - \tau)]x$ of additional consumption for children. x is the "principal" part of parental savings while rx is the "interest" and τrx is the income tax owed on the interest. The financial rate of exchange $[1 + r(1 - \tau)]$ is not related to choices or parental income, so all families in the permanent income model have a linear intergenerational budget constraint with slope $-[1 + r(1 - \tau)]$. As in the model without income taxes, expansion paths are rays emanating from the origin; consumption does not regress to the mean in percentage terms among families with the same degree of intergenerational altruism. Other than the change in slope, intergenerational budget constraints appear as they do in figure 3.11. Implications for consumption and earnings mobility in the permanent income model are therefore insensitive to the introduction of a flat-rate income tax.

$\$x$ sacrificed by parents in the form of financial transfers produces $\$[1 + r(1 - \tau)]x$ of additional consumption for children, but each dollar sacrificed for human capital investment produces $(1 - \tau)e'(h)$, where $e(h)$ is the earnings function. $e'(h)$ is the additional pre-tax earnings enjoyed because of the additional human capital investment and $\tau e'(h)$ is the additional income taxes owed on that additional pre-tax earnings. $(1 - \tau)e'(h)$ is therefore the effect of human capital investment on after-tax earnings that can be consumed by the adult child. Because the efficient human capital investment h^* equates the after-tax returns to financial and human capital transfers (that is, $(1 - \tau)e'(h^*) = [1 + r(1 - \tau)]x$), the efficient human capital investment no longer occurs at the point where the slope of the earnings function is $(1 + r)$. Instead, all families in the permanent income model invest in human capital up to the point where the slope of the earnings function is $[(1 - \tau)^{-1} + r]$. The efficient human capital investment (efficient from the point of view of the family) is less than it is in the absence of income taxation because $[(1 - \tau)^{-1} + \mathrm{r}]$ is greater than $(1 + r)$.[6] All families with children of the same ability who are subject to the flat-rate income tax are making the same human capital investments in the permanent income model. The implication that earnings regress to the mean in the permanent income model is therefore robust to the introduction of a flat-rate income tax.

Many educational and medical expenses are deductible from the U.S. federal income tax. For example, parents can purchase a better education for their children through the public school system (for example, moving

6. However, this result depends on my assumption that children do not have to pay income taxes on their inheritances, rather only on any interest that they may earn. When income taxes are also paid on inheritances, the efficient human capital investment does not depend on the income tax rate. In either case, it is still true that all families are making the same human capital investments in the permanent income model.

to a better school district) by paying additional property taxes, which are deductible from the income that is subject to federal tax. Parental time spent improving the education and health of their children, to the extent that it reduces time that parents can earn money, is another example of a parental human capital investment that is effectively deductible from federal income taxes. If one assumes that the income of parents is also taxed at a single tax rate (which can be different than the tax rate for children), the implications for the intergenerational transmission of earnings and consumption inequality are also robust to the assumption that human capital investments are deductible.

The intergenerational budget constraint in the $[c_t, c_{t+1}]$ is still linear with a flat-rate income tax, but it is less steeply sloped than in the absence of the tax. A flatter slope of the intergenerational budget constraint has an "interest rate" effect on altruism in the Mulligan model, so altruism is reduced by the income tax. However, because the intergenerational budget constraint is still linear, all of the results for altruism and intergenerational mobility derived in chapter 4 still obtain.

How does a flat-rate income tax affect the imperfect capital markets model? As in the absence of taxation, the intergenerational budget constraint consists of a curved and a linear portion. The efficient human capital investment and corresponding level of earnings for the child determine exactly where the curved portion ends and the linear portion begins. As discussed above, a flat-rate income tax affects the overall slope of the budget constraint and may affect h^* (depending on the tax deductibility of human capital investments). But a change in the overall slope of the intergenerational budget constraint does not affect the shape of the expansion path and therefore does not effect intergenerational consumption mobility. As for intergenerational earnings mobility, that still depends on whether or not a family wishes to borrow ($x_{t+1} < 0$). All of the implications of the imperfect capital markets model for intergenerational consumption and earnings mobility derived in chapter 3 are therefore robust to the introduction of a flat-rate income tax.

Graduated-Rate Taxes

A graduated-rate income tax on children changes the implications for earnings and consumption mobility. Consider, for example, a two tax bracket system. Income up to the amount $\bar{I}$ is taxed at rate τ_L, while income above the amount $\bar{I}$ is taxed at the higher rate τ_H.[7]

7. A flat-tax at rate τ on incomes above $\bar{I}$ is a special case of this two-bracket example. This special case has $\tau_L = 0$ and $\tau_H = \tau$.

Children have their pre-tax earnings and financial transfer but cannot consume it all because they must pay income taxes. When a child has pre-tax income less than $\bar{I}$ (or, equivalently, after-tax income less than $(1 - \tau_L)\bar{I}$), parents can change the child's consumption by $[1 + r(1 - \tau_L)]x$ with a financial transfer by changing their own consumption by \$$x$. A child who has income greater than $\bar{I}$ pays taxes at rate τ_H; the intergenerational rate of exchange for his family is therefore $[1 + r(1 - \tau_H)]$ rather than $[1 + r(1 - \tau_L)]$. Intergenerational borrowing and lending at interest rate r therefore produces an intergenerational budget constraint with two linear segments. Consider the solid lines in figure 5.4. One segment has slope $[1 + r(1 - \tau_L)]$ and applies to transfers that leave the child's pre-tax income less than $\bar{I}$ and after-tax income less than $(1 - \tau_L)\bar{I}$. The other segment has slope $[1 + r(1 - \tau_H)]$ and applies to transfers that leave the child's pre-tax income greater than $\bar{I}$. Figure 5.4 displays a dashed horizontal line dividing the $[c_t, c_{t+1}]$ plane into regions where the child's after-tax income and consumption is greater or less than $(1 - \tau_L)\bar{I}$. The intergenerational budget constraint changes slope at this horizontal position.

Another important effect of the graduated-rate structure is that it changes the relationship between human capital investments and the consumption of the child. Consider figure 5.3. Two after-tax earnings functions are shown as thin solid lines. The higher function is the pre-tax earnings function $e(h)$ multiplied by $(1 - \tau_L)$, which is the earnings that would be left after a flat-rate income tax at rate τ_L. The lower function is $e(h)$ multiplied by $(1 - \tau_H)$. If earnings are the only source of income, the function $(1 - \tau_L)e(h)$ determines after-tax income up to the after-tax amount $(1 - \tau_L)\bar{I}$. The after-tax earnings function therefore follows the higher function, a result which is shown in the figure by a thick curve. For pre-tax earnings above $\bar{I}$, income taxes are paid at rate τ_H; after-tax earnings accumulate according to the function $(1 - \tau_H)e(h)$. A dotted curve parallel to the lower function is therefore drawn in the figure through the higher function at the point where after-tax earnings are $(1 - \tau_L)\bar{I}$. The thick line therefore traces the rest of the after-tax earnings function along the dotted line. The two-bracket income tax introduces a kink in the after-tax earnings function.

The kinked after-tax earnings function can then be inverted and placed in the $[c_t, c_{t+1}]$ plane to show the intergenerational consumption allocations that can be reached by human capital investments alone. See, for example, the dashed curves in figure 5.4. The curves follow the slope of the after-tax earnings function and have a "kink" at the vertical position $(1 - \tau_L)\bar{I}$.

As shown with the flat-rate income tax, the efficient human capital investment depends on the income tax rate because only "interest" on the

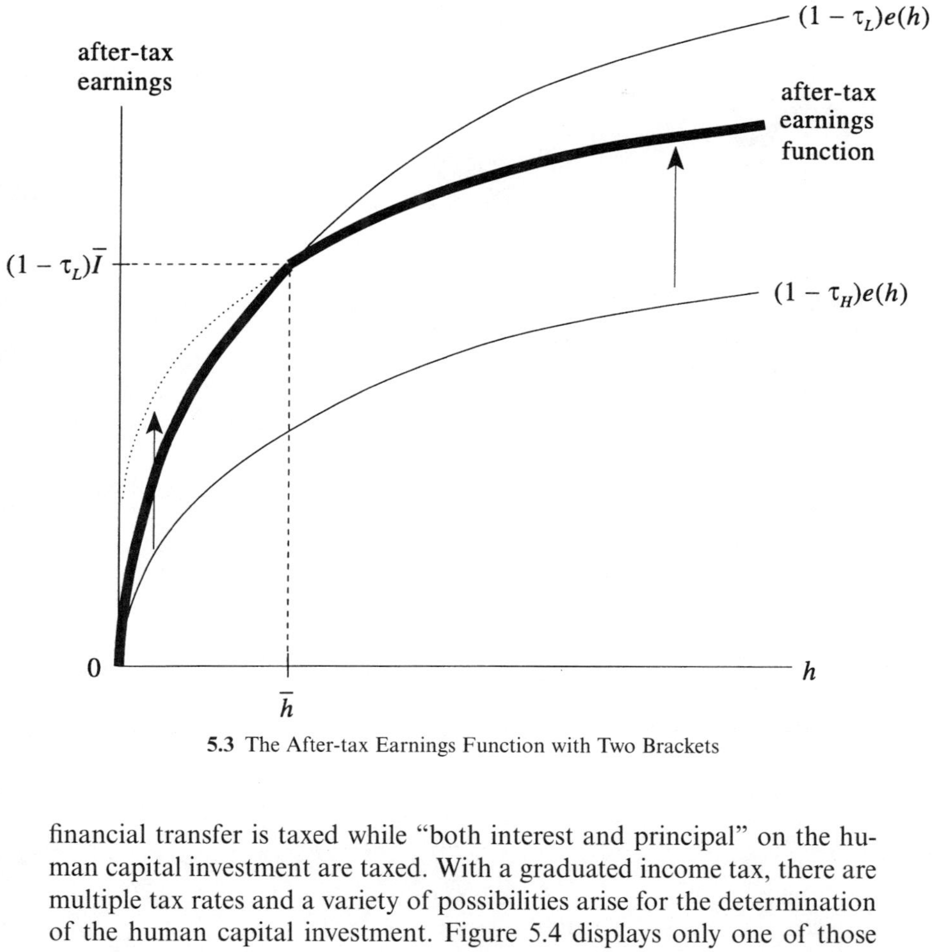

5.3 The After-tax Earnings Function with Two Brackets

financial transfer is taxed while "both interest and principal" on the human capital investment are taxed. With a graduated income tax, there are multiple tax rates and a variety of possibilities arise for the determination of the human capital investment. Figure 5.4 displays only one of those possibilities—where all families make the efficient human capital investment and it creates pre-tax earnings for children that are less than $\bar{I}$. By making the efficient human capital investment, families enjoy an intergenerational budget constraint that is also kinked at the vertical position $(1-\tau_L)\bar{I}$ and has slopes $-[1+(1-\tau_L)r]$ and $-[1+(1-\tau_H)r]$.[8]

Notice from figures 5.2 and 5.4 that the shape of the budget constraint in the permanent income model with a progressive graduated-rate income

8. A variety of other shapes of the intergenerational budget constraint are possible with a graduated-rate income tax. Even more shapes are possible when human capital investments are deductible from the computation of parental income taxes. I do not, however, explore all possible shapes arising from graduated-rate income taxation because I ultimately conclude that the U.S. income tax system approximates a flat-rate system.

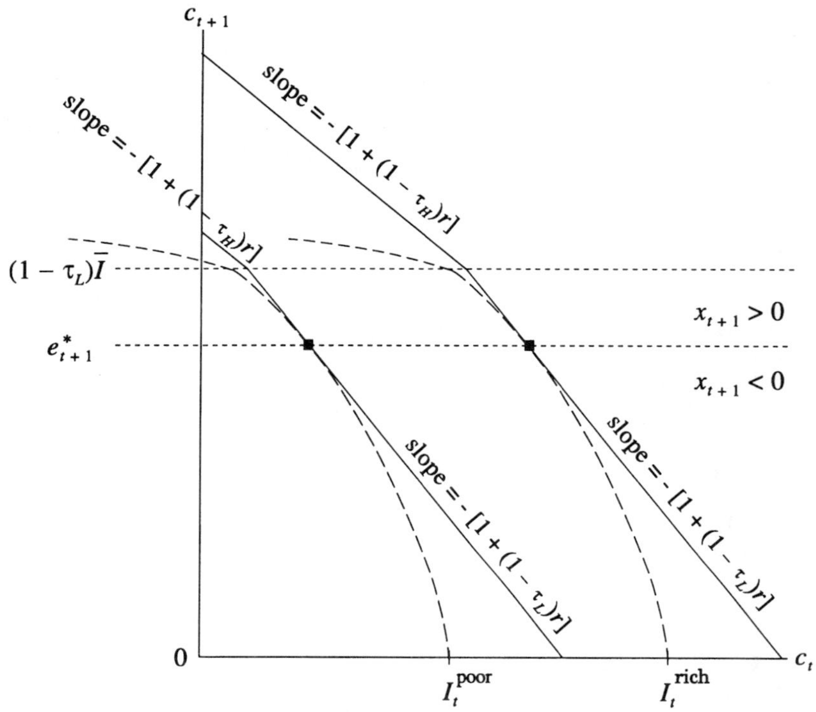

5.4 Intergenerational Budget Constraints with a Graduated-rate Income Tax

tax is similar to the shape under a graduated-rate estate tax. Both taxes produce a different straight line segment of the budget constraint for each tax bracket, although, as drawn in figures 5.2 and 5.4, only the estate tax produces a curved portion of the budget constraint for families that are between tax brackets. Because the graduated-rate income tax also has the different straight line segments for each tax bracket, consumption must also regress to the mean across progressive income tax brackets in the permanent income model when all families have the same degree of intergenerational altruism but not *within* tax brackets.[9] With a regressive income tax rate structure, consumption would regress away from the mean across tax brackets. In the Mulligan model of endogenous altruism with a permanent income constraint, the poor are more altruistic and consumption regresses to the mean both within and across progressive tax brackets.

In the imperfect capital markets model, a graduated-rate two-bracket income tax creates an intergenerational budget constraint with three seg-

9. As shown in the case of the estate tax, consumption inequality must grow over time if there is a substantial fraction of families in either the top or the bottom tax bracket.

ments: two curved and one linear or two linear and one curved. In the latter case, there are two types of "Group 1" families: one in the high tax bracket and one in the low tax bracket. Consumption regresses to the mean across tax brackets among Group 1 families but not within tax brackets.

Intergenerational earnings mobility is more complicated with a graduated-rate income tax. Two main questions need to be considered: does the efficient human capital investment vary across tax brackets, and are human capital investments deductible? The intergenerational budget constraints in figure 5.4 show only a single efficient human capital investment, which, together with its corresponding level of earnings, are displayed as squares. There are, however, other possibilities, depending on the magnitude of the tax rates τ_H and τ_L, the magnitude of the income $\bar{I}$ subject to the lower tax rate, and the shape of the earnings function. It is possible, for example, that optimal financial transfers are always zero in one or the other tax brackets, in which case earnings are very much a function of parental income.

If human capital investments are deductible from the income tax base, it is likely that the income tax *decreases* intergenerational pre-tax earnings mobility. Human capital investments are effectively cheaper for rich parents because they are in a high tax bracket and enjoy a larger tax deduction for making a human capital investment. As with the graduated-rate estate tax, parents in the high tax brackets make large human capital investments and their children enjoy high levels of pre-tax earnings.

Summary of Theoretical Results

A flat-rate income tax does not change any of the implications of the three models for intergenerational consumption and earnings mobility. A graduated-rate income tax, on the other hand, affects both intergenerational consumption and earnings mobility. In general, there is more intergenerational consumption mobility under a progressive graduated-rate income tax system. Whether or not intergenerational earnings mobility is greater under that system depends on the tax deductibility of human capital investments and other details of the system. A progressive graduated-rate income tax system can also make PI model human capital investments depend on parental income as they do in the borrowing constraints model.

Overview of the U.S. Estate, Gift, and Income Taxation

The sections on "Estate and Gift Taxation" and "Income Taxation" above derive predictions of the three models under a variety of tax systems.

Which of the hypothetical tax systems best approximates actual tax systems in the United States?

Federal Estate and Gift Taxes

Incomes, estates, and gifts are taxed in the United States. Estates and gift taxes are determined at the death of the donor and depend on the sum of the estate and all *inter vivos* gifts.[10] Because the taxes are owed by the donor—recipients do not have to pay an income or inheritance tax on their gifts—at his or her death, the tax liability created by a bequest or *inter vivos* gifts does not depend on the number of recipients. A $10 million estate bequeathed to a single child incurs the same tax liability as a $10 million estate bequeathed to ten children.

A donor may transfer up to $10,000 per year per recipient during his lifetime without incurring any federal estate or gift tax liability. A married couple can transfer up to $20,000 per year per recipient. *Inter vivos* transfers in the form of medical or education expenditures are also estate tax exempt and do not preclude the annual $10,000 or $20,000 of other tax exempt *inter vivos* gifts. In addition, a decedent can transfer another $600,000—in addition to charitable bequests and the payment of estate expenses such as debts or funeral expenses—at death without incurring an estate tax liability. Finally, any amount can be transferred to a spouse—either before or at death—without incurring an estate or gift tax liability.[11]

Notice that a substantial amount can be transferred from parents to children without paying any estate tax. Consider a couple with three children; suppose that the father dies a few months before the mother. In each of the twenty years prior to their death, the couple transfers $20,000 to each child. At the husband's death, another $200,000 is bequeathed to each child (in the name of the husband). Finally, the wife dies, leaving $200,000 to each child and the remainder of her estate to charity. This family pays no estate or gift taxes, even though $800,000 was transferred to each child for a total of $2.4 million in financial transfers! The $20,000 per year is tax free because of the annual gift exclusion and the $600,000 at the death of each parent is tax free because of the $192,800 unified estate and gift tax credit available to each parent.

Table 5.1 displays the 1995 U.S. Federal Estate and Gift tax brackets. The 0 percent bracket is shown as 0–$600,000 but, as discussed above, the

10. The division between *inter vivos* gifts and the estate does affect the timing of tax payments. See McNulty (1994) for a detailed exposition of U.S. estate and gift tax laws. See also IRS (1995a) for computation of the federal estate and gift tax for some particular examples.

11. Prior to 1981, there was a limit on the marital deduction. See McNulty (1994, chap. 13).

Table 5.1 1995 Federal Estate and Gift Tax Brackets in the United States

Estate Size			Estate Size		
Amount over	Amount not over	Marginal Tax Rate (%)	Amount over	Amount not over	Marginal Tax Rate (%)
0	600,000.*	0	2,000,000	2,500,000	49
600,000	750,000	37	2,500,000	3,000,000	53
750,000	1,000,000	39	3,000,000	10,000,000	55
1,000,000	1,250,000	41	10,000,000	21,040,000	65
1,250,000	1,500,000	43	21,040,000	∞	55
1,500,000	2,000,000	45			

Notes:

* The upper end of $600,000 for the 0% bracket is computed under the assumption that the decedent does not take advantage of the marital deduction or the annual gift exclusions. Use of the deduction and exclusions can increase the $600,000 figure to $1.2 million or more. Any change in the $600,000 figure should also be reflected in the other figures in the table.

1. Estate size is in dollars, net of annual gift exemptions and charitable and other deductions.

2. In addition to annual exemptions for inter vivos transfers, taxpayers are allowed an estate tax credit of 192,800. According to IRS (1995c, Table A), this means that no estate taxes are paid until the estate size reaches $600,000.

3. The 37–55% brackets are computed from IRS (1995c, Table A).

4. The 65% bracket derives from the phasing out of the estate tax credit and the graduated-rate schedule. See IRS (1995b, line 7) and IRS (1995c, Table A).

Source: IRS Form 1040 and instructions. IRS forms and instructions are available at http://www.irs.ustreas.gov/basic/forms_pubs/index.html

size of the smallest estate that is subject to tax depends on whether or not a decedent was able to take advantage of the marital and annual gift exclusions. With a little planning, the $600,000 shown in table 5.1 could be $1 or 2 million for a married couple. Table 5.1 shows the taxation of estates and gifts above that amount. The next $150,000 of the estate (plus gifts above the annual exclusion amount) are taxed at a 37 percent rate. Even larger estates are taxed at higher marginal rates, with the exception of estates larger than $21,040,000, which are taxed at a 55 percent rate.[12]

12. The *marginal tax rate* is the taxes paid on an additional dollar of the *tax base.* The tax base is the item being taxed: the estate in the case of an estate tax and income in the case of the income tax. The *average tax rate* is the ratio of total taxes paid to the tax base. Consider an example: a 10 percent tax on incomes above $10,000. The marginal tax rate is 0 percent for a person with $5,000 in income because an additional dollar of income for that person is not taxed. The marginal tax rate for a person with $20,000 in income is 10 percent because the 20,001st dollar of income for that person increases taxes by $0.10. Total taxes paid for the person with $20,000 in income is $1,000 (1,000 = (20,000 − 10000)*(0.10)), so the average tax rate for that person is 5 percent (0.05 = 1,000/20,000).

Table 5.1 shows that the U.S. federal estate tax has a graduated-rate structure that is somewhat "progressive" in the sense that the marginal tax rate increases with income or the size of the estate.[13] Individuals with larger estates tend to pay more taxes on an additional dollar of bequeathed wealth. However, the progressivity of the estate tax is probably not a very important force toward intergenerational mobility because the vast majority of families fall into a single estate tax bracket—the 0 percent bracket. Parents must literally make millions of dollars in financial transfers to their adult children over and above any educational and medical expenditures in order to be subject to estate taxes. Consider the fact that, over the period from 1960 through 1995, estate tax returns were filed on behalf of roughly 5 to 10 percent of adults who died after age forty-five.[14] Less than one-third of estate tax returns filed actually owe tax.[15] The estate tax appears to be relevant for a very small fraction of U.S. households.

Figure 5.5 also illustrates the quantitative unimportance of the estate tax for the vast majority of the U.S. population. The figure graphs income and estate taxes as a percentage of GDP for the period from 1940 through 1993. Federal income taxes are between 5 percent and 17 percent of GDP over the period.[16] Federal estate taxes are always less than 1 percent of GDP. The estate tax revenues are so low despite the high tax brackets because so many citizens fall into the 0 percent bracket.

Estate or inheritance taxes are also unimportant in U.S. history. With the exception of the years between 1894 and 1902 and the Civil War years, there were no federal estate taxes before 1916 and no federal gift taxes before 1924.[17] Inheritance or estate taxes could only be an important force affecting the intergenerational mobility of the most recent two or three generations in the U.S.

13. I use this definition of "progressive" based on marginal tax rates but point out that a tax system is often described to be "progressive" according to the average, rather than the marginal, tax rates. Because the average tax rate is increasing in the size of the estate (except for estates larger than $21.04 million, for which the average tax rate is 55 percent), the U.S. Estate Tax is also "progressive" according to the average tax rate definition. This chapter shows that it is the marginal tax rate definition that is relevant for intergenerational consumption mobility.

14. Number of estate tax returns from U.S. Treasury, IRS, *Statistics of Income: Estate Tax Returns,* various issues. Number of deaths by age from U.S. Commerce Department.

According to current rules, an estate tax return must be filed if a person dies with a gross estate (before deductions, exemptions, and exclusions) of $600,000 or more (U.S. Treasury, IRS, 1995a; 1995b).

15. U.S. Treasury, IRS, *Statistics of Income: Estate Tax Returns,* various issues.

16. I define federal income taxes to be the federal Individual Income Tax (including the earned income tax credit) and Social Security "contributions."

17. McNulty (1994, pp. 5–6).

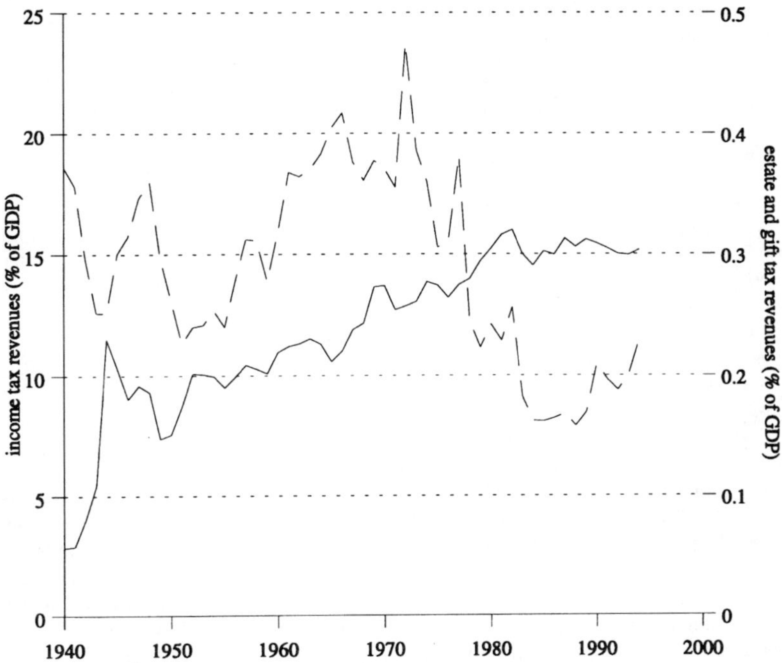

5.5 Importance of Federal Income, Estate, and Gift Tax Revenues, 1940–93
—— Income Tax (left scale) ---- Estate Tax (right scale)

Federal Income Taxes

Figure 5.5 suggests that the income tax burden is much heavier than the estate tax burden in the United States. Unlike the estate tax system, nearly all Americans are subject to a federal income tax. A married couple pays individual income taxes if it earns more than $11,250 in the year. Even if its annual income is below $11,250, a family's individual income tax burden may vary with its income because of the earned income tax credit. Every person's earnings is subject to several other "income-like" taxes, which are often labeled as "social security contributions."[18]

Table 5.2 displays the twelve different tax brackets resulting from the three forms of federal income taxation in 1994: social security "contribu-

18. The "old age and disability" portion of social security contributions is 12.4 percent of every person's first $61,200 of annual earnings (half paid by the employer, half by the employee). Medicare contributions are 2.9 percent of all earnings (half paid by the employer, half by the employee). Workers and unemployment compensation are roughly 3.1 percent of earnings (Social Security Administration, 1995, pp. 351–53).

Table 5.2 1994 Federal Individual Income and Social Security Tax Brackets in the United States

Income			Income		
Amount over	Amount not over	Marginal Tax Rate (%)	Amount over	Amount not over	Marginal Tax Rate (%)
0	4,000	7.2	103,100	122,400	43.0
4,000	5,000	14.2	122,400	151,250	33.4
5,000	9,000	21.3	151,250	167,700	38.3
9,000	11,250	14.2	167,700	261,250	39.7
11,250	49,250	28.1	261,250	290,200	43.4
49,250	103,100	40.2	290,200	∞	41.9

Notes:

1. Income is in dollars, net of tax-free retirement savings and health insurance payments and net of "employer" social security contributions.

2. Computations are for a married couple between ages 25 and 65 filing jointly and include the federal individual income tax, the earned income tax credit, and social insurance "contributions" (old age and medicare—both employer and employee portions). The couple is assumed to have no children and to take the standard deduction. Incomes of less than 122,400 are assumed to consist entirely of earnings that are split equally between husband and wife. If it were assumed instead that families itemize deductions, marginal tax rates could be as much as a percentage point higher for high income families because of the "phasing out" of deductions.

3. The 7.2 and 21.3% brackets differ from the 14.2% bracket because of the phasing in and out of the Earning Income Tax Credit. Other brackets differ because of different federal income tax brackets or because the old age portion of social insurance contributions are collected only on earnings that are less than $61,200 per worker.

4. Marginal tax rates are the same in 1995, with the dollar amounts determining the brackets increased by 2.6 percent.

Source: IRS Form 1040 and instructions. IRS forms and instructions are available at http://www.irs.ustreas.gov/basic/forms_pubs/index.html

tions," the individual income tax, and the earned income tax credit.[19] The table is computed for a married couple—both of whom earn half the family's earnings—with no children and who file IRS Form 1040 jointly. The income tax rate is the lowest, 7.2 percent, for the lowest incomes. For the

19. The marginal income tax rate is computed as suggested by Robert Barro and Chaipat Sahasakul (1986):

$$\tau \equiv \frac{s_f + s_e + \tau_{IIT}}{1 + s_f}$$

where s_f is the social security tax rate determining the "firm's" contribution (including old-age and disability and medicare payments, but not workman's compensation and unemployment insurance), s_e is the social security tax rate determining the "employee's" contribution, and τ is the marginal federal individual income tax rate (including the earned income tax credit).

most part, the marginal tax rate increases with family income. An important exception occurs when annual earnings of the husband or wife exceed the social security cap of $61,200. Since the husband and wife are assumed to earn equal amounts for the computation of table 5.2, the effect of the social security cap on the marginal tax rate is shown at a family income of $122,400. The marginal tax rate is substantially lower for families that earn more than $122,400 than for families that earn less.

Table 5.2 shows that the U.S. federal income tax system has a graduated-rate structure that is both "progressive" and "regressive." The marginal tax rate is lowest for family incomes between 0 and $49,250 and highest for family incomes between $49,250 and $122,400 or more than $261,250.[20]

Like the estate and gift taxes, a federal income tax is fairly new in U.S. history. Federal income taxes were considered to be unconstitutional until the 16th Amendment in 1913. Even when an income tax became law, most families did not pay federal individual income tax until World War II (see Mulligan 1995a). To the extent that the income tax has differed from a flat-rate tax, it has influenced the degree of intergenerational mobility only for the most recent generation or two.

Summary of the Relevant Features of U.S. Federal Estate, Gift, and Income Taxes

I have just shown that income, estate and gift taxes affect the degree of intergenerational consumption mobility through their marginal tax rate "progressivity" or "regressivity." If all are flat-rate taxes—with marginal tax rates that are neither progressive nor regressive—then all of the results from chapter 3 obtain. An examination of the U.S. federal estate, gift, and income taxes reveals that neither have very progressive graduated-rate structures. The vast majority of Americans fall into the 0 percent estate and gift tax bracket. Most Americans pay income taxes, but its rate structure is not very progressive. Because of the cap on social security taxes, the highest marginal income tax rates pertain to "middle" income brackets.

Progressivity and regressivity were irrelevant for much of U.S. history because (with the exception of the Civil War) there were no federal income, estate, or gift taxes until 1913.

Review of the Main Results

In the permanent income model of family opportunities, flat-rate income and estate taxes produce linear budget constraints with the same slope for

20. To a very close approximation, the income tax is "progressive" according to the average tax rate definition. The average tax rate begins at 7.2 percent for families with near zero income and increases to 41.9 percent for families with millions of dollars of income.

all families. Taxation affects the allocation of consumption across generations and, in the Mulligan model of altruism, each family's degree of intergenerational altruism, but does not affect any of the results for intergenerational mobility derived in chapters 3 and 4. Those implications are listed in table 4.1, but I repeat five of them below:

(1) In the permanent income model with flat-rate estate and income taxes, earnings regress to the mean according to the intergenerational persistence of ability.
(2) If all families have the same degree of intergenerational altruism in the permanent income model with flat-rate estate and income taxes, consumption does not regress to the mean in the permanent income model with flat-rate income and estate taxes.
(3) If intergenerational altruism varies across families in a way that is not associated with parental income in the permanent income model with flat-rate estate and income taxes, consumption does not regress to the mean across parental income categories.
(4) In the Mulligan model with a permanent income budget constraint with flat-rate estate and income taxes, consumption regresses to the mean across parental income categories for the bulk of the population.
(5) Consumption inequality grows over time in the permanent income model unless altruism is negatively related to parental income.

The results listed in table 4.1 for the imperfect capital markets model of opportunities are also robust to the introduction of flat-rate income and estate taxes.

Graduated-rate income and estate taxes do affect intergenerational mobility in the models of chapters 3 and 4. The introduction of a "progressive" rate structure—progressive in the sense that the marginal tax rate is higher for families with more income and larger estates—increases the degree of regression to the mean of consumption but can decrease the degree of regression to the mean of pre-tax earnings. A "regressive" rate structure—regressive in the sense that the marginal tax rate is lower for families with more income and larger estates—has the opposite effects. The graduated income and estate tax rates have their effects on intergenerational consumption and earnings mobility *across* tax brackets but not within brackets; the predictions for intergenerational mobility derived in chapters 3 and 4 still apply among families that are in the interior of the same income and estate tax brackets.

It is not clear that the graduated-rate structures of the U.S. federal estate and income taxes are actually "progressive." The vast majority of U.S. families are in a 0 percent estate tax bracket while marginal income tax rates are highest on middle-, rather than high-, income families. If the tax rates are in fact progressive, the current chapter shows that the progressivity provides yet another reason why consumption might regress to the mean across generations. All together, I have suggested four reasons why consumption might regress to the mean:

(1) Ability regresses to the mean and ability is linked to consumption because of imperfect capital markets.
(2) Intergenerational altruism varies across families in a way that is uncorrelated with parental income.
(3) Intergenerational altruism is negatively related to parental income.
(4) Estate and income tax rates are progressive.

If a graduated-rate tax system has either a top or a bottom bracket, it is not clear that the introduction of such a system can prevent the growth of consumption inequality.

Hypothesis (1) is due to Gary Becker and Nigel Tomes (1986) and others. I derive the second and third hypotheses in chapters 3 and 4, while the fourth hypothesis is explored in this chapter. The following chapters provide tests of the four hypotheses. The first is tested in chapter 8 by comparing intergenerational mobility among families that do and do not make financial transfers. The second is tested in chapter 7 by looking at intergenerational consumption mobility across parental income categories. The third is tested by looking at some implications of endogenous altruism for the charitable giving, the compensation of agents, and the distribution of resources among siblings. The fourth is tested by comparing the degree of intergenerational mobility and the dynamics of inequality across countries and in the United States before and after the institution of federal estate and income taxes.

PART 2
Empirical Arguments for Modeling Altruism

CHAPTER 6

The Evolution of Economic Inequality in the United States

Introduction

How has inequality evolved over time? Answers to this question provide some of the facts that a theory of intergenerational mobility should match. This chapter begins by describing some of the links between intergenerational mobility and the evolution of inequality over time. The rest presents evidence on two points. First, I argue that income, earnings, and wealth regress to the mean across *several* generations. The very long-term evidence complements the shorter-term—but more direct evidence—on intergenerational mobility presented in chapter 7. Second, I suggest that the very long-term trend is toward more economic equality. This second conclusion is less definite but also only indirectly related to the theoretical models presented in chapters 3 and 4.

Chapter 7 presents results from Francis Galton's (1889) style of comparisons of the income, earnings, consumption, and wealth of parents and their adult children. Although comparisons of parents and children have their obvious advantages, they also have two important disadvantages. First, it is difficult to accurately measure the income, earnings, wealth, or consumption of a particular person or of a particular family. Measurement errors can severely bias estimates of the degree of intergenerational mobility. Second, the vast majority of data sets that match the economic variables of parents and children are only for very recent history. The PSID intergenerational samples I use in chapters 7 and 8, for example, consist of adult children who are in their late twenties or thirties in the late 1980s when their economic variables are measured. Because any period of history—such as the Great Depression, wartime, or the Reagan years—

has some peculiarities, it can be dangerous to make general conclusions from only one historical period.

This chapter's study of long-term inequality trends can mitigate these two problems. On the first problem, "Links between Intergenerational Mobility and the Evolution of Inequality" shows how the evolution of inequality reveals information about the degree of intergenerational mobility even in the presence of measurement errors. The aggregated data presented in the sections on "Racial Inequality" and "Cross-region Inequality" may also alleviate measurement error problems because some measurement errors "average out" in the process of aggregation. On the second problem, the data presented dates back to 1740. The long-term trends are not derived from information on a single generation but, because the data spans the period between 1740 and 1985, includes information on ten or more generations.

"Cross-family Inequality" reviews evidence on the distribution of income, earnings, and wealth across U.S. families, arguing that inequality has declined substantially since the Civil War, with a relatively minor reversal in the last decade or two. A similar pattern is observed across ethnic groups. Wages of blacks, for example, have grown more rapidly than those of whites since the Civil War. Evidence on the distribution of income across regions of the United States is presented in "Cross-region Inequality." The regional evidence is interesting because measurement problems are less serious than—or at least different from—the problems of measuring the income of families. The section on "Cross-country Inequality" presents some evidence on the distribution of income across countries. I argue in "A Unified Approach" that inequality across families, across ethnic groups, across regions, and across countries has evolved similarly over time and that, given our knowledge of the facts, a unified theoretical explanation is more appealing. A "Review of the Main Points" provides a summary.

Links between Intergenerational Mobility and the Evolution of Inequality

The evolution of inequality over time is linked with the degree of intergenerational mobility. This section describes some of those links. The description facilitates the interpretation of the evidence on the evolution of inequality presented in the last half of this chapter.

Measuring inequality is a complicated task. Here, I report commonly used inequality statistics and sometimes comment on the robustness of my conclusion to alternative measurement strategies, but readers can find fuller discussions of measurement issues elsewhere. Anthony Atkinson provides two examples (1983; 1970).

Parental and Other Influences

The *intergenerational persistence* of income, earnings, wealth, or any other variable is the fraction of differences among parents that is typically observed among their adult children. I measure intergenerational persistence in logarithmic or percentage terms. Consider two sets of parents whose incomes differ by 50 percent. If, on average, the incomes of their children differ by 20 percent, then the intergenerational persistence of income is said to be 0.4 or 40 percent. An equivalent way of thinking about the intergenerational persistence of a variable *Y* is in terms of the regression equation 3.1, repeated below for convenience:

$$\ln Y^i_{t+1} = \alpha + \beta \ln Y^i_t + \varepsilon^i_{t+1} \tag{3.1}$$

α and β are constants. I refer to *Y* as "income," but it could refer to earnings, years of schooling, wealth, or another variable. Equation 3.1 can be thought of as generating the income of family *i*'s children (Y^i_{t+1}) according to two influences: family *i* parental income (Y^i_t) and other influences (ε^i_{t+1}). "Other influences" are, by definition, unrelated to parental income. Luck, intelligence, or a willingness to work are candidate other influences to the extent that they are unrelated to parental income. According to equation 3.1, a 1 percent difference in parental incomes is associated, on average, with a β percent difference in the incomes of children. In the 20 percent/50 percent example above, $\beta = .4$.

In principle, β could be zero. $\beta = 0$ means that parental income differences are not associated with income differences among children. If relatively high parental income were associated with relatively *low* incomes of children, then β would be negative. β can also be larger than one if parental income differences (in percentage terms) are associated with even larger income differences among children.[1] Although β could conceivably be any real number, the vast majority of empirical estimates of β are between 0 and 1. I therefore refer to the quantity $(1 - \beta)$ as the *degree of intergenerational mobility* or *the degree of regression to the mean.* More mobility therefore means less persistence, and more persistence means less mobility.

1. β is closely related to the correlation ρ between the log income of parents and the log income of children:

$$\beta = \rho \frac{sd(\ln Y_{t+1})}{sd(\ln Y_t)}$$

where *sd*(*x*) denotes the standard deviation of the variable *x*. Since *sd*(ln *Y*) is a commonly used index of inequality, it can be said the β is the intergenerational correlation of log income when inequality is not changing over time. However, I show in the text how changes in inequality over time depend on the magnitude of β.

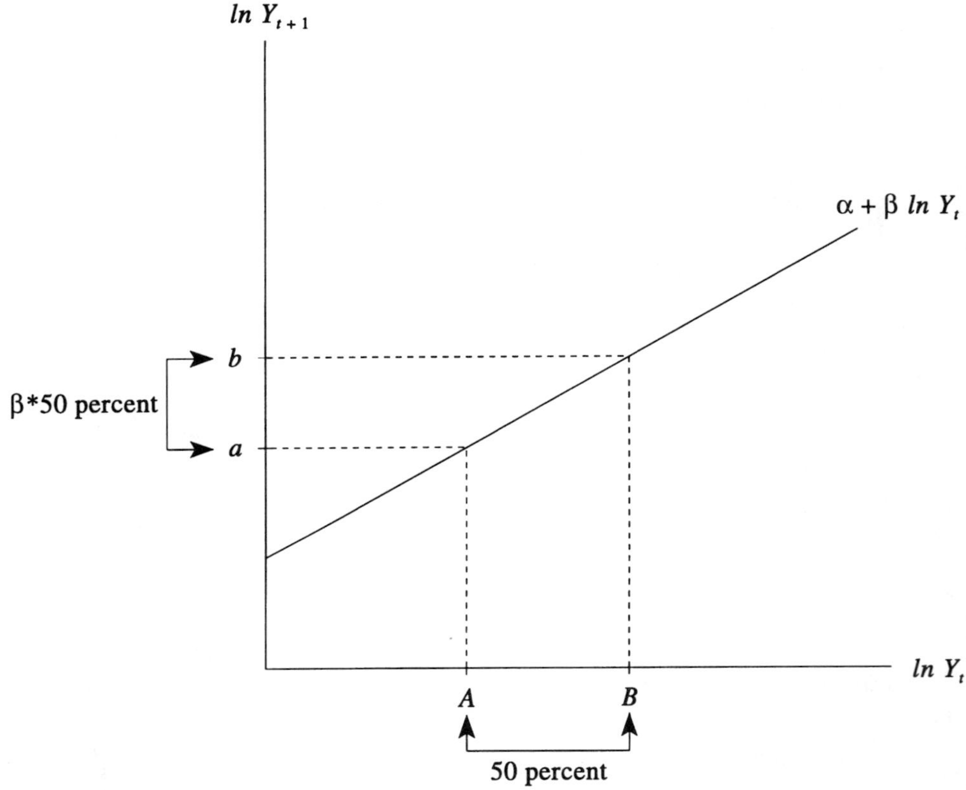

6.1 Graphical Computation of the Persistence of Inequality

$\beta = 0$, for example, implies no intergenerational persistence and a degree of intergenerational mobility of 1 (or "perfect" mobility). $\beta = 1$ implies "perfect" persistence and no mobility. β between zero and one means that there is both mobility and persistence. Incomes are said to "regress away from the mean" when $\beta > 1$.

Consider a graph of equation 3.1. Under the assumption that $\beta > 0$, figure 6.1 graphs an upward sloping line in the [ln Y_t, ln Y_{t+1}] plane. When $\varepsilon_{t+1} = 0$, the income of a child can be graphically computed from parental income by locating ln Y_t on the horizontal axis, moving vertically to the line $\alpha + \beta$ ln Y_t, and then moving horizontally to the vertical axis. This computation is done for two families in figure 6.1. If ε_{t+1} is different from zero, the quantity ε_{t+1} is added to the vertical position as a final step in the graphical computation of a child's income. The ε_{t+1}'s are, by definition, zero on average, so, on average, the log income of *A*'s child is *a* and the log income of *B*'s child is *b*. The two sets of parents *A* and *B* shown in the figure have incomes which differ by 50 percent. The graph shows that, on average, the children will have incomes that differ by β*50 percent. If there is less than perfect intergenerational persistence ($\beta < 1$), the percentage difference between children would be, on average, less than 50 percent—the percentage difference between parents.

β *and the Evolution of Inequality*

It may appear from figure 6.1 that income inequality falls when $\beta < 1$. This is not true because, when incomes evolve according to equation 3.1, inequality among any generation can be decomposed into *two* sources: that which derives from inequality among the previous generation and that which derives from unequal "other influences."[2] The magnitude of β does affect how inequality evolves over time, but one has to consider both sources of inequality. To see this, consider an economy with two types of parents. All of the first type of parents have the same log income equal to A. The second type have log income equal to B. The degree of inequality in the economy for this initial generation depends on B-A, with larger (B-A) associated with more inequality.[3] The two sources produce inequality among the next generation. First, parental income differences persist as long as $\beta \neq 0$. Second, "other influences" introduce inequality among the children of *identical* parents. The effect of the first source on the degree of inequality depends on the magnitude of β. Figure 6.1 shows that, *ignoring the "other influences,"* $\beta < 1$ means a decrease in income inequality, $\beta = 1$ means no change in inequality, and $\beta > 1$ means growing inequality. Of course, there are other influences, so both sources must be considered. Because "other influences" are always a "new" source of income inequality (that is, unrelated to the income of the previous generation), the second

2. A short algebraic proof is available when the variance of log income is used as the index of inequality. Equation 3.1 implies that inequality among generation $t + 1$ is:

$$v(\ln Y_{t+1}) = \beta^2 v(\ln Y_t) + v(\varepsilon_{t+1})$$

$v(x)$ denotes the variance of the variable x. The right-hand side of this expression is β^2 times inequality among generation t plus inequality among "other influences." There is no covariance term in the equation because, by definition, other influences are uncorrelated with parental income.

The mistaken conclusion that $\beta < 1$ implies falling inequality is known as "Galton's Fallacy" and has appeared repeatedly in economics and statistics literatures. Milton Friedman (1992) and Danny Quah (1993) point out some examples. Although Galton deserves credit for studying the intergenerational transmission of biological inequality, he does not appear to have arrived at the mistaken conclusion that bears his name. See Stephen Stigler (1986) for a brief history of Galton's contributions to statistics.

3. If, for example, there are an equal number of A's and B's and the standard deviation of log income is the index of inequality, the inequality index is equal to $(B-A)/2$.

source tends to increase inequality from one generation to the next. In the case $\beta > 1$, the result is unambiguous because both sources tend to increase inequality: inequality must grow over time. When $\beta = 1$, the first source produces no change in inequality and the second source means growing equality so, all together, inequality must grow.

The result is ambiguous when $\beta < 1$ because it depends on the relative contribution of the two influences highlighted in equation 3.1. If inequality among other influences is much larger than inequality among parents, then inequality grows over time. This can be seen in the type *A*/type *B* example above. Suppose *A* and *B* are equal or very similar. Then there is almost no inequality among the initial generation. Very unequal other influences means that there is substantial inequality among the second generation—inequality grows. At the other extreme, consider large differences between *B* and *A*, $\beta < 1$, and relatively equal "other influences." $\beta < 1$ means that the children of type *A* and type *B* parents become more similar and equal "other influences" means that little inequality is produced among type *A* children and among type *B* children. Overall, inequality falls.[4]

To summarize the results so far:

(1) If $\beta < 1$, inequality can fall or be stable.
(2) If $\beta \geq 1$, inequality must grow.

If one finds that income inequality has not grown over time, then one can conclude that (for income) $\beta < 1$. The intergenerational persistence of income is not perfect. The remainder of this chapter therefore studies evidence on the evolution of income, earnings, consumption, and wealth inequality over time.

Galton's Fallacy and Inequality across Groups

The sections "Racial Inequality" and "Cross-region Inequality" present evidence on the evolution of inequality across groups. In the first section, the groups are "blacks" and "whites," while in "Cross-region Inequality," the groups are states of the United States. As a factual matter, inequality across groups may evolve in the same way as overall inequality, but the analysis above reveals that—as a logical matter—the two need not evolve in the same way. Consider again the type *A*/type *B* example and suppose that "other influences" are very unequal relative to the difference across groups (*B*-*A*). Overall inequality grows over time in this economy because

4. The algebraic proof derives from the equation in footnote 2. From the equation, $\beta \geq 1$ obviously implies $v(\ln Y_{t+1}) > v(\ln Y_t)$. $\beta < 1$ produces growing inequality if and only if $v(\ln Y_t) < v(\varepsilon_{t+1})/(1 - \beta^2)$.

the "other influences" introduce substantial inequality among the type A children and among the type B children. However, the average log income of type A children and type B children are a and b, respectively. Inequality across the two groups for the second generation is therefore measured by (b-a), which, when $\beta < 1$, is less than (B-A). $\beta < 1$ means, in this example, that types A and B become more similar on average while overall inequality is growing. *Falling inequality across groups indicates regression to the mean but not necessarily falling overall inequality.* The evidence presented that blacks and whites have become more similar and that U.S. states have become more similar may or may not be associated with declining overall inequality, but this does indicate that there is intergenerational mobility.

My analysis above of the type A/type B example assumes that "other influences" average out within each group, but the assumption is not necessary to derive the result that falling inequality across groups indicates regression to the mean. Suppose, for example, that "other influences" average to zero in Group A but average to $\delta > 0$ in Group B. The average log income of type A children and type B children are a and $b + \delta$, respectively. Inequality across the two groups for the second generation is therefore measured by $(b + \delta - a)$. If cross-group inequality falls over time, then we must have (b-a) < (B-A), which means that β must be less than one. In other words, *falling inequality across groups indicates regression to the mean* even when "other influences" do not average out within groups.[5] An interesting application of this result is to the changing racial inequality in the United States examined later in this chapter.

Measurement Errors and the Evolution of Inequality

This section describes the links between intergenerational income (or earnings or other variable) mobility and the evolution of inequality, but how are the results interesting if income cannot be accurately measured? When the seriousness of the measurement error does not change over time and errors are uncorrelated with parental income, it turns out that the same three results derived above apply to measured inequality:

(1) If $\beta < 1$, measured overall inequality can fall or be stable.
(2) If $\beta \geq 1$, measured overall inequality must grow.
(3) If $\beta < 1$, groups become more similar in terms of the measured variable.

To prove these results, consider relationship between measured income Y_t^* and actual income Y_t:

5. I assume $\delta > 0$. In other words, "other influences" are larger for the richer group (B in my example). If instead $\delta < 0$, one would observe falling inequality across groups even when there is no regression to the mean.

$$\ln Y_t^{i*} = \ln Y_t^i + \eta_t^i \tag{6.1}$$

where η_t^i is the measurement error of family i's generation t income. Measured income inequality depends on actual income inequality and unequal measurement errors. As long as measurement error inequality doesn't change over time, measured inequality and actual inequality evolve in the same way over time. Results (1) and (2) follow. Result (3) obtains as long as measurement errors "average out" within groups.

The main results may not hold if measurement errors are correlated with income and that correlation changes over time.[6] For example, suppose rich people misreport the most income in percentage terms and that their misreporting has increased over time (for example, because tax incentives to misreport have grown over time). Measured inequality may fall while actual inequality is growing.[7]

Immigration, Intragenerational Mobility, and the Evolution of Inequality

Long-term inequality trends can provide some insights about the degree of intergenerational mobility. When tracking inequality within or across groups over a period of centuries, for example, it is clear that any trends are due either to immigration or to changing inequality across generations. After all, the people that determine inequality in say, 1800, are dead by 1980; only descendants and immigrants populate the country by 1980. However, changes over a shorter period of time, such as a decade or two, can be both intergenerational and intragenerational. Changing inequality, for example, between blacks and whites is intergenerational when younger blacks do better than the older blacks did when they were young. But black-white gaps can also narrow when all blacks—young and old—make progress relative to whites.

Although I believe that intergenerational mobility is the important determinant of long-term inequality trends, it is true as a logical matter that immigration and intragenerational mobility affect the evolution of inequality over time. I present a small amount of the evidence for determining the contribution of intergenerational mobility to long-term inequality

6. When the variance of log income is the inequality index, the algebraic proof follows from the formula for the variance of log measured income:

$$v(\ln Y_t^*) = v(\ln Y_t) + v(\eta_t) + 2c(\ln Y_t, \eta_t)$$

where $c(\ln Y_t, \eta_t)$ denotes the covariance of log actual income and the measurement error. Even if measurement error inequality ($v(\eta_t)$) is constant over time, measured inequality and actual inequality may not evolve in the same way because the covariance is changing.

7. Williamson and Lindert (1980, pp. 86–92) seriously examine this hypothesis for the twentieth century in the United States and conclude that it is quantitatively insignificant.

trends, but the reader should be cautioned that more work needs to be done in this area.

Cross-family Inequality

There are several measures of economic equality across families for various periods of U.S. history, but it is difficult to piece them together to ascertain long-term trends. Jeffrey Williamson and Peter Lindert (1980) provide one of the few analyses of the very long-term trends. I present some of their results here, piecing them together with some U.S. results reported by Alan Blinder (1980), the Census Bureau (1975), David Cutler and Lawrence Katz (1992), Claudia Goldin and Robert Margo (1992), James Smith and Finis Welch (1986), and Edward Wolff (1992) and with results for the United Kingdom as reported by Atkinson (1983) and Lindert (1986). First I display measures of the evolution of wealth inequality. Wealth inequality may have risen somewhat over the period of time from 1770 through 1860, but it is unambiguous that there have been dramatic declines in wealth inequality since 1860.[8] It is difficult to measure earnings inequality over a long historical period, but it seems likely that it declined over the period of time from 1860 through 1970 with an incomplete reversal of that trend over the last twenty years or so. Even less information is available on long-term trends of consumption inequality.

Wealth Inequality

Figure 6.2 displays the fraction of wealth held by the top 10 percent of wealthholders. The squares denote comparable measures constructed by Williamson and Lindert (1980) for the years 1774, 1860, 1870, and 1962. According to that series, the share of wealth held by the top 10 percent increased from 54 percent to 77 percent between 1774 and 1860 but fell to 36 percent by 1962. This measure of wealth inequality suggests that there was more inequality in 1774 than in 1962. The two other series provide some additional information on the first half of the time period. The triangles display the share of Massachusetts decedent wealth held by the top 10 percent of Massachusetts decedents for the years 1830, 1860, 1880,

8. In personal communications, some economic historians insist that the Williamson-Lindert results are controversial, especially those for the period of 1770 through 1860. A contribution to the debate is beyond the scope of my book. The main result from Williamson and Lindert (1980) that I emphasize—that the long-term inequality trend from the Civil War to the present is downward—is much less controversial among historians. For other studies of the period from 1770 through 1860, see Lee Soltow (1984) and Robert Margo and George Villaflor (1985). See Claudia Goldin and Lawrence Katz (1995) for a recent study of the period from 1890 to 1940.

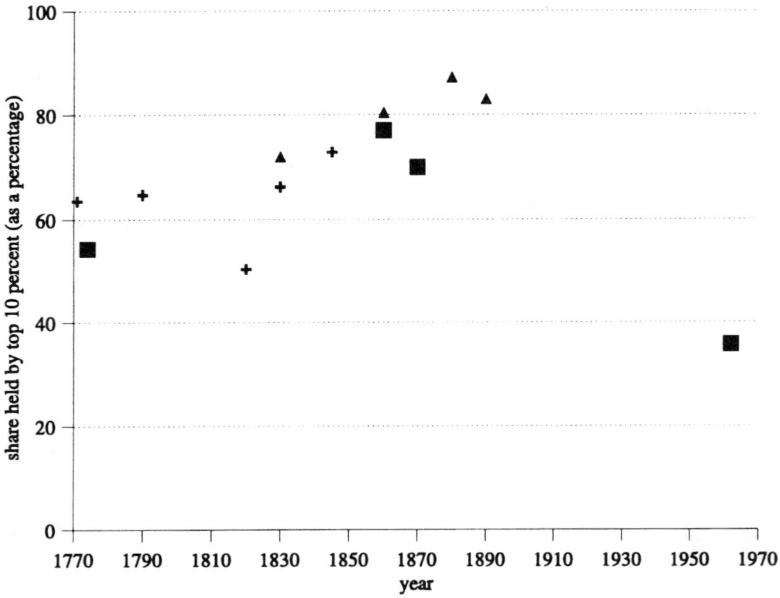

6.2 Fraction of Wealth Held by Top 10 Percent, 1771–1962
■ Williamson-Lindert series ▲ net worth of Massachusetts decedents
✚ wealth of Boston taxpayers

and 1890.[9] Crosses display a series for the population of Boston taxpayers and Boston males without property. Both series suggest increases in inequality over the period of time from 1770 through 1880.

Changes in wealth inequality, especially over the past seventy-five years, can also be seen in figure 6.3. The squares are a comparable series constructed by Williamson and Lindert for the fraction of wealth held by the top 1 percent for the years 1774, 1860, 1870, and 1962. As with their 10 percent series, inequality rises during the time frame of 1774 through 1860 and then falls by 1962. Their 1774 and 1962 fractions are 13.2 percent and 15.1 percent, respectively; the 1 percent series suggest that inequality is pretty similar in 1774 and 1962. Two other series for the top 1 percent are computed by Wolff (1992, p. 553) for the years of 1922 through 1981 and are displayed in figure 6.3. The cross series includes retirement wealth while the triangle series does not. The triangle series, for example, begins at 38 percent in 1922, declines to 30 percent in 1962, and declines further to 24 percent by 1981. Wolff's series show an unambiguous decline in wealth inequality between 1922 and 1981 and suggest that there were also

9. Williamson and Lindert (1980, p. 303).

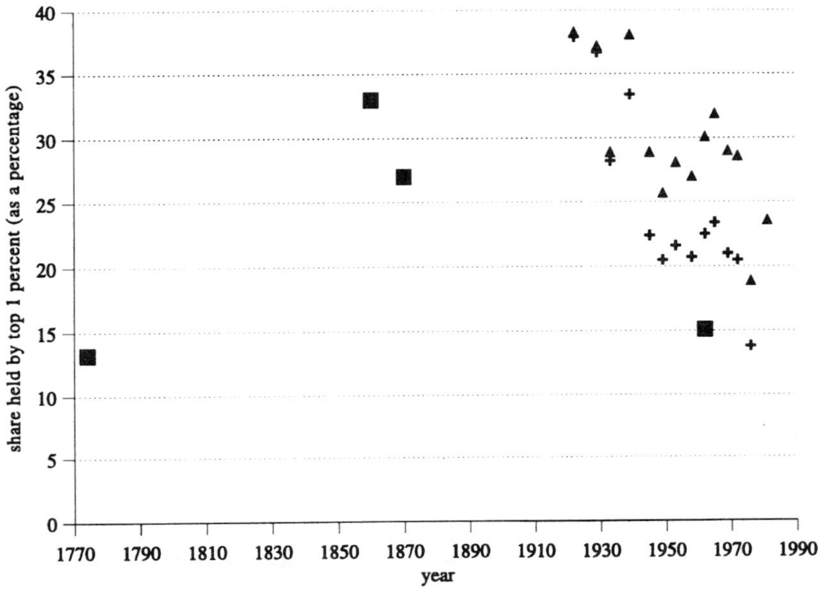

6.3 Fraction of Wealth Held by the Top 1 Percent, 1774–1981
■ Williamson-Lindert U.S. wealth series ▲ U.S. (without retirement wealth)
✚ U.S. (with retirement wealth)

declines since 1962. Taken together, the three 10 percent and the three 1 percent series shown in figures 6.2 and 6.3 suggest that wealth was more equally—or perhaps equally—distributed in 1981 than in 1774.[10]

It is easier to construct comparable measures of inequality over a long time period for the United Kingdom. Figure 6.4 displays some very long-term comparisons reported by Lindert (1986) and some comparisons for the period from 1922 to 1972 as reported by Atkinson (1983). The large squares display Lindert's series. The share of wealth held by the top 5 percent in England and Wales fell steadily from 87 percent to 84 percent over the period of time from 1740 to 1875. That share fell more rapidly over the next hundred years, standing at 50 percent in 1973.[11] Atkinson's (1983) computation of the 1972 share of the top 5 percent is fairly close to Lindert's 1973 share; Atkinson computes 56 percent and Lindert com-

10. Williamson and Lindert (1980, pp. 40–41) suggest that inequality may be most understated in 1774 because poor are undersampled. On page 58, they suggest that changing demographics have caused inequality to fall less than it would have in the twentieth century. It is therefore possible that there has been an overall inequality decline since 1774 but that it is not apparent in the figures because of these two measurement problems.

11. The 1973 share is for all of Great Britain (Lindert 1980, p. 1149).

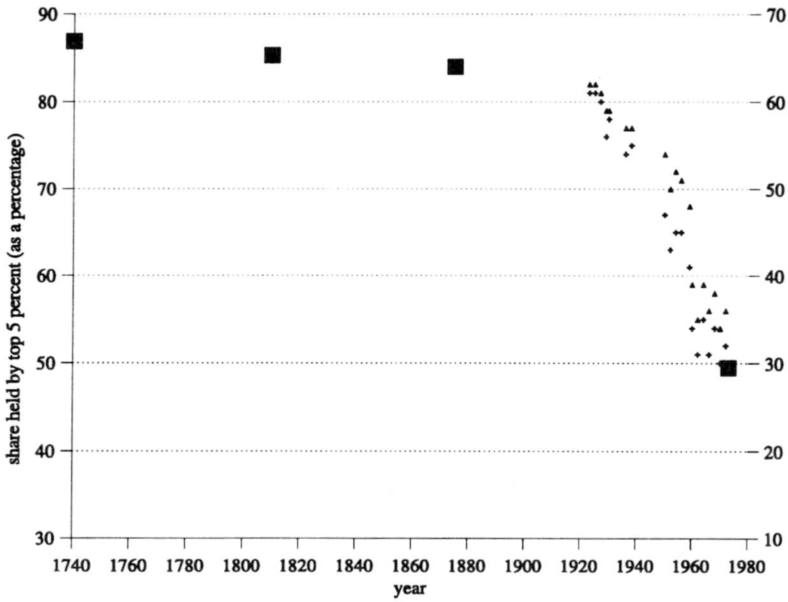

6.4 Changing Wealth Inequality in Britain, 1740–1975
■ U.K. top 5 percent (Lindert, left scale) ▲ U.K. top 5 percent (Atkinson, left scale) ✚ U.K. top 1 percent (Atkinson, right scale)

putes 50 percent. Atkinson's 1 percent and 5 percent series, displayed as crosses and triangles in figure 6.4, suggest a steady decline in inequality from 1923 through 1972.

Earnings Inequality

Measures of earnings inequality are much more difficult to obtain for long time periods. Good U.S. measures are available for the shorter time period of 1940 through 1990 when the Bureau of the Census asked citizens about their earnings. Figure 6.5 displays the log weekly wage difference between the 90th and the 10th percentiles of the male wage distributions in each of the years 1940, 1950, 1960, 1970, 1980, and 1985.[12] Wage inequality appears to have fallen dramatically in the 1940s and risen dramatically in the 1980s, with a net result of constant wage inequality over the period of 1940 to 1985. In order to obtain a rough estimate of longer-term trends, figure 6.5 also displays a measure of income inequality. The share of income received by the top 5 percent of households falls from 32 percent in 1921 to 28 percent in 1939 (the year to which the Goldin-Margo data

12. Computations by Goldin and Margo (1992, p. 2).

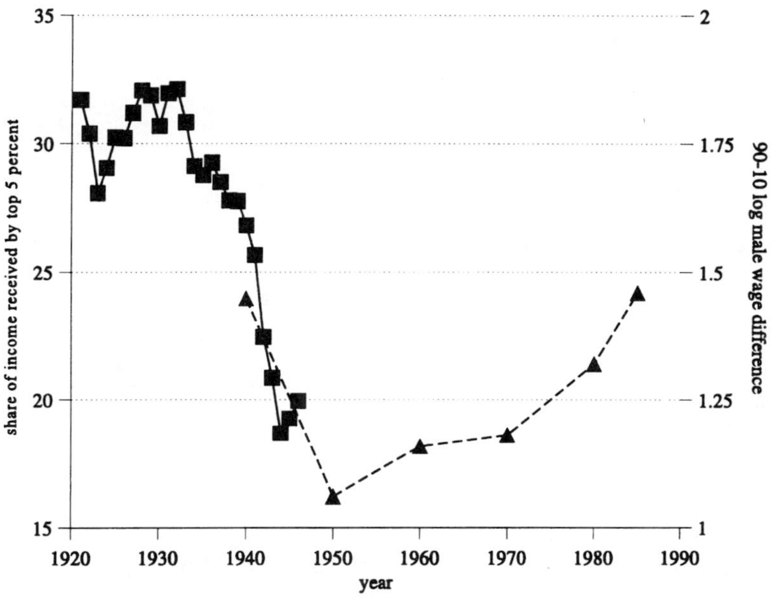

6.5 Indicators of Earnings Inequality, 1920–85
—■— income inequality (left scale) —▲— earnings inequality (right scale)

applies) and then to 20 percent by 1946.[13] To the extent that income and earning inequality move together, it appears that earnings had become more equal even before the 1940s. Despite the substantial growth of earnings inequality in the 1980s, long-term trends were probably not completely reversed.

It would be ideal to measure earnings for a representative sample of individuals as done by the Bureau of the Census since 1940. Representative samples are not available for earlier years, so Williamson and Lindert report some estimates of occupational wage ratios that may shed light on the very long-term earnings inequality trends. The wage ratios divide the typical earnings of a skilled occupation by the typical earnings of an unskilled profession. It is possible, although not necessary, that high relative earnings of skilled professions are associated with high overall inequality. For the period between 1860 and 1924, Williamson and Lindert compute the ratio of the annual income of Methodist ministers to that of nonfarm unskilled laborers. A Methodist minister was relatively well paid during some periods of history, earning four or five times more than a nonfarm

13. In order to obtain a feeling for longer-term trends, World War I and the subsequent recession are omitted from the figure. Occupational wage ratios strongly suggest that there was a sizable transitory decrease in earnings inequality during those years.

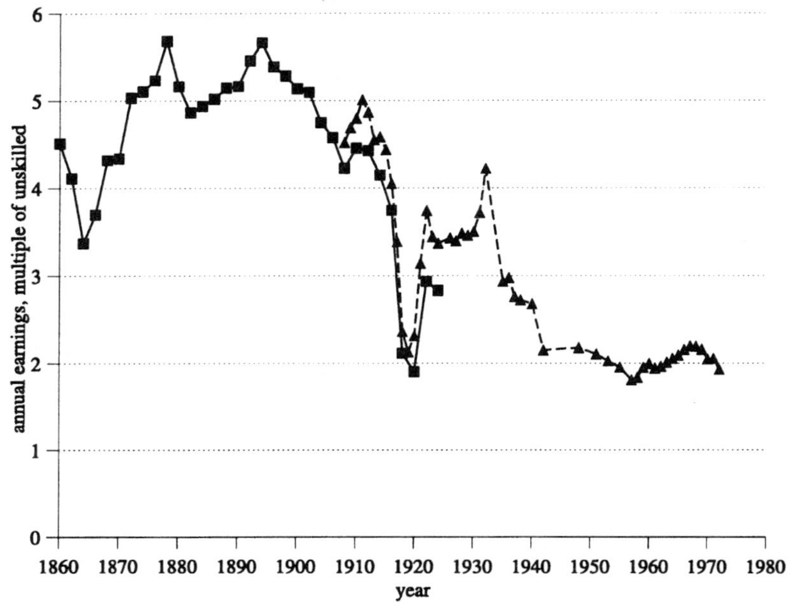

6.6 Relative Wages of Methodist Ministers and Associate Professors
—■— Methodist ministers —▲— associate professors

unskilled laborer before World War I. For the overlapping years of 1908 through 1924, figure 6.6 shows that the earnings of Methodist ministers closely tracked those of associate professors. During the 1920s and 1930s, associate professors earned three or four times the income of a nonfarm unskilled laborer. From a relative pay of 2.7 in 1940, the relative pay of an associate professor declined dramatically during the 1940s and remained stable at about 2—a pattern consistent with the evolution of the 90-10 earnings differential reported by Goldin and Margo for the years between 1940 and 1970. With a little extrapolation, the evolution of these occupational wage ratios suggest that earnings inequality declined substantially before 1940. Perhaps earnings inequality was much greater in the nineteenth century than it was in the 1980s so that recent increases in earnings inequality are only a minor reversal of a long-term trend.

Consumption Inequality

There is even less data on consumption inequality. Cutler and Katz (1992) compare the evolution of family consumption and income inequality for the years between 1960 and 1988. They argue that consumption inequality fell from 1960 to 1970, but then increased from 1970 to 1988. For example,

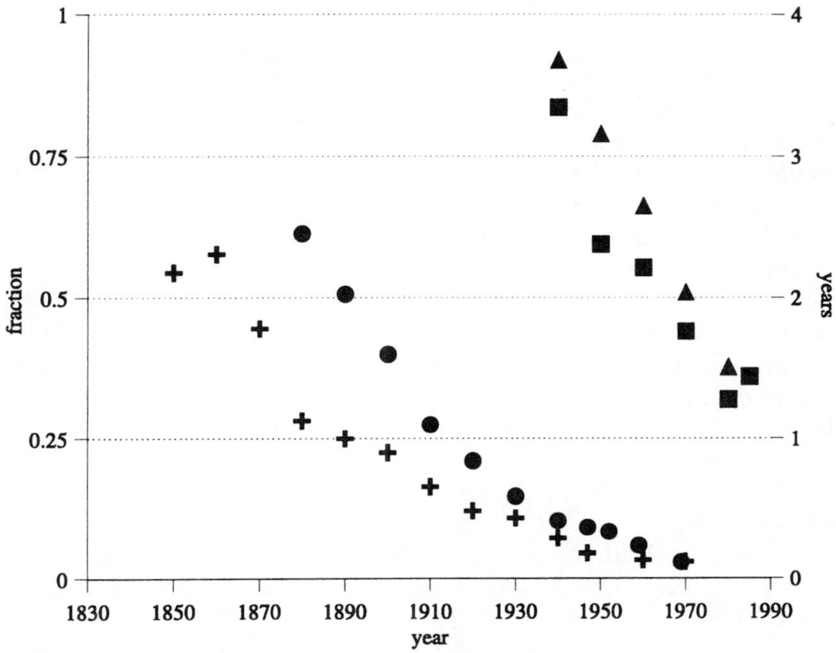

6.7 Black-White Education and Wage Gaps, 1850–1985
■ ln(white-black wage ratio) (left scale) ▲ white minus black years of schooling (right scale) ✚ white minus black school enrollment rate (left scale) ● white minus black literacy rate (left scale)

they compute consumption Gini coefficients of 0.28, 0.25, and 0.30 for the years 1960, 1970, and 1988.[14] Daniel Slesnick (1994) argues that overall consumption inequality has declined in the United States since World War II.

Racial Inequality

Slowly but surely, the economic status of blacks has become more similar to that of whites since the Civil War. Figure 6.7 graphs some indicators of black-white economic differences over the period from 1850 to 1985. The difference between the white and black school enrollment rates are shown as crosses. In 1850, 56.2 percent of school-aged whites and 1.8 percent of school-aged nonwhites were enrolled in school.[15] The difference of 54.4

14. The Gini coefficient is an index of inequality ranging from 0 to 0.5, with 0 denoting perfect equality and 0.5 denoting perfect inequality.
15. U.S. Bureau of the Census (1975, series H-434 and H-435).

percent is graphed in the figure. That difference rises slightly in 1860, but then it falls rapidly during the two decades following the Civil War. By 1880, 62 percent of school-aged whites and 33.8 percent of school-aged nonwhites were enrolled in school. The difference between the black and white enrollment rates continues to fall from 1880 to 1970, the last year of data reported by the U.S. Bureau of the Census (1975). In 1970, enrollment rates were much more similar for the two groups: 88.3 percent for whites and 85.3 percent for nonwhites.

The literacy rate provides another indicator of economic status for the period of 1870 to 1969. Thirty percent of nonwhites were literate in 1870, as compared with 91.3 percent of native whites. The difference of 61.3 percent is plotted as a circle in figure 6.7. The native white-nonwhite literacy rate difference fell in every decade over the next century. By 1969, the literacy rates were 96.4 percent and 99.3 percent for nonwhites and whites, respectively.

The enrollment and literacy data suggest substantial progress by blacks relative to whites, especially between 1860 and 1930. Data on earnings and educational attainment suggest that this progress continued until roughly 1980. In 1940, the typical white had 9.4 years of schooling, compared with 5.7 for blacks (Smith and Welch 1986, p. 27). Educational attainment reached 12.5 and 11 years for the white and black populations by 1980. The difference between the educational attainment of whites and blacks is graphed as triangles in the figure. The figure shows a difference that falls from 3.7 years to 1.5 years over the period of 1940 through 1980. Wages follow a similar pattern. Whites wages were 84 percent greater than that of blacks in 1940, but only 32 percent more in 1980.[16] The wage trend reversed in the 1980s, but the reversal was slight compared with the progress from 1940 to 1980.[17] The enrollment and literacy trends suggest that the wage reversal of the 1980s may be extremely small relative to the trends of the past century.[18]

Racial discrimination is likely to contribute to inequality between

16. James Smith and Finis Welch (1986, p. 5). They define "wages" as average weekly wages, salaries, and self-employment income of civilian men who worked at least half the year for the year prior to the Census.

17. David Card and Thomas Lemieux (1994) report that the white-black wage gap increased by four percentage points from 1979 to 1985. A earnings gap of 36 percent is therefore reported in the figure.

It can be shown that an important part of black economic progress is due to the relative success of younger black generations rather than the progress of old and young blacks together. See, for example, Smith and Welch (1986, p. 17).

18. Borjas (1994) estimates a black-white wage gap of only 47 percent in 1910, but he obtains it by assuming that blacks and whites in the same occupation earn the same wage. His data suggest that the black-white earnings gap narrowed between 1910 and 1940, but that it did so more slowly than was the case from 1940 to 1980. Becker (1971, p. 140) offers

blacks and whites. If one models discrimination as contributing to the "other influences" ε in equation 3.1, my analysis in "Galton's Fallacy and Inequality across Groups" suggests that a theory of discrimination cannot explain falling black-white wage gaps without also relying on some intergenerational mobility. Assuming that discrimination lowers the wages of blacks relative to whites, the presence of discrimination—even if that discrimination is falling over time—means that black-white inequality falls more slowly than it would in the absence of discrimination. Without intergenerational wage mobility, the black-white wage gap would not fall in the absence of discrimination, so it could not fall with it. Moreover, my findings in chapter 7 suggest that intergenerational earnings mobility within racial groups is very similar to mobility across racial groups since 1940, which implies that racial discrimination is not a quantitatively important contributor to the intergenerational persistence of wages since 1940.

I conclude the analysis of black-white differences with two other indicators of the relative economic progress of blacks over the last few decades. Figure 6.8 displays the ratio of the black home ownership rate to the white home ownership rate. That ratio first increased from 0.52 in 1940 to 0.65 in 1980 and then fell to 0.64 in 1985 (Wolff 1992, p. 555). The ratio of mean black household net worth to that of whites increased from .13 in 1962 to .24 in 1983 and stood at 0.23 in 1985. Consistent with the earnings data, the home ownership and net worth data suggest that blacks lost ground relative to whites during the 1980s but that this is only a minor reversal of an important long-term trend.[19]

Comparisons of other ethnic groups also suggest that earnings or wages regress to the mean across generations. George Borjas (1994) analyzes the wages of the adult children of early twentieth-century immigrants to the United States. He considers thirty-two nonblack ethnic groups, including Belgians, Cubans, English, French, Japanese, Polish, Spanish, and Yugoslavians. Borjas measures the log wage of adult children from the 1940 Census. These children report the birthplace of their parents, which he uses to associate the parents with an ethnic group. Borjas then estimates the parental log wage based on the occupations typically worked by members of each immigrant group in 1910, obtaining estimates of 0.4 to 0.6 for β. Ethnic groups appear to become more similar over time, although slowly.

---

similar estimates (based on fewer occupational categories) and finds no decline in the black-white earnings gap between 1910 and 1940.

19. Of course, a finding that black-white wage gaps have closed slowly but steadily over time says nothing about the "fairness" of black-white differences. A mobility finding is relevant for those interested in modeling black-white gaps in particular and economic inequality in general.

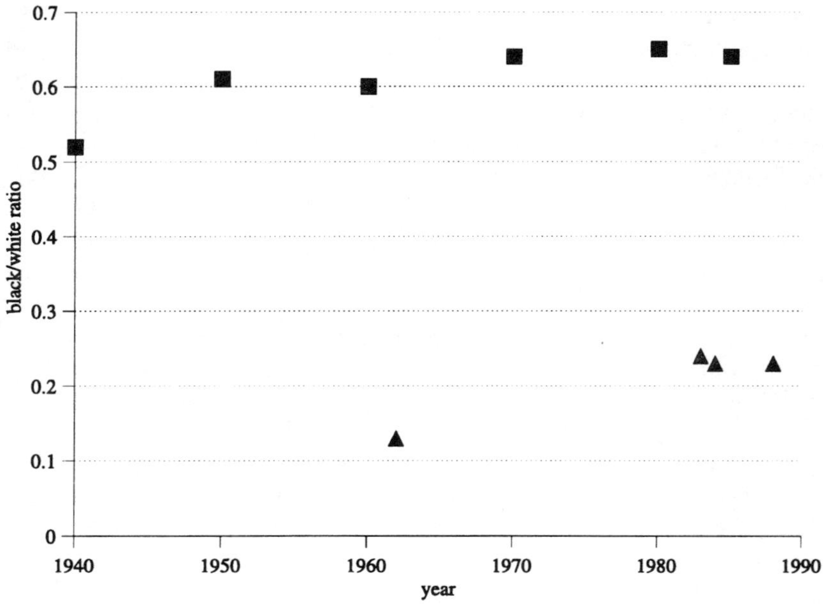

6.8 Indicators of Black-White Wealth Gaps, 1940–88
■ black-white ratio of home ownership rates ▲ black-white net worth ratio

Cross-region Inequality

The inequality across regions can tell us something about the evolution of overall inequality in the United States. An important advantage is that we can obtain a single consistent measure of inequality over a long time period—the cross-state standard deviation of log personal income per capita. Per capita personal income for forty-seven states is available on a roughly decennial basis going back to 1880. Remember that income and earnings for representative samples of families is available going back to only 1940.

Figure 6.9 reveals two important points. First, there is a long-term trend toward equality across states. Second, the Great Depression and the 1980s are relatively minor interruptions of this trend. The growing inequality across states in the 1980s only reverses a small fraction of the long-term trend. Similar trends are reported by Robert Barro and Xavier Sala-i-Martin (1991; 1992b) for regions of Europe and Japan.

The declining cross-regional inequality need not indicate a reduction in overall inequality across U.S. families. It is, without a lot of migration from poor to rich regions—inconsistent with regression away from the mean ($\beta \geq 1$) at the family level. Barro and Sala-i-Martin (1991; 1992b),

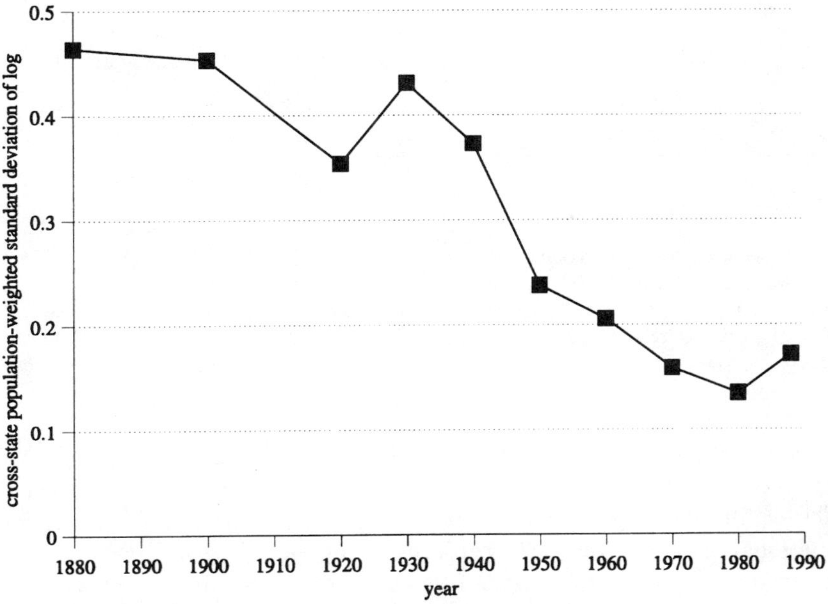

6.9 Regional Inequality, Personal Income per Capita

however, show that migration cannot explain much of the decline in regional inequality.[20]

Cross-country Inequality

Table 6.1 reports estimates of cross-country inequality of income per capita based on Robert Summers's and Alan Heston's (1991) computations. The cross-country standard deviation of the log of per capita income was 0.88 in 1960 and 1.10 in 1985. Cross-country inequality grew over the period. However, the second row of table 6.1 shows that cross-country inequality fell among the narrower sample of twenty-six European and North American countries.[21] Barro and Sala-i-Martin (1991; 1995) show that both regions and countries within Europe have become more equal since 1960. They also report direct estimates of the degree of intergenera-

20. Barro and Sala-i-Martin maintain that regions and time periods with more rapid immigration display very slightly *slower* rates of regression to the mean of incomes across regions.

21. Comparable 1950 GDP per capita data are also available for twenty-three of the twenty-six European and North American countries. The cross-country standard deviation of log GDP per capita for those twenty-three is 0.53 in 1950 and 0.35 in 1988.

Table 6.1 Inequality across Countries, 1960–85

Sample	cross-country standard deviation of log (real GDP per capita) 1960	1985
115 countries	0.88	1.10
Europe and North America	0.58	0.45

Note: There are twenty-six countries which I define to be "European and North American" and for whom comparable GDP per capita figures are available for 1960 and 1988: Austria, Belgium, Canada, Cyprus, Czechoslovakia, Denmark, Finland, France, West Germany, Greece, Iceland, Ireland, Italy, Luxembourg, Malta, Mexico, Netherlands, Norway, Portugal, Spain, Sweden, Switzerland, Turkey, United Kingdom, United States, and Yugoslavia.

tional mobility from the cross-country data, estimates which I review in chapter 7. The chapter also points out that, in order to understand what the evolution of income inequality across countries tells us about intergenerational mobility, we must know how "other influences" vary across countries in relation to income. In a cross-country analysis, "other influences" can include government activity and technological progress.

A Unified Approach

With the exception of growing inequality across a broad cross-section of countries during the past few decades, much of the evolution of inequality within and across groups is consistent with the view that consumption, earnings, and other economic characteristics regress to the mean across generations. A single model that predicts this regression to the mean would explain a great deal about the evolution of inequality. The borrowing constraints model applied to families by Gary Becker and Nigel Tomes (1986) and later applied to regions and countries by Barro and Sala-i-Martin (1992a), Barro, Mankiw, and Sala-i-Martin (1995), and others is one such model. A problem with the borrowing constraints model as a unified explanation of the evolution of inequality is that, if borrowing constraints are at all important, one would expect borrowing and lending among families to be easier than borrowing and lending among developed countries,[22] yet we see that the evolution of inequality across developed countries is very similar to the evolution of inequality within countries.[23]

22. See Martin Feldstein and Charles Horioka (1980) for a discussion and some evidence suggesting that international borrowing is more difficult than domestic borrowing.

23. I show in chapter 7 that the degree of regression to the mean of earnings or income looks similar whether one looks across or within countries.

The borrowing constraints theory counterfactually predicts that intergenerational mobility should be less across countries.

The model of the formation of altruism is another model that, because it predicts regression to the mean of consumption and earnings, is consistent with the many different kinds of evidence on the evolution of inequality presented in this chapter. I show in chapter 4 that models of altruism can explain intergenerational mobility within a country, but the model can also explain intergenerational mobility across countries. Unlike the many explanations of cross-country differences in per capita economic growth that appear in the macroeconomics literature (a macroeconomics literature that does not attempt to explain intergenerational mobility within countries), a model of altruism does not explain growth with a "rate of return" or an "interest rate" but with parental priorities.[24] Interest rates can be very similar across countries—so that there is little incentive for investors to search abroad for investments—but countries grow at different rates because parental priorities differ. In some countries, parents are very concerned for the success of their children, and they make large sacrifices to invest in their children, thereby creating economic growth, while, in other countries, parents are less concerned, and these countries, therefore, grow more slowly.

Review of the Main Points

The long-term trends of various measures of inequality tell us something about the degree of intergenerational mobility. $\beta \geq 1$ is inconsistent with stable or declining inequality. It is also inconsistent with falling inequality across ethnic groups, across regions, or across countries. This chapter reports several results that suggest that the hypothesis of $\beta \geq 1$ is false:

(1) measures of wealth inequality have fallen or have been stable over the past 200 years;
(2) measures of wealth inequality have fallen dramatically since the mid-nineteenth century;
(3) there has been little net change in earnings inequality over the last fifty years;
(4) earnings inequality appears to have fallen since the Civil War;
(5) consumption inequality has been stable or has declined since World War II;
(6) the earnings, schooling, and wealth of blacks has become more similar to that of whites since the Civil War;

24. Examples of "rate of return" based models of economic growth include Barro and Sala-i-Martin (1995) and Romer (1987).

(7) the earnings of families that immigrated to the United States in the early 1900s have slowly become more similar to the U.S. average;
(8) U.S. States have become more similar in terms of per capita income since the Civil War;
(9) European and North American countries have become more equal in terms of income per capita since 1950.

Some of these findings, especially (2) and (4), suggest that the long-term trend has been for increased economic equality. Decreasing inequality implies $\beta < 1$. The other findings need not imply that inequality has fallen over time, but they too require $\beta < 1$. Only the observation that per capita income inequality has become more unequal across a broad cross-section of countries is consistent with $\beta \geq 1$.

How different is β from 1? It is difficult to obtain a point estimate of β from the evolution of measures of overall inequality, but one can be obtained from comparisons of groups. To do so, we must assume that the "other influences" that affect a child's income over and above the effects of parental income do not vary across the groups. As reported by Barro and Sala-i-Martin (1992a), the evolution of income inequality across states since 1880 is consistent with a β for income of about 0.65.[25] The narrowing of the black-white earnings gap from 1940 to 1985 is consistent with a β for earnings of 0.59.[26] Narrowing of other ethnic gaps between 1910 and 1940 suggests a β for earnings of 0.4 to 0.6. These estimates of β for earnings and income are quite similar to the estimates of 0.5 or 0.6 that I obtain in chapter 7 with micro data on the income and earnings of adult children and their parents. "Macro" and "micro" estimates of β are studied and compared more carefully in the next chapter.

The magnitude of β is especially interesting because it is related to the degree of "equality of opportunity" in the economy. To see this, suppose we observe two sets of parents, *A* and *B*. The *A* parents have income of $20,000 per year and the *B* parents have income of $100,000 per year. *B*

25. The cross-state estimate of β is obtained by raising to the (25/108) power the coefficient from a 47-state regression of log 1988 personal income per capita on log 1880 personal income per capita.

26. The black-white estimate if β is obtained from the formula:

$$\beta = \left(\frac{\ln(Y^{w}_{1985} / Y^{b}_{1985})}{\ln(Y^{w}_{1940} / Y^{b}_{1940})} \right)^{25/45}$$

where *w* and *b* denote "white" and "black." The term in large parentheses is raised to the 45/25 power because the time period of 1940 through 1985 is forty-five years and a generation is assumed to be twenty-five years, so the period from 1940 through 1985 is 45/25 generations.

parents earn five times more than *A* parents. A β of 0.6 for income implies that, on average, the *B* children enjoy incomes that are 2.6 times larger than the *A* children. The incomes of *B* grandchildren are, on average, 1.8 times more than those of *A* grandchildren. Income differences seem to take two or three generations to substantially decay when $\beta = 0.6$—a lot longer than would be the case if β were 0.3, as has been suggested in much of the economics literature.[27] A β of 0.3 for income means that *B* children, on average, have incomes that are only 1.6 times as large as those of *A* children. The difference among grandchildren is only a factor of 1.2. $\beta = 0.3$ represents substantially more "equality of opportunity" than does $\beta = 0.6$. Chapter 7 shows that, although β is less than one, a large β is more realistic than a small one for a variety of measures of economic status.

27. Smaller estimates of β are reported by Atkinson, Maynard, and Trinder (1983), Behrman and Taubman (1985), Harbury and Hitchens (1979), Soltow (1965), and Wahl (1985). See chapter 7 for a survey of micro estimates of β.

CHAPTER 7

The Intergenerational Dynamics of Consumption, Earnings, Income, and Wealth

This chapter presents evidence on the intergenerational dynamics of consumption, earnings, income, and wealth. The newest evidence comes from my own computations using intergenerational samples from the Panel Study of Income Dynamics (PSID). I believe the empirical contributions of this chapter are fourfold. First, no one else, to date, has studied the intergenerational dynamics of consumption. I show that, contrary to the predictions of the permanent income model, consumption regresses to the mean across generations. However, I do verify the permanent income prediction that consumption is much more persistent than earnings. My second contribution is to analyze the intergenerational dynamics of consumption, earnings, income, and wealth in a single representative data set. Most previous studies focus on only one of these variables. Other studies utilize highly select samples, such as those obtained from probate records. Third, I make substantial progress on some serious measurement issues. I utilize information on the occupation, industry, schooling, and county of residence of fathers to construct instruments for parental earnings and income. Building on the result from chapter 3 that, according to the intergenerational permanent income and borrowing constraints models, parental income is an appropriate instrument for parental consumption, I report here the corresponding estimates of intergenerational consumption mobility. The main conclusions from my analysis of the measurement issues is that the intergenerational persistence of earnings has been understated in the literature, consumption and income are significantly more persistent than earnings, intergenerational mobility is very similar within and across groups, and that all measures of economic status regress to the mean across generations. Fourth, I arrive at two tentative conclusions, but they are conclusions that are important for evaluating models and government policies concerned with intergenerational mobility: intergenerational mobility in the United States has not changed with the introduction of apparently progressive income and estate taxes, and intergenerational earnings and income mobility does not vary across countries. The final two conclusions are more tentative because of an important lack of relevant research and data.

A variety of biological, economic, sociological, and statistical models of intergenerational mobility suggest Galton-style (1889) comparisons of a characteristic of an adult child with the same characteristic of his parents. All of the empirical results in this chapter are in that tradition. The characteristics of interest are consumption, earnings, income, and wealth. One unique prediction of economic models—the intergenerational permanent income model in particular—is that intergenerational mobility should be different for these different characteristics. Another set of unique predictions derived from the borrowing constraints model are the subject of the empirical analysis of the next chapter.

Like the evidence presented in chapter 6, the evidence studied here says something about the degree of intergenerational mobility. This chapter obtains estimates by comparing measures of economic status for a sample of parents and some of their adult children. The main advantage of this strategy is that sharp quantitative estimates of the degree of intergenerational earnings, income, wealth, and consumption mobility can be obtained. The sharp estimates provide for tougher tests of the theoretical models. There are two potential problems with the strategy. First, it is difficult to accurately measure the lifetime income, earnings, consumption, or wealth of any particular family. Second, data on the economic status of both parents and their adult children is difficult to obtain. The usual result of this difficulty is that only particular types of families, from a particular location, and for a particular time period are observed, which makes it difficult to generalize the results to broader populations. I believe that I make substantial progress on these two problems here and in the previous chapter. First, I use intergenerational samples from the PSID, which are fairly representative of the U.S. population. Second, I construct several good instrumental variables that can be used to correct for measurement error problems in the PSID. Third, I review a wide variety of related studies, which include families from five different countries and several different historical periods. Fourth, chapter 6 presents long-term evidence that spans several historical periods. Fifth, the evidence in chapter 6 is aggregate evidence, and it can be expected that some measurement errors are "averaged out" in the process of aggregation. All together, the evidence presented in these two chapters offers a very clear view of the degree of intergenerational mobility.

The second section describes my PSID intergenerational samples, while "PSID Results" presents Galton-style (1889) estimates of the intergenerational persistence of consumption, income, wages, and wealth. The ordinary least squares estimates are compared with a variety of instrumental variables estimates. Other related empirical studies of intergenerational mobility are reviewed in "Results from Other Data Sources," and "Review of the Main Results" reviews the results and compares them with those presented in chapter 6. An appendix to chapter 8 provides tabulations of various characteristics of the families in my intergenerational samples.

Intergenerationally Linked Data from the PSID

Data Description

The Panel Study of Income Dynamics actually began in 1968 as two studies. One was a nationally representative sample of 2,930 families drawn by the Survey Research Center (SRC). The other was a nonrepresentative sample of 1,872 low-income families drawn by the Bureau of the Census.[1] These two samples, the "SRC sample" and the "SEO sample" were combined to form the first wave of the Panel Study of Income Dynamics (PSID). Except for death and nonresponse, each member (and their offspring) of the SRC and SEO samples have been interviewed annually as part of the subsequent waves of the PSID. The Survey Research Center is still interviewing these people, and my study utilizes the 1968–89 waves.

Information is also gathered on any person who may cohabitate with one of the original sample members. Suppose, for example, that a ten-year-old girl was part of an original SRC family. She turned twenty-five in 1983 and married a thirty-year-old man with two children. If she lives with these three people, then information about them is included in the PSID. It is the children from the original wave of the PSID who, in later waves, form their own households (such as the woman in my example) that make up my intergenerational samples. These adult children are particularly interesting because we know a lot about their economic activity *and* have many years of data on their parents.

A lot of information is gathered on each PSID family, including employment, income, earnings, schooling, religion, housing, some expenditures, family background, and even attitudes. My analysis uses the data on age, earnings, schooling, employment, income, housing, and certain expenditures. I also use information from two special waves of the PSID—1984 and 1989—which inquired about wealth. Because I focus on PSID children who eventually formed their own households, all of this information is available for both the adult children and their parents. I use the information to construct measures of the economic status of parents in the years

1. See Martha Hill (1992, pp. 8–11) for more information about the design of the PSID.

between 1967 and 1972 and measures of the economic status of the adult children nearly twenty years later—from 1984 through 1989.

Annual income and annual earnings are two indicators of economic status that I measure for parents in the years from 1967 to 1971 and for adult children in the years from 1984 to 1988. Annual "earnings" are money wages and salaries earned on all jobs for the year. The "wage" is measured as annual earnings divided by annual hours worked. Annual "income" is a measure of family income which includes earnings, asset income, rent, financial transfers from relatives and others, and government transfers (for example, welfare or social security payments) for husband, wife, and others in their family. Earnings and wages are "individual" measures of economic status because they pertain to a particular person, such as a father, a mother, a son, or a daughter. Income is a family measure because it combines the income of mother and father (if they live together at the time) or the income of an adult child and his or her spouse. Single-year measures of earnings, wage, and family income are averaged over the available years of 1967 to 1971 or of 1984 to 1988 to form an estimate of lifetime earnings, wage, or family income.

Parents did not report wealth in any of the years from 1967 to 1971, but most of the children in my PSID intergenerational samples reported their wealth in 1984, 1989, or both. Of those children, many of their parents also participated in the PSID interviews of either 1984 and/or 1989. Parental and child wealth are computed for one of the two years and, if available in both years, averaged. Wealth of both parental and child households is defined to be the value of homes, real estate, vehicles, farms, businesses, and financial assets net of mortgages and other debts. Wealth is a family measure of economic status because it does not, for example, separate the wealth of spouses.

Intergenerational Samples Used in the Empirical Analysis

Most of my empirical results are robust to sample selection. This section is therefore mainly of interest for those who may want to reproduce my results.

Ideally, empirical analysis would proceed with a representative sample of the U.S. population. The SRC portion of the PSID is designed to be representative, but some of the variables of interest cannot be measured for all of the PSID-SRC respondents. I therefore begin by drawing four main intergenerational samples from the PSID.

> *Sample I:* "Full Sample" (or "All")
> Includes all children of 1968 PSID households who responded to the PSID survey while living in their own adult household (either as head, wife of head, or cohabitator with

head) in at least three of the six years from 1984 to 1989, who were born in the years 1951–61, who report their schooling, who report the number of siblings, and who report nonzero consumption in at least one of the years 1984–87 and nonzero income in at least one of the years 1984–88. Parents of these children must also report nonzero consumption in each of the years 1969–72 and nonzero income in at least one of the years 1967–71.

Sample II: "Fathers observed 1968–72"
These are the members of Sample I whose fathers were heads of the PSID households from 1968 through 1972. Sample II rules out PSID households that were headed by the mother for one or more of those years.

Sample III: "SRC Only"
These are the members of Sample I who are members of the PSID-SRC sample. Sample III rules out members of the PSID-SEO sample, which was designed to oversample the poor.

Sample IV: "Sons Only"
Sons from Sample I. Daughters are, of course, ruled out of Sample IV.

Sample I is the broadest sample available for comparing the consumption of parents and adult children without running into serious measurement error problems. For example, a broader sample could be obtained by relaxing the 1951–61 birth year restriction, thereby including children who were quite old in 1968 but who still lived with their parents or children who were quite young in 1984 and did not live with their parents. I imposed this birth year restriction to avoid overrepresenting these unusual children. Notice that all samples can include multiple children from a single 1968 PSID family. Appendix F in chapter 8 displays various characteristics of Sample I, including schooling, occupation, marital status, average age, and income of parents and children.

Sample II is interesting for measurement purposes. Multiyear measures of consumption, earnings, or income of households headed fairly continuously by a father may be a better measure of the lifetime economic status of the parents than the corresponding measures for households where a father is not always observed. Sample IV is interesting for similar reasons.

Sample III is probably the most representative sample because it excludes the poorer PSID-SEO households. Samples I, II, and IV include the PSID-SEO households and, for example, overrepresent blacks: 38.5

percent of Sample I sons and 43.3 percent of Sample I daughters are black. However, Sample III appears to slightly underrepresent blacks: only 5.9 percent of Sample III sons are black.

All of Samples I, II, III, or IV are used whenever possible. However, data availability sometimes restricts the analysis to subsamples. Four subsamples are studied.

Subsample A: "All"
All of a particular Sample (I, II, III, or IV).

Subsample B: "IV"
The members of a particular Sample whose parents reported a one-digit occupation, a two-digit industry, and county of residence. This information is used to construct instruments for parental consumption, income, and earnings.

Subsample C: "Earnings"
Members of subsample B who also report positive earnings in at least one of the years 1984–88 during which they lived in their own adult household. The head of their parental household must also report positive earnings in at least one of the years 1967–71.

Subsample D: "Wealth"
These are members of subsample B who also report positive wealth in at least one of the years between and including 1984 and 1989 during which they lived in their own adult household. The head of their parental household must also report wealth of more than $500 in at least one of the years 1984–89.

Subsample E: "Grandparent"
Members of a particular Sample whose father reported the schooling and one-digit occupation of his father.

The size of each of the subsamples is reported in table 7.1.

Measurement of Consumption

"Consumption" is the most important variable in the permanent income, borrowing constraints, and endogenous altruism models of intergenerational mobility, but (to my knowledge) no empirical studies of intergenerational mobility have measured it. I estimate the consumption of a father (or child) and his family. The PSID provides data on a household's expenditures on food for consumption at home, food eaten out, rent, mortgage

Table 7.1 Subsample Sizes

		Subsample			
Sample	All	IV	Earnings	Wealth	Grandparent
All	1781	1636	1428	956	1650
Fathers observed 1968–72	1315	1266	1224	827	1252
SRC only	874	853	766	569	843
Sons only	867	790	702	474	801

payments, property taxes and utilities.[2] Although it is not my primary measure of consumption, I experiment with the simple sum of these items as a proxy for consumption. My primary measure is constructed as a weighted average of food at home, food away from home, rent, and the value of the family's house. This weighted average is a measure of nondurable consumption because the weights are taken from a regression, using data from the Consumer Expenditure Survey, of nondurable consumption on food at home, food away from home, rent, and the value of the family's house.[3] Since several economists have used food consumption as their consumption measure, I also experiment with the sum of expenditures on food eaten away from home and food eaten at home.[4]

Both of these family measures differ from an individual's consumption. For example, it is not obvious how to correct for family composition. Children in my sample are at different stages of their life-cycles: only some are married, only some have children. Some studies have divided family expenditure by family size or by "adult equivalents" or by "family needs." However, such an adjustment ignores the possibility that sons and daughters choose to be married or to have children.

Measured consumption differs from the theoretical concept in previous chapters in another important way. Consumption is associated with a generation in the theoretical analysis; more consumption by parents means, according to the budget constraint, less transfers to the children. My mea-

2. Data is also available on money saved with food stamps, but I do not include it in my measure of consumption.

3. The Consumer Expenditure Survey regressions are reported by Jonathan Skinner (1987). Although the 1972–73 Survey was used to generate the weights for the father's consumption and the 1983 Survey for the children's consumption, the father's weights are quite similar to those used for the children.

The two regressions of nondurable consumption using Consumer Expenditure Surveys have $\overline{R}^2 = .724$ (1972–73) and $\overline{R}^2 = .680$ (1983).

4. Results with food consumption are reported in Appendix D at the end of this chapter. Results with the second alternative consumption measure are intermediate between those reported in the main text and those for food consumption.

sures of family consumption confound expenditures by parents on young children with expenditures by parents on themselves. For this reason, one may want to think of my consumption measures as indicators of adult wealth or welfare, rather than as a lifetime measure which includes childhood.

In order to get as close as possible to a lifetime measure, single-year measures are averaged for the period of 1969 through 1972 for parents and for 1984 through 1987 for adult children and then transformed to logarithms.[5]

PSID Results

Table 7.2 reports ordinary least squares estimates of β and their standard errors, where β is the coefficient on log parental status in the following regression equation:[6]

$$\ln Y_{t+1}^{i} = \beta \ln Y_{t}^{i} + X^{i}\Gamma + \varepsilon_{t+1}^{i} \quad (7.1)$$

Y_{t+1}^{i} denotes the adult economic status of child i and Y_{t}^{i} denotes the economics status of his parents. Economic status is measured as family consumption, family income, individual wage, individual earnings, or family wealth. X^{i} denotes a vector of additional regressors for family i: a constant, a dummy variable for daughters, parental and child "marriage" variables, a quadratic for the 1984 age of the child, and a quadratic for the age of the 1968 head of the child's household (either father or mother). The parental "marriage" variable is equal to the number of years that the parental household head is observed to be the father. The child "marriage" variable—included as a regressor only when Y denotes a family (as opposed to an individual) measure of economic status—is the fraction of time that the child's adult economic status is observed and that child is married or cohabitating.

Throughout the book I model each generation as a single time period. The regression equation 7.1 maintains this practice, but how can "the" economic status of particular generation be measured? A reasonable inter-

5. My primary consumption measure cannot be constructed for 1988 and 1989 because, since 1988, the PSID questionnaire no longer inquires about food and utilities expenditures.

6. A few papers in the economics literature emphasize nonlinearities in equation 7.1 when Y is measured as earnings. Examples include works by Suzanne Cooper, Steven Durlauf, and Paul Johnson (1994) and Durlauf (1996). However, I find little evidence on nonlinearities in my samples and therefore report only results from linear specifications. A linear specification is also consistent with the apparent constancy of β over time, across countries, and across groups. Even if nonlinearities were present in the general population, they may be unimportant in the PSID because the PSID includes very few of very rich.

Table 7.2. OLS Results

	Measure of Economic Status							
Sample	Family Cons.	Family Income	Family Cons.	Family Income	Individual Wage	Individual Earnings	Family Cons.	Family Wealth
All	0.55	0.47	0.54	0.48	0.32		0.49	0.33
	(0.03)	(0.03)	(0.03)	(0.03)	(0.03)		(0.04)	(0.03)
Fathers observed	0.55	0.48	0.54	0.48	0.33		0.49	0.35
1968–72	(0.03)	(0.03)	(0.03)	(0.03)	(0.03)		(0.04)	(0.04)
SRC only	0.59	0.52	0.56	0.49	0.33		0.53	0.32
	(0.04)	(0.04)	(0.04)	(0.04)	(0.04)		(0.05)	(0.04)
Sons only	0.54	0.48	0.53	0.52	0.33	0.32	0.58	0.34
	(0.04)	(0.04)	(0.04)	(0.04)	(0.04)	(0.04)	(0.05)	(0.05)
subsample	All	All	Earnings	Earnings	Earnings	Earnings	Wealth	Wealth

Notes:

1. Reported are coefficients on log parental status in a regression of log adult child's status on a dummy for daughters, parental and child marriage variables, and a quadratic in both the child and the parental head-of-household's age. The parental marriage variable is the number of years that the economic status of parents was measured and the father was present. The child marriage variable is included only for the family measures of economic status and is the fraction of years that the child's status is measured and the child is married or cohabitating. Standard errors are in parentheses.
2. "Family" measures of economics status are the entire adult household of the child (measured in some of the years 1984–89) and the entire household of his or her parents (measured in some of the years 1967–72). "Individual" measures are for the adult child (measured in some of the years 1984–88) and the head of the child's parents' household (measured in some of the years 1967–71).
3. "Wage" is annual hourly earnings, averaged over any years parent (1967–71) and child (1984–88) reported positive earnings.
4. Earnings results are not reported for samples that include both sons and daughters.

pretation of the variable Y is as *lifetime* economic status. Lifetime earnings, for example, might be measured as the average earnings received by an individual over his lifetime. However, it is not possible to observe a parent or an adult child for his entire lifetime—parents had a life before they joined the PSID and children have a life beyond the most recent wave of the PSID and the publication of this book. I therefore follow much of the empirical literature (see "Results from Other Data Sources" for a review) and make three attempts to measure lifetime economic status. First, I measure the economic status of parents and children for several years rather than a single year. A several-year average is obviously closer to a lifetime average than is a single year. Second, I try to observe parents and children when they are of similar ages. The economic status of parents is observed in the years from 1967 to 1972, when parents are roughly forty years old. The economic status of children is observed almost twenty years later in the years between 1984 and 1989 when the children are, on average, more than thirty years old. Third, age polynomials are included in the regression equation 7.1 for both parents and children.[7]

OLS estimates of the degree of consumption persistence are reported in the first column of table 7. 2. The broadest subsamples are used. The estimates of 0.54–0.59 are fairly high. They imply that more than one-half of the percentage family consumption difference between two fathers will remain between their children. Individual consumption cannot be measured, but it might regress to the mean even more slowly if an individual's *share* of family consumption were positively correlated with one's family background. This might arise, for example, because of bargaining in a marriage market among young adults who expect to inherit estates of various sizes.

According to the OLS estimates, family income is almost as persistent as family consumption. Coefficients of 0.47–0.52 are reported in the second column for the broadest subsamples.

Narrower samples are required when wages or earnings are taken as the measure of economic status. For comparability, family consumption and income results are computed with the narrower earnings subsamples and reported in columns 4 and 5. The change of subsample does not change the estimated degree of intergenerational consumption and income mobility (equivalently, the estimated degree of persistence) by more than 0.03. The OLS estimates suggest that earnings or wages are much less persistent than family consumption or income. The wage and earnings coefficients reported in columns 5 and 6 range from 0.32 to 0.33 or slightly more than half of the estimated consumption and income coefficients. The greater estimated mobility of wages and earnings as compared with consumption and income is consistent with the intergenerational permanent income model.

It is well known that errors in the measurement of parental economic status can bias estimates of the degree of intergenerational mobility.[8] Only some fraction of the reported differences among parents are actually true differences. Presumably differences among children depend on true differences among parents and not on reported differences, so one expects the economic status of children to be relatively insensitive to reported pa-

7. As a fourth attempt, I limit my samples to only children in their mid-thirties. Doing so slightly decreases the estimated degree of intergenerational mobility (by 0.05 or less), but only strengthens three main results: (1) previous studies have overestimated intergenerational mobility, (2) consumption and income are more persistent than earnings and wages, and (3) measures of economic status regress to the mean across generations. The results of my fourth attempt are not reported in the tables.

8. See Gary Solon (1992) or Anthony Atkinson, A. K. Maynard, and C. G. Trinder (1983) for a discussion of the effects of classical errors in the measurement of parental earnings.

rental status. In other words, OLS estimates of coefficients reported in table 7.2 underestimate the sensitivity of a child's status to a parent's actual status. However, it seems unlikely that measurement error would drive my finding that wages and earnings are less persistent than consumption and income. One would expect the Panel Study of Income Dynamics to live up to its name and do an excellent job of measuring income and earnings but not so good a job of measuring consumption. One expects the measurement error problem to be most serious for consumption and that the OLS estimates of consumption coefficients are the most understated.

Many readers may be convinced on logical grounds that consumption is measured most poorly, but instrumental variables results provide some additional evidence. Table 7.3 reports. In the first column, parental family

Table 7.3 IV Results

Sample	Family Cons.	Family Income	Family Cons.	Family Income	Individual Wage	Individual Earnings	Family Cons.	Family Wealth
All	0.71	0.65	0.69	0.63	0.49		0.69	0.54
	(0.04)	(0.04)	(0.04)	(0.04)	(0.04)		(0.04)	(0.05)
Fathers observed	0.68	0.65	0.68	0.63	0.49		0.68	0.52
1968–72	(0.04)	(0.05)	(0.04)	(0.04)	(0.04)		(0.05)	(0.05)
SRC only	0.77	0.71	0.72	0.71	0.53		0.75	0.43
	(0.05)	(0.06)	(0.05)	(0.05)	(0.05)		(0.06)	(0.06)
Sons only	0.72	0.63	0.68	0.60	0.50	0.48	0.81	0.53
	(0.06)	(0.06)	(0.05)	(0.06)	(0.05)	(0.07)	(0.07)	(0.07)
subsample	All	All	Earnings	Earnings	Earnings	Earnings	Wealth	Wealth

Notes:

1. Reported are coefficients on log parental status in a regression of log adult child's status on a dummy for daughters, parental and child marriage variables, and a quadratic in both the child and the parental head-of-household's age. The parental marriage variable is the number of years that the economic status of parents was measured and the father was present. The child marriage variable is included only for the family measures of economic status and is the fraction of years that the child's status is measured and the child is married or cohabitating. Standard errors are in parentheses.

2. "Family" measures of economics status are the entire adult household of the child (measured in some of the years 1984–89) and the entire household of his parents (measured in some of the years 1967–72). "Individual" measures are for the adult child (measured in some of the years 1984–88) and the head of the child's parents' household (measured in some of the years 1967–71).

3. "Wage" is annual hourly earnings, averaged over any years parent (1967–71) and child (1984–88) reported positive earnings. Earnings results are not reported for samples that include both sons and daughters. Log 1967–71 family income is the instrument for column 1 estimates. Column 2 instruments are log of mean income and earnings of 1970 Census household heads in the same age and schooling category as the PSID parental household head, log of per capita earnings, per capita personal income, and per worker earnings in the PSID household's 1970 county of residence. All nine of the Census and county instruments are used in columns 3–8. Results are very similar without race or region-based IVs.

income is used as an instrument for parental family consumption in the "All" subsamples. The estimated coefficient is 0.71 as compared with the OLS estimate of 0.55. This means that while 55 percent of reported consumption differences persist to the next generation, 71 percent of the reported consumption differences associated with income differences are transmitted to the next generation. In addition to family income, a subset of the instruments are also available for the "All" subsamples and are used to compute the IV estimates in column 2: log of mean income and earnings of 1970 Census household heads in the same age and schooling category, log of per capita earnings, per capita personal income, and per worker earnings in the PSID household's 1970 county of residence. The IV estimate of the log income β is 0.65, which is larger than the corresponding OLS estimate of 0.47.

Nine additional instruments are available in the earnings and wealth subsamples: average 1970 earnings and family income of household heads in the same sex/race/one-digit occupation category as the 1970 PSID household head (one of the parents), average 1970 earnings and family income of household heads in the same sex/age/schooling category, average 1970 earnings and family income of same-sex household heads in the same two-digit industry, average 1970 per capita personal income in the county in which the PSID family resided in 1970, average 1970 per capita earnings in the county in which the PSID family resided in 1970, and average 1970 earnings per worker in the county in which the PSID family resided in 1970. Parental family income is also used as an instrument for parental family consumption.[9] The three category family income means are not used as instruments for parental wages or earnings. The first six instruments are constructed from the 1970 1/100 Census PUMS. The three county instruments are computed from the BEA's Regional Economic Information System. All instruments are greater than zero and used in their log form.

IV results with these additional instruments are reported in columns 3 through 7 of table 7. 3. The persistence of family consumption is slightly lower in the narrower earnings sample, but the IV coefficients are still significantly higher than their OLS counterparts. Estimated coefficients from the family income equations range from 0.60 to 0.71 as compared with estimates of 0.68 to 0.72 for family consumption. Wages and earnings coefficients increase relative to their OLS counterparts, but their range of 0.49 to 0.53 is substantially different from the range of 0.68 to 0.72 for family consumption coefficients.

9. The IV point estimates of the coefficient on log parental consumption are extremely robust to the exclusion of parental family income from the list of instruments.

The possibility of measurement error is not the only reason why the IV results are interesting. Chapter 3 shows that, when families differ in their degree of intergenerational altruism in a way that is uncorrelated with income, the intergenerational permanent income model predicts regression to the mean in percentage terms of actual consumption. However, the permanent income model also predicts that consumption does not regress to the mean in percentage terms across parental income categories. According to the model, OLS estimates of the coefficient on parental consumption may be less than one, but IV estimates should be equal to one when parental income is used as an instrumental variable. The IV estimates of 0.68 to 0.77 reported in columns 1 and 3 are therefore inconsistent with the permanent income model.

"Marriage" variables are included in the regressions for the same reason that age quadratics are: measured economic status differs from actual lifetime economic status according to the marital status of parent and adult child. One expects the relationship between mismeasurement and marriage to be especially strong for family measures of economic status. For example, the family consumption of a single adult child does not seem comparable with the family consumption of a married adult child. I therefore include marriage variables in the Galton-style regressions. If marital status is itself a component of economic status, then perhaps marriage should not be included in the regressions. Results without the marriage variables, reported in Mulligan (1995b) are similar to those reported in tables 7.2 and 7.3; the intergenerational persistence of economic status is either the same or higher when marriage variables are excluded.[10]

Gary Becker and Nigel Tomes (1986) predict that grandparental economic status should enter with a negative sign in a regression of a child's status on parental status. By using the schooling and occupation to construct an estimate of grandparental income, the grandparental result can be tested with my "grandparent" subsamples. Grandparental status does in fact enter with a negative (and usually is statistically significant) sign when child and parent economic statuses are measured as consumption, income, or wages. I do not believe this grandparental result tells us much about the economics of intergenerational mobility (see chapter 3 or Goldberger [1989] for a discussion), so I do not provide a table of tests of the grandparental prediction. See Mulligan (1993, chapter 6) for an analysis with my grandparent subsamples. Jere Behrman and Paul Taubman

10. The main results are also insensitive to the exclusion of adult children who are not married the entire time that their economic status is observed. The estimated persistence of family income and individual wages is reduced by the exclusion but, because the wage is an individual measure of economic status, the reduction seems to be the result of selecting less than 50 percent of the main sample rather than the result of a correlation of marriage with mismeasurement.

(1985) and Jenny Bourne Wahl (1985) test the grandparental prediction with other data sets.

In summary, three conclusions are strongly supported by Galton-style (1889) analyses of family consumption, family income, individual wages, individual earnings, and family wealth:[11]

(1) All five measures of economic status regress to the mean across generations in percentage terms.
(2) Consumption regresses to the mean in percentage terms much more slowly across generations than does wages or earnings.
(3) Errors in the measurement of parental economic status lead to an important overestimation of the degree of intergenerational mobility.

Result (1) is inconsistent with the intergenerational permanent income model. Result (2) says that, in percentage terms, differences across families in wages or earnings close almost twice as fast as do consumption differences. Result (2) is consistent with the permanent income model but inconsistent with a borrowing constraints model where the vast majority of households are in the "constrained" category. To my knowledge, there are no noneconomic models that predict result (2).

The richness of my data set allows me to establish result (3). Time-averaging single-year measures of economic status (following Solon 1992) generates estimates of β that are larger than many of those reported in the literature. The use of several instrumental variables creates even larger estimates. The very high IV estimates are consistent with the hypothesis that earnings and other measures of economic status are often measured with substantial error.

Results from Other Data Sources

Tables 7.4, 7.5, 7.6, 7.7, 7.8, and 7.9 review previous estimates of the intergenerational persistence of economic status and compare them with my estimates. The unifying feature of many of the studies is that they use micro data that provide comparable indicators of economic status for both parents and their adult children.[12] Most are for the United States and a few utilize intergenerational samples from the PSID for which the children reach adulthood in the late 1980s. However, some data sets were obtained

11. None of the conclusions are at all sensitive to the exclusion of the marriage variables from the Galton-style regressions.

12. I omit some empirical studies of intergenerational mobility because they do not measure economic status in the same way for parents and children and therefore obtain estimates that are not strictly comparable with those reported in my tables. For example, Richard Freeman (1981) and Robert Hauser, William Sewell, and Kenneth Lutterman (1975) compare earnings of children with income of parents.

Table 7.4 Studies of the Intergenerational Persistence of Schooling Based on Observations of Parent and Adult Child

Author	β	relationships	parent/ child year	location	representative sample?	measurement error correction?
Olneck (1977)	0.45	father-son	73/73	Kalamazoo, MI	no	no
Behrman & Taubman (1985)	0.31	father-child	80/80	U.S.	father a white twin veteran	no
Lillard & Willis (1994)	0.19	father-son	1988/ 1988	Malaysia	yes	no
Lillard & Willis (1994)	0.23	father-daughter	1988/ 1988	Malaysia	yes	no
Couch & Dunn (1995)	0.27	father-son	84/84	U.S.	yes	no
Couch & Dunn (1995)	0.20	father-son	84/84	Germany	yes	no
Mulligan (1997)*	0.32	father-son	68/84–9	U.S.	yes	no
Mulligan (1997)	0.33	father-child	68/84–9	U.S.	yes	no

Notes:

* Mulligan (1997) refers to this volume.

1. β is the estimate of intergenerational persistence.

2. "Relationship" is, for individual measures of economic status (schooling and earnings), the parent and child that are compared. "father-child" means that both sons and daughters are compared with their father.

3. Years refer to the twentieth century unless otherwise noted.

4. A "representative sample" is intended to represent the entire population of the location being studied. Of course, none of the samples are truly representative.

5. The "measurement error correction" column lists attempts to correct for errors in the measurement of parental economic status.

6. Mulligan (1997—this volume) estimates are for full SRC samples except when narrowed to father-son or earnings sample as noted in the table.

in different countries, including Britain, Germany, Malaysia, Norway, and Sweden. Others apply to earlier historical periods, including children who reached adulthood in the mid-nineteenth century, the turn of the century, the 1950s, the 1960s, and the 1970s.

Schooling

Table 7.4 lists four other studies of the intergenerational persistence of schooling.[13] Michael Olneck (1977) studies families in Kalamazoo, Michigan, in 1973 and estimates $\beta = 0.45$. Behrman and Taubman (1985) study

13. I do not attempt to survey the intergenerational schooling literature as thoroughly as the earnings, income, wealth, and consumption literatures.

the offspring of a sample of U.S. white male veterans born between 1917 and 1927 and find $\beta = 0.31$. Lee Lillard and Robert Willis (1994) find $\beta = 0.19$ and $\beta = 0.23$ for sons and daughters in Malaysia. Kenneth Couch and Thomas Dunn (1995) use intergenerational samples from the U.S. PSID and the German Socioeconomic Panel (which was modeled after the PSID). They find that schooling is more persistent in the United States than in Germany. Unlike the Olneck (1977) or Behrman and Taubman (1985) samples, the Couch and Dunn samples attempt to represent national populations. I also try to obtain a sample that is representative of the United States by using the SRC portion of the PSID and obtaining estimates of 0.32 (0.33) for sons (sons and daughters pooled). None of the studies listed in table 7.4 attempt to correct for errors in the measurement of schooling, mainly because it seems that years of schooling are easy to measure. Although a stronger conclusion could be reached if table 7.4 included studies from more countries and from more historical periods, it appears that years of schooling regress to the mean fairly rapidly.

Earnings

Microdata Estimates of Intergenerational Earnings Mobility

Studies of the intergenerational persistence of earnings or wages are listed in table 7.5. Behrman and Taubman (1985) estimate a β for log earnings of 0.18 in their sample of veterans and their offspring.[14] An important shortcoming of their study is that they observe father and child at the same point in time and therefore at different stages of their life cycle. This is a problem because the fathers are, on average, sixty years old, so that many of them are retired or in the process of retiring. Much of the earnings variation across fathers is therefore not associated with lifetime earnings. Anthony Atkinson, A. K. Maynard, and C. G. Trinder (1983) are able to solve this problem because they observe the earnings of fathers in 1950 and the earnings of the adult sons in 1978 so that fathers and sons observations correspond to similar life-cycle positions. They estimate a earnings β of 0.44.

The Behrman and Taubman estimate of 0.18 and the Atkinson et al. estimate of 0.44 are not corrected for errors in the measurement of parental lifetime earnings. Atkinson, Maynard, and Trinder attempt to mitigate the problem by focusing on fathers for whom earnings reports could be verified with employers, thereby obtaining an estimate of 0.45. However, it is not clear that misreports are the only source of deviations from lifetime earnings; there can be seasonal and other transitory earnings fluctuations. Elizabeth Peters (1992), Gary Solon (1992), David Zimmerman (1992),

14. They obtain similar estimates when they separate sons and daughters (1985, p. 147).

Table 7.5 Studies of the Intergenerational Persistence of Earnings or Wages (Log) Based on Observations of Parent and Adult Child

Author	β	relationships	parent/ child year	location	representative sample?	measurement error correction?
Behrman & Taubman (1985)	0.18	father-child	80/80	U.S.	earnings > 5000, whites	
Atkinson et al (1983)	0.44	father-son	50/78	York	working class	
Atkinson et al (1983)	0.45	father-son	50/78	York	working class	employer report of earnings
Peters (1992)	0.14	father-son	66–71/ 76–81	U.S.	1 of 5 yrs w/ earnings > 0	multiyear avg.
Peters (1992)	0.13	father-daughter	67–72/ 77–82	U.S.	"	multiyear avg.
Solon (1992)	0.41	father-son	67–71/ 84	U.S.	4 years w/ earnings > 0	multiyear avg.
Solon (1992)	0.53	father-son	67/84	U.S.	earnings > 0	IV
Zimmerman (1992)	0.34	father-son	66–71/ 81	U.S.	4 years w/ earnings > 0	4-year avg.
Zimmerman (1992)	0.50	father-son	65/81	U.S.	4 years w/ earnings > 0	IV
Couch & Dunn (1995)	0.13	father-son	84–89/ 84–89	U.S.	6 years w/ earnings > 0	6-year avg.
Couch & Dunn (1995)	0.11	father-son	84–89/ 84–89	Germany	6 years w/ earnings > 0	6-year avg.
Björklund & Jantti (1993)	0.27	father-son	67–73/ 90	Sweden	5 years w/ earnings > 0	5-year avg.
Borjas (1994)	0.4–0.6	father-son	1910/ 1940	U.S.	earnings > 0 (macro)	IV. ethnic dummy
Mulligan (1997)*	0.33	father-son	67–71/ 84–88	U.S.	1 of 5 years w/ earnings > 0	multiyear avg.
Mulligan (1997)	0.50	father-son	"	U.S.	"	IV
Mulligan (1997)	0.33	father-child	"	U.S.	"	multiyear avg.
Mulligan (1997)	0.53	father-child	"	U.S.	"	IV
Mulligan (1997)	0.59	father-son	1940/ 1985	U.S.	earnings > 0 (macro)	IV, race dummy

Notes:

* Mulligan (1997) refers to this volume.

1. β is the estimate of intergenerational persistence. Mulligan (1997) and several of the other studies hold constant age polynomials for parents and children.

2. "Relationship" is the parent and child that are compared.

3. Years refer to the twentieth century unless otherwise noted.

4. A "representative sample" is *intended* to represent the entire population of the location being studied.

5. The "measurement error correction" column lists attempts to correct measurement errors of parental status.

6. Mulligan (1997) estimates are for full SRC samples except when narrowed to father-son or earnings sample as noted in the table. See tables 7.2 and 7.3 for robustness of the Mulligan estimates to sample selection.

7. Of the U.S. studies, Peters (1992) uses the NLSY while Solon (1992), Couch and Dunn (1995), and Mulligan (1997) use the PSID. Behrman and Taubman (1985) use a "twins" sample (see text).

8. Borjas (1994) and Mulligan's 0.59 are estimates of intergenerational earnings mobility across groups. Mulligan's calculation is based on Smith and Welch (1986) estimates of black-white wage gaps. See text.

Couch and Dunn (1995), and Mulligan (this volume) attempt to mitigate measurement error problems by time averaging measures of a father's earnings or wages.[15] Solon and Mulligan report estimates of 0.41 and 0.33, which are much higher than that of Behrman and Taubman. Mulligan reports a similar estimate when both daughters and sons are included. Couch and Dunn report relatively low estimates of 0.13 for the United States and 0.11 for Germany. Couch and Dunn suggest that, although the intergenerational persistence of schooling is greater in the United States than in Germany, the intergenerational persistence of earnings is not very different in the two countries. That they use quite comparable data and methods for the two countries makes their conclusion more believable. Anders Björklund and Markus Jantti (1993) conduct comparable studies of intergenerational earnings mobility in the United States and Sweden, estimating earnings β's of 0.41 and 0.27, respectively. Their Swedish estimate is reported in table 7.5 but, for the sake of brevity, their American estimate is not because their American estimate is so similar to others.

A potential problem with Solon's and Zimmerman's time averaging is that they must eliminate any father or son who does not have positive earnings in *all* of the relevant years. The strategy necessarily omits fathers and sons who tend to experience spells of unemployment that last a year or more. I relax the restriction by averaging wages over any of the five years that they are observed and then using the log in a regression—I only require that earnings be positive in one of the five years. Relaxing Solon's restriction in this way slightly lowers the estimated log earnings β. I also study income and consumption, variables which are much more likely to be positive in any given year than is earnings. Yet another useful way to bring the long-term unemployed into an analysis of intergenerational mobility is to compare actual unemployment spells of fathers and, years later, of sons. An intergenerational analysis of unemployment is very possible with my data, but I leave it for future research.[16] I suspect that my study of consumption and income and my modification of the Solon-Zimmerman strategy substantially mitigate the problem of omitting the long-term unemployed.

Solon (1992), Zimmerman (1992), and Mulligan (this volume) also use instrumental variables techniques to correct for measurement error. Solon uses schooling as his instrument and enforces the relatively strong selection criteria that fathers report positive earnings in 1967 and sons report positive earnings in 1984. Zimmerman (1992) studies wages and uses

15. Peters (1992) and Zimmerman (1992) use the NLSY. Solon (1992), Couch and Dunn (1995), and Mulligan (this volume) use the PSID.

16. Some results have recently been reported in Mulligan (1996a).

wages from other points in the father's life cycle as an instrument for a father's wage.[17] I also use wages rather than earnings and use five instruments: average 1970 earnings of household heads in the same sex/race/one-digit occupation category as the 1970 PSID household head (one of the parents), average 1970 earnings of household heads in the same sex/age/schooling category, average 1970 earnings of same-sex household heads in the same two-digit industry, average 1970 per capita personal income in the county in which the PSID family resided in 1970, average 1970 per capita earnings in the county in which the PSID family resided in 1970. My selection criteria are weaker: fathers and children need only to report positive earnings in one of five years. The Solon, Zimmerman, and Mulligan IV estimates are 0.53, 0.50, and 0.50, which are larger than their multiyear estimates.

Cross-Group Estimates of Intergenerational Earnings Mobility

Chapter 6 shows how intergenerational mobility causes inequality to decline across groups. This chapter uses the converse of this result: declining inequality across groups is used to estimate the degree of intergenerational persistence of earnings and income.

Recall equation 3.1, the basic equation describing the relationship between the economic status of parents (Y_t) and of children (Y_{t+1}). The equation is repeated below for convenience.

$$\ln Y_{t+1}^i = \alpha + \beta \ln Y_t^i + \varepsilon_{t+1}^i \tag{3.1}$$

α and β are constants. Equation 3.1 can be thought of as generating the earnings of family i's children (Y_{t+1}^i) according to two influences: family i parental earnings (Y_t^i) and other influences (ε_{t+1}^i). "Other influences" are, by definition, unrelated to parental earnings. Luck, discrimination, intelligence, government policies, or a willingness to work are candidate other influences to the extent that they are unrelated to parental income.

Equation 3.1 can be averaged within groups, where a group can be a race, a region, or a country. According to the averaged version of equation 3.1, the average log earnings of a group's children depends on the average log earnings of the group's parents and on the average "other influences" for the group. If one assumes that the other influences average to zero within each group (or, more generally, that other influences are uncorrelated with parental economic status in the group), then β dictates how

17. Zimmerman (1992) reports similar estimates for earnings, wages, and a Duncan occupational index.

inequality across groups varies over time.[18] Inequality across groups declines rapidly when β is small and slowly when β is large.

Although they use "macro" data, cross-group estimates of β can be thought of as special cases of the instrumental variable microdata estimates, where group dummy variables are used as instruments for parental earnings or wages. I therefore report the cross-group estimates together with the microdata estimates in table 7.5, noting that group dummy variables are used to correct for measurement error. Borjas, for example, studies the changing inequality across ethnic groups in the United States from 1910 to 1940. Under the assumption that "other influences" average out within groups and that all changing inequality across groups for the period is intergenerational rather than intragenerational (that is, immigrant groups catch up with the rest of the United States because children do better than parents rather than both parents and children doing better), the intergenerational persistence of earnings can be estimated from Borjas's data. Borjas estimates β's between 0.4 and 0. 6. Under the same assumptions, James Smith's and Finis Welch's (1986) black-white data can be used to estimate a β of 0.59.[19] The validity of the assumption of "other influences" averaging to zero within ethnic and racial groups is discussed later in the chapter.

Family Income

Microdata Estimates of Intergenerational Income Mobility

Table 7.6 reviews previous estimates of intergenerational family income mobility. Lee Soltow (1965) studies father-son pairs living in Sarpsborg, Norway, in 1960. James Kearl and Clayne Pope (1986) study father-son pairs living in Utah in the nineteenth century. Soltow and Kearl and Pope estimate income βs of 0.14 and 0.13, but their samples suffer from three potentially serious problems. First, the incomes of fathers and sons are observed at a single point in time so the two are at very different points in the life cycle. Second, the fact that the Norwegian sons did not move away

18. Later in the chapter, I discuss the possibility that other influences may be different for different groups.

19. The black-white estimate of β is obtained from the formula (*Y* denotes wages):

$$\beta = \left(\frac{\ln(Y^{w}_{1985} / Y^{b}_{1985}}{\ln(Y^{w}_{1940} / Y^{b}_{1940}} \right)^{25/45}$$

where *w* and *b* denote "white" and "black." The term in large parenthesis is raised to the 45/25 power because the time period of 1940 through 1985 is forty-five years and a generation is assumed to be twenty-five years, so the period of 1940 through 1985 is 45/25 generations.

from their fathers may mean that they are not typical of the Norwegian population. Third, Soltow and Kearl and Pope do not adjust for measurement error. P. de Wolff and A. R. D. van Slijpe (1973) and Atkinson, Maynard, and Trinder (1983), who obtain estimates of 0.49 and 0.38 for Sweden and Britain, are able to observe fathers and sons at similar points in the life cycle but do not correct for the effects of measurement error. Considering the methods used, the Swedish and British estimates do not seem very different from American estimates. Björklund and Jantti (1993) find somewhat more intergenerational income mobility in Sweden than in the United States, although their data methods are not strictly comparable because they measure individual Swedish incomes and U.S. family incomes. They use multiyear averages to measure economic status of fathers and sons and their Swedish estimate of β for income is 0.38.

Using multiyear averages of parental income, Peters (1992) finds the least persistence (β = 0.28) while Solon (1992) and Mulligan (this volume) find 0.48 and 0.52. Solon uses the father's schooling as an instrument for the father's family income, which increases his estimate to 0.53. I (1997) find more intergenerational persistence, especially when I use nine instruments: average 1970 earnings and family income of household heads in the same sex/race/one-digit occupation category as the 1970 PSID household head (one of the parents), average 1970 earnings and family income of household heads in the same sex/age/schooling category, average 1970 earnings and family income of same-sex household heads in the same two-digit industry, average 1970 per capita personal income in the county of PSID family residence in 1970, average 1970 per capita earnings and earnings per worker in the county of PSID family residence in 1970. Results are very similar without race or region-based IVs.

Cross-Group Estimates of Intergenerational Income Mobility

Robert Barro and Xavier Sala-i-Martin (1991; 1992a; 1992b) study the changing inequality across regions of Europe, Japan, and the United States as well as changing inequality across countries. Under the assumption that immigration is unimportant and that "other influences" average to zero for each region or country, they obtain cross-region estimates of the intergenerational persistence of income of 0.65, 0.63, and 0.50 for the United States, Europe, and Japan.[20] The cross-region estimates are quite similar to the microdata estimates reported in table 7.6, which suggests

20. The cross-region and cross-country estimates of β are obtained from a Galton-style regression—such as equation 3.1 of the log of per capita income at date $(t + 1)$ on the log of per capita income at date t. I normalize the estimates so that β is measured on a generational basis—as opposed to the annual basis reported by Barro and Sala-i-Martin.

that "other influences" do in fact average to zero for each region. However, the Barro/Sala-i-Martin cross-country estimates of β are different from the microdata and cross-region estimates. They estimate $\beta = 1.10$ for a broad cross-section of countries and $\beta = 0.79$ for twenty-two OECD countries. One way to reconcile the cross-country estimates with the cross-region and microdata estimates is to relax the assumption that "other influences" average to zero for each country. For example, government policies fall under "other influences" and, although they may be common within countries, their effects vary across countries. Barro and Sala-i-Martin obtain some data that proxies for the "other influences" and find intergenerational income persistence of 0.63 and 0.60 in a broad cross-section of countries and in a cross-section of twenty-two OECD countries.[21]

"Technological progress" may be an important "other influence" that is associated with national income but unmeasured by Barro and Sala-i-Martin. However, the nature of the association with national income is unclear and therefore makes it hard to predict how technological progress might lead to a different evolution across countries than across families within a country. One might expect that richer countries might enjoy more productive technologies, perhaps because "technology" is affected by the average education level in the nation (as in the Lucas [1988] model) or perhaps because governments of rich nations have the revenues to promote basic scientific research. In this case, intergenerational mobility across countries is less than within a country. On the other hand, "technology" might be negatively related to national income because a country can, to some degree, imitate the technologies of other countries. A country that is currently poor has a variety of rich "examples to follow," whereas the richest countries, by definition, have no richer countries to imitate. Intergenerational mobility across countries is greater than within a country in this second case.

All together the "micro" and "macro" studies of intergenerational earnings and income mobility reported in tables 7.5 and 7.6 suggest that, controlling for cross-country differences in the "other influences," intergenerational mobility is quite similar within and across groups.

Family Wealth

Table 7.7 reports the results of four previous studies of intergenerational wealth mobility. C. D. Harbury and D. M. W. N. Hitchens look at the es-

21. The use of controls for "other influences" to estimate the degree of intergenerational income mobility across groups is referred to as "estimating conditional convergence" by Barro and Sala-i-Martin.

Table 7.6 Studies of the Intergenerational Persistence of Log Family Income Based on Observations of Parent and Adult Child

Author	β	relation-ships	parent/ child year	location	representative sample?	measurement error correction?
Soltow (1965)	0.14		60/60	Norway	sons only; both live in Sarpsborg	
de Wolff & van Slijpe (1973)	0.49		38/53	Sweden	Yes	
Atkinson et al (1983)	0.38		50/78	York	working class	
Kearl & Pope (1986)	0.13		1861/ 1861	Utah	sons only	
Peters (1992)	0.28		66–71/ 76–81	U.S.	sons only	multiyear avg.
Peters (1992)	0.24		67–72/ 77–82	U.S.	daughters only	multiyear avg.
Solon (1992)	0.48		67/84	U.S.	sons only	
Solon (1992)	0.53		67/84	U.S.	sons only	IV
Björklund & Jantti (1993)	0.38	father-son*	67–73/90	Sweden	sons only	multiyear avg.
Barro & Sala-i-Martin (1991)	0.65		1880/ 1988†	U.S.	48 states	IV, state dummy
Barro & Sala-i-Martin (1992a)	0.63		1950/ 1985†	Europe	73 regions	IV, region dummy
Barro & Sala-i-Martin (1992b)	0.50		1930/ 1987†	Japan	47 prefectures	IV, region dummy
Barro & Sala-i-Martin (1992a)	0.79		1960/ 1985†	OECD	20 countries	IV, country dummy
Barro & Sala-i-Martin (1992a)	1.10		1960/ 1985†	World	98 countries	IV, country dummy

Notes:

* Björklund and Jantti (1993) measure individual income rather than family income.

† Coefficient, normalized to generational units, from a regression of log income (or GDP) per capita in the final year on log income (or GDP) per capita in the initial year.

continued

tates of British fathers who died in 1902 and follow as many of their sons as possible until their death. They estimate a log wealth β of 0.46. Paul Menchik (1979) undertook a similar study for parents who died in Connecticut in the 1930s and 1940s.[22] He estimates a log wealth β of 0.76. Kearl and Pope obtain an estimate of 0.27 for Utah Mormons in the nineteenth century. All three studies utilize very special samples, however. The

22. Menchik combines the estates of mothers and fathers whenever possible.

Table 7.6—*Continued*

Author	β	relation-ships	parent/ child year	location	representative sample?	measurement error correction?
Barro & Sala-i-Martin (1992a)	0.60		1960/ 1985‡	OECD	20 countries	IV, country dummy
Barro & Sala-i-Martin (1992a)	0.63		1960/ 1985‡	World	98 countries	IV, country dummy
Mulligan (1997)**	0.52		67–71/ 84–88	U.S.	Yes	multiyear avg.
Mulligan (1997)	0.71		67–71/ 84–88	U.S.	Yes	IV

Notes:

** Mulligan (1997) refers to this volume.

‡ Coefficient on log initial income, normalized to generational units, from a regression of log income (of GDP) per capita in the final year on log income (or GDP) per capita in the initial year, school enrollment in the initial year, average government consumption spending as a fraction of GDP, number of coups and political assassinations, and the investment purchasing power ratio. See Barro and Sala-i-Martin (1992a) for more description of the variables.

1. β is the estimate of intergenerational persistence. Mulligan (1997) and several of the other studies hold constant age polynomials for parents and children.

2. "Relationship" is, for individual measures of economic status (schooling and earnings), the parent and child that are compared. "father-child" means that both sons and daughters are compared with their father.

3. Years refer to the twentieth century unless otherwise noted.

4. A "representative sample" is *intended* to represent the entire population of the location being studied. Of course, none of the samples are truly representative.

5. The "measurement error correction" column lists attempts to correct for parental status measurement errors.

6. Mulligan (1997) estimates are for full SRC samples except when narrowed to father-son or earnings sample as noted in the table. See tables 7.2 and 7.3 for robustness of the Mulligan estimates to sample selection.

Menchik (1979) and Kearl and Pope (1986) samples are very special because they require that fathers and sons die in the same state. Harbury and Hitchens (1979) and Menchik (1979) samples only include very wealthy families. None of these three studies make any adjustments for the possibility of measurement error.

Wahl (1985) studies the wealth of parent-child pairs that can be located in the 1860 and 1870 Censuses. Her sample families represent a broad cross-section of Americans, although the sample is not explicitly designed to be representative. She uses occupation and several demographic and locational variables as instruments for parental wealth, finding log wealth β estimates of 0.36 and 0.58. My IV estimates are 0.50 for sons only and 0.43 for sons and daughters pooled.

Table 7.7 Studies of the Intergenerational Persistence of Log Family Wealth Based on Observations of Parent and Adult Child

Author	β	relation-ships	parent/child year	location	representative sample?	measurement error correction?
Harbury & Hitchens (1979)	0.46		1902/ son's death	Britain	sons only large estates	
Menchik (1979)	0.76		30s, 40s/ child's death	CT	large estates, children also died in CT by 1976	
Kearl & Pope (1986)	0.27		1861/1861	Utah	sons only	
Wahl (1985)	0.36		1860	U.S.	?	IV
Wahl (1985)	0.58		1870	U.S.	?	IV
Mulligan (1997)*	0.32		84,89/84,89	U.S.	wealth reported in 1 of 2 years	multiyear avg.
Mulligan (1997)	0.43		84,89/84,89	U.S.	wealth reported in 1 of 2 years	IV
Mulligan (1997)	0.40		84,89/84,89	U.S.	sons only, wealth reported in 1 of 2 years	multiyear avg.
Mulligan (1997)	0.50		84,89/84,89	U.S.	sons only, wealth reported in 1 of 2 years	IV

Notes:

* Mulligan (1997) refers to this volume.

1. β is the estimate of intergenerational persistence. Mulligan (1997) and several of the other studies hold constant age polynomials for parents and children. Wahl (1985) is the only wealth study that did not report a log-log functional form; her β is computed at the mean from her level-level coefficient.

2. "Relationship" is, for individual measures of economic status (schooling and earnings), the parent and child that are compared. "father-child" means that both sons and daughters are compared with their father.

3. Years refer to the twentieth century unless otherwise noted.

4. A "representative sample" is *intended* to represent the entire population of the location being studied. Of course, none of the samples are truly representative.

5. The "measurement error correction" column lists attempts to correct for errors in the measurement of parental economic status.

6. Mulligan (1997) estimates are for wealth SRC samples.

7. The Wahl (1985) sample is not based on a sample survey designed to mimic U.S. demographics, but does include individuals from a variety of locations, occupations, and wealth categories.

Table 7.8 Studies of the Intergenerational Persistence of Log Family Consumption Based on Observations of Parent and Adult Child

Author	β	relation-ships	parent/child year	location	representative sample?	measurement error correction?
Mulligan (1997)*	0.59		69–72/ 84–87	U.S.	Yes	multiyear avg.
Mulligan (1997)	0.77		69–72/ 84–87	U.S.	Yes	IV

Notes:

* Mulligan (1997) refers to this volume.

1. β is the estimate of intergenerational persistence. Mulligan (1997) and several of the other studies hold constant age polynomials for parents and children.
2. "Relationship" is, for individual measures of economic status (schooling and earnings), the parent and child that are compared. "father-child" means that both sons and daughters are compared with their father.
3. Years refer to the twentieth century unless otherwise noted.
4. A "representative sample" is *intended* to represent the entire population of the location being studied. Of course, none of the samples are truly representative.
5. The "measurement error correction" column lists attempts to correct for errors in the measurement of parental economic status.
6. Mulligan (1997) estimates are for full SRC samples. See tables 7.2 and 7.3 for robustness of the Mulligan estimates to sample selection.

Family Consumption

This study is the only one to compute the degree of intergenerational consumption mobility. My estimates of β are as large as 0.81, which is larger than any study has found for earnings, income, or wealth.

Occupation

Sociologists were intensely interested in intergenerational or social mobility long before economists were.[23] An important part of the sociological literature includes quantitative estimates of "occupational mobility."[24] It is beyond the scope of this chapter to carefully review the occupational mobility literature, but I offer a few comments on that literature and how it relates to my study of the transmission of economic status.

A problem with empirical studies of occupational mobility is that their

23. See Reinhard Bendix and Seymour Lipset (1966) for an early collection of several interesting studies of social mobility.

24. Blau and Duncan (1967), Featherman and Hauser (1978), and Zimmerman (1992) are three very interesting studies of occupational mobility in the United States.

measures of economic or "social" status are often only very roughly related to "economic status" as represented in the economic models of intergenerational mobility presented in chapter 3 or to "social status" as represented in sociological models. For example, Seymour Lipset and Hans Zetterberg (1956), Thomas Fox and S. M. Miller (1965), and William Goode (1966) present quantitative estimates of intergenerational movements between two broad working classes: "manual" and "nonmanual." One society is considered to be more mobile than another if sons in the former society are more likely to belong to a different working class than their fathers. "Manual" and "nonmanual" classifications obviously provide only a very rough indication of a person's economic status. A great advantage of these kinds of measures of occupational mobility over the consumption, earnings, income and wealth mobility estimates that I present above is that the measures of occupational mobility can be obtained for many different countries and for many different time periods.

Table 7.9 presents Goode's (1966) mobility index for eighteen different countries. His index is computed from estimates of intergenerational transitions between the manual and nonmanual working classes. Although it is difficult to translate Goode's estimates into an estimate of intergenerational earnings mobility as defined in this and previous chapters, one thing is obvious from table 7.9—there is earnings mobility in a wide variety of countries. In each of the eighteen countries reviewed by Goode there is a sizable fraction of sons of manual-laborer fathers who became nonmanual workers.

It is possible to use occupation to obtain a better measure of economic or social status than is provided by the crude "manual"–"nonmanual" characterization. Zimmerman (1992) and others have used the Duncan occupational index. The Duncan index is an indirect measure of earnings, but it has some advantages over many direct earnings measures. First, the Duncan index may measure lifetime earnings better than does a single year's earnings because occupation is subject to fewer transitory fluctuations. Second, the Duncan index can be interesting because it may capture "nonpecuniary" aspects of jobs, such as prestige and pleasant working conditions, that make workers happy but need not be related to measured earnings. In regressions of a son's log Duncan index on his father's, Zimmerman (1992) finds a coefficient of about 0.3.

Measures of occupational mobility for several countries strongly support my conclusion that economic status regresses to the mean across generations. It is difficult, however, to relate the occupational mobility results to two other conclusions—that measurement error has led to an important overstatement of the degree of intergenerational mobility and that consumption is less mobile than earnings.

Table 7.9 Occupational Mobility in Eighteen Countries

Country	manual into nonmanual	Immobility Index
Great Britain	24.8	234
USSR	34.9	244
Australia	24.1	261
Denmark	24.1	262
France	30.1	264
Brazil	29.4	277
USA	28.8	279
Sweden	25.5	284
Netherlands	19.6	290
Japan	23.7	297
Norway	23.2	308
West Germany	20	355
India	27.3	368
Belgium	5.7	398
Puerto Rico	14.3	401
Hungary	14.5	500
Finland	11	691
Italy	8.5	747

Notes:

1. "Immobility index" is $100*x/y$ where x = share of sons of nonmanual fathers who became nonmanual and y = share of sons of manual fathers who became nonmanual.
2. "Manual into nonmanual" is $100*y$.
3. Countries are sorted according to the immobility index.

Source: Goode (1966, Table 1b).

Review of the Main Results

Previous studies of intergenerational earnings mobility have typically found a log earnings β in the range of 0.1 to 0. 4. However, Solon (1992) and others have suggested that the lower estimates suffer from measurement error bias. Couch and Dunn (1995) and Björklund & Jantti (1993) provide the only direct cross-country comparisons, finding roughly equal intergenerational earnings mobility in the United States and Germany but more earnings mobility in Sweden. Indirect comparisons of estimates of intergenerational mobility across countries do not reveal important cross-country differences. Income mobility estimates have typically been larger—in the neighborhood of 0.4 to 0.5, although direct comparisons of log earnings and log income β's are not always possible because they are not estimated with the same samples. Log wealth β's have also been larger, although they have almost always been estimated for samples of only very wealthy families.

I add to the existing literature in several ways. First, I make a variety of corrections for measurement error, including time-averaging and the use of several different instrumental variables. It is overwhelmingly clear that these techniques result in substantially higher estimates of the degree of intergenerational persistence. The intergenerational persistence of log wages is probably as high as 0.5. The corrections produce log income β's of about 0.6 and log consumption β's as large as 0.8. I estimate the intergenerational persistence of these various measures of economic status with a single sample of families, so direct comparisons of their magnitudes are available. Consumption regresses to the mean most slowly. Income regresses to the mean more rapidly and earnings or wages regress to the mean most rapidly. Because my estimates of β confirm only the highest estimates reported in previous studies, I must argue that the degree of intergenerational mobility has been overstated. Half—rather than one-third—of parental wage differences are typically observed among adult children.

Measurement error is not the only reason that previous studies have overstated the degree of intergenerational mobility. Previous studies have not looked at an important indicator of economic status—consumption. Consumption is very persistent across generations, with almost 80 percent of consumption differences persisting until the next generation.

Four Strongly Supported Conclusions

Chapters 6 and 7 present a wide variety of evidence on the intergenerational transmission of inequality. I arrive at four main conclusions: (1) the intergenerational persistence of earnings or wages has, mainly because of measurement errors, been understated by many previous microdata studies; (2) consumption, income, and wealth regress to the mean more slowly than do earnings and wages; (3) all measures of economic status regress to the mean across generations; and (4) intergenerational mobility is very similar within and across groups. Table 7.10 reviews my conclusions and the data that support them.

There are three types of evidence supporting the idea that measurement errors lead to an important overstatement of the degree of intergenerational earnings or wage mobility. The most direct evidence is micro data from the PSID, where enough information is available to time-average the parental data and to construct good instrumental variables. The slow narrowing of the black-white wage gap over the period of time from 1910 through 1985 is some aggregate evidence suggesting that wages regress to the mean fairly slowly. In fact, the estimate of 0.59 for the log wage β that was obtained in chapter 6 from the 1940 through 1985 black-white wage gaps is quite similar to the instrumental variables estimate of 0.53 that

Table 7.10 Four Quantitative Results on the Degree of Intergenerational Mobility

Claim	Supporting evidence
(1) the intergenerational persistence of earnings or wages has, mainly because of measurement errors, been understated by previous microdata studies	• U.S. micro data (PSID, NLSY) • black-white wage gaps 1910–85 • ethnic wage gaps 1910–40
(2) consumption, income, and wealth regress to the mean more slowly than do earnings and wages	• U.S. micro data (PSID, NLSY) • U.S. regional differences 1880–1988 • U.S. micro data from 1870 • Utah Mormon records 1860–70 • Connecticut probate records
(3) all measures of economic status regress to the mean across generations	• U.S. micro data (PSID, NLSY) • U.S. probate records 1774–1962 • U.S. cross-sectional wealth surveys 1922–81 • U.S. cross-sectional consumption surveys 1960–88 • U.S. cross-sectional earnings surveys 1940–85 • U.S. income tax records 1913–85 • narrowing black-white wage gap 1910–85 • narrowing ethnic wage gaps 1910–40 • declining cross-state inequality 1880–1988 • declining regional inequality in Europe (1880–1988) and Japan (1930–87) • British probate records 1740–1973 • Occupational mobility in eighteen countries (mid 1900s)
(4) intergenerational mobility is very similar within and across groups	• narrowing black-white wage gap 1940–80 • narrowing ethnic wage gaps 1910–40 • U.S. micro data (PSID, NLSY) • U.S. regional income differences 1880–1988 • European (1950–85) and Japanese (1930–87) regional income differences

Solon (1992) and I obtain with PSID micro data. George Borjas's (1994) estimates for other ethnic groups also suggest a log earnings β of 0.4 to 0. 6. These estimates are much larger than the estimates of 0.1 or 0.2 that have been previously obtained from micro data.

Income, wealth, and especially consumption appear to regress to the mean less rapidly than do earnings and wages. The PSID micro data again provide the easiest comparisons. I estimate log consumption β's as large as 0.8, which is larger than even the 0.59 obtained from the black-white wage gaps from the 1940–85 time period. In a single PSID sample, for example, I estimate a log wage β of 0.53, a log income β of 0.71, and a log consumption β of 0.72. Log wealth β's are between 0.5 and 0.6 in the PSID and are even larger in some probate studies.

With the exception of a broad cross-section of countries, all of the evidence presented in chapters 6 and 7 suggest that all measures of economic status regress to the mean across generations. Consumption regresses the most slowly, but it still regresses to the mean. 0.84 is about the largest log consumption β that I found in the PSID. Cross-sectional consumption data for the period of 1960 through 1988 suggest that consumption inequality does not grow over the long term, so that β cannot be as large as 1. A variety of cross-sectional wealth surveys from the United Kingdom and the United States suggest that wealth inequality has not grown over the long term so that it too must regress to the mean. Income inequality as measured from U.S. tax returns and from aggregate data on regional incomes has fallen over time. The failure to find long-term growing inequality in any of these various data sources strongly suggests that all of the measures of economic status must regress to the mean across generations.

Intergenerational mobility appears to be similar within and across groups. In other words, the poor catch up with the rich within a group (for example, poor white Americans catch up with rich white Americans) at about the same speed as poor groups catch up with rich groups. For example, Solon (1992), Zimmerman (1992), Mulligan (1996b), and others have estimated the intergenerational persistence of earnings or wages to be about 0.5 in micro data. Since the microdata samples consist mainly of white Americans, the 0.5 estimate is an estimate of intergenerational mobility "within a group."[25] If the same parameter applies across groups—which, in terms of the regression equation 3.1, requires that "other influences" ε, such as discrimination, average to zero within groups or be uncorrelated with average group income—then one should be able to use the 0.5 estimate to predict changing inequality across groups. The black-white wage gap, for example, was 84 percent in 1940 (Smith and Welch 1986, p. 5). By 1980, forty years and 1.6 generations have passed.[26] If the same parameter applies across groups, then the black-white wage gap should close by 50 percent per generation or 67 percent over 1.6 generations; the predicted wage gap for 1980 is 28 percent. In fact, the black-white wage gap has closed slightly more slowly over the period: it stood at 32 percent in 1980 (Smith and Welch 1986, p. 5). Twenty-eight out of thirty-two per-

25. Using my "All, Earnings" sample from the PSID, I estimate the intergenerational persistence of wages to be 0.49 for whites and 0.43 for blacks (these are IV estimates). The hypothesis that intergenerational earnings mobility is the same for blacks and whites cannot be rejected at the 95 percent confidence level.

26. I assume that each generation is separated by twenty-five years. 1.8 = 45/25.

centage points of the 1980 black-white wage gap can be explained by the fact that parents of black workers in 1980 were poorer than parents of white workers. Four percentage points are unexplained and may be due to discrimination in the labor market in 1980.[27]

I report in chapter 6 estimates by Borjas (1994) of intergenerational earnings mobility across ethnic groups for the period from 1910 to 1940. His estimates of β range from 0.4 to 0.6, which are similar to the within-group estimates of Solon (1992), Zimmerman (1992), Mulligan (1996b), and others. An important exception to my finding of similar intergenerational mobility within and across groups are the suggestions by Becker (1957) and Borjas (1994) that the black-white wage gap closed more slowly over the period of time from 1910 through 1940. The slow narrowing of the black-white gap over the early period is, in terms of the regression equation 3.1, consistent with the idea that "other influences" ε, such as discrimination, were especially important for blacks in 1940.

Solon (1992) and Mulligan (1996b) find the intergenerational persistence of family income to be as large as 0.6 in micro data. 0.6 is similar to the intergenerational persistence of family income across countries and regions that is implied by estimates in the macroeconomics literature.[28]

27. If we redo the calculation for the period of 1940 through 1985 or from 1940 to 1990, roughly ten percentage points are unexplained. The 1940–80 calculation may be more relevant from the point of view of intergenerational models because the widening of black-wage gap since 1980 may have to do with "short-run" forces that are unrelated to the intergenerational model. See, for example, Card and Lemieux (1994) for a discussion of some of those nonintergenerational forces. On the other hand, the 1940–85 calculation may be more comparable with the within-group estimates by Solon (1992), Zimmerman (1992), and Mulligan (this volume) because those papers study the earnings of adults in the mid 1980s.

Of course, the fact that blacks were poorer than whites in 1940 has to do with discrimination. My calculation may only separate the effects of past and present discrimination. For a different and more detailed calculation—but one with very similar results—see work by Derek Neal and William Johnson (1996).

28. Barro and Sala-i-Martin (1991; 1992b; 1995) estimate that per capita income gaps narrow at the rate of 2 percent per year across American regions, across European regions, and across Japanese regions. Assuming that generations are separated by twenty-five years, 2 percent per year is almost exactly 0.60 per generation. They find a slower rate than 2 percent per year across OECD countries. However, correcting for differences in some of the "other influences" across countries produces the result that per capita income gaps narrow at the rate of 2 percent per year across countries.

Another possible interpretation of the evidence in this section—one that is inconsistent with my interpretations (1) and (4)—is that previous microdata studies do *not* understate intergenerational persistence and that there is much less intergenerational mobility across groups than within groups. Because it deemphasizes measurement error, this alternative explanation has problems with some of the details of Solon's (1992) study, but might explain the high persistence estimates of Solon (1992), Zimmerman (1992), and Mulligan (1996) as artifacts of the uniqueness of the 1980s as a period in the history of inequality.

Two Tentative Conclusions

Is it possible that "progressive" income and estate taxes explain much intergenerational mobility in the United States? Two conclusions from my analysis of the persistence of inequality in chapters 6 and 7 suggest that the answer is "no." First, intergenerational mobility in the United States does not seem to have increased with the introduction of apparently progressive income and estate taxes since 1913. Figure 6.9, for example, suggests that regional income inequality in the United States declined just as rapidly before 1920 as after.[29] Microdata estimates of intergenerational wealth mobility before 1920 by Harbury and Hitchens (1979), Kearl and Pope (1986), and Wahl (1985) suggest very similar intergenerational mobility in the earlier period. Second, intergenerational earnings and income mobility may not vary across countries. Estimates of intergenerational income, earnings and wealth for Britain, Germany, and Sweden do not seem to be very different from estimates for the United States. An exception is the study by Björklund and Jantti comparing the United States and Sweden.[30] Estimates of occupational mobility reported in table 7.9 seem to be quite similar, with the exceptions of Belgium, Puerto Rico, Hungary, Finland, and Italy. However, much more research on both nineteenth-and twentieth-century comparisons and cross-country comparisons of intergenerational mobility and the progressivity of tax systems are necessary to arrive at a strong conclusion regarding the unimportance of taxes for intergenerational mobility.

Appendix D: Some PSID Results with an Alternative Measure of Consumption

Table 7.11 estimates intergenerational consumption mobility using food consumption (the sum of expenditures on food eaten at home and food eaten away from home). Jonathan Skinner (1987) shows that his proxy for nondurable consumption (which I use in the text) is a much better predictor of actual nondurable consumption than is food consumption. Given that food consumption is a highly error-ridden measure of nondurable consumption, it is therefore not surprising that OLS estimates of the intergenerational persistence of food consumption—displayed in columns 1 and 3 in table 7.11—are smaller than the corresponding estimates of the

29. See Sala-i-Martin (1990) for some direct evidence for the hypothesis that government transfers cannot explain much of the decline of regional income inequality.

30. Soltow's (1965) study of income mobility in Sweden produces a very low estimate of β, but it is not clear that his sample and methods are comparable with those of the studies that I cite for the United States.

Table 7.11 OLS and IV Results for Food Consumption

	Estimation Method			
Sample	OLS	IV	OLS	IV
All	0.32	0.64	0.35	0.57
	(0.04)	(0.06)	(0.04)	(0.06)
Fathers observed	0.36	0.61	0.35	0.56
1968–72	(0.04)	(0.06)	(0.04)	(0.06)
SRC only	0.37	0.70	0.35	0.55
	(0.04)	(0.09)	(0.05)	(0.07)
Sons only	0.35	0.63	0.37	0.52
	(0.05)	(0.09)	(0.05)	(0.08)
subsample	All	All	Earnings	Earnings

Notes:

1. Reported are coefficients on log parental family food consumption in a regression of log adult child's family food consumption on a dummy for daughters, parental and child marriage variables, and a quadratic in both the child and the parental head-of-household's age. The parental marriage variable is the number of years that the economic status of parents was measured and the father was present. The child marriage variable is included only for the family measures of economic status and is the fraction of years that the child's status is measured and the child is married or cohabitating. Standard errors are in parentheses.
2. Food consumption is measured in some of the years 1984–87 for adult children and in 1969–72 for parents.

intergenerational persistence of Skinner's proxy for nondurable consumption that I report in the text.

IV estimates of the intergenerational persistence of food consumption are substantially higher than the OLS estimates but somewhat smaller than the estimates reported in the text using Skinner's proxy. Nevertheless, the main conclusions from the text are robust to the use of food expenditure as the measure of consumption. In particular, consumption regresses to the mean across generations, consumption is more persistent than earnings, and previous studies appear to have overstated the degree of intergenerational mobility.

CHAPTER 8

Borrowing Constraints and the Persistence of Inequality

The borrowing constraints model described in chapter 3 is the most standard economic model of intergenerational mobility.[1] This chapter tests some of the implications of the intergenerational borrowing constraints model. In particular, the presence of borrowing constraints affects the rate of regression to the mean of consumption and earnings or wages in the following ways:

(1) Among families that are making financial intergenerational transfers, consumption does not regress to the mean at all.
(2) Earnings regress to the mean *more* rapidly among families that are making financial transfers.
(3) Earnings of adult children are less unequal across families that make financial transfers.
(4) Richer parents are more likely to make financial transfers to children.

Notice that these implications distinguish two groups of families—one that makes financial transfers and another that does not. The second group wishes to borrow against the earnings of children in order to finance parental consumption and human capital investments for children (that is, make negative rather than positive financial transfers), but they cannot do so because of the assumed borrowing constraint. These implications are an interesting contrast to the permanent income model—where all families make financial transfers of some kind—as well as more mechanical models of intergenerational mobility, such as those reviewed by Arthur

1. The borrowing constraints assumption is at the center of the Becker and Tomes (1986), Bénabou (1994), Durlauf (1996), Glomm and Ravikumar (1992), Loury (1981), and Tamura (1991) models of intergenerational mobility.

Goldberger (1989) that make no distinction between families that do and do not participate in financial markets. More subtle versions of these hypotheses are also considered.

Consider the following generational model of a economic characteristic X:

$$\ln X^i_{t+1} = \begin{cases} (constant) + \gamma \ln X^i_t + \varepsilon^i_{t+1} & \textit{if } \ln c^i_{t+1} \geq \ln e^{i*}_{t+1} \\ \dfrac{\beta}{\gamma}(constant) + \dfrac{\gamma - \beta}{\gamma}\phi \ln e^{i*}_{t+1} & \\ & \textit{if } \ln c^i_{t+1} < \ln e^{i*}_{t+1} \\ + \beta \ln X^i_t + \dfrac{\beta}{\gamma}\varepsilon^i_{t+1} & \end{cases} \quad (8.1)$$

X can be interpreted as either consumption or earnings. e^{i*}_{t+1} denotes that level of the child's consumption where parents switch from human capital transfers to financial transfers. e^{i*}_{t+1} varies across families because it depends on the ability of the child. ε^i_{t+1} includes surprises, family-specific degrees of intergenerational altruism, and measurement errors. The (constant) term is the same across families and, under the consumption interpretation, depends on the common component of altruism and the expected rate of return on financial assets. $\phi = 1$ ($\phi = 0$) when X is measured as consumption (earnings).

Under both the consumption and earnings interpretations of X, the intergenerational mobility parameter is allowed to differ for two groups. The first group consists of families of children who consume more than the efficient level of earnings. The second group consists of all other families. According to the permanent income model, intergenerational mobility should be the same for the two groups. The borrowing constraints model, on the other hand, predicts that borrowing constraint will bind for the second group of families. As summarized by items (1) and (2) above, earnings are predicted to be less mobile in the second group and consumption is predicted to be more mobile. A unique prediction of the borrowing constraints model is therefore that $\beta \neq \gamma$.

The model shown in equation 8.1 assumes a particular functional form—the log of a child's consumption (or earnings) is assumed to be linearly related to the log of his parents' consumption (or earnings). I choose this functional form for two reasons. First, it is the most common specification reported in the empirical literature.[2] More important, the

2. Examples include those provided by Gary Solon (1992), who regresses a son's log earnings on the log of his father's earnings, and those used by Paul Menchik (1979), who regresses the log of a son's wealth on the log of his father's wealth.

model shown in equation 8.1 is consistent with the qualitative features shown in figures 3.7 and 3.13 of *both* the permanent income and borrowing constraints models. To see this for the case when X is measured as consumption, consider figure 8.1. The left panel graphs two expansion paths in the [ln c_t, ln c_{t+1}] plane according to the mathematical model 8.1. Notice that the panel is similar to figure 3.13 except that a logarithmic scale is used. If one begins at low levels of income (and therefore low levels of consumption for both generations) and considers increases in income by following a single expansion path, the expansion path has slope β for low levels of income. If $\beta < 1$, then the ratio c_{t+1}/c_t is falling as income rises. When one reaches the level of income corresponding with log child consumption of log e^{i*}_{t+1}, parents make financial bequests and the expansion path increases its slope from β to γ. If $\gamma = 1$, then the ratio c_{t+1}/c_t is constant along this segment of the expansion path. If $\beta < \gamma < 1$, then the ratio falls but less rapidly than on the β-sloped portion of the path.

The right panel graphs the same information in the [c_t, c_{t+1}] plane under the assumption that $\beta < \gamma = 1$. Notice that, qualitatively, it is identical to figure 3.13. Beginning at the origin, the ratio c_{t+1}/c_t falls as income rises. At the level of income corresponding with child consumption of e^{i*}_{t+1}, parents make financial bequests, and the ratio c_{t+1}/c_t remains constant for further increases in income. This shows that the mathematical model 8.1 shares all of its qualitative properties with the model displayed in figure 3.13.

The different intergenerational models analyzed in chapters 3 through 5 can be thought of as special cases of the mathematical model 8.1, where those models differ from each other according to their predictions for β and γ. They also have different predictions for how the error term ε_{t+1} should be related to parental consumption and other variables. Those predictions are summarized in table 8.1. The rest of this chapter is concerned with statistical tests of the validity of those predictions.

Eight different cases are displayed in the table according to whether there is an unobserved component of altruism, whether there are borrowing constraints, and whether intergenerational altruism is related to parental income. Consider the upper left portion of the top panel, which corresponds to no borrowing constraint, no unobserved component of altruism, and altruism that is independent of parental income. Because there is no borrowing constraint, one must have $\gamma = \beta$. $\gamma = 1$ because intergenerational altruism is independent of parental income. cov(ε_{t+1}, x_{t+1}) = 0 because there is no unobserved component of altruism. Introducing a borrowing constraint corresponds to a movement to the right-hand column in table 8.1 and means that $\beta < \gamma$. Allowing intergenerational altruism to be negatively related to parental income means that $\gamma < 1$,

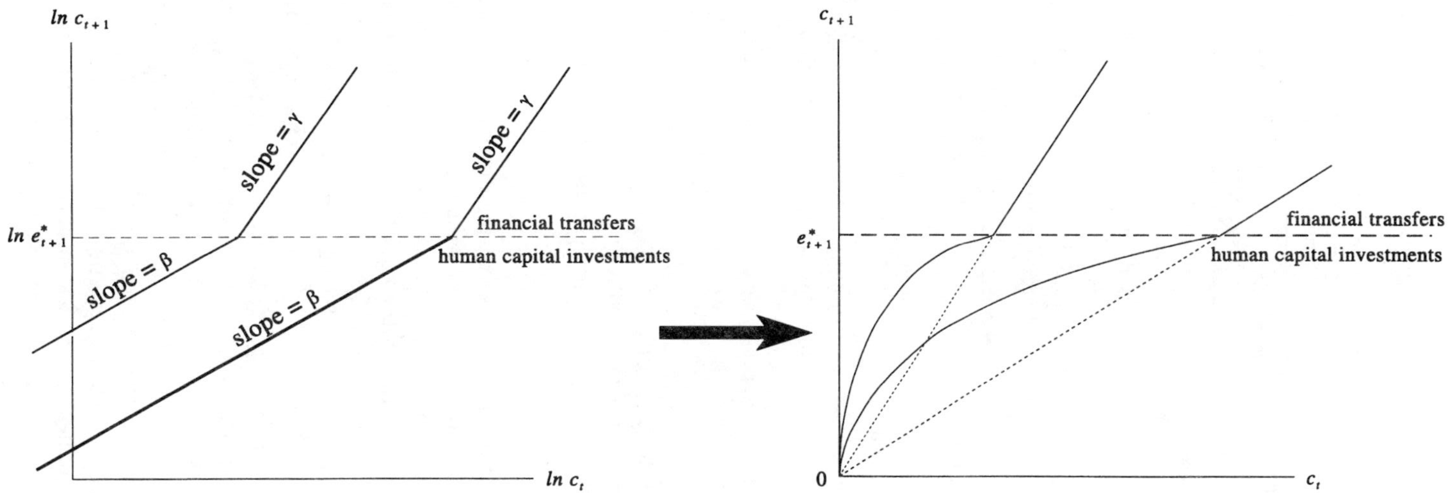

8.1 Expansion Paths for the Mathematical Model: the [ln c_t, ln c_{t+1}] and [c_t, c_{t+1}] Planes

Table 8.1 Predictions of Eight Intergenerational Consumption Models

	Permanent Income	Borrowing Constraint
	No unobserved component of altruism	
IG altruism independent of parental income	$\gamma = 1$ $\beta = 1$ $\text{cov}(\varepsilon_{t+1}, x_{t+1}) = 0$	$\gamma = 1$ $\beta < 1$ $\text{cov}(\varepsilon_{t+1}, x_{t+1}) = 0$
IG altruism a (−) function of parental income	$\gamma < 1$ $\beta = \gamma$ $\text{cov}(\varepsilon_{t+1}, x_{t+1}) = 0$	$\gamma < 1$ $\beta < \gamma$ $\text{cov}(\varepsilon_{t+1}, x_{t+1}) = 0$
	Unobserved components of altruism	
IG alruism independent of parental income	$\gamma = 1$ $\beta = 1$ $\text{cov}(\varepsilon_{t+1}, x_{t+1}) > 0$	$\gamma = 1$ $\beta < 1$ $\text{cov}(\varepsilon_{t+1}, x_{t+1}) > 0$
IG altruism a (−) function of parental income	$\gamma < 1$ $\beta = \gamma$ $\text{cov}(\varepsilon_{t+1}, x_{t+1}) > 0$	$\gamma < 1$ $\beta < \gamma$ $\text{cov}(\varepsilon_{t+1}, x_{t+1}) > 0$

Notes:

1. $\text{cov}(\varepsilon_{t+1}, x_{t+1})$ denotes the population covariance between the consumption error term and financial transfers. Groups-specific linear regression estimates are subject to "selection bias" when $\text{cov}(\varepsilon_{t+1}, x_{t+1}) \neq 0$. The bias is likely to be larger for the smaller group.
2. β and γ are the parameters in equation 8.1 when X is measured as consumption.
3. e^*_{t+1} is assumed to be the same for all families. If e^*_{t+1} varies in a way that is uncorrelated with parental income, then Group 2 regression estimates of β are subject to "selection bias." See chapter 3 for more discussion and Han and Milligan (1997) for algebraic and numerical analyses.

which can be seen in table 8.1 by moving down to the lower portion (of either the top or bottom panel). Introducing unobserved components of altruism means that the unobserved determinants of a child's consumption—shown as ε_{t+1} in the mathematical model—will be correlated with the giving of financial bequests. This final point can be seen in the table by moving from the upper panel to the lower panel.

Table 8.2 summarizes the predictions of two intergenerational earnings mobility models: earnings regress to the mean across generations regardless of borrowing constraints ($\beta, \gamma < 1$), and earnings regress to the mean more rapidly among families that make financial transfers.

Tables 8.1 and 8.2 review implications of the models analyzed in chapters 3 through 5 for intergenerational consumption and earnings mobility, but those models also make predictions for cross-sectional consumption and earnings inequality. Table 8.3 summarizes. When intergenerational altruism is independent of parental income, consumption inequality grows

Table 8.2 Predictions of Two Intergenerational Earnings Models

Permanent income	Borrowing Constraint
$\gamma = \beta < 1$ $\text{cov}(\varepsilon_{t+1}, x_{t+1}) < 0$	$\gamma < \beta < 1$ $\text{cov}(\varepsilon_{t+1}, x_{t+1}) < 0$

Notes:

1. $\text{cov}(\varepsilon_{t+1}, x_{t+1})$ denotes the population covariance between the earnings error term and financial transfers.
2. β and γ are the parameters in equation 8.1 when X is measured as earnings or wages.
3. e^*_{t+1} is assumed to be the same for all families. If e^*_{t+1} varies in a way that is uncorrelated with parental earnings, then Group-specific estimates of β and γ are subject to "selection bias." If e^*_{t+1} is correlated with parental earnings, then Group 2 estimates of β are subject to "omitted variable bias."

Table 8.3 Predictions for Consumption and Earnings Inequality

	Permanent income	Borrowing Constraint
IG altruism independent of parental income	• consumption inequality grows without bound • child earnings inequality is independent of x_{t+1}	• consumption inequality grows more rapidly in Group 1 • child earnings inequality is greater among the borrowing constrained
IG altruism a (−) function of parental income	• consumption inequality does not grow without bound • child earnings inequality is independent of x_{t+1}	• child earnings inequality is greater among the borrowing constrained

Note: x_{t+1} denotes financial transfers from parents to child.

without bound in the permanent income model and more rapidly in Group 1 in the borrowing constraints model. As discussed in chapter 6, these predictions are closely related to the $\gamma = 1$ prediction. Intergenerational altruism that is negatively related to parental income means that richer parents tend to give a smaller fraction of their resources to their children—a force which produces regression to the mean and stabilizes inequality in both the permanent income and borrowing constraints versions of the models. Borrowing constraints do affect the degree of earnings inequality; earnings are more unequal among the adult children of financially constrained families than among the children of families that make financial transfers ($x_{t+1} \neq 0$).

Two Data Sources

I use data on PSID parents and their adult children to obtain estimates of γ, β, and cov(ε_{t+1}, x_{t+1}) and therefore suggest which of the models summarized in tables 8.1, 8.2, and 8.3 might be more realistic. In addition to the PSID, I use two waves of the Federal Reserve's Survey of Consumer Finances (SCF) to look at the relationship between the receipt of financial transfers and earnings inequality among adult children. The SCF is not an intergenerational sample—it does not include information on the economic situation of both parents and their adult children—but it does provide information on adults who have (and have not) received or expected to receive an inheritance. Without the ability to make intergenerational comparisons, the SCF has the disadvantage that the implications (1) and (2) cannot be tested. However, the SCF does provide an additional data source for testing (3) and (4). Moreover, the SCF offers more information about inheritances, so tests of (3) are more convincing.

I divide my PSID and SCF samples into two groups:

Group 1: Adult children who have received, or expect to receive, an inheritance of $25,000 or more.
Group 2: Adult children who have not received, and do not expect to receive, an inheritance of $25,000 or more.

According to a literal interpretation of the theory, Groups 1 and 2 should be defined according to $x_{t+1} > 0$ and $x_{t+1} = 0$. A financial inheritance of $500 would place a family in Group 1 according to the literal interpretation. This may not be a satisfactory way to map the data into the model because the *only* role for inheritances in the model is to provide for the consumption of children. In reality, inheritances may serve other purposes. This may be especially true for very small inheritances, which, for example, may be received by children to pay funeral expenses of parents. I therefore define Groups 1 and 2 according to $x_{t+1} \geq \$25,000$ and $x_{t+1} < \$25,000$.

The adult children in my PSID sample were in their thirties at the time that they reported their inheritance or expectation of an inheritance. Some of these children, of course, are not expecting an inheritance but—due to unforeseen circumstances—may receive an inheritance later in life. Or some children may expect an inheritance but never actually receive one. Nevertheless, I believe that it is the *expectation* of an inheritance that is most relevant to the Becker-Tomes model. Remember that the purpose of measuring inheritances is to determine whether or not parents were financially constrained *when human capital investments were made for the children.* It is very likely that the parents of an adult child who, between the ages of twenty-five and forty, has received or expects to receive an inheritance were not financially constrained when they were making human capital investments for the child. Because financial surprises can occur as parents and child age, it is less likely that the parents of an adult child of age fifty or sixty who receives or expects to receive an inheritance were financially unconstrained many years earlier when human capital investments for the child were made. Figure 8.2 displays a histogram of the amounts inherited by adult children in my intergenerational PSID sample. Both actual and expected inheritances are included in the tabulation. The data is grouped on a proportional scale, with the brackets defined as \$1–249, \$250–499, \$500–999, \$1,000–1,999, \$2,000–3,999, \$4,000–7,999, \$8,000–15,999, \$16,000–31,999, \$32,000–63,999, \$64,000–127,999, \$128,000–255,999, \$256,000–511,999, and \$512,000 and above. Twenty-four percent of the overall sample is tabulated in the figure; the other 76 percent neither have nor expect an inheritance.

Figure 8.3 displays data from the 1989 Survey of Consumer Finances. Because the Survey of Consumer Finances oversamples the rich, the SCF respondents are more likely to have received or to expect an inheritance

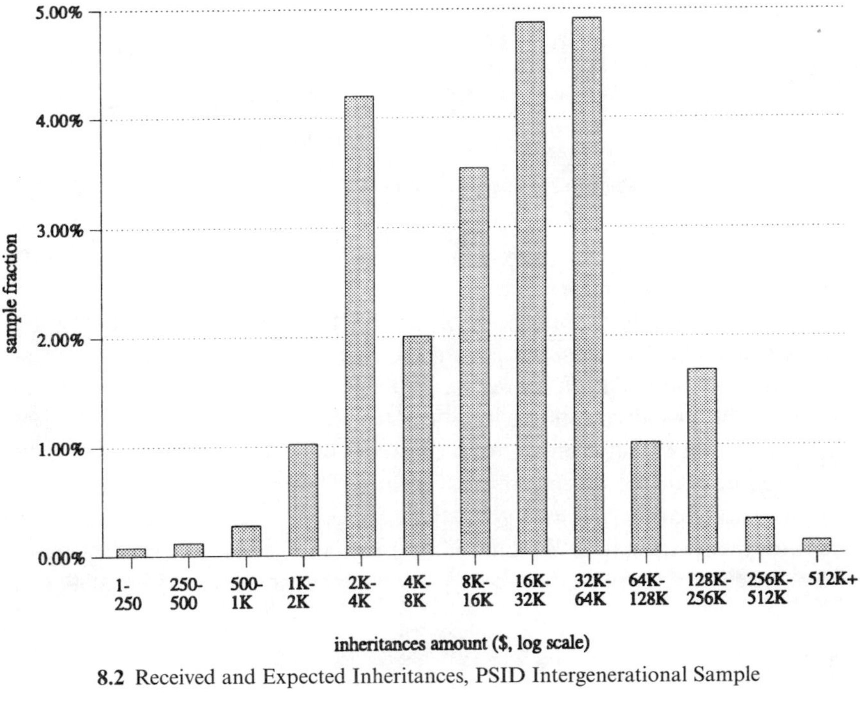

8.2 Received and Expected Inheritances, PSID Intergenerational Sample

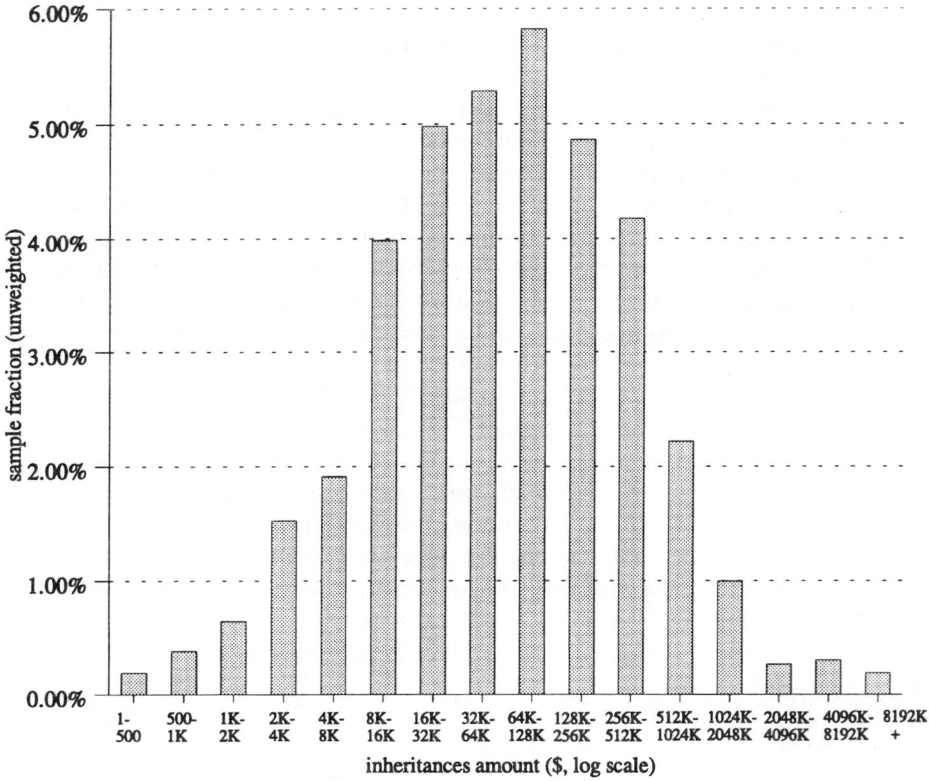

8.3 Inheritances Received or Expected by 1989 SCF Respondents Aged 25 to 35

and, among those who have, inheritances are larger than in the PSID sample.

It is not possible to determine which PSID respondents received their inheritance from a parent or grandparent rather than a friend or distant relative, but information from the SCF suggests that inheritances from parents and grandparents are the most common.[3] Table 8.4 shows that 78 percent of adults between the ages of twenty-five and thirty-five who have received inheritances received them from parents or grandparents.

Figures 8.2 and 8.3 also suggest that, although several adult children in my intergenerational PSID sample and my SCF cross-sectional samples have received or expected to receive inheritances in excess of $25,000, it is

3. Presumably inheritances from parents and grandparents are those most relevant for intergenerational models.

Table 8.4 Relationship to Bequeathors in the SCF (Inheritor between the ages of 25 and 35)

relationship	share of inheritances
parent	47%
grandparent	31%
aunt or uncle	7%
sibling	1%
friend	5%
other	9%

Note: SCF respondents are weighted to represent the entire U.S. population aged 25 to 35.

unlikely that more than a few were subject to the progressive Federal Estate Tax. In 1987, the Federal Estate Tax applied to estates (net of charitable and other deductions) in excess of $600,000.[4] An estate of $600,000 after charitable and other deductions could, for example, be divided among three nondeductible beneficiaries (for example, three children) without being subject to the Federal Estate Tax. If one of these children reported truthfully to the PSID (and the $200,000 was his only inheritance), an inheritance of $200,000 would appear in figure 8.2.[5] Most of the inheritances shown in the figures are less than $200,000, so it seems unlikely that a graduated-rate Federal Estate Tax is an important force producing regression to the mean among Group 1 families in any of my samples.

Because of the estate tax, the amount of inheritances probably understate the quantity of financial transfers. Estate and gift taxation can be avoided by spreading financial transfers over time in amounts less than $20,000 per year per beneficiary. Donors can also pay for the medical or educational expenses of a beneficiary without being liable for an estate or gift tax.

How do the inheritances in my PSID sample compare with those in the U.S. population as a whole? It is hard to answer this question precisely,

4. An "estate" is all of the property of a decedent. An "inheritance" is the receipt of property by a *particular* beneficiary from a decedent. The estate is therefore the taxes plus the sum of all beneficiaries' inheritances.

The Federal Estate Tax has changed several times over its history. I point out a few recent years: the tax applied to estates (net of charitable and other deductions) in excess of $60,000 in 1976, $120,667 in 1977, and $600,000 after 1986 (McNulty 1994, pp. 6–7).

5. If families use the marital deduction, these figures can double. A couple can have a taxable estate of $1.2 million and not pay estate taxes. For example, they could have three children that receive inheritances of $400,000 each. As I mention below, these figures still don't include the annual exclusion of *inter vivos* gifts.

but there are a couple of qualitative similarities between my sample and the overall U.S. population. First, a majority of people never receive an inheritance. Second, very few families pay inheritance taxes. That these are true for the U.S. population is suggested by the fact that, over the period of 1960 through 1995, estate tax returns were filed on behalf of roughly 5 to 10 percent of adults who died after age forty-five.[6] Less than one-third of estate tax returns filed actually owe tax.[7]

Another way to get an idea about the representativeness of the PSID sample is to compare it with the 1989 SCF sample. Like PSID respondents, SCF respondents answer questions about inheritances in 1989. The SCF also oversamples richer families, so the SCF data sets include a larger number of Group 1 families than does the PSID sample. The Federal Reserve reports the sampling weights, so one can determine whether the PSID and the SCF are sampling similar populations.[8] For example, 15 percent of adult children from the PSID-SRC intergenerational sample have received an inheritance; 4 percent have inheritances that exceed $25,000.[9] By comparison, 16 percent of 1989 SCF respondents between the ages of twenty-five and thirty-five have received inheritances while 7 percent have received inheritances that exceed $25,000.[10] The PSID-SRC and weighted SCF figures are quite similar, so I see no reason to strongly suspect that the PSID is unrepresentative of inheritances.

Because the SCF oversamples richer families, it allows one to study behavior for a variety of income groups. For example, one can investigate the Becker-Tomes hypothesis that inheritances occur in richer families. Figure 8.4 breaks 1989 SCF families into 100 family income groups. For each group, the fraction of families that have received or expect to receive more than $25,000 of inheritances is computed. Note that richer families

6. Number of estate tax returns from U.S. Treasury, IRS, *Statistics of Income: Estate Tax Returns,* various issues. Number of deaths by age from U.S. Commerce Department.

According to current rules, an estate tax return must be filed if a person dies with a gross estate (before deductions, exemptions, and exclusions) of $600,000 or more (U.S. Department of the Treasury, IRS, 1995a; 1995b).

7. U.S. Treasury, IRS, *Statistics of Income: Estate Tax Returns,* various issues.

8. Both are *intended* to draw a sample from the entire U.S. population, but—because not all contacted families respond—it is possible that the samples turn out to be unrepresentative. Nonresponse is likely to be a bigger problem for the PSID where families are asked to participate in the survey for many years in a row.

9. These PSID figures do not included expected inheritances. Thirty-one percent of adult PSID-SRC children report positive actual or expected inheritances; 16 percent report actual and expected inheritances that total $25,000 or more.

10. The SCF figures are weighted to account for the oversampling of rich families. The unweighted percentages are 19 percent and 9 percent, respectively. The weighted percentages are 38 percent and 31 percent when both actual and expected inheritances are included.

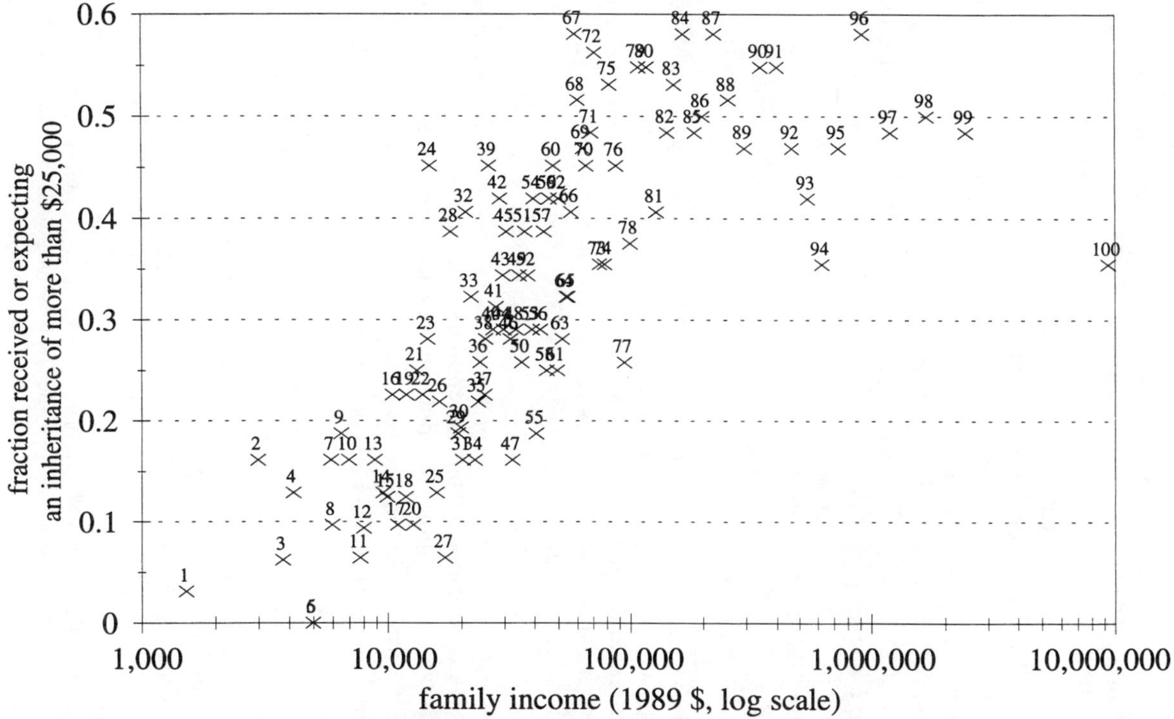

8.4 Receipt of Inheritance versus the Family Income of the Recipient

are more likely to receive inheritances.[11] Less than 20 percent of families with less than \$20,000 annual income receive or expect to receive sizable inheritances. Roughly 30 percent of families with annual incomes of \$20,000 through \$100,000 receive or expect to receive sizable inheritances. About 50 percent of families with an annual income of more than \$100,000 receive or expect to receive sizable inheritances.

The Becker-Tomes prediction (4) appears to be correct. A finding of a strong relationship between family income and receipt of an inheritance also suggests that parental income—and not the ability of children—is an important determinant of the way in which parents transfer resources to children. If the ability of the child primarily determined whether a child received a human capital or a financial transfer, then low-income children would be receiving inheritances.[12] This result is relevant for interpretation of some of the results reported below.

Simple Regression Results for Consumption

I regress the log of the adult child's consumption on the log of the parents' consumption, marriage variables and age polynomials for the parents and the children, and a gender dummy for the adult child. The regressions are estimated separately for the two groups to obtain separate estimates of β and γ. Four results are suggested by table 8.5. First, as was suggested in table 7.2, consumption is more persistent across generations than is earnings. Second—and this was also seen in table 7.2, more persistence of consumption is observed when parental income is used as an instrument for parental consumption. The difference between the OLS and IV estimates is consistent with unobserved components of altruism or with errors in the measurement of parental consumption. Third, there is a slight indication that—as predicted by the imperfect capital markets models—consumption regresses to the mean more slowly among families that are making financial bequests ($\beta < \gamma$). This is suggested by the IV results for the SRC sample. The coefficient on parental log consumption is 0.90 for Group 1 and 0.74 for Group 2. OLS and other IV results, on the other hand, do not suggest $\beta < \gamma$.[13] Fourth, log consumption appears to regress

11. The definition of family income here includes asset income that may accrue from past inheritances. However, figure 8.3 shows that those inheritances are not large enough to produce so much income, such that most of the family income variation in figure 8.3 is not from inheritances.

12. See chapter 3 or Appendix A for a derivation of this result in a mathematical model.

13. Recall from table 8.1 that, in the permanent income model, $\beta = \gamma$ but Group-specific estimates of β and γ are subject to downward selection bias when there are unobserved components of altruism. Since Group 1 is smaller than Group 2, it is likely that the selection bias is more serious in Group 1. In this case, the permanent income model is consistent with an estimated γ that is *less* than estimated β.

Table 8.5 Separate Regression Results for Consumption

			OLS		IV	
Sample	Sample Size		Group 1: $x_{t+1} \geq$ \$25,000	Group 2: $x_{t+1} <$ \$25,000	Group 1: $x_{t+1} \geq$ \$25,000	Group 2: $x_{t+1} <$ \$25,000
All	219	1562	0.45	0.55	0.65	0.70
			(0.08)	(0.03)	(0.12)	(0.04)
Fathers observed	169	1146	0.43	0.56	0.57	0.68
1968–72			(0.09)	(0.03)	(0.12)	(0.04)
SRC only	135	739	0.63	0.58	0.90	0.74
			(0.10)	(0.04)	(0.15)	(0.06)
Sons only	106	761	0.41	0.55	0.65	0.71
			(0.12)	(0.05)	(0.17)	(0.06)

Notes:

1. Results are obtained from the "All" subsample.

2. Reported are coefficients on log parental family consumption in a regression of log adult child's family consumption on a dummy for daughters parental and child marriage variables, and a quadratic in both the child and the parental head-of-household's age. Standard errors are in parentheses.

to the mean even among those families making sizable financial transfers. Group 1 coefficients on log parental consumption range from 0.57 for the "fathers observed" sample to 0.90 for the SRC only sample. A Group 1 coefficient of one can be rejected in most cases, whereas the models with exogenous altruism suggest a coefficient of one. According to the regression results, there appears to be a situation of $\beta = \gamma < 1$, which is inconsistent with intergenerational altruism that is independent of parental income and with borrowing constraints.

Analysis of Selection Bias

In order for the regressions reported in table 8.5 to deliver valid estimates of β and γ, there must not be important differences across families in unobserved components of intergenerational altruism. Otherwise Groups 1 and 2 would fail to be random samples.[14] Poor Group 1 families would tend to have higher than average rates of intergenerational altruism while rich Group 1 families would have more or less average rates. It would therefore appear that, within Group 1, consumption of the child varies less with parental consumption than is dictated by the parameter γ. Nonrandomness has similar effects on Group 2 regression estimates of β because

14. Another selection bias occurs in Group 2 when e^{*}_{t+1} varies across families.

rich Group 2 families have lower than average rates of intergenerational altruism. Because OLS estimates of both β and γ are biased downward, it is unclear how selection affects estimates of $(\gamma - \beta)$, although one expects the bias of γ to be greater because Group 1 is smaller than Group 2. It is more clear that selection may generate OLS estimates of γ that are less than one when in fact $\gamma = 1$.

Correcting for the possible nonrandomness of the Group 1 sample is not easy. I propose three separate strategies:[15]

(1) Assume that the unobserved component of altruism is lognormally distributed across PSID families.
(2) Consider regressions of $\ln c_{t+1}$ on $\ln c_t$ in a sample that pools both Groups 1 and 2.
(3) Examine the evolution of cross-family Group 1 variance of consumption from generation to generation.

I report the results of the three approaches in the remainder of this section.

Maximum Likelihood Estimates

Table 8.6 reports maximum likelihood estimates of γ and β based on the assumption that the unobservables of the model—unobserved components of altruism, measurement errors, earning ability, and income surprises—are lognormally distributed across families. The maximum likelihood estimates are not very different from the regression estimates. First, most estimates of γ (Group 1) are somewhat smaller than estimates of β (Group 2)—a finding inconsistent with important effects of borrowing constraints on the degree of intergenerational mobility. Second, estimates of γ are smaller than 1. Because they do not differ substantially from the regression estimates, the maximum likelihood estimates suggest that there is not an important covariance between financial bequests and the degree of intergenerational altruism. Remember from table 8.1 that $\beta = \gamma < 1$ and $\text{cov}(\varepsilon_{t+1}, x_{t+1}) = 0$ is consistent with a permanent income model with intergenerational altruism that varies across families in a way that is strongly correlated with parental income. Even with $\gamma > \beta$, borrowing constraints cannot explain all intergenerational mobility because $\gamma < 1$.

15. A fourth strategy would be to separate families according to parental income or to estimate nonlinear versions of equation 7.1. According to the borrowing constraints model, intergenerational consumption (earnings) mobility should fall (rise) with parental income since more Group 1 families are associated with high parental income. As I reported in chapter 7, I find no evidence of such nonlinearities, although some other earnings studies have.

Table 8.6 Maximum Likelihood Estimates

Sample	Sample Size		No instruments for parental consumption: Group 1: $x_{t+1} \geq$ \$25,000	No instruments for parental consumption: Group 2: $x_{t+1} <$ \$25,000	Parental income as an instrument for parental consumption: Group 1: $x_{t+1} \geq$ \$25,000	Parental income as an instrument for parental consumption: Group 2: $x_{t+1} <$ \$25,000
All	219	1562	0.46	0.54	0.38	0.76
			(0.11)	(0.03)	(0.13)	(0.05)
Fathers observed 1968–72	169	1146	0.43	0.55	0.36	0.73
			(0.13)	(0.03)	(0.14)	(0.05)
SRC only	135	739	0.63	0.58	0.78	0.73
			(0.31)	(0.04)	(0.17)	(0.06)
Sons only	106	761	0.42	0.55	0.58	0.72
			(0.13)	(0.05)	(0.19)	(0.07)

Notes:

1. Results are obtained from the "All" subsample.

2. Reported are coefficients on log parental family consumption in a "regression equation" of log adult child's family consumption on a dummy for daughters, parental and child marriage variables, and a quadratic in both the child and the parental head-of-household's age. Standard errors are in parentheses.

3. The statistical model also includes a "selection equation" and, in the IV case, a "prediction equation" for parental consumption. Likelihood functions are displayed in Appendix E.

Pooled versus Separate Regressions

The regression estimates of β shown in table 8.5 are subject to downward selection bias. If Groups 1 and 2 are pooled and a single intergenerational persistence parameter is estimated, there is no selection problem, but that parameter is presumably an average of β and γ. Another approach to the selection problem, therefore, is to compare the estimates of β shown in table 8.5 with a pooled estimate. Under the joint hypothesis of selection bias and $\beta < \gamma$, the pooled estimate should be larger. Instead, the pooled IV estimates of 0.71, 0.68, 0.77, and 0.72 are very similar to the IV estimates for Group 2 shown in table 8.5 (0.70, 0.68, 0.74, 0.71). If $\gamma = \beta$ and there is a selection bias, then the pooled estimates reported in tables 7.2 and 7.3 should not be very different from the Group-specific estimates reported in table 8.5.

Growing Consumption Inequality in the Two Groups

There are four factors that determine measured consumption inequality among children in each of the two groups. The first is parental consump-

Table 8.7 The Intergenerational Transmission of Consumption Inequality in Groups 1 and 2

	Group 1: $x_{t+1} \geq \$25,000$		Group 2: $x_{t+1} < \$25,000$	
Sample	inequality among sons	inter-generational growth	inequality among sons	inter-generational growth
All	0.49	1.28	0.57	1.40
Fathers observed 1968–72	0.47	1.24	0.53	1.23
SRC only	0.47	1.37	0.50	1.27
Sons only	0.49	1.26	0.59	1.44

Note: Consumption inequality within each generation of group is measured at the standard deviation of log consumption that cannot be explained by age and marriage variables. The ratio of consumption inequality for sons to that for fathers is also displayed in the table.

tion inequality because the consumption of parents and children are correlated. Second, unequal "other influences" create inequality among children. Third, measurement error can cause measured inequality to seem larger than actual consumption inequality. Fourth, "selection bias"—the tendency for poor Group 1 parents to be more altruistic than average and for rich Group 2 parents to be less altruistic than average—reduces inequality among children within each Group. Suppose that inequality in "other influences" and "measurement errors" are the same in the two Groups. Notice that, according to the borrowing constraints model, $\gamma > \beta$, so parental consumption inequality contributes more to consumption inequality among children in Group 1. If the selection bias is not too different in the two groups in terms of its contribution to inequality among children, then the borrowing constraints model predicts that consumption inequality grows more rapidly (or falls more slowly) across generations for Group 1 families because consumption inequality is more persistent for that Group. If, in addition, parental consumption inequality is similar in the two groups, then one expects there to be more consumption inequality in Group 1. Table 8.7 displays consumption inequality and the intergenerational growth of measured consumption inequality—the ratio of the standard deviation of measured log consumption of adult children to the standard deviation of the measured log consumption of fathers—in each of the two Groups and for each of the four PSID samples.[16] Measured consumption inequality grows across generations—probably because con-

16. The standard deviation of log consumption is corrected for any consumption inequality that can be explained by the age and marriage variables.

sumption is less accurately measured for sons—but the growth of consumption inequality does not appear to be greater for Group 1 families. Consumption inequality grows more rapidly in Group 2 for the "All" and "Sons only" samples while growth is more rapid in Group 1 for the "SRC only" sample. Consumption inequality is greater for Group 2 in all samples.

Simple Regression Results for Wages

The borrowing constraints model also has predictions for the persistence of wages in the two groups. Group 1 families invest the efficient level of human capital, which differs across families only because ability differs. Earnings therefore regress to the mean at the same rate as ability in Group 1. In Group 2, however, ability is not the only source of correlation between the earnings or wages of parents and children. Parental earnings also affects parental income, which affects the human capital investment of constrained families. This additional source of dependence of a child's adult earnings on that of his parents in Group 2 suggests that earnings or wages may regress to the mean more slowly in Group 2 than in Group 1. Table 8.8 reports separate estimates of the dependence of a child's wage on that of his or her father for the two Groups. Neither OLS nor IV estimates are very different for the two groups. The SRC and sons samples are exceptions to some degree, with more intergenerational wage mobility

Table 8.8 Separate Regression Results for Wages

Sample	Sample Size		OLS		IV	
			Group 1: $x_{t+1} \geq$ \$25,000	Group 2: $x_{t+1} <$ \$25,000	Group 1: $x_{t+1} \geq$ \$25,000	Group 2: $x_{t+1} <$ \$25,000
All	185	1243	0.33	0.32	0.42	0.49
			(0.08)	(0.03)	(0.11)	(0.04)
Fathers observed	159	1065	0.33	0.32	0.46	0.48
1968–72			(0.08)	(0.03)	(0.13)	(0.04)
SRC only	115	651	0.31	0.33	0.35	0.54
			(0.10)	(0.04)	(0.14)	(0.06)
Sons only	90	612	0.41	0.32	0.61	0.50
			(0.13)	(0.04)	(0.19)	(0.05)

Notes:

1. All estimates are for the "Earnings" subsample.
2. Reported are coefficients on log parental wage in a regression of log adult child's wage on a dummy for daughters, parental and child marriage variables, and a quadratic in both the child and the parental head-of-household's age. Standard errors are in parentheses.
3. See chapter 7 for a discussion of the instruments used for the parental wage.

in Group 1 for the SRC sample and more mobility for Group 2 in the "sons only" sample.

It is also clear from tables 8.5, 8.6, and 8.8 that consumption is more persistent than earnings or wages in *both* Group 1 and Group 2. The difference in Group 1 is predicted by the borrowing constraints model because Group 1 families look like permanent income families. However, an important difference between the persistence of consumption and earnings in Group 2 is not predicted by the borrowing constraints model.

The separate regression results for wages are also subject to selection bias. To see this, consider the error term in the earnings equation for Group 1. Because Group 1 children enjoy the efficient human capital investments, differences between their earnings and the earnings of their parents are mainly due to differences in the ability of the two generations. A very unable child from a poor family is more likely to be in Group 1 than is an able child from a poor family because the efficient human capital investment is smaller for the unable child. Nearly all children from rich families are likely to be in Group 1, so the error term ε_{t+1} is positively correlated with parental earnings among the Group 1 families and OLS estimates of γ are biased upwards. A similar argument applies to Group 2, so OLS estimates of β are biased upwards.[17] Three strategies that can be used to correct for selection bias are similar to those used in the section on "Analysis of Selection Bias":

(1) Assume that the earnings error term is lognormally distributed across PSID families.
(2) Consider regressions of $\ln e_{t+1}$ on $\ln e_t$ in a sample that pools both Groups 1 and 2.
(3) Compare cross-family Group 1 and Group 2 wage inequality.

Table 8.9 reports the results from approach (1). There is a bit more wage mobility in Group 1, although there are some exceptions. The IV point estimates of the intergenerational persistence of wages for the "All sample" are 0.32 for Group 1 and 0.49 for Group 2, point estimates which are substantially different. However, the point estimates for the "Sons only" sample are also different, with the larger estimates for Group 1. It is therefore unclear from the results in table 8.9 that the borrowing constraints model tells us much about intergenerational wage mobility.

The regression estimates of β shown in table 8.8 are subject to upward selection bias. If Groups 1 and 2 are pooled and a single intergenerational persistence parameter is estimated, there is no selection problem, but that

17. Parental altruism also appears in the error term for Group 2. Children from rich unaltruistic families are more likely to be in Group 2 than are children from rich altruistic families.

Table 8.9 Maximum Likelihood Estimates for Wages

Sample	Sample Size		No instruments for parental earnings		Instruments for parental earnings	
			Group 1: $x_{t+1} \geq$ \$25,000	Group 2: $x_{t+1} <$ \$25,000	Group 1: $x_{t+1} \geq$ \$25,000	Group 2: $x_{t+1} <$ \$25,000
All	185	1243	0.22	0.32	0.32	0.49
			(0.09)	(0.03)	(0.14)	(0.04)
Fathers observed 1968–72	159	1065	0.34	0.32	0.28	0.51
			(0.15)	(0.03)	(0.15)	(0.04)
SRC only	115	651	0.31	0.35	0.34	0.57
			(0.10)	(0.04)	(0.17)	(0.06)
Sons only	90	612	0.42	0.32	0.61	0.49
			(0.17)	(0.04)	(0.23)	(0.06)

Notes:

1. Results are obtained from the "All" subsample.
2. Reported are coefficients on log parental wage in a "regression equation" of log adult child's wage on a dummy for daughters, parental and child marriage variables, and a quadratic in both the child and the parental head-of-household's age. Standard errors are in parentheses.
3. The statistical model also includes a "selection equation" and, in the IV case, a "prediction equation" for parental consumption. Likelihood functions are displayed in Appendix E.
4. See chapter 7 for a discussion of the instruments used for the parental wage.

parameter is presumably an average of β and γ. Another approach to the selection problem is therefore to compare the estimates of β shown in table 8.8 with a pooled estimate. Under the joint hypothesis of selection bias and $\beta > \gamma$, the pooled estimate should be smaller. Instead, the pooled IV estimates of 0.49, 0.49, 0.53, and 0.50 are very similar to the IV estimates for Group 2, as shown in table 8.8 (0.49, 0.48, 0.54, 0.50).

The next section tackles the selection bias problem using approach (3).

Inheritance and Earnings Inequality

The borrowing constraints model also predicts that earnings inequality is related to inheritance. Among families that are making financial transfers, earnings of adult children are unequal—but only to the extent that the children have different innate abilities.[18] Ability also affects the earnings of children of borrowing constrained families—but so does parental income. The human capital investments in children of this second group of

18. Unequal ability produces unequal earnings in potentially two ways. First, ability has a direct effect on earnings. Second, ability may affect the rate of return to human capital investments and therefore the ultimate human capital investment made by parents.

Table 8.10 Inheritance and Earnings Inequality among Sons

Data source	Group 1: $x_{t+1} \geq \$25{,}000$ share	sd (ln w)	90/10	Group 2: $x_{t+1} < \$25{,}000$ share	sd (ln w)	90/10	Addendum: $x_{t+1} > 0$ share	sd (ln w)	90/10	Addendum: $x_{t+1} = 0$ share	sd (ln w)	90/10
	actual and expected inheritances											
PSID IG sample	13%	0.59	1.51	87%	0.54	1.32	28%	0.54	1.31	72%	0.55	1.41
89 SCF age 25–35	32%	0.57	1.26	68%	0.60	1.50	41%	0.70	1.53	59%	0.51	1.32
89 SCF age 36–64	29%	0.78	1.72	71%	0.61	1.36	38%	0.75	1.52	62%	0.61	1.34
	actual inheritances only											
PSID IG sample	2%	0.26	0.91	98%	0.55	1.34	12%	0.55	1.30	88%	0.54	1.34
89 SCF age 25–35	7%	0.71	1.38	93%	0.59	1.39	19%	0.65	1.51	81%	0.57	1.36
89 SCF age 36–64	13%	0.93	1.97	87%	0.63	1.38	25%	0.80	1.71	75%	0.62	1.39

Notes:

1. "90/10" is the log of the ratio of wages at the 90th and 10th percentiles.
2. In order to represent the U.S. male population, the PSID sample includes SRC sons only.
3. SCF samples are weighted to represent the overall U.S. population. Only men are included.
4. The SCF shares in the table differ slightly from those in the text because age is defined as the son's age in the table and as the respondent's age in the text. Also, female-headed households are excluded from the calculations in the table.
5. Only ten observations are included in the PSID-SRC sample of sons with actual inheritances of more than $25,000.

families therefore have a source of variation other than ability: parental income. Earnings should therefore be more unequal among the borrowing constrained families.[19]

Table 8.10 reports a measure of earnings inequality among Group 1 and Group 2 families in the two data sources. There is no evidence that earnings are more equal among adult children of families that make financial transfers. The first row of the table reports measures of wage inequality among sons from the PSID when x_{t+1} is defined according to both actual and expected inheritances. There actually appears to be more wage in-

19. This result does not obtain for all parameterizations of the Becker-Tomes model. It does obtain under the auxiliary assumption that the variance across families of the efficient human capital investment is small.

equality across the sons of Group 1 families! The standard deviation of the log wage is 0.59 and the 90–10 wage differential is 1.51 compared with 0.54 and 1.32 for Group 2. Inequality within the two groups is much less different when defined according to $x_{t+1} > 0$ and $x_{t+1} = 0$. In the PSID sample, it is difficult to determine whether this result is robust to the distinction between actual and expected inheritances. The fourth row of the table defines x_{t+1} according to actual inheritances only. However, it is difficult to measure earnings inequality for Group 1 sons because only ten PSID-SRC sons enjoy actual inheritances of more than $25,000. Earnings inequality is slightly greater for the $x_{t+1} > 0$ versus the $x_{t+1} = 0$ group.

The PSID sons are fairly young—between the ages of twenty-five and thirty-five. It is possible that a comparison of *lifetime* earnings inequality for Groups 1 and 2 is distorted by a focus on young men because life-cycle earnings growth is related to the overall level of lifetime earnings. Data from the SCF provides some information on this possibility. The SCF provides some large Group 1 samples because it oversamples the rich. It also includes men of all ages. The second and third rows of table 8.10 report measures of wage equality and their relationship to inheritance when x_{t+1} is defined according to actual and expected inheritances. The second row is most comparable with the first because it includes only men between the ages of twenty-five and thirty-five. From this row, it is difficult to determine how wage inequality is related to inheritance—it depends on how Group 1 is defined ($x_{t+1} > \$25{,}000$ versus $x_{t+1} > 0$) and the measure of wage inequality. However, the results are unambiguous for the older men; wage inequality is greater among sons receiving inheritances. Results are also unambiguous in the fifth and sixth rows of the table where x_{t+1} is measured according to actual inheritance only. My main result that wage inequality fails to be greater among the children of "borrowing constrained" families therefore does not appear to be an artifact of the PSID or of a focus on younger men.

Results from Other Data Sources

Parents Do Borrow Against the Earnings of Children

Although this chapter emphasizes some very direct evidence against the borrowing constraints model, there is also some indirect evidence against the borrowing constraints model that appears in chapters 6 and 7 and in the results of other researchers. First, it is not clear that parents are completely unable to "borrow" against the earnings of their children. The care for elderly parents by adult children is very similar to the borrowing that is assumed not to exist in the borrowing constraints model: young parents make investments that raise earnings of children and then later some of those earnings are transferred back to elderly parents in the form of resources devoted to their care.[20] Although the care for elderly parents by adult children may have declined in recent years (Michael, Fuchs, and Scott 1980), the historical practice shows that families are in fact able to arrange for the transfer of resources from children to parents, an arrangement which is assumed to be impossible in the borrowing constraints model.

Intergenerational Mobility Within and Across Groups

Second, one would expect borrowing and lending to be easier among families who live near each other than among families that live in different regions or in different countries.[21] Since there are more local borrowing opportunities than international borrowing opportunities, one would expect it to be easier for the children of a poor family in a rich country or region to advance their status than for those in a poor country or region to catch up to those in a rich one. However, the empirical analysis in chapters 6 and 7 suggests instead that intergenerational mobility is quite similar within and across groups, whether those groups are defined to be ethnic groups, regions, or countries. An explanation of intergenerational mobility that relies on borrowing constraints seems at odds with the similar mobility within and across groups.

Cross-Country Comparisons of Intergenerational Mobility

It is possible that some government policies alleviate borrowing constraints by, for example, sponsoring job training programs or assisting students with the financing of formal schooling. If borrowing constraints are an important determinant of intergenerational mobility and government policies vary across countries or over time, then one expects more intergenerational earnings mobility and less intergenerational consumption mobility in those countries and time periods that have more government policies which alleviate borrowing constraints.

Even when measured as a fraction of national income, educational expenditures by federal, state, and local governments in the United States have increased dramatically in the last seventy-five years.[22] Has intergenerational earnings mobility increased and intergenerational consumption

20. See Robert Michael, Victor Fuchs, and Sharon Scott (1980) for some measures of the importance of the care for elderly parents by adult children.

21. Martin Feldstein and Charles Horioka (1980) and others suggest that there is in fact little net international borrowing and lending.

22. U.S. Council of Economic Advisors (various issues).

mobility declined? There is limited evidence on the degree of intergenerational mobility a century ago, but the evidence surveyed in chapter 7 suggests the intergenerational mobility was not much different seventy-five or one hundred years ago.[23]

There is limited research comparing intergenerational mobility and government programs to facilitate the financing of human capital investments across countries or regions. In two studies, Kenneth Couch and Thomas Dunn (1995) and Anders Björklund and Markus Jantti (1993), argue that, because of government policies, schooling is easier to finance in Germany and Sweden than in the United States. Couch and Dunn find that the intergenerational persistence of schooling is greater in the United States than in Germany but that the intergenerational persistence of earnings is similar in the two countries. Björklund and Jantti (1993) find more intergenerational earnings mobility in Sweden than in the United States. P. de Wolff and A. R. D. van Slijpe (1973) find an estimate of the degree of Swedish intergenerational income mobility that is quite similar to other estimates for the United States while Goode (1966) reports somewhat less occupational mobility for Sweden. Mulligan (1996b) estimates similar degrees of intergenerational mobility for individual states in the United States that have somewhat different policies for providing public education.

Probate Records

Nigel Tomes (1981) is also concerned with the testing of some of the uniquely economic implications of Becker and Tomes (1986). In particular, Tomes has a probate sample where the correlation between an adult child's educational attainment and his or her parent's income is stronger for children not receiving a financial inheritance. I am able to extend

23. The post–World War II GI Bill was one potentially important government policy that alleviated intergenerational borrowing constraints. Were the postwar earnings of World War II GI's less sensitive to parental income? There is not yet any direct evidence on this (direct evidence would be a data set with the earnings of GIs and their parents), although the analyses of Behrman et al. (1980) and Jere Behrman, Robert Pollak, and Paul Taubman (1989) suggest that the GI Bill is associated with somewhat less earnings inequality among GI's. This result might be interpreted as evidence in favor of the borrowing constraints model, although a life-cycle version of the perfect capital markets model (in other words, breaking the single generational period into several life-cycle periods along the lines of Yoram Ben Porath's work [1967]) also predicts less earnings inequality because time spent fighting a war is time that an able young man cannot make the efficient human capital investments that would allow him to have more earnings than other GIs in his cohort. Behrman et al. also find a greater sensitivity of GI schooling to parental schooling.

Tomes's result in several ways. First, I look at a sample from the PSID that is much more representative of U.S. families than are probate samples. Second, I look at intergenerational earnings correlations in addition to schooling correlations. I am therefore able to rule out the possibility that determinants of earnings other than formal schooling vary with the presence of financial transfers in such a way as to counteract the excess sensitivity of schooling to parental income among "no inheritance" families. Third, I use instrumental variables techniques to mitigate measurement error problems with the estimation of the degree of intergenerational mobility. Fourth, I measure the variable for which economic approaches to inheritance have the strongest predictions—consumption. Fifth, I am able to study how earnings inequality is related to inheritance.

To compare with Tomes's work, table 8.11 reports some relationships between schooling, earnings, parental income, and inheritance for my PSID and SCF samples. (A related literature such as Cameron and Heckman (1996) looks at educational attainment as a function of parental income and tuition costs. Such implications of the borrowing constraints

Table 8.11 Tomes's Test with PSID and SCF Data

Sample	Sample Size		Child's schooling as a function of parental income		Addendum: "Rate of Return" to Schooling	
			Group 1: $x_{t+1} \geq$ \$25,000	Group 2 $x_{t+1} <$ \$25,000	Group 1: $x_{t+1} \geq$ \$25,000	Group 2: $x_{t+1} <$ \$25,000
All	185	1243	2.01	2.16	0.123	0.124
			(0.41)	(0.14)	(0.020)	(0.007)
Fathers observed	159	1065	2.00	2.13	0.122	0.121
1968–72			(0.44)	(0.14)	(0.022)	(0.008)
SRC only	115	651	1.25	3.19	0.126	0.108
			(0.50)	(0.23)	(0.026)	(0.010)
Sons only	90	612	1.90	2.28	0.116	0.115
			(0.71)	(0.20)	(0.029)	(0.009)
1989 SCF	518	1012	N/A	N/A	0.090	0.071
ages 25–35					(0.013)	(0.007)
1989 SCF	1617	2962	N/A	N/A	0.138	0.086
ages 36–64					(0.007)	(0.004)

Notes:

1. PSID results are obtained from the "Earnings" subsample.
2. SCF regressions are weighted according to each household's sampling weight.
3. "Child's schooling as a function of parental income" reports the coefficient from a regression of adult child's years of schooling on the log of parental income, where parent's occupation, region, and schooling are used to predict income.
4. "Rate of Return to Schooling" reports the coefficient from a regression of the log of the adult child's hourly wage on the adult child's schooling.

model are not derived in this book, so the tests of those implications are not reviewed here.)

Some of Tomes's results can be found in the PSID. Like Tomes, I regress an adult child's schooling on (log) parental income separately for Group 1 and Group 2 and report the estimated coefficients in the first two columns of table 8.11. Note that my sampling and estimation procedures differ from Tomes's in two important ways. First, Tomes uses probate records, which do not represent the overall U.S. population as well as does the PSID. Second, I enjoy much better measures of parental income. Parental income is measured when children are young (presumably when schooling decisions are being made) and is observed in several consecutive years. Furthermore, I am able to use instrumental variables procedures to correct for any additional measurement error.[24] The table displays results that are qualitatively similar to Tomes's: schooling appears to be more sensitive to parental income among Group 2 families. It is interesting that this is practically the only intergenerational mobility difference I have detected between Groups 1 and 2.

A key result from the Becker-Tomes borrowing constraint model is that differences in educational attainment between Groups 1 and 2 should show up as earnings differences among the adult children, yet important differences were not detected in tables 8.8, 8.9, 8.10, and 8.11. Do some of the schooling differences fail to translate into earnings differences? Or are the PSID data special? The second two columns of table 8.11 report some results that might help to reconcile my results and Tomes's. These two columns show that, in a regression of an adult child's wage on his or her years of schooling, the coefficient on schooling (or "rate of return to schooling" as referred to in the labor economics literature) is larger for Group 1. I suggest two alternative explanations of Tomes's results. First, some of the excess sensitivity of schooling to parental income among poorer families may be due to the consumption component of schooling. It is possible that all families make efficient human capital investments but that richer Group 2 families purchase more schooling for its consumption value. Second, it is possible that all families make efficient or nearly efficient human capital investments, but the form of those investments—schooling versus experience versus networking versus other ways of increasing earnings—is related to the economic status of the family.[25] Despite Tomes's results, the vast majority of the predictions of the Becker-Tomes model cannot be verified in the PSID or the SCF.

24. See chapter 7 for more discussion of measurement error corrections in my PSID samples.

25. Jere Behrman (1987a; 1987b) explicitly models several dimensions of human capital investment, suggesting that one dimension, such as schooling, may be a poor proxy for the overall human capital investment.

As I discuss in chapter 3, Tomes's test of the borrowing constraint model is related to regressions of an adult child's wage on investments in his human capital made by his parents and on his parents' income. The borrowing constraints model in most cases predicts that the partial correlation with parental income is negative. Mulligan (1996b) argues that the more common empirical finding is a positive partial correlation.

Another study attempting to use measures of financial transfers to identify "Group 1" families was done by Jere Behrman, Robert Pollak, and Paul Taubman (1995). They use the PSID, but rather than using inheritances, they study *inter vivos* transfers (financial transfers made while parents are still alive). Families with parents that make *inter vivos* transfers to children are designated as "Group 1" (or, in their terminology, "very high resource") families. They do not study intergenerational mobility, but they do focus on the distribution of resources among siblings—a topic analyzed in chapter 11.

Review of the Main Results

Although I verify Tomes's finding that the sensitivity of a child's educational attainment to parental income is related to inheritance, I find very little evidence that intergenerational consumption or earnings mobility is related to inheritance. Consumption regresses to the mean among families making financial transfers. Consumption and earnings regress to the mean in similar ways in Group 1 versus Group 2 families. Earnings inequality seems to be no different among the adult children of these two groups. All of these findings are at odds with the predictions of the borrowing constraints model.

Is it possible that my failure to find different intergenerational mobility in "Group 1" and "Group 2" is the result of my failure to correctly identify families as either Group 1 or Group 2? There are three possible mistakes that might occur in the designation of families as "Group 1" or "Group 2": (*a*) some Group 1 families are incorrectly designated as Group 2, (*b*) some Group 2 families are incorrectly designated as Group 1, and (*c*) both types of families are incorrectly designated. Since the borrowing constraints model predicts that the intergenerational mobility of Group 1 families is so different from Group 2 families and different from a pooled sample of Group 1 and Group 2 families, my strategy for designating families is to commit mistake (*a*), but to avoid mistakes (*b*) and (*c*). I study adult children who, *between the ages of twenty-five and thirty-five,* report their expectations about inheritance. I suspect that an adult child of that age who expects a sizable inheritance is quite unlikely to have parents who were either too poor or too unwilling to transfer resources to children such that the efficient human capital investment was not affordable.[26] If the human capital investment of a child who does expect a sizable inheritance is less than efficient, why didn't parents reduce the inheritance and increase the human capital investment? In other words, I am quite confident that the families I designate as "Group 1" are in fact Group 1. Some additional Group 1 families may have been misdesignated as Group 2 but, unless *most* of my "Group 2" families are in fact Group 1 (which means that just about every family is Group 1—but why then is the borrowing constraints model interesting?), the borrowing constraints model predicts that consumption should not regress to the mean and that intergenerational earnings mobility should be greater among my Group 1 families.

Although this chapter emphasizes some very direct evidence against the borrowing constraints model, there is also some indirect evidence against the borrowing constraints model that appears in chapters 6 and 7 and in the results of other researchers. First, it is not clear that parents are completely unable to "borrow" against the earnings of their children. Second, an explanation of intergenerational mobility that relies on borrowing constraints seems at odds with the similar mobility within and across groups. Third, intergenerational mobility does not seem to vary across countries or over time in a way that is correlated with government programs designed to facilitate the financing of schooling.

Borrowing constraints do not appear to be an important determinant of intergenerational mobility. The empirical results in this chapter are interesting for students of the Becker-Tomes model but also help to answer an interesting and important policy question: "How would economic inequality be affected by a government policy that removed financial barriers to educational attainment?" If borrowing constraints are an important barrier to educational attainment, it is puzzling that the Groups 1 and 2 in my empirical analysis are not very different. Group 1 families appear to have adequate financial resources while Group 2 families may not, yet intergenerational mobility and earnings inequality seems to be the same in both groups. I suggest that a government policy designed to remove financial barriers would certainly benefit some families, but it would not have an important effect on earnings inequality. My conclusion is not based on a claim that government policies cannot achieve their stated goals but on my observation that intergenerational mobility and earnings inequality are unrelated to borrowing constraints. Rather than reducing inequality, government subsidization of schooling may only have the effect

26. I suspect that the marginal human capital investment for many children is the completion of high school, attending college, or the completion of college—an investment which occurs between the ages of sixteen and twenty-four. The marginal investment decision was therefore made only a few years before the children in my sample reported their inheritance.

of transferring resources from taxpayers to (*a*) educators and (*b*) richer families who are more likely to choose many years of schooling for their children.

Appendix E: Likelihood Functions Used in the Statistical Analysis

Eight different likelihood functions are used in the empirical analysis: four for consumption and four for wages. The four for wages are perfectly analogous to those for consumption, so only the consumption likelihood functions are reported here. Of the four likelihood functions for consumption, two use instrumental variables and two do not. Two likelihood functions are used to determine the parameters for Group 1 and two others are used to determine the parameters for Group 2.[27]

E.1 No Instrumental Variables

Estimation of Group 1 Parameters

According to the imperfect capital markets model, we have:

$$x^i_{t+1} > 0 \quad \textit{if} \quad \ln c^i_{t+1} = \gamma \ln c^i_t + X^i_t \Gamma + \varepsilon^i_{t+1} \geq \ln e^{*i}_{t+1}$$

$$x^i_{t+1} = 0 \quad \textit{if} \quad \ln c^i_{t+1} < \ln e^{*i}_{t+1} \qquad (8.2)$$

where i denotes families and t denotes generations. X_t is a vector of additional regressors which include age polynomials and marriage variables. The error term ε_{t+1} includes altruism and the unanticipated portion of the child's ability. e^* is the efficient level of earnings, is assumed to be unobserved, and is allowed to vary across families. The statistical model above is a special case of the well-known "Heckit" model, with the first equality defining the "regression equation" and the $\geq$ inequality defining the "selection equation." The likelihood function for the Heckit model is reported, for example, in STATA Corporation (1994, p. 394).

Maximum likelihood estimates of γ and their standard errors are reported in the first column of table 8.6.

Estimation of Group 2 Parameters

According to the imperfect capital markets model, we have (using the same notation as above):

27. Each likelihood function is maximized separately, even though those that contain the parameters for Group 1 also share some parameters with those that contain the parameters for Group 2. Joint estimation of pairs of likelihood functions would be more efficient and permit tests of overidentifying restrictions, but I do not pursue the joint estimation in this book.

$$x^i_{t+1} > 0 \;\; if \;\; \ln c^i_{t+1} \geq \ln e^{*i}_{t+1}$$

$$x^i_{t+1} = 0 \;\; if \;\; \ln c^i_{t+1} = \beta \ln c^i_t + X^i_t\tilde{\Gamma} + \frac{\beta}{\gamma}\varepsilon^i_{t+1} + \left(1 - \frac{\beta}{\gamma}\right)\ln e^{*i}_{t+1} < \ln e^{*i}_{t+1} \quad (8.3)$$

$\tilde{\Gamma}$ is a different parameter vector than Γ ($\tilde{\Gamma} = \Gamma/\gamma$). Again we have a special case of the Heckit model, with the final equality defining the "regression equation" and the final inequality defining the "selection equation."

Maximum likelihood estimates of β and their standard errors are reported in the second column of table 8.6.

E.2 Instrumental Variables for Parental Status

Estimation of Group 1 Parameters

The likelihood function is different with instrumental variables because, in addition to a "regression equation" and a "selection equation," there is a "prediction equation" for parental status:

$$\ln c^i_t = Z^i_t\phi + \sigma_3\zeta^i_{t+1} \quad (8.4)$$

Z is a vector of instruments and ϕ is a vector of parameters.

A likelihood function $L_1(\gamma, \Gamma, \phi, \ln \bar{e}^*, \sigma_1, \sigma_2, \sigma_3, \rho_{12}, \rho_{23}, \rho_{13})$ is maximized to estimate γ and the other parameters, where $\ln \bar{e}^*$ is the average log efficient earnings, σ_1 is the standard deviation of the "selection equation's" error term ($\ln e^*_{t+1} - \varepsilon_{t+1}$), σ_2 is the standard deviation of the "regression equation's" error term (ε_{t+1}), σ_3 is the standard deviation of the "prediction equation's" error term ($\sigma_3\zeta_{t+1}$), and ($\rho_{12}, \rho_{23}, \rho_{13}$) are the corresponding correlations. That likelihood function is defined below:

$$L_1(\gamma, \Gamma, \phi, \ln \bar{e}^*, \sigma_1, \sigma_2, \sigma_3, \rho_{12}, \rho_{13}, \rho_{23}) \equiv$$

$$\sum_{i|x^i_{t+1}=0} \Pi^i_0(\gamma, \Gamma, \phi, \ln \bar{e}^*, \sigma_1, \sigma_2, \sigma_3, \rho_{12}, \rho_{13}, \rho_{23})$$

$$+ \sum_{i|x^i_{t+1}>0} \Pi^i_1(\gamma, \Gamma, \phi, \ln \bar{e}^*, \sigma_1, \sigma_2, \sigma_3, \rho_{12}, \rho_{13}, \rho_{23})$$

$$\Pi^i_0(\gamma, \Gamma, \phi, \ln \bar{e}^*, \sigma_1, \sigma_2, \sigma_3, \rho_{12}, \rho_{13}, \rho_{23}) \equiv \ln \Phi\left(\frac{\ln \bar{e}^* - X^i_t\Gamma - \gamma Z^i_t\phi}{\sigma_1}\right)$$

$$\Pi^i_1(\gamma, \Gamma, \phi, \ln \bar{e}^*, \sigma_1, \sigma_2, \sigma_3, \rho_{12}, \rho_{13}, \rho_{23}) \equiv$$

$$-\ln \sigma_2 - \ln \sigma_3 - \ln 2\pi - \frac{1}{2}\ln(1 - \rho^2_{23})$$

$$-\frac{1}{2|\Sigma|}\left[\left(\sigma_{yy} - \frac{\sigma^2_{xy}}{\sigma_{xx}}\right)(\ln c^i_{t+1} - \gamma Z^i_t\phi - X^i_t\Gamma)^2 + \left(\sigma_{zz} - \frac{\sigma^2_{xz}}{\sigma_{xx}}\right)(\ln c^i_t - Z^i_t\phi)^2\right.$$

$$+ 2\left(\sigma_{yz} - \frac{\sigma_{xy}\sigma_{xz}}{\sigma_{xx}}\right)(\ln c_t^i - Z_t^i\phi)(\ln c_{t+1}^i - \gamma Z_t^i\phi - X_t^i\Gamma)\Bigg]$$

$$+ \ln \Phi\left(\sqrt{\frac{1-\rho_{23}^2}{|\Sigma|}}\left[\frac{\gamma Z_t^i\phi + X_t^i\Gamma - \ln \bar{e}^*}{\sigma_1}\right.\right.$$

$$\left.\left. + \frac{\sigma_{xy}(\ln c_{t+1}^i - \gamma Z_t^i\phi - X_t^i\Gamma) + \sigma_{xz}(\ln c_t^i - Z_t^i\phi)}{\sigma_{xx}}\right]\right)$$

$$|\Sigma| \equiv 1 + 2\rho_{12}\rho_{13}\rho_{23} - \rho_{12}^2 - \rho_{13}^2 - \rho_{23}^2$$

$$\sigma_{xx} \equiv 1 - \rho_{23}^2,\ \sigma_{xy} \equiv \frac{\rho_{13}\rho_{23} - \rho_{12}}{\sigma_2},\ \sigma_{xz} \equiv \frac{\rho_{12}\rho_{23} - \rho_{13}}{\sigma_3},\ \sigma_{yy} \equiv \frac{1-\rho_{13}^2}{\sigma_2^2},$$

$$\sigma_{yz} \equiv \frac{\rho_{12}\rho_{13} - \rho_{23}}{\sigma_2\sigma_3},\ \sigma_{zz} \equiv \frac{1-\rho_{12}^2}{\sigma_3^2} \qquad (8.5)$$

Maximum likelihood estimates of γ and their standard errors are reported in the third column of table 8.6.

Estimation of Group 2 Parameters

Again we have a regression equation, a selection equation, and a prediction equation. The prediction equation is the same as above. The regression and selection equations change as they did in the no instruments case. The resulting likelihood function $L_2(\beta, \ldots)$ is maximized to estimate β and the other parameters. That likelihood function is defined below:

$$L_2\left(\beta, \tilde{\Gamma}, \tilde{\phi}, \frac{\beta}{\gamma}\ln \bar{e}^*, \tilde{\sigma}_1, \tilde{\sigma}_2, \tilde{\sigma}_3, \tilde{\rho}_{12}, \tilde{\rho}_{13}, \tilde{\rho}_{23}\right) \equiv$$

$$\sum_{i|x_{t+1}^i > 0} \tilde{\Pi}_0^i\left(\beta, \tilde{\Gamma}, \tilde{\phi}, \frac{\beta}{\gamma}\ln \bar{e}^*, \tilde{\sigma}_1, \tilde{\sigma}_2, \tilde{\sigma}_3, \tilde{\rho}_{12}, \tilde{\rho}_{13}, \tilde{\rho}_{23}\right)$$

$$+ \sum_{i|x_{t+1}^i = 0} \tilde{\Pi}_1^i\left(\beta, \tilde{\Gamma}, \tilde{\phi}, \frac{\beta}{\gamma}\ln \bar{e}^*, \tilde{\sigma}_1, \tilde{\sigma}_2, \tilde{\sigma}_3, \tilde{\rho}_{12}, \tilde{\rho}_{13}, \tilde{\rho}_{23}\right)$$

$$\tilde{\Pi}_0^i\left(\beta, \tilde{\Gamma}, \tilde{\phi}, \frac{\beta}{\gamma}, \ln \bar{e}^*, \tilde{\sigma}_1, \tilde{\sigma}_2, \tilde{\sigma}_3, \tilde{\rho}_{12}, \tilde{\rho}_{13}, \tilde{\rho}_{23}\right) \equiv \ln \Phi\left(\frac{X_t^i\tilde{\Gamma} + \beta Z_t^i\tilde{\phi} - \frac{\beta}{\gamma}\ln \bar{e}^*}{\sigma_1}\right)$$

$$\Pi_1^i\left(\beta, \tilde{\Gamma}, \tilde{\phi}, \frac{\beta}{\gamma}, \ln \bar{e}^*, \tilde{\sigma}_1, \tilde{\sigma}_2, \tilde{\sigma}_3, \tilde{\rho}_{12}, \tilde{\rho}_{13}, \tilde{\rho}_{23}\right) \equiv$$

$$- \ln \tilde{\sigma}_2 - \ln \tilde{\sigma}_3 - \ln 2\pi - \frac{1}{2} \ln(1 - \tilde{\rho}_{23}^2)$$

$$- \frac{1}{2|\tilde{\Sigma}|}\Bigg[\left(\tilde{\sigma}_{yy} - \frac{\tilde{\sigma}_{xy}^2}{\tilde{\sigma}_{xx}}\right)(\ln c_{t+1}^i - \beta Z_t^i\tilde{\phi} - X_t^i\tilde{\Gamma})^2 + \left(\tilde{\sigma}_{zz} - \frac{\tilde{\sigma}_{xz}^2}{\tilde{\sigma}_{xx}}\right)(\ln c_t^i - Z_t^i\tilde{\phi})^2$$

$$+ 2\left(\tilde{\sigma}_{yz} - \frac{\tilde{\sigma}_{xy}\tilde{\sigma}_{xz}}{\tilde{\sigma}_{xx}}\right)(\ln c_t^i - Z_t^i\tilde{\phi})(\ln c_{t+1}^i - \beta Z_t^i\tilde{\phi} - X_t^i\tilde{\Gamma})\Bigg]$$

$$+ \ln \Phi\left(\sqrt{\frac{1 - \tilde{\rho}_{23}^2}{|\tilde{\Sigma}|}}\left[\frac{\frac{\beta}{\gamma} \ln \bar{e}^* - \beta Z_t^i\tilde{\phi} - X_t^i\tilde{\Gamma}}{\tilde{\sigma}_1}\right.\right.$$

$$\left.\left.+ \frac{\tilde{\sigma}_{xy}(\ln c_{t+1}^i - \beta Z_t^i\tilde{\phi} - X_t^i\tilde{\Gamma}) + \tilde{\sigma}_{xz}(\ln c_t^i - Z_t^i\tilde{\phi})}{\tilde{\sigma}_{xx}}\right]\right)$$

$$|\tilde{\Sigma}| \equiv 1 + 2\tilde{\rho}_{12}\tilde{\rho}_{13}\tilde{\rho}_{23} - \tilde{\rho}_{12}^2 - \tilde{\rho}_{13}^2 - \tilde{\rho}_{23}^2$$

$$\tilde{\sigma}_{xx} \equiv 1 - \tilde{\rho}_{23}^2,\ \tilde{\sigma}_{xy} \equiv \frac{\tilde{\rho}_{13}\tilde{\rho}_{23} - \tilde{\rho}_{12}}{\tilde{\sigma}_2},\ \tilde{\sigma}_{xz} \equiv \frac{\tilde{\rho}_{12}\tilde{\rho}_{23} - \tilde{\rho}_{13}}{\tilde{\sigma}_3},\ \tilde{\sigma}_{yy} \equiv \frac{1 - \tilde{\rho}_{13}^2}{\tilde{\sigma}_2^2},$$

$$\tilde{\sigma}_{yz} \equiv \frac{\tilde{\rho}_{12}\tilde{\rho}_{13} - \tilde{\rho}_{23}}{\tilde{\sigma}_2\sigma_3},\ \tilde{\sigma}_{zz} \equiv \frac{1 - \tilde{\rho}_{12}^2}{\tilde{\sigma}_3^2} \qquad (8.6)$$

Maximum likelihood estimates of β and their standard errors are reported in the fourth column of table 8.6.

Appendix F: Summary Statistics for PSID Samples

This appendix lists characteristics of the 1,781 parent-child pairs (867 sons and 914 daughters) used in the regressions of tables 7.2, 7.3, 8.5, 8.6, 8.8, 8.9, 8.10, and 8.11.

Table A.1 Sample Characteristics—Group 1 ($x_{t+1} \geq \$25,000$)

	Sons and Daughters				
	N	Mean	Std. Dev.	Min.	Max.
age in 1986	219	31.8	2.57	27	36
avg. family income, (1984–88)	219	34,460	23,736	543	191,891
avg. nondurable consumption, (1984–87, estimated)	219	16,101	9,004	689	66,375
avg. hourly "wage," (1984–88)	214	9.25	6.95	0.80	69.72

	Head of Parental Household				
	N	Mean	Std. Dev.	Min.	Max.
age in 1968	219	42.3	7.51	29	67
avg. family income, (1967–71)	219	32,995	21,582	5,949	119,037
avg. nondurable consumption, (1969–72, estimated)	219	18,772	7,673	5,125	40,624
avg. hourly "wage," (1967–71)	196	11.03	6.80	1.60	44.41

Note: Data (except age and schooling) converted to 1982 dollars using the CPI for all items (U.S. Council of Economic Advisers, 1992).

Table A.2 Sample Characteristics—Group 2 (x_{t+1} < $25,000)

	Sons and Daughters				
	N	Mean	Std. Dev.	Min.	Max.
age in 1986	1562	31.3	2.63	25	36
avg. family income, (1984–88)	1562	26,277	18,893	79	270,242
avg. nondurable consumption, (1984–87, estimated)	1562	12,947	6,914	135	64,630
avg. hourly "wage," (1984–88)	1492	8.09	5.08	.16	53.04

	Head of Parental Household				
	N	Mean	Std. Dev.	Min.	Max.
age in 1968	1562	40.0	7.32	22	74
avg. family income, (1967–71)	1562	28,054	19,561	3,575	234,521
avg. nondurable consumption, (1969–72, estimated)	1562	17,008	7,541	3,537	50,476
avg. hourly "wage," (1967–71)	1340	10.06	7.49	0.15	90.84

Note: Data (except age and schooling) converted to 1982 dollars using the CPI for all items (U.S. Council of Economic Advisers, 1992).

Table A.3 Race

	All		SRC Only	
race	sons	daughters	sons	daughters
White	61.1	54.9	94.1	87.5
Black	38.2	43.1	5.7	11.3
Other, not reported	0.7	2.0	0.2	1.2
Total	100.0%	100.0%	100.0%	100.0%

Table A.4 Number of Siblings

Number	All	SRC Only
0	4.0	3.1
1	9.6	15.5
2	15.3	22.9
3	17.5	21.6
4	12.5	12.7
5	10.2	6.9
6	8.5	8.1
7	7.3	4.0
8	3.8	0.7
9	4.6	2.5
10	2.0	0.5
11	1.9	0.6
12	1.5	0.5
13+	1.4	0.6
Total	100.0%	100.0%
Mean	4.5	3.4

Table A.5 Birth Order (with mother)

Order	Percent
1st	21.5
2nd	19.3
3rd	17.0
4th	10.7
5th	6.6
6th	4.0
7th	3.2
8th	2.1
9th	0.9
10th+	1.3
not reported	13.6
Total	100.0

Table A.6 "Marital" Status—Adult Children

Percentage of the time when consumption is measured that person is "married"	Parental Household Head	Sons	Daughters
0%	17.8	26.9	34.4
1–25%	2.4	5.7	4.7
26–50%	2.9	7.0	5.5
51–75%	2.8	7.3	6.4
76–99%	0.0	0.0	0.0
100%	74.1	53.2	49.1

Note:

(1) A person is "married" if he or she cohabitated with an adult of the opposite sex.

(2) Example: a parent who is married 50 percent of the time when consumption is measured is "married" in two of the four years (1969–72) that consumption is measured.

Table A.7 Schooling

brackets	years coded	sons	daughters	fathers	mothers
0–5, with difficulty reading	1			1.5	0.1
0–5	4	0.1	0.1	5.5	2.3
6–8	7	1.4	1.3	27.3	16.4
9–11	10	18.1	12.7	17.0	20.6
12 only	12	23.3	28.1	27.0	37.5
12 plus nonacademic training	13	18.5	21.0	1.9	3.4
some college	14	16.7	16.7	7.4	8.1
college grad.	16	17.4	15.2	8.4	6.5
advanced or professional degree	18	4.5	4.8	4.0	2.3
not reported		0.0	0.0	0.2	3.0
Total		100.0%	100.0%	100.0%	100.0%
mean years coded		13.2	13.2	10.7	11.1

Notes:

1. Exact years of schooling completed are coded for children but are bracketed for parents.
2. Only fathers and mothers were classified according to their ability to read.
3. "Years Coded" refers to the years of schooling assigned (by the author) to each parental bracket for regression analysis.

Table A.8 Occupation

One-Digit Occupation Category	sons	daughters	parental household head
professional, technical and kindred	16.2	18.6	10.4
managers, administrators (except farm)	14.4	8.3	6.7
self-employed businessmen	NA	NA	3.7
clerical and sales	8.5	29.5	9.7
craftsmen, foremen and kindred	22.2	1.5	16.2
operatives and kindred	19.0	8.0	18.4
laborers (including farm)	6.8	1.1	19.3
farmers and farm managers	0.9	0.1	4.6
misc. (military, household work, etc.)	9.5	18.8	2.0
no response	0	0	0
not working/not in the labor force	2.8	14.1	9.1
Total	100.0%	100.0%	100.0%

Notes:

1. The final category is "not working" for sons and daughters and "not in the labor force" for fathers and mothers.

2. Occupation response is from 1986, 1987, 1988, or 1989 for sons and daughters (whenever they were working) and 1968 for parental household head.

3. Self-employed sons or daughters are coded according to the activities that they perform at work rather than as a separate occupation.

PART 3
Arguments from Other Disciplines

CHAPTER 9
The Biological Origins of Altruism

The model of chapter 4 argues that intergenerational altruism is not a universal constant but adjusts to circumstances. Chapters 3 through 8 motivate the model by arguing that such a model of altruism offers more accurate predictions for intergenerational mobility than do existing economic models. However, I believe there are other motivations for the model. One motivation comes from the field of sociobiology. Sociobiologists have argued that their analysis has much to say about the origins of social behavior in general and altruism in particular, but I show that their arguments have implications for the *endogeneity* of altruism. A theory of the origins of altruism is, in my view, also a theory of the endogeneity of altruism.

The first section outlines the merits and demerits of sociobiological reasoning. I then apply the reasoning to uncover determinants of altruism. This chapter is more mathematical than the preceding chapters, with the mathematical models showing exactly how biological and economic analysis might be integrated.

On Evolutionary Reasoning and Economic Analysis

Sociobiological arguments are used to motivate the endogeneity of altruism. Before doing so, I comment on evolutionary reasoning, how it can contribute to economic analysis, and how it cannot. My comments in this section reflect the arguments of some other economists, including Ingemar Hansson and Charles Stuart (1990) and Jack Hirshleifer (1977).

Economists usually have little to say about the specification of preferences, leaving the study of preferences to psychologists. One justification for their silence is that preferences, to the extent that they vary across individuals, are unpredictable. Restrictions on preferences are therefore kept to a minimum. Properties like concavity, additivity, separability, or constant elasticities may be made for analytical convenience—subject to a disclaimer, of course. Nonsatiation, altruism, and other stronger restrictions on preferences may be justified on introspective grounds. The evocation of one's introspection is nonetheless kept to a minimum.

However, evolutionary biology has predictions for the formation of preferences.[1] Moreover, evolutionary reasoning, in which agents act as if they maximized an objective subject to constraints, is natural for economists. Evolutionary reasoning supposes that an organism's genetic characteristics—including, in the case of humans, emotions and mental processes—are "chosen" so as to maximize the reproductive success of that organism.[2] While biologists are not always clear about how the choice is constrained, they do imply that genetic traits can change only incrementally.

In order to understand how evolutionary reasoning can help us learn about preferences, it is important to understand the mechanics behind the metaphorical "choices" that are "intended" to maximize reproductive success. First, changes in the characteristics of an organism—which begin as genetic mutations—occur only very *slowly,* over thousands of years. That is because favorable mutations, which probably do not occur very frequently to begin with, can only be selected through their differential contribution to the mutant organism's reproductive success. In other words, the smallest unit of time worth thinking about in an evolutionary context is a generation. The slow action of evolution suggests how evolutionary reasoning should be integrated with economic analysis: evolution first determines preferences which are then *taken as given* in an economic analysis.

Second, organisms do not *actually* choose their genetic characteristics; genetic characteristics are only thought of *as if* they were chosen so as to maximize reproductive success.[3] The precise mechanism that motivates

1. In fact, some psychologists (those who study the formation of preferences) see their field as merely a branch of evolutionary biology! Two of them, Martin Daly and Margo Wilson, "are inspired by the potential of selection thinking as metatheory for psychology" (Daly and Wilson 1988, p. 9).

2. Reproductive success is often referred to as "fitness." Although fitness can have connotations other than reproductive success, I will regard the two terms as synonyms.

When I label human emotions and mental processes as "genetic characteristics," I do not intend to take an extreme stand in the nature versus nurture debate. I hope that my discussion of biological potentiality, biological determinism, and economic analysis below will clarify this point.

3. For instance, no serious biologists think that a female kangaroo has ever thought to herself, "my pouch is a really handy way to care for my offspring," yet a serious biologist could argue that pouches exist because they are an effective way to care for offspring.

fitness maximizing behavior does not have to be, and in general will not be, a conscious fitness maximizing calculus. In fact, the more likely mechanism is pleasure. Organisms pursue those activities which give them pleasure.[4] Those organisms whose mental or neurological systems yield pleasure from activities that promote fitness will, because they pursue reproductive success indirectly through the pursuit of pleasure, be naturally selected. In the case of humans, for whom economists often summarize pleasure with a utility function, utility will be intimately related to—and perhaps indistinguishable from—reproductive success. An example is sexual desire: people often engage in sexual activity not because they consciously realize that they are promoting reproductive success, but because it gives them pleasure. Why is sexual activity pleasurable? Because it promoted reproductive success.

I have argued that (1) evolution shapes genetic characteristics only slowly and (2) that, in the words of Hansson and Stuart, "utility mirrors fitness" (1990, p. 542). However, the second point should be qualified by the first. People enjoy activities that *historically* promoted reproductive success: utility mirrors fitness with a lag. If there is a sudden (according to the evolutionary clock) reduction in the fitness value of an activity, people will still enjoy—and therefore pursue—that activity, although evolutionary reasoning predicts that eventually people will cease to enjoy that activity. In other words, traits that had fitness value in the premodern era need not have fitness value today. For example, a preference for fatty foods probably promoted fitness in the days when caloric intake was barely above subsistence levels while today such preferences do not serve to extend life. Because evolution acts only slowly, one can still expect genes with questionable fitness value today, like a preference for fatty foods, to be a feature of modern preferences because such preferences had fitness value for much of human history. Natural selection is adaptive:

> Selection shapes the minds and bodies of organisms to the particular conditions within which selection has been operating. Adaptation is not prospective. The apparent purpose in organismic design depends on the persistence of essential features of historical environments. (Daly and Wilson 1988, p. 7)

Stephen Jay Gould argues against some applications of evolutionary reasoning to human behavior. Gould argues that the evolutionary principle "utility mirrors fitness with a lag" is, in his words, "an untestable

4. In the special case of humans, the conscious pursuit of pleasure can be thought of as utility maximization.

speculation about unrecoverable behavior patterns of distant ancestors."[5] In other words, he feels that we have too little information about historical determinants of fitness. While it is not so obvious that historical determinants of fitness are completely mysterious, one can think of other reasons to discount his argument. First, are evolutionary stories of preference formation any less testable than introspective ones? Other than joint tests of preferences and constraints, introspection is, to my knowledge, the only other way economists can distinguish hypotheses about preferences. Second, a theory that explains the behavior of animals as well as that of humans seems to be intellectually more appealing than one uniquely tailored for human beings; economists (should) prefer theories that explain a wide range of behavior.

One might object to a theory of the evolutionary formation of preferences because it must attribute an individual's preferences to his genetic composition, thereby assuming away half of the field of psychology.[6] I believe that such an objection is unfounded; an evolutionary theory can allow the "nurture" component and free will to play roles in human decision-making. The argument is familiar to economists. First, unlike psychologists, economists are not primarily concerned with any particular individual's behavior but with the behavior of people *on average.* As long as the influences of free will and "the environment" are more idiosyncratic than are the influences of genetic composition, the more systematic evolutionary determinants of preferences will help us to understand average behavior. Individual preferences that significantly deviate from any genetic predisposition can therefore be consistent with average preferences that appear as if they were genetically determined. Second, one may want to extend evolutionary arguments beyond determinants of genetic composition to determinants of culture.[7] Finally, many economists do believe that at some deep level preferences are genetically determined. In particular, George Stigler and Gary Becker (1977) argue that it is useful to think of *all* human beings as having identical preferences—a rather extreme version of a story of the genetic determination of preferences!

5. See Stephen Jay Gould (1992, p. 52). Here Gould is arguing against the kin selection theory (see my "An Altruism Function Derived from Evolutionary Reasoning") as a theory of the origins of human altruism. Reading between the lines of Gould's paper, I find that he believes that the kin selection theory does not explain *human* behavior as he sees it. Two evolutionary psychologists, Martin Daly and Margo Wilson, offer some suggestive evidence to the contrary.

6. The naive theory that all behavior can be attributed to an organism's genetic composition has been called "biological determinism" by Stephen Jay Gould (1977).

7. See Christopher Badcock (1991, pp. 252ff) for a discussion. The idea is that selection occurs at levels of aggregation higher than a gene or an organism.

An Altruism Function Derived from Evolutionary Reasoning

The "evolutionary reasoning" outlined above might help economists think about preferences. The reasoning, when applied to the problem of altruism, yields a "Discriminating Altruist Corollary." The principle says that altruism should be conditional on characteristics of the recipient. If an individual felt the same degree of concern for all people, that individual would enjoy less reproductive success than others who were genetically predisposed to be concerned for others only according to certain characteristics. Evolutionary reasoning concludes by predicting that, over time, the appropriately discriminating altruists would outnumber the indiscriminate ones. The argument is then illustrated in a mathematical model of altruism and fitness maximization.

The Corollary is so named because the relevant characteristics are left unnamed. I therefore follow my discussion of the Corollary by outlining some existing theories of the evolutionary benefits of altruism, theories which propose specific personal attributes that can be interpreted as the "characteristics" alluded to by the Discriminating Altruist Corollary. The first theory to be considered is the biologist's kin selection theory of altruism, which notes that altruism, while perhaps detrimental to individual survival, can promote reproductive success. As opposed to the kin selection theory, Becker's Rotten Kid Theorem argues that altruism may in fact be beneficial to the altruist's fitness. I show that both approaches suggest that certain factors influence the rate of return to altruism (in the sense of fitness) and therefore, according to the Discriminating Altruist Corollary, are fundamental determinants of altruism.

The Discriminating Altruist Corollary

Economists model individuals as utility maximizers or "pleasure seekers," whereas biologists might think of individuals as "fitness maximizers." The two views can be reconciled by admitting that individuals do maximize utility, but evolution selects those individuals and their utility functions according to fitness. Thus, the surviving utility functions tend to look like fitness objectives.

Preferences have several features, which are often modeled as parameters, that are of interest to economists. Examples are risk-aversion, prudence, and altruism. The Discriminating Altruist Corollary uses evolutionary reasoning to analyze one feature of preferences—altruism.

> *The Discriminating Altruist Corollary*
> If the rate of return to altruism, in terms of reproductive success, is a function of characteristics of the recipient, then

> altruists who condition their altruism on those characteristics (or observable proxies) will achieve greater reproductive success than nondiscriminatory altruists. All altruists must eventually be of the discriminating variety because discriminating altruists are favorably selected.

The model below will formalize this result.

First, agents are utility maximizers. They not only derive pleasure from their own consumption (*c*), but they may enjoy the happiness of another person.

$$\text{pleasure} = u(c) + a(z)V(h) \tag{9.1}$$

The degree of an agent's concern for his friend's happiness (V) is modeled by the altruism function $a(z)$, which depends upon a Z-dimensional vector z characteristics of his friend. Agents may have no idea why their concern depends upon z—they are genetically predisposed to feel that way.

An agent is endowed with y units of resources, which he can spend on his own consumption or on a transfer h to his friend. The production possibilities are described by the function $B(c, h, y, a)$, which allows for the possibility that altruism might enhance the production of consumption goods. Agents' choices maximize the altruistic pleasure function subject to the production possibilities.[8]

$$\max_{c,h} \; [u(c) + a(z)V(h)]$$

$$\text{s.t} \quad B(c, h, y, a) = 0, \quad c, h \geq 0$$

$$\text{with} \quad u', V' > 0, \quad u'', V'' < 0$$

$$B_c, B_h < 0, \quad B_{ch} = 0, \quad B_y > 0, \quad B_a, B_{ah} \geq 0, \quad B_{ac} \leq 0 \tag{9.2}$$

The optimal choices are:

$$c = g_1(a, y), \quad h = g_2(a, y), \tag{9.3}$$

g_2 is increasing in a as long as solutions are interior and the various restrictions on the pleasure functions and the production possibilities hold.[9]

Pleasure-seeking agents are behaving according to g_1 and g_2. Those that reproduce will be those that, as an accidental byproduct of pleasure seeking, achieved highest fitness. In other words, the surviving altruism function will be that which maximizes fitness subject to pleasure-seeking behavior.[10]

8. My formulation rules out strategic interactions, but the main result—that a theory of the origins of altruism has predictions for the endogeneity of altruism—can also be derived in a model with strategic interactions.

9. Inada conditions for $u(c)$ and $V(h)$ (and a positive a) would guarantee interior solutions.

10. I assume that in the initial population there was at least one agent for every possible $a(z)$ function.

$$\text{surviving } a(z) = \underset{a}{argmax}[f_0(c) + f(h, z)]$$

$$\text{s.t.} \quad \text{z given}$$

$$c = g_1(a, y), \quad h = g_2(a, y), \tag{9.4}$$

where f_0 denotes the contribution of one's own consumption to fitness and f denotes the contribution of transfers. Notice that the contribution of transfers depends on the characteristics z if the cross-derivatives of f are nonzero. I assume f_0 is strictly increasing and weakly concave and that f is strictly increasing and weakly concave in h.

The slope of the surviving altruism function is shown below. z_j denotes the jth characteristic and the "denominator" is a positive number when the above maximization problem is concave.[11]

$$\frac{\partial a}{\partial z_j} = \frac{\frac{\partial g_2}{\partial a}}{\text{denominator}} \frac{\partial^2 f(h, z)}{\partial z_j \partial h} \gtrless 0 \text{ as } \frac{\partial^2 f(h, z)}{\partial z_j \partial h} \gtrless 0 \quad j = 1, \ldots, J \tag{9.5}$$

This is exactly the Discriminating Altruist Corollary: surviving altruism functions are sensitive to characteristics that influence the contribution of transfers to fitness. A detailed proof of the Discriminating Altruist Corollary can be found in Mulligan (1993).

What exactly are the characteristics z? For that matter, why does h influence fitness at all? Since other authors have attempted to answer these questions, some of their theories are outlined in the following subsections.

Kin Selection and the Rate of Return to Altruism

How can altruism, the concern of one agent (the altruist) for the welfare of another (the recipient), have fitness value? After all, altruism by definition requires that the altruist have concern for something other than his own personal well-being. What stopped "selfish" agents from dominating altruistic ones in the Darwinian battle for survival? The primary sociobiological answer is that evolution selects *genes* not individuals.[12] The genetic

11. Nonconvexity of the decision rules g_1 and g_2 in a are sufficient, but not necessary, to guarantee that the maximization of fitness (as a function of altruism) subject to $c = g_1$ and $h = g_2$ is a concave problem.

12. That evolutionary selection operates at a genetic level as opposed to higher levels (for example, organisms, populations, or species) is often debated as a general principle of evolutionary biology. However, even opponents of genetic selection admit that it is a powerful model of the particular problem of altruism. See, for example, Gould (1992, pp. 50–51) for one opponent's discussion. See David Haig (1993) for a proponent's view.

Genetic selection is sometimes criticized on the grounds that it is not complicated enough, that "one gene—one trait" models are too simple. Economists' standard justifications for the simplicity of their models are well known; I do not repeat them here.

hypothesis is the foundation of the *kin selection* theory of altruism.[13] According to the theory, altruistic behavior has fitness value as long as the recipients of altruism tend to be "related" to the altruist, namely, that they tend to share the altruistic gene. Notice that what a social scientist calls altruism—the concern of one individual for another's welfare—an evolutionary biologist calls selfishness because the former takes the individual as primitive while the latter takes the gene as primitive.

The kin selection theory predicts that a gene which causes its carrier to be concerned with the welfare of others in accordance with their degree of kinship will be selected in favor of a gene that causes less discriminatory altruistic behavior. The latter gene has less survivability because its carrier tends to make transfers to agents without the gene.[14] By contrast, conditional altruism has the advantage of minimizing altruistic acts toward nonrelatives. In its additively separable form, the welfare of a discriminatory altruist (agent $i = 0$) is:

$$V_0 = u(c_0) + \sum_{i=1}^{N} a(z_i)V_i \tag{9.6}$$

The altruist's objective includes his own personal well-being $u(c_0)$—which depends on his own consumption c_0—as well as the welfare of his N acquaintances.[15] Acquaintance i's welfare receives weight $a(z_i)$, which depends on a measure (or vector of measures) of the kinship of 0 and i.

13. Scott Boorman's and Paul Levitt's book (1980) includes an exposition of the kin selection theory of altruism. Biologists define altruism to be "behavior which promotes the reproductive success of the recipient at a cost to the reproductive success of the altruist" (Badcock 1991, p. 25). I refer the reader to my earlier discussion of the relationship between utility and reproductive success in humans. For many purposes, utility and reproductive success are indistinguishable; altruism as defined by economists is not so different from altruism as defined by biologists.

An important alternative to the kin selection theory of altruism is the theory of reciprocal altruism. A discussion of reciprocal altruism is beyond the scope of this chapter and is probably not highly relevant to intergenerational altruism, the primary application of my theory of altruism in this study. Under some interpretations, my examination of the Rotten Kid theorem below touches on the concept of reciprocal altruism.

14. Discriminatory altruists are more likely win a struggle for survival against nonaltruists than are nondiscriminatory altruists because the nondiscriminatory altruists would transfer more resources to the nonaltruists. Similarly, discriminatory altruists should tend to win a battle for survival against nondiscriminatory altruists.

15. It is likely that the recipient is also concerned with the altruist's welfare. I will abstract from "two-sided" altruism, with three justifications. The first is to simplify the analysis and focus on a few particular effects. Second, two-sided altruism may be the least relevant in the special case of intergenerational altruism. When "intergenerational transfers" are defined broadly, including expenditures on health and education, the bulk of intergenerational transfers are from parents to children. Third, I will be focusing on the time argument of the altruism function. The bulk of the interaction between parents and their children occurs

I argue that, because individuals cannot always observe kinship, altruism responds to proxies for kinship. z in equation 9.6 therefore denotes proxies for kinship. Such proxies may be professed kinship—an imperfect proxy when paternity is uncertain—or similarities of appearance, attitudes, and mannerisms. To the extent that populations are geographically viscous, a measure of proximity like the amount of time that two people have spent together also proxies for kinship. For example, I have in mind that when an altruist meets somebody that he has never seen before, he puts very little weight on the stranger's welfare.[16] Such discrimination against strangers is naturally selected because, with high probability, the stranger is not kin. I rewrite the altruist's objective as:

$$V_0 = u(c_0) + \sum_{i=1}^{N} a(kinship_i, appearance_i, attitudes_i, paternal\ uncertainty, q_i)V_i \quad (9.7)$$

q_i, the amount of time that 0 spends with i, enters as a measure of i's proximity to 0. I associate "expected kinship" with "professed kinship" together with an estimate of paternal uncertainty. For example, the professed kinship of an allegedly close relative would be adjusted downwards substantially when his paternal uncertainty is high. Adam Smith may not have had biological arguments in mind (although see 1982 [1790], VI.ii.I.3), but he indicated that, holding constant the frequency of interaction, the benevolence of intergenerational relations is decreasing in paternal uncertainty.

> A jealous husband, indeed, notwithstanding the moral connection, notwithstanding the child's having been educated in his own house, often regards, with hatred and aversion, that unhappy child which he *supposes* to be the offspring of his wife's infidelity. (1982 [1790], VI.ii.I.13, italics added)

Rotten Kids and the Rate of Return to Altruism

Sociobiology has yielded two results. First, we should not be surprised that modern preferences exhibit altruism since such preferences may have had fitness value during the process of human evolution. Second, because altruism that is conditional on kinship may have even greater fitness value

---

when the parents are adults and the children are children. One could argue that altruism is a concept most applicable to adults, that children are still learning how to be concerned for the welfare of another.

See Miles Kimball (1987) for an analysis of two-sided, exogenous intergenerational altruism.

16. He may show some concern for the stranger's welfare if he observes some of the other proxies for kinship, such as he and the stranger sharing similar attitudes.

than does less discriminatory altruism, one should not be surprised to observe that people weight the welfare of others according to proxies for the degree of their kinship. Becker's (1976) paper strengthens the first result by proposing an alternative to the kin selection theory. I extend Becker's reasoning to strengthen my second result, that altruism should be conditional on something.

Becker proposes another reason why altruistic preferences could promote survivability. He noticed that rational recipients of altruism realize that the transfer that they receive from the altruist depends on their own actions. Because a recipient's welfare will tend to be a normal good for the altruist, the recipient will refrain from taking actions that marginally benefit himself but substantially harm the altruist. The recipient is motivated to do so because the altruist's transfer is indirectly conditional on the recipient's actions. Recipients of altruism therefore simulate altruism—they act as if they valued the altruist's objective. Notice that Becker's "Rotten Kid" argument does not require an active punishment motive on the part of the altruist.

The Rotten Kid Theorem implies that altruistic preferences, because they influence the actions of others, can be beneficial to the altruist as well as to the recipient! Since it cannot be beneficial in the Rotten Kid sense for an altruist to weight the welfare of a Rotten Kid whose rotten actions are of no consequence, the Rotten Kid Theorem implies that the benefits of altruism depend on the social proximity of the altruist and the Rotten Kid recipient. Preferences, such as those displayed in equation 9.6, which allow for the degree of altruism to depend on the social proximity of the recipient should therefore be selected in favor of preferences which are less discriminatory.

Summary

The Discriminating Altruist Corollary builds on existing theories of the origins of altruism to show that we should expect altruism to be endogenous. Altruism should depend on the characteristics of the recipient of transfers. One of those characteristics is the amount of time during which altruist and recipient interact. It is the time argument of the "altruism function" that I study in chapter 4 to build a model of intergenerational mobility, in chapter 11 to build a model of inequality within the family, in chapter 12 to analyze charitable giving, and in chapter 13 to study principal-agent problems.

CHAPTER 10
Classical Discussions of Altruism

In addition to the fields of economics and biology, the motivation for endogenous altruism—and some of the implications of my economic model—can be found in the field of philosophy. I review some of the work of David Hume, Adam Smith, John Rae, and others. These classical philosophers/economists argued that altruism or sympathy is endogenous and is formed as the result of costly actions. Moreover, they derive some implications of their approach that are similar to some results from chapter 4. It appears that my idea of endogenizing altruism is quite old, although a deliberate application of the model to economic issues such as intergenerational mobility, inequality, and the principal-agent problem may be novel.

Altruism Is Formed as the Result of Costly Actions

By what mechanism does an altruist enjoy the welfare of another? In his *Theory of Moral Sentiments,* Adam Smith contemplates the mechanics of altruism:

> As we have no immediate experience of what other men feel, we can form no idea of the manner in which they are affected, but by conceiving what we ourselves should feel like in the situation. . . . [our senses] never did, and never can, carry us beyond our own person, and it is by the imagination only that we can form any conception of what are [our brother's] sensations (1982 [1790], I.i.I.2)[1]

1. There is some dispute among historians about the relationship between altruism and Smith's concept of "sympathy." While recognizing that an association with altruism of any of the several benevolent passions discussed by Smith would be incorrect, I believe that some of his thoughts do pertain to altruism as defined here. A connection between altruism and Smith's sympathy can be seen in his discussion of giving, which I cite later in this chapter.

Altruism or sympathy has its costs as well as its benefits. On the benefit side, one can enjoy the utility of others. However, that enjoyment can only be realized after some investment has occurred. Smith claims that imagination is the necessary investment. Presumably imagination is produced with the time of the altruist, information about the recipient, and perhaps some experience or "imagination capital" that the altruist has accumulated from past altruistic feelings. Smith suggests that time is an important component of the investment and that time may enhance altruism or sympathy through the accumulation of information and familiarity:

> After himself, the members of his own family, those who usually live in the same house with him, his parents, his children, his brothers and sisters, are naturally the objects of his warmest affections. . . . He is more *habituated* to sympathize with them. He *knows better* how everything is likely to affect them, and his sympathy is more precise and determinate, than it can be with the greater part of other people. It approaches nearer, in short, to what he feels for himself. (1982 [1790], VI.ii.I.2, italics added)

Other classical philosopher/economists seem to agree that altruism, or something close to altruism, varies in important ways according to the frequency of personal interaction. David Hume argued that personal interaction is much more relevant than any judgment of merit or propriety.

> Whoever is united to us by any connexion is always sure of a share of our love, proportion'd to the connexion, without enquiring into his other qualities. . . . When we have contracted a habitude and intimacy with any person; tho' in frequenting his company we have not been able to discover any very valuable quality, of which he is possess'd; yet we cannot forbear preferring him to strangers, of whose superior merit we are fully convinc'd. (1878, pp. 140–41)

One could argue that Hume and Smith refer to something slightly different than altruism as I have defined it, but there is no doubt that F. Y. Edgeworth had altruism in mind. Edgeworth does not postulate a dependence of altruism on the frequency of interaction from an imagination story as I do—he just observes a correlation. Consider a passage from his *Mathematical Psychics:*

> his neighbor's happiness as compared with his own neither counts for nothing, nor yet "counts for one," but counts for a fraction. We must modify the utilitarian integral by multiplying each pleasure, except the pleasures of the agent himself, by a fraction—a factor doubtless diminishing with what

> may be called the *social distance* between the individual agent and those of whose pleasures he takes account. (1932 [1881], pp. 102–3, italics added)

The discussions of Smith, Hume, and Edgeworth are consistent with the idea that people are predisposed toward selfishness but that selfishness is often overcome through the time and effort of the altruist.[2]

Altruism Increases with Schooling?

Adam Smith appeared to believe that schooling or some other form of intellectual development increases a person's capacity for altruism.[3]

> The man whose whole life is spent in performing a few simple operations . . . generally becomes as stupid and ignorant as it is possible for a human creature to become. The torpor of his mind renders him, not only incapable of relishing or bearing a part in any rational conversation, but of conceiving any generous, noble or tender sentiment. (1981 [1776], V.i.f.51)

John Rae appears to agree:

> The strength of the intellectual powers, giving rise to reasoning and reflective habits, forms another important element in the determination of the course of human action. These habits in opposition to the passions of the present hour, bring before us the future, both as concerns ourselves, and others . . . (1905 [1834], p. 57)

People with more schooling enjoy, on average, higher wages while Smith and Rae argue that schooling enhances altruism. Does this overturn the "substitution effect" result from chapter 4 that a higher wage *decreases* the degree of altruism? The substitution effect from chapter 4 still holds even if schooling enhances altruism, as long as schooling enhances wages *more* than it enhances a person's ability to be altruistic. To see this, remember that chapter 4 modeled the cost of accumulating altruism as $w\theta(a)$ where w is the wage, a is altruism, and $\theta(a)$ is a function that allows for the marginal cost of altruism to vary with the level of altruism. Holding constant the wage, Smith and Rae suggest that altruism is cheaper to accumulate for people with schooling. In other words, schooling reduces the value of $\theta(a)$. However, as long as the positive effect of schooling on the wage w

2. An innate predisposition toward selfishness is also a common concept in the social psychology "moralization" literature, where it is referred to as "egocentrism." See Roger Brown (1986) for an overview.

3. I was informed of this reference to moral sentiments in the *Wealth of Nations* by David Sally. See his discussion of Smith's view of altruism in Sally (1995).

is greater than the negative effect of schooling on $\theta(a)$, then the total cost of altruism $w\theta(a)$ increases with schooling.

Chapter 4 shows that a higher wage has both "substitution" and "total resource" effects but, because the "substitution" and "total resource" effects are of the same magnitude and the parental wage determines only a fraction of total family resources, the net effect of a higher wage is to decrease altruism. This result may not hold if schooling has an important effect on the cost of altruism because, under the Smith-Rae hypothesis, schooling has a less than proportional effect on the net cost of altruism $w\theta(a)$.

Smith Derives the "Interest Rate Effect"

Chapter 4 derives an "interest rate effect" on intergenerational altruism. When the interest rate is high, providing consumption for children is cheaper and, because altruism and consumption by children are complements, altruism is encouraged. In other words, the *price of giving affects the degree of concern.* One interpretation of the "price of giving" is that it measures the "effectiveness" of the transfer. In other words, the "relative price of giving" effect means that *altruists allocate their altruism where their transfers are most effective.* This result was observed by Adam Smith:

> When the happiness or misery of others depends in any respect upon our conduct, we dare not, as self-love might suggest to us, prefer the interest of one to that of many. The man within [ourselves] immediately calls to us, that we value ourselves too much and other people too little. . . . When the happiness or misery of others, indeed, in no respect depends upon our own conduct . . . we do not always think it so necessary to restrain, either our natural and, perhaps, improper anxiety about our own affairs. (1982 [1790], III.3.5–7)

Not only does the amount of benevolent behavior respond to the effectiveness of that behavior, observes Smith, but so does the *degree of concern.* Although Smith may have a somewhat different explanation for his observation, his observation is consistent with an important prediction of my model of altruism: altruism responds to the effectiveness of transfers. Doctors will tend to care about those who need medical attention, instead of those who need, say, legal assistance.

Summary

Adam Smith, David Hume, John Rae, and others thought about motives for giving. They did not conclude that the desire to give is a fixed universal constant but argued instead that the desire depends on circumstances. They argue—and I explicitly model—that it is costly to *enjoy* giving. Time is an important part of that cost.

Smith and Rae also suggest that schooling enhances the desire to give. I show the conditions under which this effect can exist and my main results still obtain.

Smith observes that the *desire* to give responds to the price of giving, an observation that is consistent with the "interest rate effect" derived in chapter 4 and the "relative price of giving effect" derived in chapter 11.

PART 4
Other Applications of Endogenous Altruism

CHAPTER 11

Intergenerational Altruism and Inequality within the Family

While the child neutrality assumption is useful to isolate certain effects of altruism formation on the intergenerational transmission of inequality, this chapter derives more results for inequality by considering differences among siblings. The model of altruism predicts that parents can aggravate inequality within the family, that divorce reduces parental concern for children, and that parental concern for children discourages divorce.

The model has somewhat different implications for the intragenerational distribution of resources than do standard models. I emphasize what the implications mean for interpreting several empirical studies of family transfers, such as those showing that birth order, family size, family composition, and some childhood variables are correlated with economic outcomes later in children's lives.[1] I question several interpretations of evidence on intergenerational transfers.

This chapter considers "parents" who choose altruism and transfers for each of two children. However, other interpretations are available. For example, one could think of a donor who is choosing among several charities. Issues of free-riding (off of other donors) and imperfect information are probably especially important for the analysis of giving outside of the family and are explored in more detail in the next two chapters.

The chapter consists of four sections. "Accumulating Altruism for Several Children" modifies the model of chapter 4 to allow parents to treat siblings differently. The results of the model are used in the following section to address the question "Do Parents Mitigate or Aggravate Inequality within the Family?" I show that, although the standard model of altruism suggests that parental transfers should mitigate inequality within the fam-

1. See, for example, Donald Cox (1987) and Peter Lindert (1977).

ily, a model with endogenous altruism can predict that parents aggravate inequality. I offer new interpretations of a variety of evidence on family transfers. "Divorce, Parental Altruism, and Child Welfare" introduces divorce into the model and shows that a noncustodial parent might care more about the consumption of his stepchildren than the consumption of children from a previous marriage. The main results of the chapter are reviewed in the last section. An appendix presents a mathematical version of the models analyzed in this chapter. An understanding of the analysis in chapter 4 is required to follow the arguments in this chapter.

Accumulating Altruism for Several Children

The basic Mulligan model presented in chapter 4 features either one child per family or multiple children that are treated symmetrically. Parents in the basic Mulligan model chose parental consumption, consumption per child, and child-oriented resources per child. I extend that model in this chapter to allow parents to treat children differently. "Statement of the Full Problem" presents the problem, describing parental behavior and arguing that the problem consists of two stages. The intergenerational allocation of resources is determined in stage one and the intragenerational allocation is determined in stage two. The main results of the chapter are derived from an analysis of this second-stage problem. The second-stage problem is detailed in "Setup of the Second-Stage Problem" and the last half of the section derives implications of the model, including: "total resource," "interest rate," "substitution," "relative price of giving," "relative price of caring," and "happiness" effects.

Statement of the Full Problem

Families are assumed to have two children, whom I name "Child 1" and "Child 2."[2] Parents in the model choose parental consumption, consumption for child 1, consumption for child 2, child-oriented resources for child 1, and child-oriented resources for child 2. Those five goods are denoted $(c_t, c_{1,t+1}, c_{2,t+1}, q_1, q_2)$.

Setup of the Second-Stage Problem

The full problem can be broken into two stages. In the first stage, parents decide how much to consume c_t and the total amount to spend on child-oriented resources Q. In the second stage, remaining consumption C_{t+1} and child-oriented resources Q are allocated among the two children. In

2. The main results extend to families with more than two children. See Mulligan (1993, chapter 4).

other words, the first-stage problem concerns the *inter*generational allocation of resources while the second stage concerns the *intra*generational allocation.

For the first-stage problem, one can expect the main results reported in chapter 4 to obtain. For example, an increase in total family resources will—for a given parental wage and a given interest rate—increase the amount of child-oriented resources Q purchased by parents. The novel results to be reported in this chapter are therefore for the second-stage problem—the allocation of resources among children.

Like the model of chapter 4, the second-stage model is analyzed in three steps. First, preferences and constraints for consumption resources are derived, with particular attention to the effect of child-oriented resources. Second, preferences and constraints for child-oriented resources are derived. Third, effects of total family resources, the interest rate, the relative price of giving, and other variables on the willingness and opportunity to accumulate altruism are analyzed.

Parental Preferences for Intragenerational Allocations

Suppose that the same child-oriented resources are allocated to each child: $q_1 = q_2$. For now, assume that equal child-oriented resources means that parents have equal concern for each child's consumption.[3] With equal concern for each child, one can draw parental indifference curves in the $[c_{1,t+1}, c_{2,t+1}]$ plane. The consumption of child 1 is measured on the horizontal axis and the consumption of child 2 is measured on the vertical axis. The difference between indifference curves displayed in figure 11.1 and those displayed in previous chapters is that the consumption of children is measured on *both* axes. In contrast, parental consumption (c_t) is measured on the horizontal axis and average consumption of children (c_{t+1}) is measured on the vertical axis in the diagrams of previous chapters. Measuring consumption of children on both axes makes sense for our analysis of the *intra*generational allocation of consumption in this chapter. Previous chapters were concerned with the *inter*generational allocation of consumption.

Because parental concern for each child is assumed to be equal, the indifference curves displayed in figure 11.1 are symmetric around the 45-degree line. In other words, the indifference curves would be unchanged if instead $c_{2,t+1}$ were measured on the horizontal axis and $c_{1,t+1}$ on the vertical axis—a sensible property for indifference curves that are supposed to model identical concern for each child.

Notice that indifference curves are curved in the $[c_{1,t+1}, c_{2,t+1}]$ plane.

3. This assumption is relaxed later in the chapter.

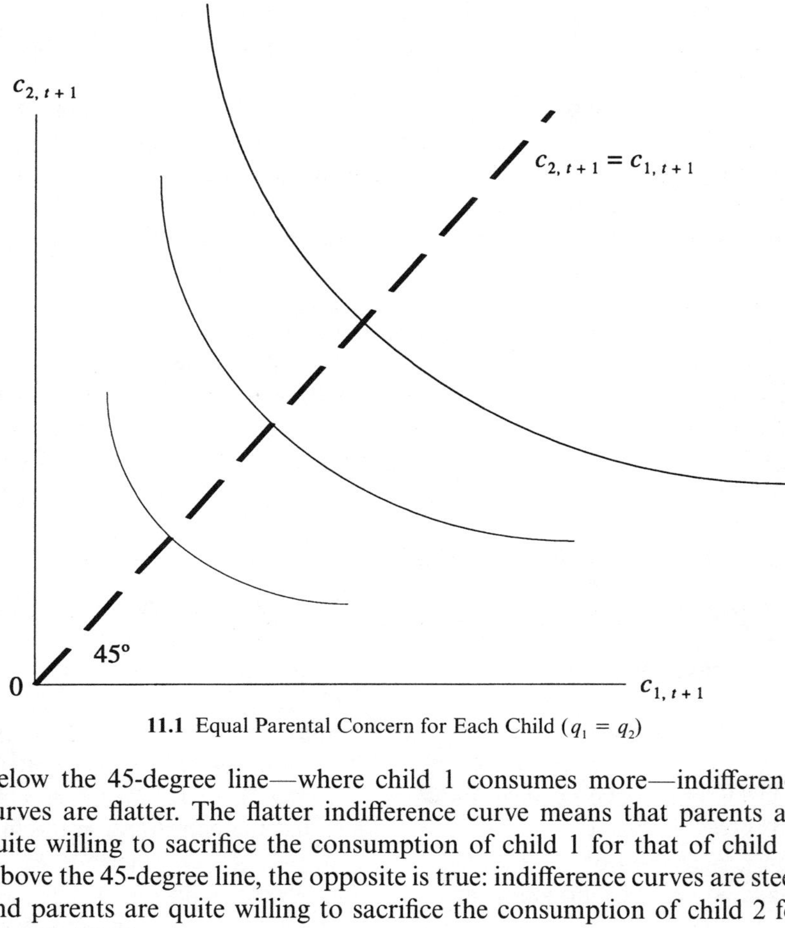

11.1 Equal Parental Concern for Each Child ($q_1 = q_2$)

Below the 45-degree line—where child 1 consumes more—indifference curves are flatter. The flatter indifference curve means that parents are quite willing to sacrifice the consumption of child 1 for that of child 2. Above the 45-degree line, the opposite is true: indifference curves are steep and parents are quite willing to sacrifice the consumption of child 2 for that of child 1.

If q_1 is greater than q_2, then parents are more concerned with the consumption of child 1. A large q_1 therefore has the effect of shifting indifference curves to the southeast in the $[c_{1,t+1}, c_{2,t+1}]$ plane such as the dashed indifference curves shown in figure 11.2. Solid curves are displayed for small q_1.

Compare the two sets of indifference curves in figure 11.2. At allocation *A*, the dashed indifference curves are steeper than the solid curves. In other words, parents are more willing to give up the consumption of child 1 for the consumption of child 2 when q_1 is small.

To facilitate the exposition, I assume that indifference curves in the $[c_{1,t+1}, c_{2,t+1}]$ plane are L-shaped. The L-shape represents a very strong parental preference for moderate allocations of consumption *among* the

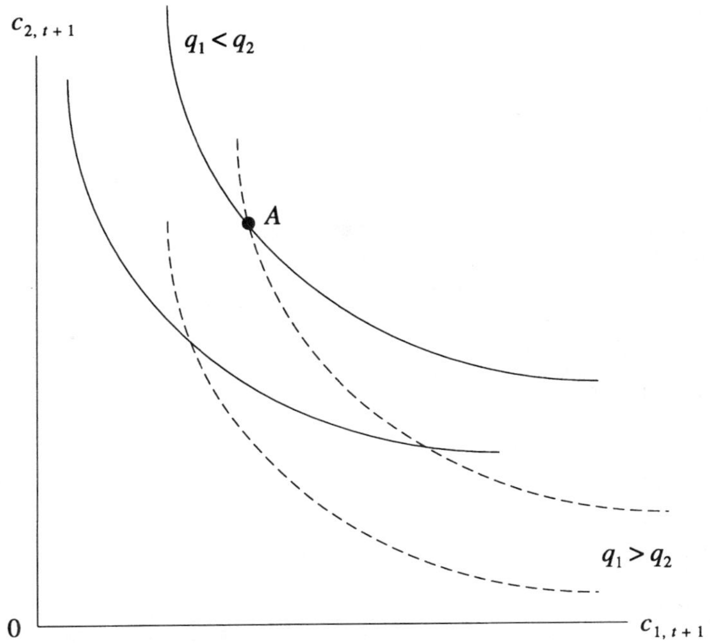

11.2 Effect of Unequal Child-oriented Resources on Parental Preferences

children, but many of the results derived for the L-shaped curves also extend to more gently curved indifference curves, such as those shown in figure 11.2. With the L-shaped curves, a reallocation of child-oriented resources has the effect of shifting the ray of preferred proportions. Consider figure 11.3. The ray of preferred proportions is relatively flat when more child-oriented resources are allocated to child 1 and relatively steep when more are allocated to child 2.

Constraints on the Intragenerational Allocation of Consumption

In the second-stage problem, C_{t+1} units of consumption are available to be allocated among the two children. It is assumed that the price of child 1's consumption is 1 (a normalization) and the price of child 2's consumption is R. The budget constraint in the $[c_{1,t+1}, c_{2,t+1}]$ plane is drawn as the solid line with slope $-1/R$ in figure 11.4. Parents can choose the allocation $(C_{t+1}, 0)$ so that child 2 consumed nothing. Or parents can reallocate consumption from child 1 to child 2, which, because the price of child 2's consumption is R, moves them along the solid budget constraint in the figure.

Because parents are older than children, the relative price of c_t and c_{t+1}

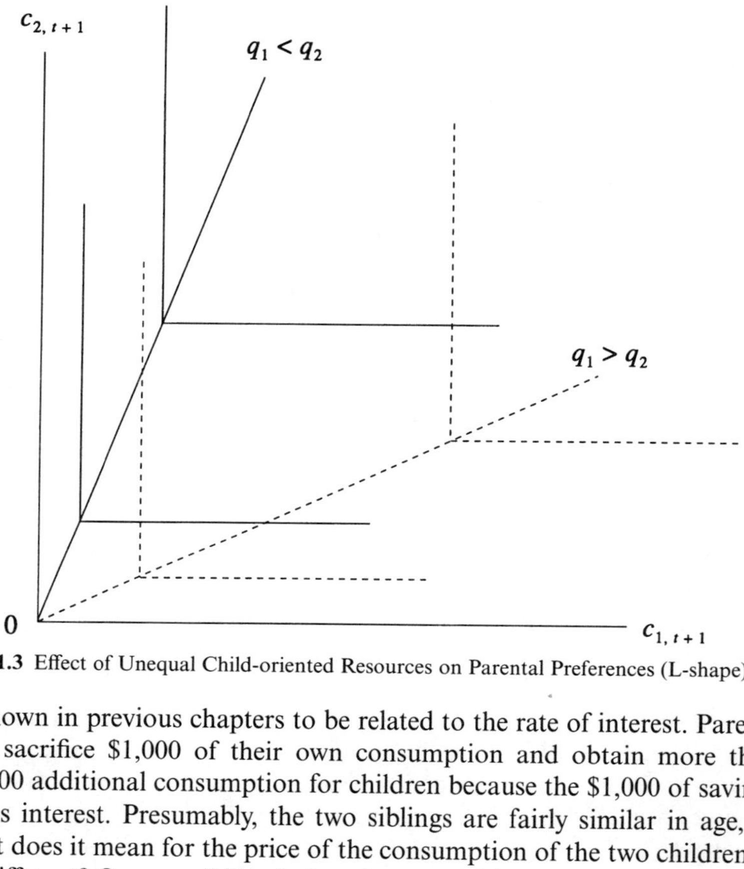

11.3 Effect of Unequal Child-oriented Resources on Parental Preferences (L-shape)

is shown in previous chapters to be related to the rate of interest. Parents can sacrifice $1,000 of their own consumption and obtain more than $1,000 additional consumption for children because the $1,000 of savings earns interest. Presumably, the two siblings are fairly similar in age, so what does it mean for the price of the consumption of the two children to be different? One possibility is that the two children consume very different goods (for example, one consumes in a city and another in a rural area). Another possibility is that transfers to the two children are taxed at different rates by the government. It is shown later in this chapter that the relative price R can also reflect different conditions under which a parent gives to each child. For example, a divorced parent may live with child 1 but not with child 2, and these different conditions for the children effectively means that consumption is, from the parent's point of view, more expensive for child 2. Borrowing constraints for a family with children of different abilities can also create different prices of giving because the rate of return to human capital investments varies across siblings.

Constraints on the Allocation of Child-Oriented Resources

The intragenerational consumption allocation chosen by parents is easily displayed in the $[c_{1,t+1}, c_{2,t+1}]$ plane—parents choose the point on the

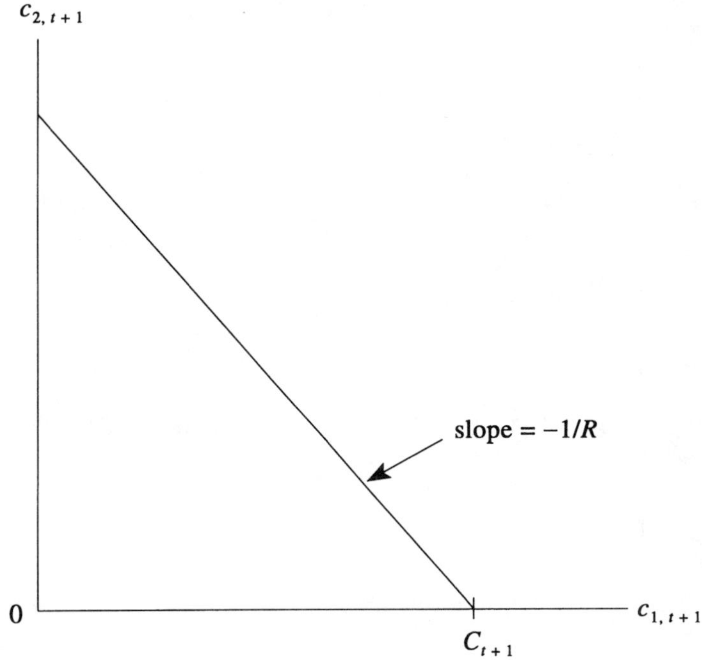

11.4 Constraints on Intragenerational Consumption Allocations

budget constraint shown in figure 11.4 that coincides with the ray of preferred proportions. However, the ray of preferred proportions is determined by the intragenerational allocation of child-oriented resources.

In the second-stage problem, Q units of child-oriented resources are available to be allocated among the two children. It is assumed that the price of child 1's child-oriented resources is 1 (a normalization) and the price of child 2's is p. The budget constraint in the $[q_1, q_2]$ plane is drawn as the solid line with slope $-1/p$ in figure 11.5. Parents can choose the allocation $(Q, 0)$ so that no resources are oriented toward child 2. Or parents can reallocate from child 1 to child 2, which, because the price of child 2's child-oriented resources is p, moves them along the solid budget constraint in figure 11.5.

Parents' Chosen Allocation of Child-Oriented Resources

Because parents allocate consumption among children in a fixed proportion that is determined according to the allocation of child-oriented resources, one can draw parental indifference curves in the $[q_1, q_2]$ plane. Parents choose the feasible allocation (q_1, q_2) that achieves the highest utility, which—as shown in figure 11.6—must be an allocation where an indifference curve is tangent to a budget constraint in the $[q_1, q_2]$ plane.

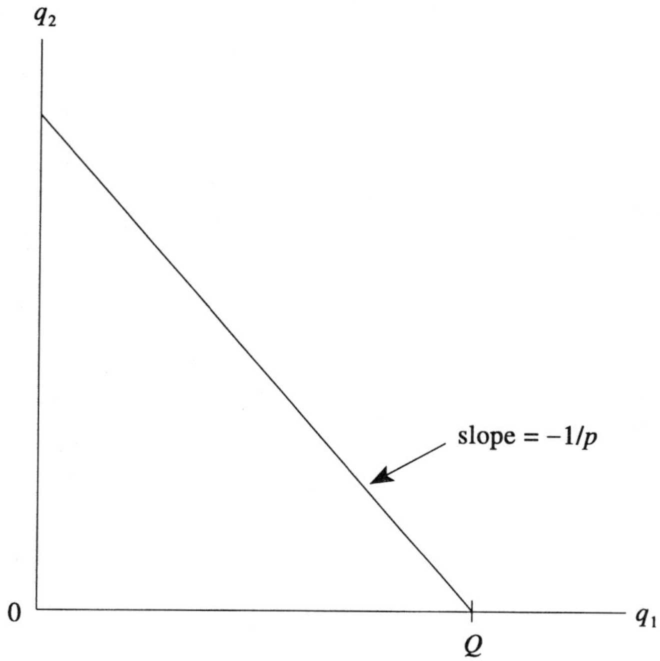

11.5 Constraints on q_1 and q_2

Four properties of those indifference curves can be derived from the single-child model of chapter 4. The four assumptions from the single-child model are:

(1) more altruism raises the desired proportion c_{t+1}/c_t;
(2) if the accumulation of altruism were costless, all parents would prefer more;
(3) at a given level of altruism, the willingness to pay for altruism is proportional to child consumption c_{t+1};
(4) holding constant c_{t+1}, the willingness to pay for altruism is less when altruism is greater.

To derive properties of indifference curves in the two-child model from the assumptions (1)–(4) single-child model, one observation is required:[4]

$$\text{willingness to sacrifice } q_2 \text{ for } q_1 = \frac{\text{willingness to sacrifice } q_2 \text{ for } C}{\text{willingness to sacrifice } q_1 \text{ for } C} \tag{11.1}$$

4. The validity of the observation can be seen in a simple example. Suppose you are willing to sacrifice four bananas for one orange or two apples for one orange. Then you value apples twice as much as bananas: you are willing to sacrifice two bananas for one apple.

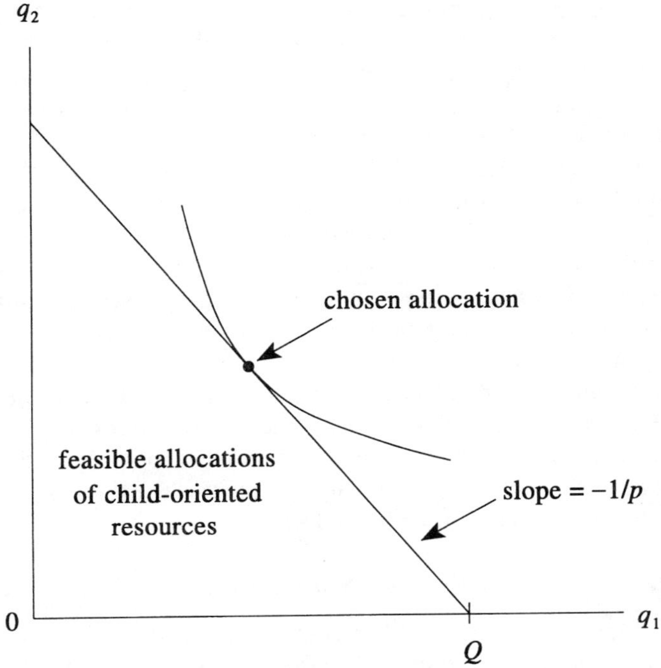

11.6 Allocation of Child-oriented Resources

where C is total consumption resources for the family. The willingness to sacrifice q_2 for q_1 determines the slope of the indifference curves in the $[q_1, q_2]$ plane. The assumptions (1) through (4) tell us about the willingness of parents to sacrifice q_1 or q_2 for C, so, according to the formula above, they can be used to compute the slope of the indifference curves in the $[q_1, q_2]$ plane.

The properties (5) through (8) can be derived for indifference curves in the $[q_1, q_2]$ plane:

(5) more q_2 relative to q_1 raises the desired proportion $c_{2,t+1}/c_{1,t+1}$;
(6) if the accumulation of altruism for each child were costless, all parents would prefer more;
(7) at a given intragenerational allocation of children-oriented resources, the willingness to sacrifice q_2 for q_1 is proportional to $c_{2,t+1}/c_{1,t+1}$;
(8) holding constant $c_{2,t+1}$ and $c_{1,t+1}$, the willingness to pay for q_2 is less when q_2 is greater.

Consider (5). Assumption (1) says that q_2 raises the desired proportion $c_{2,t+1}/c_t$ and that q_1 raises the desired proportion $c_{1,t+1}/c_t$, so the desired proportion $c_{2,t+1}/c_{1,t+1}$ must be increasing with q_2 and decreasing with q_1. Property (6) is trivial. From assumption (3), the numerator in equation 11.1 is proportional to $c_{2,t+1}$ and the denominator is proportional to $c_{1,t+1}$, so the ratio is proportional to $c_{2,t+1}/c_{1,t+1}$—this proves property (7). Property (8) follows from assumption (4).

Before I derive the effects of total family resources and the various prices on the distribution of resources among siblings, I display conditions under which children are treated equally. Suppose $p = R = 1$. In other words, the price of child-oriented resources is the same for both children and the price of consumption is the same for both children. If parents are not biased toward one child or another, then the symmetry of the problem suggests that both children are treated equally when $p = R = 1$. Notice that this result is independent of C_{t+1} and Q. If total family resources or the interest rate or the price of child-oriented resources were to change without changing $p = R = 1$, then one would expect the aggregate resources devoted to children to change but for those resources to continue to be equally distributed among children.

Total Resource, Interest Rate, and Substitution Effects

What is the effect of total family resources on the allocation of resources among children? The analysis of the single-child model suggests that total family resources affect aggregate consumption by children C_{t+1} and aggregate child-oriented resources Q. First, I derive the effect of total family resources through its effect on Q. Figure 11.7 shows that an increase of aggregate child-oriented resources from Q to Q' produces a *parallel* shift of the budget constraint in the $[q_1, q_2]$ plane. If preferences were homothetic, then Q would affect the overall level of q_1 and q_2, but not their ratio q_2/q_1.[5] However, preferences need not be homothetic, so more Q might increase the ratio q_2/q_1 or might decrease it. The only unambiguous result in this regard is when $p = R = 1$: q_2/q_1 must be one for any value Q.

Total family resources may also have an effect on the aggregate consumption of children C_{t+1}. However, figure 11.6 shows that C_{t+1} does not shift the budget constraint in the $[q_1, q_2]$ plane because the position of the constraint only depends on Q and p. C_{t+1} also fails to affect the position of the indifference curves in the $[q_1, q_2]$ plane. To prove this, one must study the willingness to pay for q_2 at a given allocation (q_1, q_2). According to property (7), that willingness to pay depends on the ratio $c_{2,t+1}/c_{1,t+1}$. From figure 11.3 and property (5), one sees that the ratio $c_{2,t+1}/c_{1,t+1}$

5. By definition, homothetic preferences are displayed as indifference curves with slopes that are constant along a ray. A parallel shift of the budget constraint therefore cannot shift the chosen allocation off its original ray, so the ratio q_2/q_1 remains constant.

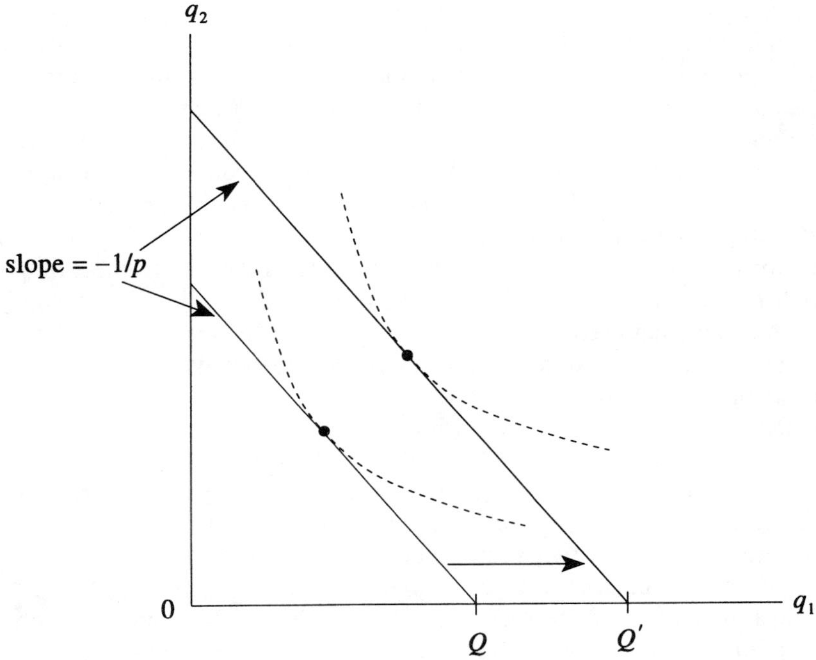

11.7 Effect of Q on q_1 and q_2

depends only on q_1 and q_2 (and not C_{t+1}), so that at a given allocation (q_1, q_2) one has a given ratio $c_{2,t+1}/c_{1,t+1}$ and therefore a given willingness to pay regardless of C_{t+1}. C_{t+1} does not affect the position of either the budget constraint or the indifference curves in the [q_1, q_2] plane and therefore cannot, for given Q, affect q_1 or q_2.

Total family resources, the interest rate, and the overall price of child-oriented resources all affect the allocation of consumption and child-oriented resources among children through their effects on Q and C_{t+1} in the first-stage problem. With homothetic preferences for q_1 and q_2 or with $p = R = 1$, total family resources, the interest rate, and the overall price of child-oriented resources do not affect the relative treatment of children.

"Relative Price of Giving" Effect

The relative price of transferring resources to the two children, R, does affect their relative treatment. R can differ from one, perhaps because the two children consume different goods (for example, one consumes in a city and another in a rural area), because transfers to the two children are taxed at different rates by the government, or because parental transfers occur under different conditions.

R affects the slope of the budget constraint in the $[c_{1,t+1}, c_{2,t+1}]$ plane, but not the constraint in the $[q_1, q_2]$ plane. However, higher R increases the slope of the indifference curves in the $[q_1, q_2]$ plane and therefore motivates a reallocation of child-oriented resources toward child 1. The effect of R on the willingness to sacrifice q_2 for q_1 follows from the complementarity result of chapter 4. Like the ski trips and ski equipment of chapter 4, q_2 and c_2 are complements. An increase in the relative price of c_2 (R) discourages purchases of q_2. Another way to show that the willingness to pay for q_2 depends on R is to show that R affects the effectiveness of q_2. High R produces a very flat budget constraint in the $[c_{1,t+1}, c_{2,t+1}]$ plane, which means that even a large increase in q_2 (and thereby a large shift of the ray of preferred proportions) cannot be associated with a large increase in $c_{2,t+1}$. The inflexibility of $c_{2,t+1}$ at high R matters because the willingness to pay for q_2 is proportional to $c_{2,t+1.}$

For given Q and C_{t+1}, a higher R decreases the ratio q_2/q_1. Figure 11.3 shows that the ratio $c_{2,t+1}/c_{1,t+1}$ must decrease. R may have an effect on the aggregates Q and C_{t+1} chosen in the first-stage problem, but the analysis in the previous section shows that (to a good approximation) Q and C_{t+1} do not effect either the ratio q_2/q_1 or the ratio $c_{2,t+1}/c_{1,t+1}$. A higher R must therefore produce a redistribution of both child-oriented and consumption resources toward child 1, the child whose consumption has become relatively cheap.

"Relative Price of Caring" Effect

The relative price of child-oriented resources, p, also has an affect on the relative treatment of children. p might differ from one because one child lives relatively far away from parents so that it is difficult for parents to spend time with him and thereby accumulate child-oriented resources.

It is easy to show that a higher p produces a reallocation of child-oriented resources toward child 1. A higher p produces a flatter budget constraint in the $[q_1, q_2]$ plane but does not affect the position of indifference curves. Because of the curvature of the indifference curves in the $[q_1, q_2]$ plane, the flatter budget constraint means that chosen q_2 falls relative to q_1. Lower q_2 relative to q_1 shifts the ray of preferred proportions in the $[c_{1,t+1}, c_{2,t+1}]$ plane, decreasing the ratio $c_{2,t+1}/c_{1,t+1}$.

For given Q and $C_{t+1,}$ a higher p decreases the ratios q_2/q_1 and $c_{2,t+1}/c_{1,t+1}$. p may also have an effect on the aggregates Q and C_{t+1} chosen in the first-stage problem, but the analysis in the previous section shows that (to a good approximation) Q and C_{t+1} do not effect either the ratio q_2/q_1 or the ratio $c_{2,t+1}/c_{1,t+1}$. A higher p must therefore produce a redistribution of both child-oriented and consumption resources toward child 1, the child for whom child-oriented resources have become relatively cheap.

"Relative Happiness" Effect

I assume throughout the book that parents care about the *consumption* of children and, all other things being equal, prefer an equal distribution of consumption among children. However, it is probably more realistic to assume that parents care about *happiness* rather than consumption per se. My analysis of consumption is consistent with this more realistic assumption under three conditions: (1) more consumption produces more happiness for parents and children, (2) the relationship between consumption and happiness does not depend on parental income, and (3) the relationship between consumption and happiness is the same for all siblings. The first two conditions justify the analysis of the single-child consumption models in previous chapters while the additional third condition is required to justify the analysis of this chapter. What follows explores the consequences of relaxing the requirement that the relationship between consumption and happiness is the same for all siblings.

When parents are concerned with happiness rather than consumption, one needs to begin by drawing their indifference curves as a function of the happiness of each child rather than as a function of consumption. Suppose that the same child-oriented resources are allocated to each child: $q_1 = q_2$. Assume that equal child-oriented resources means that parents have equal concern for each child's happiness. With equal concern for each child, one can draw parental indifference curves in the $[u_{1,t+1}, u_{2,t+1}]$ plane, where $u_{1,t+1}$ and $u_{2,t+1}$ are the happiness of each child, respectively.

The happiness of child 1 is measured on the horizontal axis and the happiness of child 2 is measured on the vertical axis in figure 11.8. Because parental concern for each child is assumed to be equal, the indifference curves displayed in figure 11.8 are symmetrical around the 45-degree line. In other words, the indifference curves would be unchanged if instead $u_{2,t+1}$ were measured on the horizontal axis and $u_{1,t+1}$ on the vertical axis—a sensible property for indifference curves that are supposed to model identical concern for each child. Parents are assumed to have a strong preference for moderation, so indifference curves are L-shaped. A relatively large q_2 shifts the ray of preferred proportions upward.

If both children were equally happy for any given level of consumption, then parental preferences could also be represented with indifference curves in the $[c_{1,t+1}, c_{2,t+1}]$ plane. The 45-degree ray of preferred proportions representing equal happiness in the $[u_{1,t+1}, u_{2,t+1}]$ plane would be associated with the 45-degree ray of preferred proportions representing equal consumption in the $[c_{1,t+1}, c_{2,t+1}]$ plane. Suppose instead that child 1 is more happy than child 2 for a given level of consumption. Suppose further that the differences are proportional—child 1 is, say, 50 percent

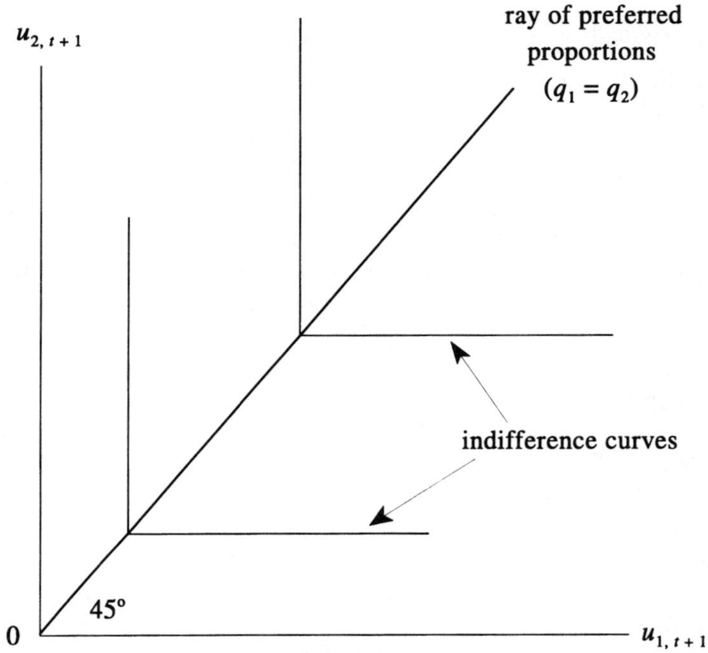

11.8 Identical Concern for the Happiness of Children

happier than child 2 for any given level of consumption. Then the 45-degree ray of preferred proportions representing equal happiness in the $[u_{1,\,t+1}, u_{2,\,t+1}]$ plane is associated with a ray of preferred proportions in the $[c_{1,\,t+1}, c_{2,\,t+1}]$ plane that is steeper than 45° because, to make both children equally happy, child 2 needs more consumption. q_1 and q_2 still shift the ray of preferred proportions in the $[c_{1,\,t+1}, c_{2,\,t+1}]$ plane as shown in figure 11.3, but $q_1 = q_2$ is now associated with a ray that is different from 45°. See figure 11.9.

As before, the chosen allocation of child-oriented resources can be determined by studying the budget constraint and indifference curves in the $[q_1,q_2]$ plane. The budget constraint is as in figure 11.5, with slope $1/p$ and intersecting the horizontal axis at Q. Indifference curves are similar to those shown in the figure, but the willingness to pay for child-oriented resources depends on the relative *happiness* of children rather than the relative consumption. In other words, we have properties (5)′–(8)′ rather than properties (5)–(8):

(5)′ More q_2 relative to q_1 raises the desired proportions $u_{2,\,t+1}/u_{1,\,t+1}$ and $c_{2,\,t+1}/c_{1,\,t+1}$.

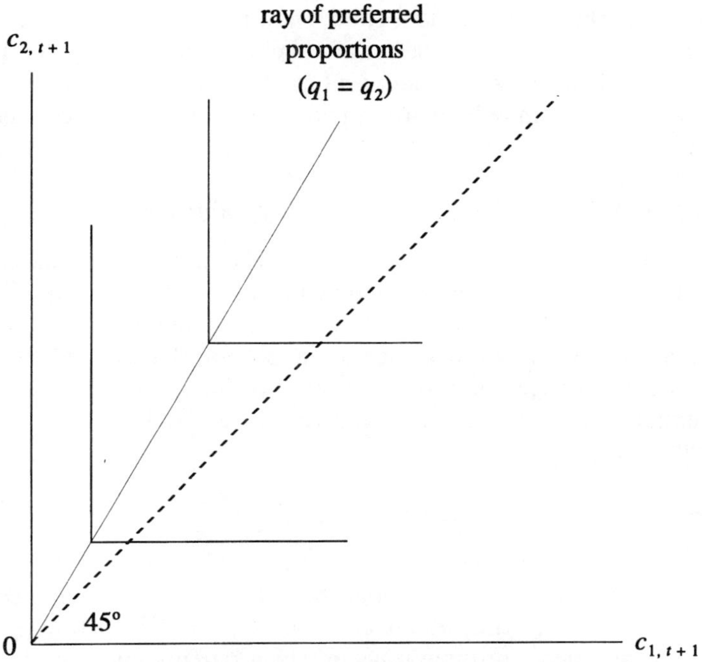

11.9 Equal Concern for Happiness, Unequal Concern for Consumption

(6)′ If the accumulation of altruism for each child were costless, all parents would prefer more.

(7)′ At a given intragenerational allocation of children-oriented resources, the willingness to sacrifice q_2 for q_1 is proportional to $u_{2,t+1}/u_{1,t+1}$.

(8)′ Holding constant $u_{2,t+1}$ and $u_{1,t+1}$, the willingness to pay for q_2 is less when q_2 is greater.

If $q_1 = q_2$ and $R = p = 1$, then the ray of preferred proportions in the $[u_{1,t+1}, u_{2,t+1}]$ plane is the 45-degree line, both children are equally happy, and child 2 consumes more. For a *given* allocation of child-oriented resources, parents mitigate unequal happiness in the family by giving additional consumption to the less happy child.[6] However, endogenous altruism produces another force. Parents' willingness to pay for child-oriented resources depends on the *happiness* of the child. Child-oriented resources and happiness are complements like the ski trips and ski equipment of chapter 4. Parents are therefore more willing to purchase child-oriented

6. This is a result that depends on a strong parental preference for moderation. See Mulligan (1993, chapter 4) for a discussion.

resources for the happier child—child 1 in this case—which shifts the ray of preferred proportions back toward the 45-degree line in the $[c_{1,\,t+1}, c_{2,\,t+1}]$ plane. In other words, endogenous altruism can aggravate unequal happiness in the family by causing parents to care more about the happier child.[7]

Do Parents Mitigate or Aggravate Inequality within the Family?

I show in this section how the standard model of altruism and the endogenous altruism model can offer different answers to the question, "Do parents mitigate or aggravate inequality within the family?" I offer new interpretations of a variety of evidence on family transfers, including studies of bequests, primogeniture, the treatment of handicapped children, the differential treatment of married and unmarried adult children, and the strategy of beggars.

Mitigation of Inequality in the Standard Model

The standard model of the altruistic allocation of consumption—in which altruism is exogenous—predicts that parents tend to mitigate inequality in the family. To see this, let altruism be exogenous by setting $q_1 = q_2$. With $q_1 = q_2$, there are three ways in which parents mitigate inequality among children:[8]

(1) Parents allocate equal consumption to children with equal happiness.
(2) Parents transfer more resources to children with lower earnings.
(3) Parents allocate more consumption to less happy children.

With $q_1 = q_2$ and each child equally happy at a given level of consumption, the ray of preferred proportions is the 45-degree line in the $[c_{1,\,t+1}, c_{2,\,t+1}]$ plane, so, regardless of economic opportunities, parents allocate the same consumption to each child. This proves result (1). To prove result (2), remember from chapter 3 that each child consumes his earnings plus a parental transfer. If the consumption of both children is the same and their

7. This result does not depend on the assumed proportionality of the happiness difference between child 1 and child 2. See Appendix G or Mulligan (1993, chapter 4) for a proof.

8. Some of the particular results depend on the strong parental preference for moderation. It is also possible that, in the presence of borrowing constraints, parents aggravate in inequality in the standard model (see Behrman, Pollak, and Taubman 1995 for a discussion), but the basic conclusion of this section—that endogenous altruism tends to aggravate inequality within the family *relative* to standard models—is robust to generalizations of the model. See Mulligan (1993, chapter 4) for some proofs.

earnings are different, then the parental transfer must be larger for the child with less earnings. Result (3) is the "relative happiness" effect.

Endogenous Altruism Tends to Aggravate Inequality

Altruistic parents mitigate inequality within the family in standard models where altruism is exogenous. However, the accumulation of altruism can aggravate inequality within the family. Four additional results may obtain when parents choose to accumulate altruism:

(4) Parents allocate less consumption and child-oriented resources toward a child whose consumption is more expensive.
(5) Parents allocate less consumption and child-oriented resources toward a child whose child-oriented resources are more expensive.
(6) Parents allocate fewer child-oriented resources to less happy children.
(7) Parents may target concern and consumption toward a few children.

Result (4) is the "relative price of giving effect," result (5) is the "relative price of altruism" effect, and result (6) is the "relative happiness" effect.

Result (7) follows from the complementarity model. If the complementarity between child-oriented resources and consumption of a child is sufficiently strong, parents may treat children very differently.[9] Consider the ski example from chapter 4. Let the ski equipment and ski trips be the analogues to the consumption and child-oriented resources of child 1 and let golf equipment and golf trips be the analogues to the consumption and child-oriented resources of child 2. In this example, imagine that skiing and golf may not be very different in terms of their ability to make a consumer happy but, because of the complementarity of trips in equipment and the fact that incomes are limited, it makes sense to concentrate on just one sport. It may not make sense to take an equal number of ski and golf trips and have an equal amount of ski and golf equipment. Some people may concentrate on skiing, taking a lot of trips and buying a lot of equipment, while only taking one golf trip and buying only basic golf equipment. Others may concentrate on golf. The analogy with the stated problem is that the complementarity of child-oriented resources and consumption may cause families to concentrate on one child (or a few children).

9. In terms of the mathematical model of Appendix G, "sufficiently strong" complementarity means that second-order conditions fail in some regions of the choice set.

Interpreting Evidence on Family Transfers

Because the usual model of altruism tends to predict that parents mitigate inequality in the family, the prediction has been the focus of several empirical studies. A variety of results have been found. Nigel Tomes (1981), for example, argues that poorer siblings enjoy larger inheritances from parents. Paul Menchik (1980; 1988) and Mark Wilhelm (1990), on the other hand, argue that inheritances are equally divided among siblings. Peter Lindert's (1977) study of the achievement of siblings by birth order suggests that siblings are not treated equally. Donald Cox (1987) shows that unmarried children and adult children who live with their parents receive greater parental transfers than their siblings. B. Douglas Bernheim, Andrei Shleifer, and Lawrence Summers (1985) suggest that adult children who spend more time with their aging parents enjoy larger bequests. Jere Behrman, Robert Pollak, and Paul Taubman (1995) study financial transfers from parents to adult children in the PSID and Wilhelm (1990) studies large estates subject to federal tax in 1982, showing that parental financial transfers do not seem to fully compensate children with low earnings.[10] Donald Cox and Mark Rank (1992) find that adult children with low earnings may be more likely to receive large financial transfers from parents. Casual observation suggests that at least some handicapped children enjoy more parental attention and resources than nonhandicapped siblings. On the other hand, some parents may abort an unborn child who is expected to be handicapped.

Are these findings consistent with a model of altruistically motivated transfers? Findings such as Tomes's (1981)—that parental transfers tend to mitigate inequality—may be consistent with the usual model of exogenous altruism. However, the other findings, such as those of Menchik (1980), Lindert (1977), Bernheim, Shleifer, and Summers (1985), and Behrman, Pollak, and Taubman (1995), suggest that parents fail to use transfers to mitigate inequality and seem to be inconsistent with the usual model.

Although inconsistent with the usual model, our results (4) through (7) suggest that findings of parental aggravation of inequality may be consistent with our model of endogenous altruism. Strong complementarities between child-oriented resources and consumption by children may lead to parents to focus resources on a few children, such as sons or the first-born. First-born children also have a monopoly on parental time before

10. There are several other studies of the allocation of resources within the family including Lazear and Michael (1988), Pitt and Rosenzweig (1990), Rosenzweig and Schultz (1982), and Schultz (1982), but the evidence presented in those studies are less directly related to the theoretical models of interest here.

the second sibling arrives so, to the extent that the time that parents and children spend together involves the accumulation of child-oriented resources, parents may become more concerned with the success of the firstborn.[11] Adult children who live with parents or who visit parents often may also contribute to the accumulation of child-oriented resources.

The usual model of altruism can explain why parents of a handicapped child may devote extra resources to him, but—since altruism is truly exogenous—it cannot explain why parents might try to abort a handicapped fetus. Our model of endogenous altruism explains this as parents who *anticipate* that, with time, they will become attached to their children. Whether ethically defensible or not, some of these parents decide that it is better to avoid becoming attached to a handicapped child and instead focus their love and concern on another healthy child who may be more capable of being happy. This is the "relative happiness" effect reported in the previous section.

One interpretation of the "relative price of giving" R is that it measures the "effectiveness" of the transfer.[12] In other words, the "relative price of giving" effect means that *altruists allocate their altruism where their transfers are most effective.* This result was observed by Adam Smith,

> When the happiness or misery of others depends in any respect upon our conduct, we dare not, as self-love might suggest to us, prefer the interest of one to that of many. The man within [ourselves] immediately calls to us, that we value ourselves too much and other people too little. . . . When the happiness or misery of others, indeed, in no respect depends upon our own conduct . . . we do not always think it so necessary to restrain, either our natural and, perhaps, improper anxiety about our own affairs. (1982 [1790], III.3.5–7)

Not only does the amount of benevolent behavior respond to the effectiveness of that behavior, observes Smith, but so does the *degree of concern.* Although Smith may have a somewhat different explanation for his observation, his observation is consistent with an important prediction of this chapter: altruism responds to the effectiveness of transfers. For example, doctors will tend to love those who need medical attention, instead of those who need, say, legal assistance.

Another application of the relative price of giving effect is the differential parental treatment of married and unmarried adult children observed by Cox (1987). It can be cheaper to give to an unmarried child because

11. See C. Y. Cyrus Chu (1991) for another "increasing returns" explanation of primogeniture.

12. I thank Gary Becker for suggesting this interpretation of the transfer price.

free-riding in-laws are involved with married children. To see this, notice that a transfer made by one set of parents (say the husband's) to the married couple may reduce transfers made by the wife's parents, although not necessarily dollar-for-dollar. From the husband's parents' point of view, it is as if transfers to their married son are more expensive than those to unmarried children because they must sacrifice more than a dollar to increase the consumption of the married couple by a dollar. Free-riding of other potential donors is the topic of the next section and of chapter 12.

Altruism and Insurance in the Family

The standard model of exogenous altruism predicts that shocks to the income of one family member should be fully shared by the entire family. If, for example, one member of a five-person family looses $1,000, all five members of the family should reduce their consumption by roughly $200. The exogenous altruism model is very much like an insurance model in this way. However, the "full insurance" behavior is not the result when altruism is endogenous. If parents are hit with a favorable income surprise and that shock increases their value of time, the cost of accumulating altruism increases relative to the increase in total family resources, parental altruism falls, and parents allocate a smaller fraction of their resources to children. Thus it appears, as Joseph Altonji, Fumio Hayashi, and Larry Kotlikoff (1992) find, that parents do not "adequately" share their income surprise with their children. If, instead, children receive the income shock, the extra income increases total family income without affecting the cost to parents of accumulating altruism. Parental altruism increases and parents devote a larger fraction of total family resources to children. It therefore appears that parents consume "too little" of the additional income enjoyed by children. Although the endogenous altruism model may not fully explain the results of Altonji, Hayashi, and Kotlikoff (1992), it is no longer true that altruism and insurance are identical when altruism is endogenous.

The Beggar's Strategy

Another application of the "relative happiness effect" is to the behavior of beggars and potential donors. Let's interpret the "parents" in our model as potential donors and the "children" as potential recipients of donations including children, relatives, friends, charities, and beggars. If beggars are the least happy of the potential recipients, the "relative happiness effect" of our model predicts that potential donors will refrain from accumulating altruism for beggars. This behavior of potential donors can involve avoiding eye contact with a beggar or avoiding viewing him at all.

If for some reason a potential donor does accumulate altruism for a beggar on a par with that accumulated for other recipients, I have shown that donors might make the largest transfers to the least happy recipient—the beggar. If beggars know that potential donors behave this way, they may try to capture the attention of potential donors with the hope that some altruism might be accumulated. The potential donors, on the other hand, are trying to avoid eye contact—eye contact presents the danger that altruism might accumulate—because they feel that their altruism is better spent on happier recipients.

Divorce, Parental Altruism, and Child Welfare

So far, the analysis assumes that two parents make decisions about consumption and child-oriented resources together. Cooperation of mother and father is a realistic model for some married couples, but it is probably quite unrealistic for a mother and father who are divorced. Here I model the formation of parental altruism by a father who is divorced from his wife—she has custody of their child—and show that divorced fathers are less likely to care about their children.[13]

In my model, resources allocated to children of divorced parents are determined in two stages:

Stage 1: The father decides on his degree of altruism and on the amount of money to give to the child.
Stage 2: With the knowledge of father's transfer, the mother decides how much to consume and how much to give to the child.

To simplify the exposition, I assume that the mother's degree of intergenerational altruism is exogenous. I denote consumption by father, mother, and child as (c_d, c_m, c_k), respectively. I assume that a father is able to anticipate how his actions affect the mother's choices in the second stage, so I analyze the second stage of the problem first.[14]

The mother cares about her consumption and the consumption of her child. Because her altruism is exogenous, her indifference curves in the

13. Custody of the child—not gender—is the important theoretical distinction between "fathers" and "mothers" in my model.

14. In the language of game theory, my analysis of the second stage first assumes a Stackelberg equilibrium concept. In particular, I assume that a mother does not try to threaten a father with the starvation of their child in order to convince the father to transfer more. In a "one-shot" game, the threat would not be credible because the father knows that the mother is altruistic and therefore will not starve the child. However, threats by the mother may be credible in a "repeated" version of this game. For a discussion of repeated games and equilibrium concepts, see Drew Fudenberg and Jean Tirole (1991).

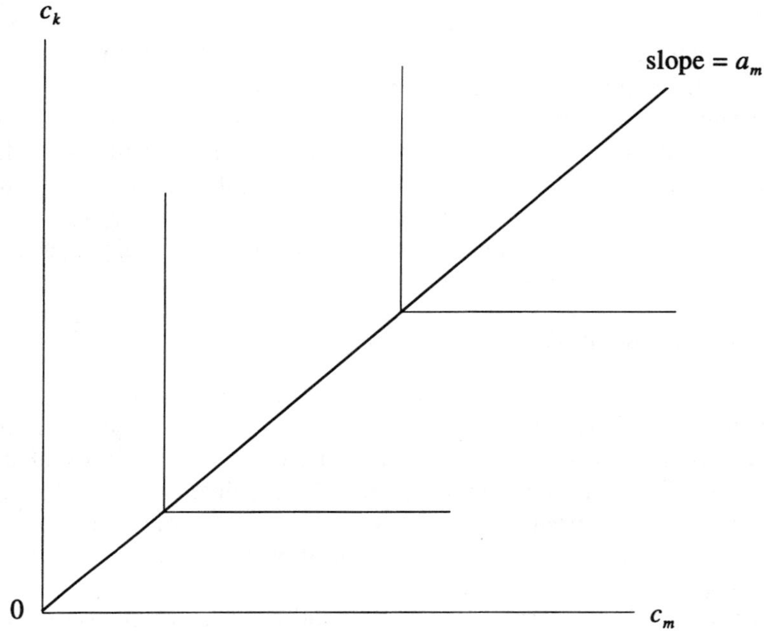

11.10 A Divorced Mother's Indifference Curves

$[c_m, c_k]$ plane have a single ray of preferred proportions whose slope I denote a_m. Figure 11.10 displays the divorced mother's indifference curves.

A mother has her own resources A_m and the transfer from the child's father x. Clearly it is feasible for the mother to consume A_m and the child to consume x, an allocation which is displayed as a square dot in figure 11.11. If the consumption of mother and child have the same price, then the mother can sacrifice a dollar of her own consumption to increase the child's consumption by a dollar or vice versa.[15] The feasible consumption allocations in the $[c_m, c_k]$ plane can therefore be displayed as a line with slope one passing through (A_m, x) as shown by the solid line in figure 11.11.

What happens to consumption by the child when the father contributes an additional \$100? As shown in figure 11.11, the maternal budget constraint shifts to the right in a parallel fashion by \$100. The mother determines the consumption allocation according to the ray of preferred proportions, which means that both the consumption of mother and child increase. Since c_m increases, it must be the case that c_k increases by less

15. The intergenerational price of consumption can be allowed to include an interest rate, as in chapters 3 and 4, without changing any of the results.

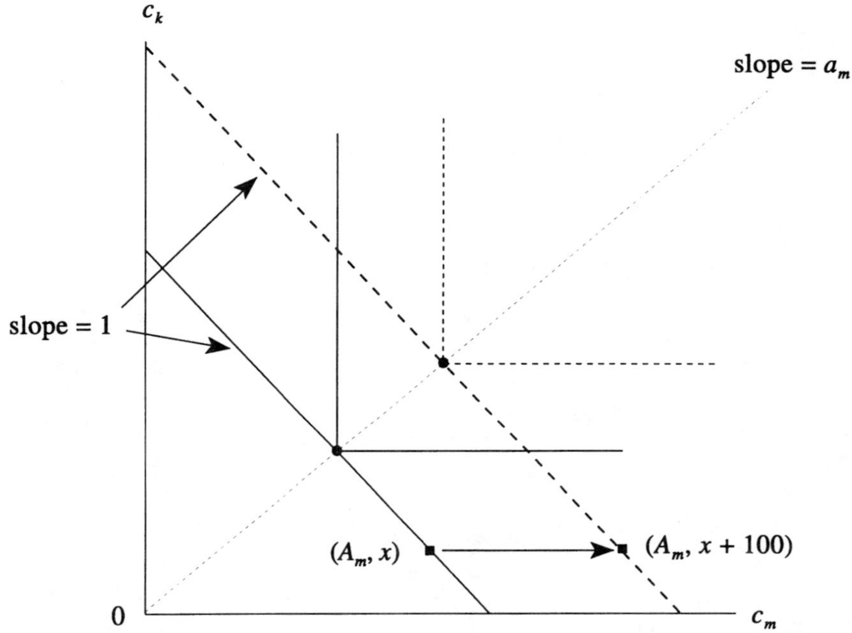

11.11 Effect of the Paternal Contribution on the Divorced Mother's Decision

than \$100.[16] *So, for his \$100, the father gets less than \$100 of additional consumption by the child; the price of child consumption is, from the point of view of the father, greater than one.* The key difference between a married and a divorced father in my model is that the divorced father faces a higher price of child consumption.[17]

Price of Paternal Giving—Exogenous Altruism

The father, who has resources A_d, cares about his consumption and the consumption of his child. His indifference curves in the $[c_d, c_k]$ plane have a ray of preferred proportions whose slope I denote as a_d. Figure 11.12 displays an indifference curve and the corresponding ray of preferred proportions for the father. For the purposes of exposition, a_d is taken as given in this section and treated as an object of choice in the next section.

Because the mother consumes part of the transfer that a father gives to the child, the price of the child's consumption is greater than one from the

16. Mathematically, c_m increases by $100^*(1 + a_m)$ and c_k increases by $100^*am_{(1 + am)}$.

17. The effect of divorce on the price of giving has been studied by Yoram Weiss and Robert Willis (1985) and others. The novelty here is to study the effect of the price of giving on altruism.

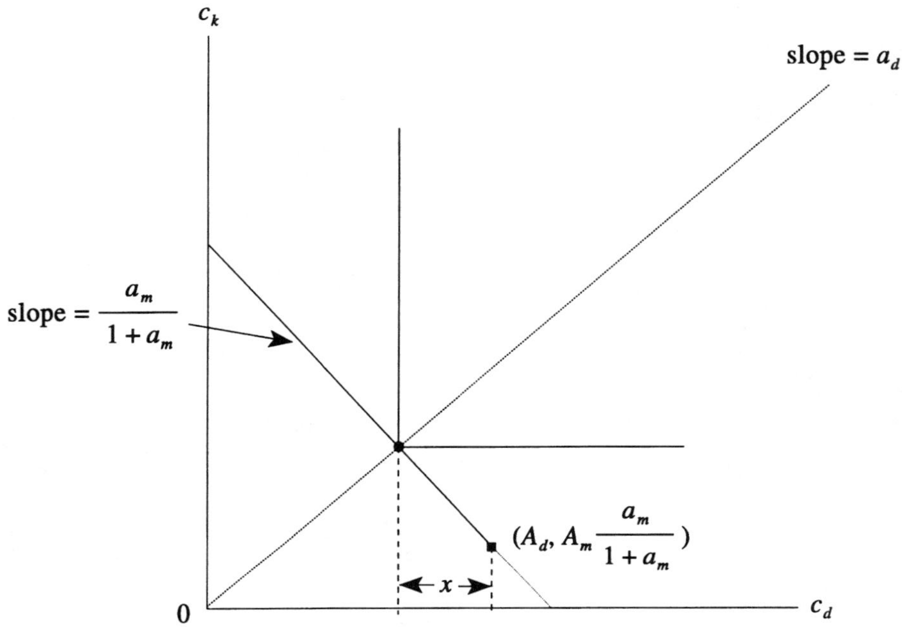

11.12 A Divorced Father's Consumption Choice

father's point of view. Mathematically, that price is $1 + (1/a_m)$, where a_m is the slope of the mother's ray of preferred proportions. The slope of the father's budget constraint in the $[c_d, c_k]$ plane must therefore be the reciprocal of that price, $a_m/(1 + a_m)$. To determine the position of the budget constraint, consider the case that the father makes no transfer. The father consumes his resources A_d and the mother and child share the mother's resources A_m. Since the mother's ray of preferred proportions has slope a_m, the child's share of the mother's resources is $A_m a_m/(1 + a_m)$. This feasible allocation $(A_d, A_m a_m/(1 + a_m))$ is shown in figure 11.12 as a square dot. The father's budget constraint passes through the square dot and has a slope of $a_m/(1 + a_m)$, such as the solid line shown in figure 11.12.

Notice that the father's transfer can be computed graphically in figure 11.12 in much the same way that transfers are computed in chapter 3. The father transfers what he does not consume $(A_d - c_d)$, which can be measured as the horizontal distance between the square dot and the consumption allocation, the round dot. That horizontal distance is marked x in the figure, where x denotes the quantity of consumption resources transferred by the father to the child.

The father's budget constraint is shown as a dashed line to the right of the square dot in figure 11.12 because it is assumed that negative transfers ($c_d > A_d$) are not possible. If the father's ray of preferred proportions passes below the square dot, then the father's chosen consumption allocation will be the square dot.

Notice that more altruism by the mother shifts the square dot to the right and increases the slope of the father's budget constraint in the $[c_d, c_k]$ plane, which means that both father and child consume more. More altruism by the father shifts his ray of preferred proportions upward, which increases c_k, decreases c_d, and (because the transfer increases) increases c_m.

Paternal Altruism Formation

To see how divorce affects intergenerational altruism, remember from chapter 4 how intergenerational altruism is formed by parents who are married (and cooperate). The main difference is that the price of child consumption from the point of view of a father who cooperates with his wife is one. This means that his budget constraint is steeper in the $[c_d, c_k]$ plane. From the "relative price of giving" effect derived in "Accumulating Altruism for Several Children," one can predict that fathers will accumulate more concern for children in marriage than out of marriage. Our complementarity model produces this result: child-oriented resources and the consumption of the child are complements, so more expensive consumption means less accumulation of child-oriented resources.

Consider a father with a natural child from a previous marriage and a stepchild from a current marriage. The price of consumption of the stepchild is (assuming that the father can cooperate with his new wife) one, while the price of consumption of the natural child is greater than one (because the natural child's mother consumes part of the father's transfer). The different prices of giving encourage the father to accumulate altruism for his stepchild and not for his natural child. See Barry Hewlett (1992) for some evidence suggesting that the concern of fathers for natural children often declines after divorce and loss of custody.

Divorce can also have a total resource effect. Family resources can be lost not only because divorce lawyers must be paid but also because two separate households must be maintained. As shown in chapter 4, the effect of a decrease of total family resources is to reduce the accumulation of altruism.

My result that marriage encourages intergenerational altruism suggests that marriage and altruism are complements. With a complementarity between altruism and marriage, an increase in altruism (for example, because the interest rate is high) encourages marriage and discourages divorce.

Other Applications

There are two other applications of this two-stage model. One was discussed in "Do Parents Mitigate or Aggravate Inequality within the Family?": the differential treatment of married and unmarried adult children. The wife's parents are the analogue to the mother in this example. A larger transfer by the husband's parents reduces transfers made by the wife's parents, which increases the cost to the husband's parents of transferring resources to their son and his wife. Our model predicts less altruism and fewer transfers by the husband's parents.

A second application is to the effect of merit goods on altruism. Gary Becker (1991) *assumes* that the consumption of *merit goods*—such as going to church or "saying no to drugs"—by children increases the altruism of parents. Rather than *assuming* this result, it can be *derived* from the two-stage model. Suppose that parents care about their own consumption c_t and the consumption of merit goods by their child c_M. In the first stage, parents choose their degree of altruism (their ray of preferred proportions in the $[c_t, c_M]$ plane) and their transfer to the child. In the second stage, the child spends fraction $a_M/(1 + a_M)$ of his resources on merit goods and the fraction $1/(1 + a_M)$ on other goods. The price of merit goods from the point of view of parents is therefore $1 + 1/a_M$. A child with a higher a_M consumes more merit goods, thereby lowering the price of merit goods from the point of view of his parents, which encourages his parents to accumulate altruism.

Review of the Main Results

Parents choose altruism and transfers for each of two children in the model of this chapter. The model can also be interpreted as a donor who is choosing among several charities.

Total family resources and the interest rate do not affect the distribution of resources among siblings, but the relative price of giving, the relative price of caring, and the relative happiness of the two children do. When altruism is endogenous—as modeled in this chapter—parental transfers can either mitigate or aggravate inequality within the family, a result which suggests new interpretations of a variety of evidence on family transfers.

The "relative price of giving" effect on altruism and transfers is emphasized in the final section of the chapter. I show how divorce or the consumption of nonmerit goods can discourage the accumulation of intergenerational altruism by parents.

Appendix G: A Mathematical Model of Altruism with Several Children

A mathematical model of the formation of intergenerational altruism that allows parents to treat siblings differently is presented in this appendix. The first section specifies the full problem, describing parental choices and showing how the problem can be broken into two stages. Solutions to the second-stage problem are characterized in the following section.

G.1 Preferences and Permanent Income Constraints

In the full problem with two children, there are five goods (c_t, $c_{1,t+1}$, $c_{2,t+1}$, q_1, q_2). c_t is consumption by parents, $c_{1,t+1}$ is consumption by child 1, and $c_{2,t+1}$ is consumption by child 2. q_1 and q_2 are child-oriented resources oriented toward child 1 and 2, respectively. Total family resources A_t, can be spent on the five goods:

$$A_t = c_t + \frac{c_{1,t+1}}{1+r} + R\frac{c_{2,t+1}}{1+r} + p_1q_1 + p_2q_2 \qquad (11.2)$$

R is the relative price of $c_{1,t+1}$ and $c_{2,t+1}$. p_2/p_1 is the relative price of q_1 and q_2 and is denoted p.

Parental preferences for the five goods are:

$$V(c_t, c_{1,t+1}, c_{2,t+1}, q_1, q_2) \equiv \min\{f(q_1 + q_2)c_t, g(q_1)\mu c_{1,t+1}, g(q_2)c_{2,t+1}\} \quad (11.3)$$

μ denotes the relative ability of child 1 to produce utility from consumption. For $\mu > 1$ ($\mu < 1$), child 1 is more (less) happy than child 2 at the same level of consumption.

Choices for the five goods that maximize $V(c_t, c_{1,t+1}, c_{2,t+1}, q_1, q_2)$ subject to the budget constraint 11.2, must also solve another maximization problem:

$$\max[\min\{g(q_1)\mu c_{1,t+1}, g(q_2)c_{2,t+1}\}]$$

$$\text{s.t.}$$

$$q_1 + pq_2 = Q$$

$$c_{1,t+1} + Rc_{2,t+1} = C_{t+1} \qquad (11.4)$$

This simpler maximization problem can be thought of as the second stage of the full problem. In the first stage, parents decide how much to consume and the total amount to spend on child-oriented resources ($Q = q_1 + pq_2$). In the second stage, remaining consumption C_{t+1} and child-oriented resources Q are allocated among the two children.

G.2 Characterization of the Solution to the Second-Stage Problem

For given q_1 and q_2, parents allocate consumption to the two children in fixed proportions $c_{2,\,t+1} = \mu g(q_2)/g(q_1)$. Using the fixed proportion, one can derive a reduced form utility function in terms of q_1 and q_2:

$$v(q_1, q_2) \equiv \mu \frac{g(q_2)}{1 + R\mu \dfrac{g(q_2)}{g(q_1)}} C_{t+1} \tag{11.5}$$

The reduced form utility function also depends on the total amount of consumption resources (C_{t+1}), which are taken as given in the second-stage problem. Variables such as total family resources A_t and the interest rate r affect the second-stage problem only through their effect on C_{t+1} and Q.

The willingness to pay for q_1 is the slope of the indifference curves of $v(q_1, q_2)$:

$$\text{willingness to pay for } q_1 = \frac{\dfrac{\partial v}{\partial q_1}}{\dfrac{\partial v}{\partial q_2}} = R\mu \frac{g(q_2)}{g(q_1)} \frac{g'(q_1)/g(q_1)}{g'(q_2)/g(q_2)} \tag{11.6}$$

The slope of the budget constraint in the $[q_1, q_2]$ plane is $1/p$, so the willingness to pay above is equated to $1/p$ at the chosen allocation (q_1, q_2).

Proposition 1. All families treat children equally (in terms of consumption and child-oriented resources) when $R = p = \mu = 1$.

Proof: Given the symmetry of the second-stage problem for $R = p = \mu = 1$, the proposition is not surprising. It can be proven by first showing that $q_1 = q_2$ satisfies the first-order condition 11.7 when $R = p = \mu = 1$. $q_1 = q_2$ then implies that the fixed proportion is $c_1 = c_2$.

Proposition 2. If $g(q)$ is a Cobb-Douglas function, q_2/q_1 is independent of Q.

Proof: The first-order condition determining the optimal q_2 in the second-stage problem is:

$$\frac{\dfrac{\partial v}{\partial q_1}}{\dfrac{\partial v}{\partial q_2}} = R\mu \frac{g(q_2)}{g(q_1)} \frac{g'(q_1)/g(q_1)}{g'(q_2)/g(q_2)} = \frac{1}{p} \tag{11.7}$$

With Cobb-Douglas $g(q)$, this condition determines the ratio q_2/q_1 as a function of R and μ only.

Corollary: If $g(q)$ is a Cobb-Douglas function, q_2/q_1 and c_2/c_1 are independent of total family resources and the interest rate.

Proof: Proposition 2 shows that, with a Cobb-Douglas $g(q)$, the first-order condition $(\partial v/\partial q_1)/(\partial v/\partial q_2) = 1/p$ determines the ratio q_2/q_1 as a function R and μ only. From the fixed proportions, $c_2/c_1 = \mu g(q_2)/g(q_1)$, which, with a Cobb-Douglas $g(q)$, depends only on μ and the ratio q_2/q_1.

Proposition 3. A higher price of consumption for a child reduces his share of consumption and child-oriented resources.

Proof: Substituting the constraint $q_1 = Q - pq_2$ into the first-order condition 11.7 and differentiating with respect to R shows that $dq_2/dR < 0$. It follows that higher R decreases q_2/q_1 and since $c_{2,\,t+1} = \mu g(q_2)/g(q_1)$, $c_{2,\,t+1}/c_{1,\,t+1}$.

Proposition 4. More child-oriented resources and perhaps more consumption are allocated to the child who is happier for a given level of consumption.

Proof: Substituting the constraint $q_1 = Q - pq_2$ into the first-order condition 11.7 and differentiating with respect to R shows that $dq_2/d\mu < 0$. It follows that higher μ decreases q_2/q_1, although perhaps not $c_{2,\,t+1}/c_{1,\,t+1}$.

Proposition 5. A higher price of child-oriented resources for a child reduces his share of consumption and child-oriented resources.

Proof: Substituting the constraint $q_1 = Q - pq_2$ into the first-order condition 11.7 and differentiating with respect to R shows that $dq_2/dp < 0$. It follows that higher p decreases q_2/q_1 and since $c_{2,\,t+1}/c_{1,\,t+1} = \mu g(q_2)/g(q_1)$, $c_{2,\,t+1}/c_{1,\,t+1}$ falls.

CHAPTER *12*

Altruism and Giving beyond the Family

Transfers of resources across families are an important part of economic activity and have important effects on economic inequality.[1] Those transfers include welfare programs and contributions to churches, schools, and hospitals. Some are voluntary charitable giving and others are enforced or encouraged by the government. This chapter uses the model of the formation of altruism proposed and developed in chapters 4 and 11 to derive predictions for voluntary giving within and beyond the family. "Government Transfers and Parental Altruism" models the effect of a government welfare program on parental altruism and the welfare of children. I show that, although children of welfare families can benefit from the additional resources provided by the program, a welfare program may affect the formation of intergenerational altruism by parents. Some of the activities of charities are analyzed in "Private Charities and Endogenous Impure Altruism." Charitable activities often suffer from a "free-rider" problem: the objective of the charity is desirable to many people but the giving of a typical donor can only have a very small effect on the charity's objective. This environment is different from giving within the family because the sacrifices of parents can and almost always do have a very large effect on the welfare of children. Beginning with the model of chapter 4, this second section studies how the free-rider problem makes the formation of altruism beyond the family different from the formation of altruism within the family. "Charitable Giving over Time" makes predictions for the evolution over time of aggregate charitable giving.

1. Charles T. Clotfelter (1985, pp. 3–7) estimates that charitable giving is more than 2 percent of GNP and that, including volunteer work, nonprofit organizations employ well over 10 percent of the U.S. labor force.

Chapter 4 emphasizes the effects of three variables on the formation of altruism: total resources, the value of time, and the interest rate. The value of time matters because it is an important component of the price of altruism. The interest rate dictates the price of giving in the model of chapter 4. More total resources increases altruism, a higher price of altruism lowers it, and a higher price of giving lowers it. Here I use these three results and derive some others to make predictions about the effects of public and private charitable activities. An understanding of the analysis in chapter 4 is therefore required to follow the arguments in this chapter.

Government Transfers and Parental Altruism

Chapter 5 studies the effect of income and estate taxation on intergenerational altruism and intergenerational mobility. This section studies some effects from the other side of the government ledger: its spending programs. In particular, the U.S. government has a variety of programs, including food and medical assistance to single mothers and subsidized education, intended to boost the consumption of children. I derive some predictions of my model for the consumption of children and the accumulation of altruism and compare them with the standard model.

I first focus on education subsidies. Then I look at government programs that provide a minimum level of consumption for children. Because all government programs must be paid for with taxes of some kind, I then begin to combine the analysis of taxes from chapter 5 with the analysis of spending programs from this chapter.

I include my analysis of government transfer programs with my analysis of charitable giving because, at least to some extent, government welfare and education programs are like nationally sponsored charities. The key difference between the two is that governments use their power to tax to obtain revenue for their transfer programs while private charities must solicit voluntary donations.

Education Subsidies

Suppose a government program were to subsidize the formation of human capital, perhaps by matching parental expenditures on education. A subsidy program of this kind has the effect of increasing the level and slope of the earnings function. Consider the earnings functions shown in figure 12.1. Without a government subsidy, parental expenditures on the human capital of children (h_{t+1}) produce earnings of children (e_{t+1}) according to the solid curve shown in the figure. When the government matches parental expenditure, government funds are added to the parental expenditure so any h_{t+1} produces more earnings for children. This effect of the govern-

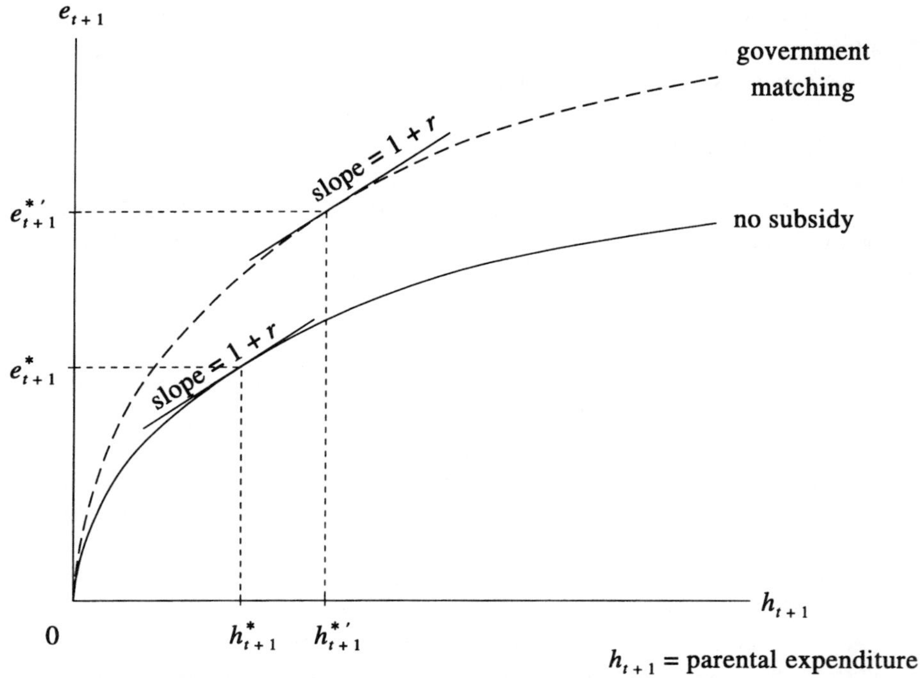

12.1 Education Subsidies and Earnings Functions

ment subsidy amounts to an upward shift of the earnings function as shown in figure 12.1. The shift is larger for a large parental expenditure h because the government contribution is proportional to h.

In the permanent income model of opportunities, the human capital investment chosen by parents (h^{*}_{t+1}) occurs at the point where the slope of the earnings function equals $(1 + r)$. Because the government subsidy effectively increases the slope of the earnings function, parents increase the human capital investment and children enjoy more earnings.

What is the effect of the subsidy on consumption and altruism? Because the government subsidy encourages human capital investment, it effectively shifts upwards the earnings endowment (e_t, e_{t+1}) in the [c_t, c_{t+1}] plane. However, remember from chapters 3 and 4 that, because the rate of interest determines the slope of the intergenerational budget constraint in the [c_t,c_{t+1}] plane, a shift of the earnings endowment does not change that slope. Nor does the government subsidy affect the price of accumulating altruism. So there is only a "total resource effect" on altruism. The introduction of the government subsidy increases the consumption by parents, consumption by children, and the accumulation of altruism because of the "total resource effect." The ratio c_{t+1}/c_t increases because altruism increases.

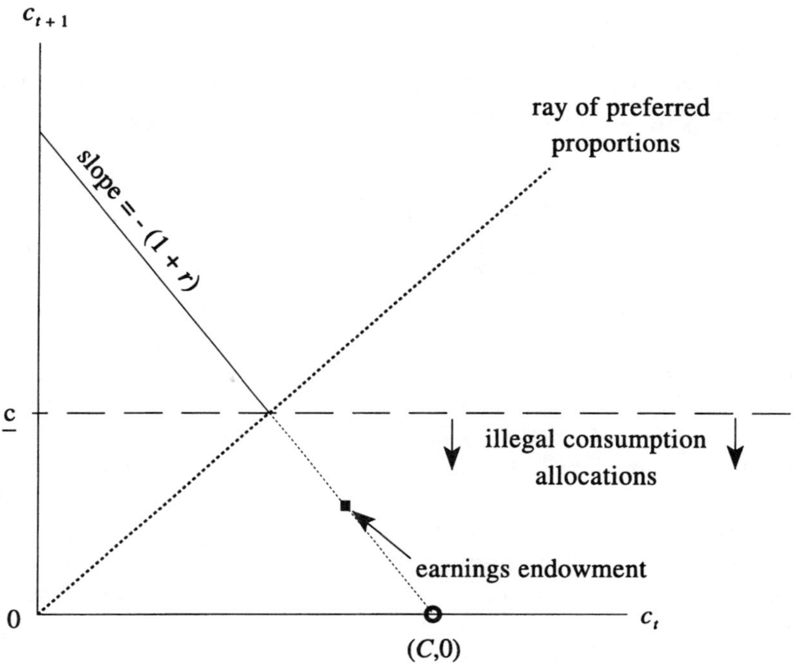

12.2 Government-guaranteed Consumption for Children

Education subsidies must be financed with tax revenues. Therefore my final consideration in this section is of some of the possible tax systems that might be used to raise the revenue for an education subsidy in order to work out the full effect of the program on consumption and altruism.

Government-guaranteed Consumption for Children

Another government policy that might be intended to help children is to require parents to provide for some minimum level of consumption for the child.[2] To see the effect this would have on family decisions, one needs to study the effect on the intergenerational budget constraint. Let (e_t, e_{t+1}) be the earnings endowment shown as a square in figure 12.2. Without the government program, the intergenerational budget constraint in the $[c_t, c_{t+1}]$ plane is a line with slope $-(1 + r)$ passing through the earnings endowment and extending to the point $(C, 0)$.[3] If the government requires

2. Throughout the book, I interpret c_{t+1} as adult consumption by children and c_t as adult consumption by parents. Another interpretation for c_{t+1} that is especially appropriate for this section is the *childhood* consumption by children.

3. Remember from chapter 4 that C is consumption resources or total family resources A minus the cost $\theta(a)$ of accumulating altruism.

that parents provide for a minimum level $\underline{c}$ of consumption for children, than allocations below the horizontal dashed line are not permitted and the intergenerational budget constraint consists only of the solid line. The allocation (C, 0), for example, is not a feasible choice under the government program because it does not provide the minimum consumption level for the child. How does the government regulation affect the accumulation of altruism? If, in the absence of the regulation, the parental ray of preferred proportions in the $[c_t, c_{t+1}]$ plane is at or above that shown in figure 12.2, the parents already provide the minimum consumption level for children and the regulation does not affect them. Suppose instead that the ray of preferred proportions were below. There are two effects on the incentives for parents to invest in altruism. First, the parental willingness to pay for altruism is proportional to the consumption of children, which increases as a result of the regulation. Parents might therefore increase their altruism, perhaps to the point indicated by the ray of preferred proportions shown in the figure. However, there can be another effect. Holding constant consumption resources C, the regulation takes parents off their ray of preferred proportions—they must sacrifice their own consumption in order to provide more for their child. One way that parents might return to their ray of preferred proportion is to *reduce* their accumulation of altruism, which, because that accumulation is costly, frees up resources for consumption, which shifts the budget constraint to the right in the $[c_t, c_{t+1}]$ plane. The ray of preferred proportions shifts downward with less altruism, but the resources gained might be large enough that the new proportions are affordable with $c_{t+1} > \underline{c}$.

Together with a regulation on the minimum consumption for children, a government program may also provide the necessary resources to poor families. Medicaid and school lunch programs are examples of government programs that attempt to provide a minimum consumption level for children. The increase in total family resources resulting from the government provision is an additional effect that tends to increase altruism.

The government provision of resources to poor families also has several other effects because the government transfers are often contingent on characteristics of the recipient. For example, mainly poor unmarried mothers are eligible for AFDC (Aid for Families with Dependent Children), and they are the largest block of recipients of Medicaid (U.S. House of Representatives 1994). Moreover, the amount of government aid is larger for mothers with more children. These contingencies affect the behavior of recipients, providing incentives for young women to be unmarried, fail to earn income, and have more children.[4] I show in chapter 4 that

4. See Hilary Williamson Hoynes (1995), Robert Moffitt (1994), Mark Rosenzweig (1995), and T. Paul Schultz (1994) for some studies of these effects of AFDC and Medicaid.

higher fertility can lower altruism per child and consumption per child. I show in chapter 11 that children of unmarried parents may enjoy less consumption and altruism. A government program that lowers the value of a mother's time, on the other hand, can promote the accumulation of altruism to the extent that child-oriented resources are time-intensive. So the net effect of a government transfer program can be to either increase or decrease intergenerational altruism.

Combined Effects of Spending and Tax Programs

The education subsidy tends to increase altruism and the consumption of children because of a "total resource effect." The government-guaranteed minimum consumption can also have a total resource effect. However, both programs must be financed by taxes. To the extent that the taxes are levied on the families that receive the subsidy or are subject to the minimum consumption regulation, then there is a *negative* total resource effect on altruism and consumption by children. The net total resource effect may actually be to decrease altruism and consumption by children. An estate or income tax also changes the slope of intergenerational budget constraints, which, via the "interest rate effect," discourages parents to provide consumption for their children and to accumulate altruism. An income tax can also decrease the value of taxpayers' time, which, to the extent that child-oriented resources are time-intensive, encourages the formation of altruism.

Parents transfer resources to children in two ways in the permanent income model: human capital and financial transfers. An economy-wide education subsidy could therefore mean an important reallocation of intergenerational transfers from financial to human capital transfers. With fewer families willing to save in the form of financial assets, the rate of interest on financial assets increases, which increases consumption by children and the incentive to accumulate altruism.

If the taxes are levied on, say, rich families and the government program is targeted toward poor families, then the introduction of the program would increase the consumption and altruism of the poor and decrease the child consumption and altruism of the rich. Targeted government programs will therefore have a larger effect on the altruism and consumption by children of the targeted families.

Private Charities and Endogenous Impure Altruism

I suggest in chapter 11 that my model of intergenerational altruism also applies to the giving of resources from one family to another. Charities that intend to promote the welfare of children will have the effects of the government welfare programs analyzed above. The focus here is not on the effect of transfers on the altruism of recipients (as in the discussion on government transfers) but on the effect of the financing of charitable activities on the generosity of donors.

Free-riding in Private Charities

Consider a model with two goods: private consumption c and the "success" of a charity G. The success of the charity is determined by the sum of donations. For example, a charity might attempt to cure a disease and is more likely to be successful when more research money is available.

Let N denote the number of donors to a particular charity. An individual donor i cares not only about his consumption c_i and the success of the charity G, but also his own contribution to the charity g_i. His concern for the success of the charity has been referred to in the economics literature as "pure altruism" while the donor's concern for his own donation is labeled "impure altruism."[5] Notice that there is a "free-rider" problem with pure altruism but not with impure altruism. When a donor contributes to the success of a charity, pure altruists are happier because they are glad to see the success of the charity increase while impure altruists do not care because their consumption and their own personal donation are their only concerns. It is therefore possible for a purely altruistic donor to get a lot of enjoyment from a charity without making a substantial donation himself because the charity is successful as a result of the donations of others. I assume that a donor may care about the charity but not the other donors, so donors do not consider the effect of their donation on the happiness of other donors. This failure to consider other donors is referred to as the "free-rider" problem in economics.[6]

Endogenous Pure and Impure Altruism

Setup of the Model

I allow donors to have both pure and impure altruistic motives, modeling the relative importance of pure and impure altruism with L-shaped indifference curves in the $[g_i, G]$ plane. Figure 12.3 displays two sets of indifference curves. With the solid set, the ray of preferred proportions is steep (with slope $= b$), so "pure" altruistic motive is stronger; the donor is relatively more concerned with the success of the charity. The "impure"

5. See James Andreoni (1990) for references and an analysis of a model with both pure and impure altruism. My contribution to the analysis is to endogenize impure altruism in much the same way that I endogenize pure altruism in previous chapters.

6. See Howard Margolis (1982) for a discussion of altruism, free-riding, and charities and for additional examples of behavior that is affected by the free-rider problem, including political behavior and academic work.

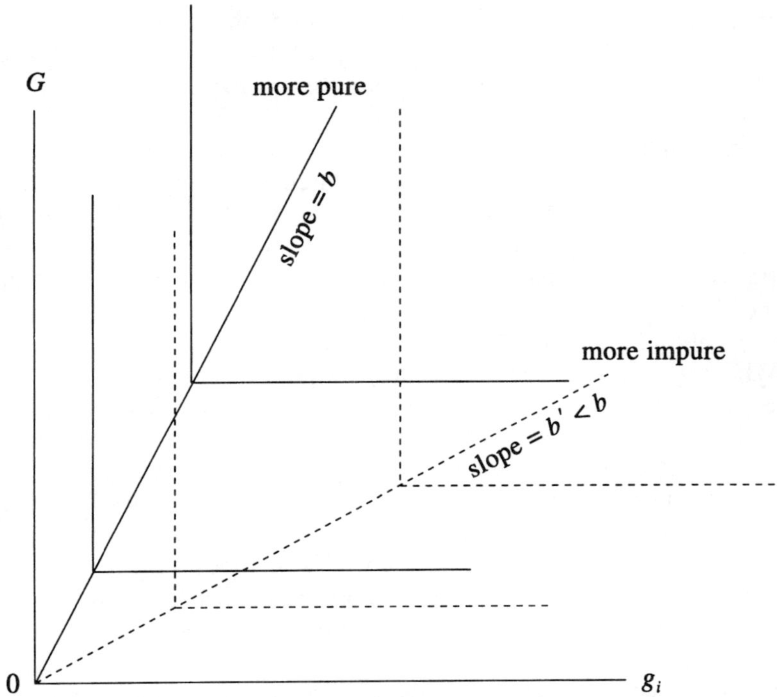

12.3 Modeling the Relative Importance of Pure and Impure Altruism

altruistic motive is stronger according to the dashed set of preferences. The important difference between pure and impure altruism is that the perfectly pure altruist does not care how the charity is successful—whether it is his donations or the donations of others—while the perfectly impure altruist cares only about his own contribution and not at all about the donations of others.

The most important assumption about preferences is that the ray of preferred proportions can be affected by charities. Charities can spend resources to *promote impure altruism,* which has the effect of shifting downward a donor's ray of preferred proportions in the $[g_i, G]$ plane.[7] Advertising is a notable way in which charities shift the ray of preferred proportions. For example, a famous U.S. charity, "Save the Children," collects almost $100 million per year with a "sponsorship" advertising campaign.[8]

7. I use the term "impure altruism" to remain consistent with a previous economics literature, not as a pejorative term. In fact, Andreoni (1988) and others have argued that "impure altruism" is a major force sustaining important, dedicated, and beneficial charities that could not be sustained if "pure altruism" prevailed.

8. American Broadcasting Companies (1995).

Donors contribute money to sponsor a particular child. Information about that child is provided for a "Save the Children" sponsor. By emphasizing a link between a *particular* donor and a *particular* recipient, the sponsorship strategy encourages a donor to focus on his contribution. Of course, the advertising campaigns cost money that does not directly benefit the charity's cause. In the Save the Children example, resources may be spent to dress, clean, and photograph children in order to satisfy sponsors rather than spending those resources on food, education, or medical goods. The benefit of such resources is indirect in that it affects the "preferences" of donors—each donor is encouraged to focus on the results of his contribution, which can increase the size of the contribution.

What are the feasible choices in the $[g_i, G]$ plane? The sum of donations G is obviously the donor i's donation plus the contributions of all other $N - 1$ donors. I assume that the donation of the other donors cannot be influenced by donor i, so that a \$1 increase in the donation of i increases the aggregate donations G by \$1 and—because donor i has limited resources A—decreases i's private consumption c_i by \$1. Donor i has preferences over the three variables c_i, g_i, and G, so he chooses the feasible allocation (c_i, g_i) that he prefers most. Because the contributions of the other $N - 1$ donors affect G, those other contributions also affect donor i's choices.

I assume that the other $N - 1$ donors make decisions in a manner similar to donor i, choosing the preferred feasible allocation (c, g). For simplicity, I assume for the moment that all donors are identical; all have the same preferences and the same resources A. Because all donors have the same preferences, opportunities, and decision-making process, all must ultimately choose the same donation. Identical donations for all means that $G = Ng$: the sum of donations G is the individual donation g times number of donors N. $G = Ng$ not a restriction on individual choices but an equilibrium outcome. Each donor is free to make a contribution that is different from those of the others but chooses not to do so.

Large versus Small Charities

Potential equilibrium outcomes can be displayed in the $[g_i, G]$ plane as a ray with slope N, as shown in figure 12.4. There are two important cases to consider in the model. In the first case $N > b$; the ray of potential equilibrium outcomes is steeper than the ray of preferred proportions. The equilibrium ray is flatter $(N' < b)$ in the second case. In the first case, $(N > b)$, notice that impure altruism dominates decisions by the donor. Consider the allocation B. Because $N > b$, the allocation B lies above the ray of preferred proportions and a change in the success of the charity G

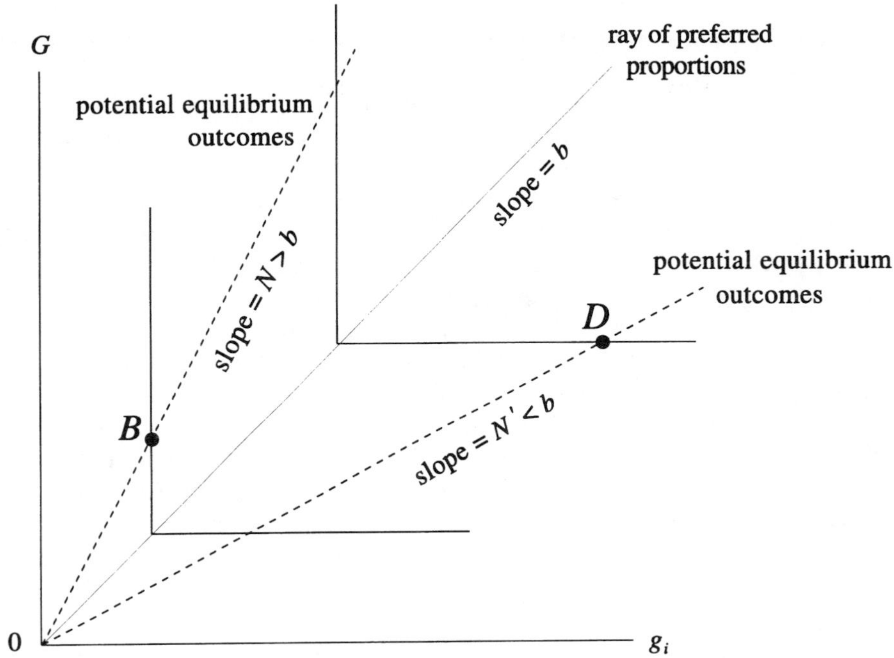

12.4 Equilibrium Outcomes and Preferred Proportions of Pure and Impure Altruism

cannot change his utility if his own donation g_i is held constant. This can be proven graphically because a change in G holding g_i constant is a vertical movement that keeps the allocation on the same indifference curve. In other words, holding constant his own consumption, the donor at allocation *B* only gains from a higher donation from himself rather than greater success of the charity. For this donor, *a change in b increases his donation.* The impure altruistic motive is the only relevant motive at allocation *B*, so it can help a charity to encourage impure altruism, shifting the ray of preferred proportions downward.

In the second case ($N' < b$), pure altruism dominates decisions by the donor. Consider the allocation *D*. Because $N' < b$, the allocation *D* lies below the ray of preferred proportions and a change of donor *i*'s donation cannot change his utility if *G* is held constant. This can be proven graphically because a change in g_i holding *G* constant is a horizontal movement that keeps the allocation on the same indifference curve. In other words, holding constant his own consumption, the donor at allocation *D* does not care whether it is he or other donors who contribute the necessary resources to achieve *G*. For this donor, *a change in b has no effect on his donation.* The impure altruistic motive isn't relevant at allocation *D*, so it does not help a charity to encourage impure altruism—shifting the ray of preferred proportions downward—unless the shift were so far as to bring the ray of preferred proportions below the ray of potential equilibrium outcomes ($N > b$). Only when the ray of preferred proportions is below can shifts have effects on donations. So the smaller N is, the more the ray of preferred proportions must be shifted before donations are affected and, because changing preferences is costly, the less likely the charity is likely to find the promotion of impure altruism to be economical.

Large charities in the model should tend to enjoy more donations per donor because a large charity is more likely to enjoy large effects on donations of the promotion of impure altruism. For this reason, people may be more likely to "donate" to large causes—such as fighting in a national war or voting in a national election—than to "donate" to smaller causes. The endogeneity of pure and impure altruism may also explain why Mark Isaac, James Walker, and Arlington Williams (1994), A. Schram and F. van Winden (1991), and others have found experimental subjects to donate more to large-group causes than to small-group causes. However, there is no explicit promotion of impure altruism in those experiments.

Heterogenous Donors

I assume that all donors are identical to show that the ray of potential equilibrium outcomes has slope N, but the assumption is easily modified. Suppose that all donors are identical except for donor i who, perhaps because he is poorer, donates half of what the other donors do. The ray of potential equilibrium outcomes then has slope $(2N - 1)$.[9] A ray with slope $(2N - 1)$ is steeper than a ray with slope N, so smaller donors are likely to have a ray of preferred proportions that is below the ray of potential equilibrium outcomes, which means that the promotion of impure altruism is more likely to have an effect. Notice that "large" and "small" donors are defined here *relative* to other donors to the charity.

Because the promotion of impure altruism is more likely to have an effect on smaller donors, should charities target such promotions toward small donors? There are two considerations. First, an effect is more likely among small donors. Second, a given effect generates more donations among larger donors. The second result follows from the fact that doubling the donation of a big donor is better than doubling the donation of a small one. The first effect can dominate for small charities. Suppose, for example, that the ray of potential equilibrium outcomes is above the ray

9. By definition, $G = g_i + (N - 1)g_{\sim i}$, where $g_{\sim i}$ is the average donation of donors other than i. With an equilibrium outcome of $g_i = g_{\sim i}/2$ (as opposed to $g_i = g_{\sim i}$), we have $G = (2N - 1)g_i$.

of preferred proportions for small donors and below for rich donors. Then a small promotion of impure altruism has an immediate effect on small donors and no effect on large donors. The second effect dominates for large charities when the ray of potential equilibrium outcomes is above the ray of preferred proportions for all donors.

Individual donors may choose to promote their own impure altruism. Whether they do so or not depends on the cost of doing so and the extent to which impure altruism distracts from pure altruism. If individual donors do promote their own impure altruism, then their private promotions are affected by the promotions of charities. The promotions of charities will substitute for the individual-level promotions, which dampen the former's effects. Since smaller donors are less likely to be able to afford promoting their own impure altruism, charity promotions are more likely to have an effect on them. "Large" and "small" donors are defined here in absolute terms, not relative to other donors to the charity.

Predictions for the Financing of Public Goods

The theoretical model produces six results:

(1) Larger charities are more likely to promote impure altruism.
(2) In percentage terms, the promotion of impure altruism has a larger effect on smaller donors.
(3) Impure altruism should be more prevalent among smaller donors to small charities.
(4) Impure altruism should be more prevalent among larger donors to large charities.
(5) When impure altruism is individually formed, the promotion of the impure altruism of smaller donors is more effective.
(6) Through the promotion of impure altruism, large charities can enjoy larger average donations.

Result (1) follows from my analysis of figure 12.4. A slightly different derivation of the ray of potential equilibrium outcomes produces results (2) through (4). Result (5) allows for individual-level promotion of impure altruism.

"Save the Children" is an important example of how charities can promote impure altruism. Certain types of patriotism provide another example. During World War II, it was common for the U.S. government to advertise the effects of the contribution of citizens to the war effort. Of course, any one citizen could not change the outcome of the war, but many government advertisements had a "sponsorship" flavor like the modern "Save the Children" charity. Figure 12.5 displays a poster from World War II. The poster was displayed in factories that made war materials. The

12.5 Promotion of Impure Altruism during World War II (Source: Nelson 1995)

focus of the poster is not the effect of shoddy manufacturing on the overall outcome of the war but its effect on a *particular* soldier. Other posters emphasized the effects of hard work and well-kept secrets by citizens on the family of a particular soldier. Figure 12.5 is an example of a government promoting impure altruism in order to encourage patriotic donations by citizens.

Charitable Giving over Time

Chapter 4 emphasizes the effects of three variables on the formation of altruism: total resources, the value of time, and the interest rate. The value of time matters because it is an important component of the price of altruism. The interest rate dictates the price of giving in the model of chapter

4. More total resources increases altruism, a higher price of altruism lowers it, and a higher price of giving lowers it. Moreover, it is shown in chapter 4 that proportional changes in total resources and the price of giving have no effect on altruism. When altruism pertains to charitable giving, my discussion adds two other variables to the list: the size of the charity and the size of the donation.

All five variables change over time with economic growth. What are the effects on altruism and charitable giving? Economic growth has raised both total family resources and the value of time but probably in a roughly proportional way. If the formation of altruism is 100 percent time-intensive, there is little net effect on the formation of altruism. If the formation of altruism is less than 100 percent time-intensive, the net effect will be for charitable giving to grow over time. Because many charitable contributions are income tax deductible, the price of giving to charity depends on prevailing income tax rates. Income tax rates have generally risen over time, which makes it cheaper to donate to charities, which encourages the formation of altruism. The number of donors to any particular charity might grow with the overall population, which should encourage impure altruism. Taken together, all of these forces suggest that charitable altruism should grow over time, with the fraction of resources donated to charities growing as well.

Summary of the Main Results

Government tax and transfer programs have offsetting effects on intergenerational altruism, but less ambiguous predictions are available in a model of private charities. The model emphasizes the endogenous formation of pure and impure altruism, deriving several results:

(1) Larger charities are more likely to promote impure altruism.
(2) In percentage terms, the promotion of impure altruism has a larger effect on smaller donors.
(3) Impure altruism should be more prevalent among smaller donors to small charities.
(4) Impure altruism should be more prevalent among larger donors to large charities.
(5) When impure altruism is individually formed, the promotion of the impure altruism of smaller donors is more effective.
(6) Through the promotion of impure altruism, large charities can enjoy larger average donations.
(7) Charitable giving should grow over time.

It remains to be shown whether or not these predictions accurately describe changes in charitable activity across charities, over time, and across countries.

Howard Margolis (1982) also has a model of charitable giving with both pure and impure motives (which he refers to as "goods" and "participation" altruism). My model differs from the Margolis model analytically because I endogenize the relative weighting of pure and impure motives. As my analyses of fertility in chapter 4 and of inequality within the family in chapter 11 suggest, a theory of endogenous altruism can produce predictions about the number and type of charities (or "children") to which a donor gives, whereas participation in a group is taken as exogenous in the Margolis analysis. From a positive point of view, the models differ in their predictions of the income elasticity of giving; Margolis (1982) predicts that the rich donate a larger fraction of their resources to charity.

Appendix H: A Mathematical Model of Pure and Impure Altruism

H.1 Preferences and Budget Constraints

A charity has N donors, the ith of which has A_i resources to split between his own consumption c_i and his donation g_i.

$$c_i + g_i = A_i \tag{12.1}$$

The success of the charity G is the sum of the donations net of expenditures on goods that promote impure altruism:

$$G \equiv \sum_{i=1}^{N} (g_i - q_i) \equiv g_i + (N-1)g_{\sim i} - Q \tag{12.2}$$

where $g_{\sim i}$ is defined to be the average donation of all donors other than i. Q is aggregate resources devoted to the promotion of impure altruism.[10]

Donor i derives utility from both pure and impure altruism. He prefers his donation and the success of the charity to be in fixed proportions and the fixed proportion depends on the goods used to promote i's impure altruism q_i. In other words, the altruistic portion of his utility takes the form:

$$v(g_i, G) \equiv \min\{b(q_i)g_i, G\}$$
$$b'(q_i) < 0 \tag{12.3}$$

The ray of preferred proportions in the $[g_i, \text{G}]$ plane has slope $b(q_i)$, which can be decreased by expenditures on goods that promote impure altruism.

10. In the text, it is assumed that the success of the charity is the sum of donations *without* netting out promotions of impure altruism. The appendix shows that this difference does not effect any qualitative results.

H.2 Characterization of Chosen Donations

Donors also have a selfish portion of their utility function which depends on consumption. Donor i prefers the selfish and unselfish portions in fixed proportions:

$$V(c_i, g_i, G) \equiv \min\{fc_i, v(g_i, G)\} = \min\{fc_i, b(q_i)g_i, G\} \qquad (12.4)$$

Each donor maximizes his utility 12.4 subject to his budget constraint 12.1, taking the donations of others ($g_{\sim i}$) and promotions of impure altruism ($q_{\sim i}$, q_i) as given. The chosen consumption and donation of donor i are:

$$\text{If } (N-1)g_{\sim i} - Q < (b_i - 1)fA_i/(f+b_i)$$

$$c_i = \frac{1}{1+f}[A_i + (N-1)g_{\sim i} - Q]$$

$$g_i = \frac{f}{1+f}A_i - \frac{1}{1+f}[(N-1)g_{\sim i} - Q] \qquad (12.5)$$

$$\text{If } (N-1)g_{\sim i} - Q \geq (b_i - 1)fA_i/(f+b_i)$$

$$c_i = \frac{b(q_i)}{b(q_i)+f}A_i$$

$$g_i = \frac{f}{b(q_i)+f}A_i \qquad (12.6)$$

H.3 Nash Equilibrium Donations

If we assume that all donors have the same preferences and the same resources A, then a Nash equilibrium involves $g_i = g_{\sim i}$ for all i. The form of the Nash equilibrium depends on the relationship between $b(q)$ and N.

Case 1: $N - b > (1 + b/f)Q/A$

(roughly $N > b$)

$$g = \frac{f}{b(q)+f}A \qquad (12.7)$$

Case 2: $N - b < (1 + b/f)Q/A$

(roughly $N < b$)

$$g = \frac{f}{N+f}A + \frac{1}{N+f}Q \qquad (12.8)$$

Only in Case 1 can a slightly larger Q increase the success of the charity.[11] In that case, it pays to promote impure altruism more heavily when the average donation is larger.

Notice that, because more q decreases $b(q)$ and therefore utility, donors in the model have no private incentive to affect their preference for impure altruism.

H.4 Average Donation versus the Size of Charities

Larger charities tend to enjoy larger average donations because their investments in the impure altruism of their donors are more potent. Consider two charities of size N and N' and assume that donors to the two charities are equally wealthy. The first charity is large enough that investments in impure altruism have an immediate effect on donations; $N > b(0)$. The second charity is small enough that it does not pay for it to invest in impure altruism; $N' < b(0)$ and $Q' = 0$. The donations g and g' to each charity can be computed from the formulas above:

$$g = \frac{f}{b(q) + f} A$$

$$g' = \frac{f}{N' + f} A \qquad (12.9)$$

Promotion of impure altruism by the larger charity can produce $b(q) < N'$ even though $b(0) > N'$. $b(q) < N'$ delivers the result $g > g'$.

11. Q increases donations in both cases, but the higher donations in Case 2 do not pay for the expenditures on the promotions of impure altruism.

CHAPTER 13
Altruism and the Principal-Agent Problem

It is common in human interactions to be concerned with the actions of others. How can we induce someone (an "agent") to behave in a way that we prefer? One possibility is to pay the agent for taking the appropriate action. However, it can be difficult to verify his action and therefore difficult to offer financial incentives for correct behavior. This chapter explores the possibility of forming an altruistic relationship with the agent so that he is directly concerned with the effects of his actions on others even without financial incentives.

"The Standard Principal-Agent Problem" presents the standard principal-agent model and provides some examples. The formation of the agent's altruism for the principal—which I refer to as "investments in loyalty"—is modeled in "The Principal-Agent Problem with Endogenously Loyal Agents." "Corporate Loyalty and Executive Compensation" applies the model.

The Standard Principal-Agent Problem
Examples

Suppose, for example, I want to hire a real estate agent to sell my house. More effort on the part of the agent increases my likelihood of obtaining a good price for the house. There are other factors that affect the price I ultimately get for the house—factors beyond my control or that of my agent. If I obtain a low price for the house, I cannot be 100 percent sure whether this is just bad luck or whether my agent was too lazy. What type of contractual arrangement should I make with the agent to obtain the best profit from the sale of my house (net of the agent's compensation)? This type of problem has been studied extensively in the economics literature, where it has been generically referred to as the *principal-agent problem.*[1] The "principal" in my example is the homeowner and the "agent" is the real estate agent.

In general, there is a principal who is concerned with a product y that depends on two factors: (1) the unobservable action, x, of the agent and (2) other unobservable factors, ε:

$$y = x + \varepsilon \tag{13.1}$$

All else equal, effort is undesirable for the agent. How should the agent be compensated by the principal? One possibility is for the principal to pay a flat fee to the agent, but then the agent has no incentive to exert effort as he earns the flat fee no matter what he does. Another possibility is to strongly link the agent's pay to the quantity of the final product, y. However, this second possibility is a problem if the other unobservable factors—and therefore output and the agent's compensation—are random and the agent is risk-averse. A risk-averse agent demands compensation not only for exerting effort but also for facing risk.

Consider another sales example. A widget manufacturer hires a salesperson to sell one million widgets. Nobody is sure how much customers are willing to pay. Strong efforts by the salesperson result in a higher price. In this example, y is sales revenue, x is the salesperson's effort, and ε are other widget market factors. If the salesperson is paid only a base salary that does not depend on how much he sells, then it is unlikely that he will sell very hard. However, a very low base salary and a very high commission rate may not work either because the salesperson is unwilling to bear so much risk without some guarantee of a positive payoff (after all, he must buy groceries!).

Computation of the Optimal Compensation Scheme

Solutions to principal-agent problems involve compensation w for the agent that is tied in some way to the final product. For concreteness, I refer to a simple salesperson's contract:

$$w = b + c * y, \; c > 0 \tag{13.2}$$

y is the final product and w is the compensation. b can be thought of as the "base salary," since it is earned even if $y = 0$. Compensation increases with y according to the "commission rate" c. On average, compensation is $b + c^*x$ because—on average—output is x. The agent cares about his average compensation ($b + c^*x$), his effort (x), and the risk that he faces.

1. See Michael Spence and Richard Zeckhauser (1971) for an early mathematical exposition of the problem and Bengt Holmstrom and Paul Milgrom (1994) for a recent analysis.

As an approximation, we can represent the utility of the agent as:

$$u = (b + c * x) - v(x) - \sigma c$$
$$v'(x) > 0,\ v''(x) > 0 \qquad (13.3)$$

The first term in equation 13.3 is expected pay, which obviously increases utility. The second term $v(x)$ represents the disutility of effort. The third term $-\sigma c$ represents the disutility of risk. The parameter σ indexes uncertainty about ε, which creates more risk for the agent according to the commission rate, c. As an index of uncertainty, σ could be the variance of ε or some other measure of the range of possible values that the agent might expect ε to take. The agent's pay is not risky if the commission rate is zero and very risky if the commission rate is high.

The agent has an outside opportunity that yields him utility $\bar{u}$. Any arrangement that arises between the principal and the agent must therefore yield utility of at least $\bar{u}$ for the agent, or he will take his outside opportunity rather than work with the principal.

The principal cares about expected profits:[2]

$$\text{expected profits} = \pi = x - (b + c * x) \qquad (13.4)$$

The first term is effort, which, on average, determines output. The second term $-(b + cx)$ reflects the average compensation that will be paid to the agent. Profits are the difference between output and payments to the agent.

What compensation scheme (that is, a combined base salary/commission rate package) will a principal offer his agent? Two forces must be considered. First, the compensation scheme affects the choice of effort by the agent. At one extreme, a zero commission rate gives the agent no reason to exert effort. At the other extreme, a very high commission rate means a very high payoff to effort for the agent. Second, the agent has outside opportunities. If he is offered a low base pay and a high commission and the work is risky, he may be happier going to another job with less risk or a higher base pay.

These two forces suggest an important result: *commission rates are inversely related to risk.* Why? Consider a zero commission rate and some base pay b. Consider raising c and lowering the base pay so that expected compensation is constant. First, there is more effort and the agent is less happy—but this effect is present in both risky and risk-free situations. Second, the agent faces more risk and the additional risk is proportional

2. The principal is not risk-averse. In the case of corporate shareholders (principals) and corporate executives and salespeople (agents), this assumption is quite realistic because shareholders can diversify their risk by holding the shares of many different corporations.

to the riskiness of the project. So principals in an uncertain environment must maintain a high base pay when they raise the commission rate to compensate the agent for the additional risk he faces (if the agent were not so compensated, he would look for another job). A principal in a risk-free environment can drop the base pay when he raises the commission rate because the higher commission rate does not confront the agent with more risk. Raising the commission rate is effectively more expensive for principals in an uncertain environment, so one expects them to keep their commission rates low.

The Principal-Agent Problem with Endogenously Loyal Agents

The presence of risk makes it costly to provide financial incentives to agents. Without financial incentives, selfish agents do not exert effort. Is there any way that a selfish agent can be made less selfish so that he also cares about the principal's welfare? Following the model of chapter 4, I assume that there are resources—which I call *principal-oriented resources*—which increase the altruism or loyalty of the agent toward the principal.[3] Purchases of principal-oriented resources are "investments in loyalty." Under these circumstances, the agent cares about *both* his own private welfare ($u = (b + c^*x) - v(x) - \sigma c$) *and* the expected profits of the principal ($\pi = x - (b + c^*x) - \theta(a)$). The more the principal invests in loyalty, the greater weight the agent places on expected profits in his choice of effort. $\theta(a)$ is expenditures of the firm on principal-oriented resources, which, holding constant output and wage compensation, reduce the principal's profits.

Even without a financial incentive (that is, a commission rate greater than zero), a loyal agent will exert effort because he cares about the welfare of the principal. Principals therefore try to make their agents loyal, taking into account that principal-oriented resources are costly.

With the opportunity to accumulate principal-oriented resources, principals have two ways to encourage effort: loyalty and financial incentives. Financial incentives are more costly in a risky environment because the agent must be compensated for bearing risk, so loyalty is the relatively attractive way to encourage effort in risky environments. This is the main result of the chapter: *principals use lower commission rates and encourage more loyalty in riskier environments.* Appendix I presents a mathematical proof of the result.

What happens to base pay in risky environments? The commission rate is low and loyalty is high. As long as an agent is not terribly happy about the principal's efforts to make him more loyal (so that he does not view

3. For another model of the formation of loyalty, see George Akerlof (1983).

the loyalty itself as substantial compensation), the base pay must be high in risky environments to compensate for the low payoff to effort and for being "remolded" into a loyal employee.

Throughout the book, I have argued that the formation of altruism is time-intensive. Should loyalty be less common among agents whose time is very valuable? There are two effects of the value of an agent's time on the incentives for a principal to invest in loyalty. First is the obvious effect that the time-intensive formation of loyalty is more costly when time is valuable. Second, loyalty produces more work effort by agents, which produces more output according to (*a*) the number of hours that the agent works and (*b*) the agent's productivity. Increasing the work effort of somebody who works long hours or is otherwise very productive is better than increasing the effort of somebody who does not work much. Because a worker's productivity and his value of time are closely related, the productivity and value of time effects may cancel out. What is left is the prediction that less investment in loyalty should occur for part-time employees. If the accumulation of loyalty is not time-intensive, then the productivity effect dominates and firms invest in loyalty more intensively for productive employees.

Although investments in loyalty may not respond to the value of time, they should respond to other determinants of the price of principal-oriented resources.

Corporate Loyalty and Executive Compensation

The principal-agent model with endogenously loyal agents is used to understand some important human behavior, including the compensation of executives and nepotism.

One important application of the principal-agent model is to executive compensation.[4] The "principals" are the corporate shareholders who would like to see high profits. High profits are produced in part with a hard-working executive—the "agent" in this example—but the effort of an executive may not be observable. Executives are often compensated with stock options. Since the stock options are a function of the profits of the corporation, they act as the "commission rate" in our model.

The commission rate is lower and base pay is higher in the model with loyal agents than in the standard principal-agent model where loyalty is not a force encouraging work effort. Michael Jensen and Kevin Murphy (1990) have argued that, as an empirical matter, commission rates seem to be too low and base pay too high relative to those predicted by a standard principal-agent model. This finding is consistent with my model, although

4. Many of the results here can also be applied to the compensation of salespeople.

it is also consistent with a model where loyalty exists but is exogenous. My principal-agent model with *endogenously* loyal agents has the unique prediction that commission rates are low while loyalty and base pay are high *in firms whose fortunes are very uncertain.* My prediction can be tested by comparing different kinds of firms—some risky and other less risky (where risky might be defined in terms of historical variations in a firm's earnings or stock returns relative to its industry)—and measuring the gap between the actual commission rate and the commission rate predicted by the standard principal-agent model.[5] If my model is correct, the gap should be larger for riskier firms.

How is corporate loyalty formed? Employees may naturally become loyal to a firm by spending many years with that firm. "Purchases of principal-oriented resources" are observed in this case by a firm that is especially eager to hire executives from within. Executives hired from the outside may be more productive according to some "objective" criteria, but shareholders forego the extra productivity to hire a more loyal veteran of the corporation. Nepotism can be another form of investment in loyalty. The cost of nepotism is that relatives of shareholders are likely to be less productive than the best executive available from the outside, but a relative of a shareholder is more likely to keep the shareholder's interests in mind. A third example of investments in loyalty are company picnics or corporate logos. These items, if used carefully, can instill pride in employees and encourage them to remember the firm's interests. Again, risky corporations should be more likely to make investments in loyalty—including nepotism, the hiring of insiders, and the encouragement of company pride. If employees are more loyal when they feel "treated fairly," "fair" (but otherwise costly) treatment of employees is a fourth example of investments in loyalty.

Julio Rotemberg (1994) analyzes altruism (which is not quite loyalty) and work effort in firms. Although he does not model loyalty as I do, his analysis is related in two ways. First, he reviews much of the available evidence on the relationship between "human relations" and productivity in firms. Second, because he states more precisely the types of human relations that a firm might encourage and how those relations translate into worker productivity, some of his models might be loosely interpreted as stories of the shape of my $\theta(a)$ function. What I emphasize that Rotemberg does not is that the *endogeneity* of loyalty has predictions for when loyalty will *substitute* for financial incentives.

5. A firm's risk should probably be defined relative to its industry because, in many cases, an executive can be compensated according to the performance of his firm relative to the industry without affecting the financial incentive for the executive to work hard.

Review of the Main Results

The standard principal-agent problem is modified to allow for the endogenous formation of the agent's loyalty to the principal. Through purchases of "principal-oriented resources" or "investments in loyalty," loyalty is substituted for financial incentives in risky environments. Even though investments in loyalty may be time-intensive, the value of time does not directly affect investments in loyalty. Other determinants of the cost of loyalty are important.

The model applies to a wide variety of market and nonmarket interactions, but one example is analyzed here—corporate loyalty and the compensation of executives. I predict that observable investments in loyalty—such as nepotism, hiring executives from within, and the encouragement of corporate pride and costly attempts to "treat workers fairly"—should be higher in firms with uncertainty about profits relative to the industry. Actual commission rates should be below those predicted by the standard principal-agent model, with the gap being largest for the most risky firms.

The model of altruism and the principal-agent problem in this chapter is not fully developed, but the predictions derived from it suggest that it is worth studying further. For example, the principal-agent relationship here occurs only once, rather than being repeated over time, as is perhaps a more realistic description of many relationships. The model might also be extended to relationships other than the shareholder-executive relationship, such as to the care of children (where parents are the "principal" and child-care providers are the "agents") or physician-patient relationships (where patients are "principals" and physicians are "agents").

Appendix I: A Mathematical Model of Altruism and the Principal-Agent Problem

Altruism or "loyalty" is introduced into a standard principal-agent problem. Behavior in the model occurs in three stages:

(1) Given the uncertainty of output (indexed by σ) and a reservation utility of agents $\overline{u}$, the principal chooses a base pay b, a commission rate c, and loyalty a.
(2) The agent chooses work effort x to maximize expected utility $u(x; a, b, c, \sigma)$.
(3) Output $y = x + \varepsilon$ is realized. Profits are $(1 - c)y - b - \theta(a)$ and the agent's compensation is $w = b + cy$. $\theta(a)$ is the cost of motivating the loyalty level a.

Firms are aware of these three stages and choose a, b, and c in order to maximize expected profits $(1 - c)x - b - \theta(a)$. The functional form of the utility function $u(x; a, b, c, \sigma)$ is:

$$u(x; a, b, c, \sigma) = g(a)[b + cx - \sigma c - v(x)] + f(a)[(1 - c)x - b - \theta(a)]$$

$$g(a) \geq f(a) \geq 0, f'(a) > 0, v'(x) > 0, v''(x) > 0,$$

$$\frac{d}{da}\left[\frac{f(a)}{g(a)}\right] > 0, \; \frac{d^2}{da^2}\left[\ln \frac{f(a)}{g(a)}\right] < 0, \; \frac{d^2}{da^2} \ln f(a) > 0, \; \frac{d^2}{da^2} \ln g(a) > 0 \quad (13.5)$$

The terms in the left-hand square brackets represent the "selfish" sources of utility for the agent: expected compensation $b + cx$, the disutility of risk-bearing $-\sigma c$, and the disutility of effort $-v(x)$.

$\bar{u} > 0$, small $f(a)/g(a)$, σ, $v(x)$, $\theta(a)$ and $g' < 0$ are sufficient to guarantee that second-order conditions hold.

The marginal product of effort is one, and $v'(x)$ is the marginal cost of effort. Assuming that the project is productive enough to deliver more than the reservation utility for the agent, the efficient level of effort satisfies $v'(x) = 1$. If effort were observed, the principal would offer only a base salary to any worker or to an agent who put forth the efficient effort that provides the reservation utility to the agent. A commission is not desirable in the observable case because it is not needed to motivate effort and because the commission rate confronts the agent with risk which he dislikes.

Effort is not observable by the principal, so a positive commission rate is required to motivate effort. The effort x chosen by the agent in stage (2) satisfies:

$$v'(x) = \frac{f(a)}{g(a)} + \left(1 - \frac{f(a)}{g(a)}\right)c \quad (13.6)$$

The agents sets his marginal utility of effort to a weighted average of the efficient marginal utility (one) and his expected compensation for effort (the commission rate). The weights are determined by the ratio $f(a)/g(a)$, which can be thought of as the degree of "loyalty" or "altruism." Zero loyalty is $f(a)/g(a) = 0$, imperfect loyalty is $f(a)/g(a) \in (0, 1)$, and perfect loyalty is $f(a)/g(a) = 1$. With perfect loyalty, the agent exerts the efficient effort even though his effort cannot be verified by the principal.

The principal anticipates the agent's second-stage decisions knowing that the loyalty a and the commission rate c affect the chosen effort. The principal chooses a, b, and c to maximize expected profits subject to the constraint that the agent obtain at least the reservation utility level $\bar{u}$. Formally, the principal's maximization problem is:

$$\max_{a,b,c}\left[(1-c)\psi\left(\left(1-\frac{f(a)}{g(a)}\right)c+\frac{f(a)}{g(a)}\right)-b-\theta(a)\right]$$

$$g(a)[b+cx-\sigma c-v(x)]+f(a)[(1-c)x-b-\theta(a)]\geq\bar{u}$$

s.t. $$\left(1-\frac{f(a)}{g(a)}\right)c+\frac{f(a)}{g(a)}=v'(x) \quad (13.7)$$

where ψ is the inverse of the marginal utility of effort function $v'(x)$.

Proposition 1. "Loyalty" a is an increasing function of σ. If $v''' \geq 0$, or σ is sufficiently small, the principal's optimal commission rate c is a decreasing function of σ, the index of uncertainty.

Proof: The principal's first-order condition with respect to a yields:

$$\frac{da}{d\sigma}=\frac{1-c}{-(\text{SOC})}\,\frac{\dfrac{d}{da}\left[\dfrac{f(a)}{g(a)}\right]}{1-\dfrac{f(a)}{g(a)}} \quad (13.8)$$

If the second-order conditions hold, then (SOC) must be negative and a is an increasing function of σ.

The principal's first-order condition with respect to c yields:

$$v'(x)+\sigma v''(x)=1 \quad (13.9)$$

Under the conditions of the proposition, this first-order condition implicitly defines x as a decreasing function of σ. Moreover, that function depends only on the shape of the v function. Since x is increasing in loyalty a and the commission rate c, more σ and less x means either less loyalty or less c. Less loyalty is ruled out above, so more σ must lead to less c.

CHAPTER 14
Conclusions

A model of the formation of altruism and its application to intergenerational mobility and other human behavior are the main theoretical contributions of this book. This concluding chapter reviews the model of the formation of parental priorities as well as the resulting theory of intergenerational mobility and lists some of the empirical failures of standard economic models of intergenerational mobility that I document in the empirical chapters. Several other implications of endogenous altruism derived in the book are untested at this time but are itemized here for future empirical research.

I also review some of the main criticisms of altruistic models that have appeared in the economics literature. I argue that they are not criticisms of my model. "Problems with Altruism as a Motive for Human Behavior" addresses an audience of mainly economists and can be skipped by those who are uninterested in a fairly esoteric debate among economists.

Although I make progress on the modeling of intergenerational mobility, my work also raises new questions, which are briefly discussed in the concluding section.

A Model of the Formation of Parental Priorities

I present a theory of intergenerational mobility in which parental priorities are the primary determinant of the relative success or "consumption" of children. Parents are predisposed toward selfishness but take costly actions to overcome their selfishness and become willing to sacrifice their own success for the success of their children. I refer to these costly actions as the "accumulation of altruism" or the "purchase of child-oriented resources" and believe them to be mainly time-intensive. Spending time with children is a necessary condition for a parent to care about the welfare of a child. The model of altruism can also be applied to interpersonal relationships outside of the family, with "donor" replacing "parent" and "recipient" replacing "child."

Spending time with children can increase a parent's willingness to sacrifice for them, a process which I model in a very mechanistic way. Although it is important that parents recognize that such a process occurs, it is not important that the process be perfectly predictable. My mechanistic model is purely an expositional device like the mechanistic models of the effect of schooling on earnings or models of the effect of advertising on the demand for a product. I no more believe that the formation of preferences is perfectly foreseeable than anybody believes that a college education necessarily increases a person's earnings by exactly 42 percent or that a Budweiser advertisement during the Super Bowl results in the sale of exactly 110,000 additional cans of beer.

A Theory of Intergenerational Mobility

The accumulation of altruism is an example of the "formation of preferences," although my theory is based on the standard complementarity model from economics. Altruism is a complement with the success of children. A decline in the price of either of these two goods therefore increases the demand for both. A low parental value of time, a determinant of the cost of accumulating altruism, therefore encourages both altruism and consumption by children. Divorce, a low interest rate, or high estate and income tax rates, determinants of the relative price of a child's consumption, also discourage altruism and consumption by children. Holding constant these prices, additional family income or wealth increases altruism and consumption by children.

Altruism per child also depends on the number of children, with more children increasing aggregate altruism but decreasing altruism per child. The bearing and rearing of children is also time-intensive. A low value of time, a high interest rate, or high values of family income encourage fertility.

According to the model, intergenerational mobility is different among families for whom income is primarily "earned" versus families for whom income is primarily "unearned." The value of time is the more important determinant of altruism and consumption by children among "earned" income families. To the extent that family size is constant across earned income classes, poor families accumulate more altruism per child while rich families accumulate less. Per capita consumption therefore regresses to the mean across generations while consumption inequality can fall over time.

If the wealth effect on fertility is strong enough among "unearned" income families, then their consumption also regresses to the mean. As overall fertility declines over time and fertility varies less across families, the wealth effect on child-oriented resources dominates the wealth effect on fertility and consumption regresses away from the mean among "unearned" income families with parents that work.

Chapter 4 derives the wealth and price effects that generate my key results from an economic model, but those effects also appear in the analyses of other disciplines. Chapter 9 derives some of the results in a sociobiological model. I show in chapter 10 that philosophical discussions by Adam Smith, David Hume, and others also produce some of the main effects that generate my results.

Failures of Existing Economic Models

The "permanent income" and "borrowing constraints" models are the dominant models of intergenerational mobility in economics. Both models predict that earnings regress to the mean across generations, but so does Francis Galton's (1889) much more simple and believable model of intergenerational mobility. Galton simply stated that a characteristic of a child, such as height, is positively correlated with the same characteristic of his parents. Tall parents tend to have tall children. However, children are not, on average, as tall relative to other children as their parents are relative to other parents. Galton estimated that the intergenerational persistence of height to be between one-third and two-thirds.

Modern researchers have obtained estimates of the intergenerational persistence of a variety of economic characteristics, such as log earnings, that are also between one-third and two-thirds. Do economic models of intergenerational mobility make predictions that are any better than those made by Galton over a hundred years ago? Economic models do make a variety of predictions that are different from Galton's model, but many of them are incorrect. Using data from a variety of sources, I show in chapters 6 through 8 that the permanent income and borrowing constraints models have important counterfactual predictions. The permanent income model counterfactually predicts that consumption inequality grows over time. The borrowing constraints model counterfactually predicts that intergenerational consumption and earnings mobility are different among families that make financial transfers to children.

Chapters 6 and 7 also show that the evolution of inequality is similar across countries, regions, and families. The similarities suggest a unified theory of the evolution of inequality. Both Galton's very simple model and my model of the formation of altruism as applied to intergenerational mobility are such theories.

Many existing economic models of intergenerational transfers also predict that parental transfers should mitigate inequality within the family. Parents in the models transfer more resources to less fortunate children. "Compensatory" transfers are a part of actual family behavior, but there is also a variety of behavior that cannot be understood with the compensatory model.

Chapters 6 and 7 bring together a wide variety of evidence that show that intergenerational mobility is limited. More than 50 percent of earnings differences among parents are passed on to children. Approximately 80 percent of parental consumption differences are inherited. Although a slow process of intergenerational mobility does not directly refute or invalidate many of the models presented in this book, the slow process is inconsistent with existing estimates in the economics literature.

My finding of less intergenerational consumption mobility than intergenerational income mobility is consistent with the idea that lifetime consumption is not equal to lifetime earnings. Some parents consume substantially less than their lifetime earnings, passing on financial resources to their children. Laurence Kotlikoff and Lawrence Summers (1981) provide more direct evidence that, in fact, lifetime consumption and lifetime earnings are not equated person by person and emphasize that the important magnitude of intergenerational financial transfers means that capital accumulation cannot be understood without a theory of intergenerational transfers. My model of endogenous intergenerational altruism is one such theory.

Can intergenerational mobility be explained by progressive income and estate taxes? Chapter 5 derives the implications of a standard economic model of intergenerational mobility with progressive estate and income taxes. The evidence reviewed in chapters 6 and 7 suggest that progressive taxation cannot explain very much intergenerational mobility. The "progressive tax" model of chapter 5 as well as the "permanent income" and "borrowing constraints" models of chapter 3 are the primary alternatives to my model of parental priorities that are presented in this book.

The theoretical and empirical results imply that the wages of blacks will eventually catch up with those of whites, incomes of southern Americans or southern Italians will eventually catch up with those of northern Americans or northern Italians, but only slowly. For example, my estimates imply that blacks will still earn 5 percent less than whites in the year 2100. My results also suggest that a government program that helps families finance education may not improve intergenerational mobility or earnings inequality but will instead serve as a subsidy to educators and the richer families who are more likely to provide several years of schooling for their children.

Other Implications of Endogenous Altruism

The model of the formation of altruism also has predictions for a variety of other human behaviors. Chapters 11 through 13 derive those implications, twelve of which are listed below:

(1) Parents are more likely to abort handicapped children. Parents who have handicapped children may allocate more resources to them.
(2) People avoid contact with beggars but, conditional on contact, want to give them resources.
(3) Divorced parents without custody of children devote a small—or even zero—fraction of their resources to those children.
(4) Parents transfer more resources to single adult children and to children with whom they spend more time.
(5) Larger charities are more likely to promote "impure" altruism. "Pure" altruism is more likely to be the dominant motive in small groups such as the family.
(6) Charitable giving grows over time.
(7) Executives of corporations with more idiosyncratic risk are more loyal, receive a higher base pay, and receive fewer performance incentives relative to the principal agent model.
(8) Firms with more idiosyncratic risk are more likely to hire managers from within the company or managers who are related to shareholders.
(9) Through the promotion of impure altruism, larger charities can collect larger average donations.
(10) With endogenous altruism, income shocks are less than perfectly insured in the family.
(11) Divorce decreases altruism, savings, and long-run economic growth.
(12) Wage-tax financed pay-as-you-go social security increases altruism, savings, and long-run economic growth.

Problems with Altruism as a Motive for Human Behavior

Because I model the formation of altruism, one might expect my model to share several implications with the standard or "exogenous" models of altruistically motivated transfers that have appeared in the economics literature. Four implications of exogenous altruism models are emphasized in the economics literature:

(1) Consumption of different family members should be highly correlated over time.

(2) Altruistically motivated intergenerational transfers should compensate poorer children.
(3) Government transfers should not affect behavior.
(4) Private charities are unsustainable.

The altruism hypothesis is often thought to be contradicted because implications (1) through (4) appear to be counterfactual.

Implication (1) can be derived in an exogenous altruism model where families learn about their resources over time. If someone in the family receives good news about income, the consumption of all family members should increase proportionally. This implication is tested by Joseph Altonji, Fumio Hayashi, and Larry Kotlikoff (1992) and is rejected. That parents care about the consumption of family members rather than about income produces implication (2): family members who earn less income must be given a larger transfer in order to achieve a moderate distribution of consumption within the family. Implication (3) is a logical extension of Robert Barro's (1974) Ricardian Equivalence Theorem and the related result by Gary Becker (1974). I show in chapters 3 and 11 how, in the standard model of exogenous altruism, the allocation of consumption in the family depends only on total family resources and relative prices of consumption. If the government takes from one member of the family and gives to another, then total family resources are unchanged. If the relative prices are also unchanged, then none of the family consumption decisions change. B. Douglas Bernheim (1986) and Bernheim and Kyle Bagwell (1988) produce implication (3) as a logical extension of the Barro and Becker result by suggesting that many families are linked together by marriage so that properly defined extended families (that is, the set of people who are altruistically linked to each other in some way) is very large. If altruism motivates transfers within the family, Bernheim and Bagwell argue, a great number of government transfers—all government transfers if all families are eventually intermarried—between families are "within an extended family" and therefore do not affect consumption decisions. Result (4) has been emphasized by Howard Margolis (1982) and follows from the fact that "pure altruists" care only about their own consumption and the success of the charity but not about their own donation.

There are three important reasons why empirical rejections of implications (1) through (4) are consistent with the usefulness of my model of altruism. First, the distinction between "pure" and "impure" altruism is necessary to derive (1) through (4) but not crucial for the derivation of many of my main implications. It is straightforward to reinterpret my model as one of the formation of impure altruism. Second, even with "pure" altruism, the altruistic transfer motive may not be operative. A theory of altruism is still relevant for behavior when transfer motives are not always operative, while implications (1) and (3) need not hold.

A third reason that implications (1) through (4) are not fundamental implications of my model is that, even when the altruism in my model is pure, results (1) through (4) need not obtain. Consider result (1). If parents are hit with a favorable income surprise and that shock increases their value of time, the cost of accumulating altruism increases relative to the increase in total family resources and parents allocate a smaller fraction of their resources to children. Thus it appears, as Altonji, Hayashi, and Kotlikoff (1992) find, that parents do not "adequately" share their income surprise with their children. If, instead, children receive the income shock, the extra income increases total family resources without affecting the cost of accumulating altruism. Parental altruism increases and parents devote a larger fraction of total family resources to children. It therefore appears that parents consume "too little" of the additional income enjoyed by children.

I show in chapter 11 that, although there is a tendency for parental transfers to mitigate inequality within the family when altruism is exogenous, there is also a tendency for altruism to aggravate inequality within the family when altruism is endogenous. Implication (3) can also be violated in either the exogenous and endogenous altruism models because there are some families that never intermarry or because government transfers also affect either the cost of accumulating altruism or the relative price of consumption of different extended family members.

Once one admits that altruism responds to market and other forces, it is no longer believable that the kind of altruism that exists within the family is the same kind of altruism that operates outside of the family. I build a model in chapter 12 of the formation of pure and impure altruism. Charitable organizations are aware of the free-riding problems with pure altruism and therefore try to encourage the impure altruism of donors. Implication (4) no longer obtains when altruism is endogenous.

Future Research on Altruism and Intergenerational Mobility

Testing Other Implications of the Theory

The standard economic models of intergenerational mobility have several important counterfactual predictions. I propose that intergenerational mobility is better understood by modeling part of "tastes"—the desire of parents to sacrifice for children. Modeling altruism has several implications for intergenerational mobility, but I also show that the model has predictions for a variety of other behaviors, including the distribution of resources within the family, charitable giving, and the compensation of agents. Testing all of the implications is beyond the scope of this book, but such testing is a good direction for future research. I suggest, for example, that one might measure the amount of time parents and children spend together and use that as a measure of parental altruism. I also show how to test the idea that loyalty might be more important than financial incentives in firms with very uncertain profits.

New Models of Intergenerational Mobility

My empirical work also suggests other ways of modeling intergenerational mobility. Consider, for example, the relationship between the adult consumption and earnings of sons or daughters and the consumption and earnings of their fathers. Not surprisingly, earnings of sons are more strongly related to earnings of fathers than are the earnings of daughters; table 14.1 displays an earnings persistence of 0.45 for sons and 0.39 for daughters. More surprising is that adult family consumption is equally persistent across generations for both sons and daughters. In other words, the son of a rich father tends to earn a lot while the daughter may not, but both sons and daughters of rich fathers tend to enjoy high adult consumption levels. This result may reflect an unimportance of human capital investments in the persistence of consumption across generations, or it may reflect the importance of marital sorting. Daughters of a rich father may not earn a lot, but they are likely to marry a man who does. The matching of daughters with similar sons-in-law is consistent with the findings of David Lam and Robert Schoeni (1993; 1994) and Anthony Atkinson, A. K. Maynard, and C. G. Trinder (1983) and may be a very important determinant of intergenerational mobility.

Both the "unimportant human capital" and the "marital sorting" explanations of table 14.1 emphasize forces that are either absent or unimport-

Table 14.1 Intergenerational Persistence for Sons and Daughters

	Log Earnings	Log Consumption
Sons	0.45	0.68
	(0.07)	(0.05)
Daughters	0.39	0.69
	(0.11)	(0.05)

Notes:

1. Reported are IV coefficients on log parental status in a regression of log adult child's status on a dummy for daughters, parental and child marriage variables, and a quadratic in both the child and the parental head-of-household's age.

2. The sample is my PSID "All Earnings" sample. See chapter 7 for more details about the sample and instruments.

ant in the vast majority of economic models of intergenerational mobility. I hope that future research explores further the roles of financial transfers and assortative mating.

Another useful modeling strategy is to link a model of intergenerational occupational mobility with a model of intergenerational earnings, consumption, and wealth mobility. Such a model would connect a very large sociology literature on occupational mobility over time and across countries with an economic literature on earnings and wealth inequality. Although parents and children often choose occupations for purely financial reasons, the formation of preferences is also likely to be an important part of the story. The values and attitudes that make a parent relatively successful at an occupation are likely to be passed on to children. I expect the tools of economics to be helpful in modeling the kinds of preference formation relevant for intergenerational occupational mobility.

New Models of Intergenerational Altruism

My approach to modeling the formation of intergenerational altruism emphasizes personal interactions in the family. Interactions outside of the family, except as they occur in an idealized marketplace, are not an important part of my theory of intergenerational altruism. However, my analyses of charitable giving and corporate loyalty suggests that the basic approach does extend to extrafamilial interactions. Modeling extrafamilial interactions and intergenerational mobility together may be a fruitful research strategy. One potential model is a "keeping up with the Joneses" model where intergenerational consumption allocations are determined not only by parental income, the interest rate, and other determinants of a family's budget set, but also a desire by each family for its children to consume like the children of other families. This "keeping up with the Joneses effect" produces regression to the mean of consumption across generations even when capital markets are perfect and government redistribution is absent. However, future work on this approach must resolve two issues. First, why is the keeping up with the Joneses effect more important for consumption by children rather than consumption by parents? "Keeping up with the Joneses" may mean that families want *parents* to consume like other parents and that consumption regresses *away* from the mean even when capital markets are perfect and government redistribution is absent (note that family resources are limited so it is not feasible for both the parents and children of a poor family to imitate the consumption of a rich family)! Second, one needs to know more about intergenerational mobility within and across groups. Intergenerational consumption mobility is different within and across groups in both versions of the "keeping up with the Joneses" model because, by definition, the consumption of others is the same for everyone in the same group but different for people from different groups. Although he does not analyze consumption, George Borjas (1992) argues that intergenerational mobility is different within and across ethnic groups. However, I offer a measurement error interpretation of Borjas's findings in chapters 6 and 7 and argue that intergenerational mobility is in fact similar within and across groups.

"Impure" altruism has been used to study a variety of issues in economics, including charitable giving and political behavior. Future research might investigate the implications of impure *intergenerational* altruism for intergenerational mobility. I suspect that a theory of impure intergenerational altruism would predict some intergenerational consumption mobility and more intergenerational earnings mobility. Interest, estate taxes, and income taxes might have different effects on intergenerational mobility than in a theory of "pure" intergenerational altruism.

Impure intergenerational altruism would also produce a tendency for parents to make equal gifts to siblings with different incomes rather than compensating children with lower incomes. Since some parental transfers do in fact compensate poorer children, a fully realistic theory would have to combine the "pure" and "impure" motives in some way. Margolis (1982) provides such a theory, but he obtains a "superior goods" result: the rich give away a greater fraction of their resources. When applied to intergenerational transfers, I suspect that the superior goods result would produce a tendency for consumption to regress away from the mean across generations because rich parents would give a relatively high fraction of their resources to their children.

New Data Sources

The bulk of the intergenerational earnings data is for the modern United States, but a thorough investigation of questions such as "How do taxes and education policies affect intergenerational mobility?" requires evidence from a variety of time periods and from a variety of countries. For example, I display in chapter 7 the results of a study of nineteenth-century intergenerational mobility—the nineteenth century is a period with little or no income and estate taxation—but it would be better to see a couple of studies. More studies of consumption would also be extremely useful for obtaining insights into the validity of economic models.

A GUIDE TO MATHEMATICAL NOTATION

1. Mathematical Notation Appearing in the Main Text

Function/ Parameter	Description
c_t	consumption by parents
c_{t+1}	consumption per child
Y_t	a characteristic of parents
Y_{t+1}	a characteristic of a child
α	constant term
β	degree of intergenerational persistence
$1 - \beta$	degree of intergenerational mobility
ρ	intergenerational correlation
e_t	earnings of parents
e_{t+1}	earnings per child
●, ○	consumption allocation
■, □	earnings endowment
x_t	financial transfer from grandparents to parents
x_{t+1}	financial transfer from parents to child
U_1, U_2, U_3	utility levels
h_{t+1}	human capital transfer from parents to child
h^*_{t+1}	efficient human capital transfer from parents to child
e^*_{t+1}	earnings associated with h^*_{t+1}
B_t	earnings ability of parents
B_{t+1}	earnings ability of child
B^*_{t+1}, B_{t+1}	two types of earnings ability of a child, the former affecting the slope of the earnings function, the latter affecting the level

ε_{t+1}	other influences on a child's characteristic (unassociated with parents' characteristic)
I_t	parental income
q_t	child-oriented resources
$\overline{q}$	maximum affordable child-oriented resources
A	"Total family resources" ≡ present value of family earnings
C	"Consumption resources" (permanent income model) ≡ present value of family consumption = total family resources net of expenditures on child-oriented resources
C_t	"Consumption resources" (imperfect capital markets model) ≡ parental income net of expenditures on child-oriented resources
w_t	wage rate of parents
w_{t+1}	wage rate of child
a	degree of intergenerational altruism per child
$\theta(a)$	cost of accumulating altruism in the amount a
$\underline{a}$	degree of intergenerational altruism obtained with no expenditure on child-oriented resources
n_t	fertility of parents
d_t	"fixed" cost of having a child
δ_t	net cost of having a child $\equiv d_t - w_{t+1}/(1 + r)$
C_{t+1}	aggregate consumption of children $\equiv n_t c_{t+1}$
$a(n)$	intergenerational altruism per child as a function of fertility
$na(n)$	aggregate intergenerational altruism as a function of fertility
τ	an income or estate tax rate
τ_L, τ_H	low and high tax rates
τ_{IIT}, s_f, s_e	Individual Income Tax rate, social security tax rates determining a firm's contribution and an employee's contribution
$\overline{x}$	the minimum estate size subject to the higher estate tax rate
h^{**}_{t+1}	human capital investment where the slope of the earnings function is equal to $(1 + r - \tau)$, where τ is the higher estate tax rate
e^{**}_{t+1}	earnings associated with h^{**}_{t+1}
$\overline{I}$	the minimum income subject to the higher income tax rate
X^i_t	a vector of additional regressors in a child's status equation

Γ	a vector of coefficients corresponding to the additional regressors
γ, β	intergenerational persistence for Groups 1 and 2
ϕ	either 1 or 0
h	a transfer from altruist to recipient
z	a vector of characteristics of the recipient
$B(c, h, y, a)$	function describing production possibilities of the discriminating altruist model
$g_1(a, y)$, $g_2(a, y)$	decision rules for the altruist
$f(h, z)$	fitness function
$c_{1, t+1}$, $c_{2, t+1}$	consumption by child 1 and 2
q_1, q_2	child-oriented resources corresponding to child 1 and 2
R, p	relative price of consumption and child- oriented resources for child 1 and 2
C_{t+1}, Q	total consumption and child-oriented resources allocated to the two children
A_m, c_m, a_m	divorced mother's resources, consumption, and altruism
c_k	child's consumption
A_d, c_d, a_d	divorced father's resources, consumption, and altruism
N	number of donors to a charity
g_i, $g_{\sim i}$	i's donation, average donation of all those other than i
G	success of the charity
b, b'	parameters indicating the relative preference for pure and impure altruism
y	total output in the principal-agent model
x	the agent's effort
ε	unanticipated portion of output in the principal-agent model
w	agent's compensation
b, c	agent's base pay and commission rate
$v(x)$	agent's disutility of effort
σ	index of uncertainty in the principal-agent model
π	expected profits

2. Mathematical Notation Appearing in Mathematical Appendices Only

Function/ Parameter	Description
r_t	generational interest rate on financial transfers from grandparents to parents
r_{t+1}	generational interest rate on financial transfers from parents to children
B_t	earnings ability of parents as anticipated by grandparents
B_{t+1}	earnings ability of child as anticipated by parents
λ_{t+1}	unanticipated earnings ability of child (unanticipated by parents)
μ_λ	mean of log of unanticipated earnings ability
σ_λ^2	variance of log of unanticipated earnings ability
ε_{t+1}	unanticipated component of log of unanticipated earnings ability $\equiv \ln \lambda_{t+1} - \mu_\lambda$
χ_{t+1}	unanticipated return on financial assets (unanticipated by parents)
α	constant degree of intergenerational altruism
σ	intergenerational elasticity of substitution
β	degree of intergenerational earnings mobility (imperfect capital markets model) $\equiv \nu/[\nu + \sigma(1 - \nu)]$
A_t	"total family resources" $\equiv$ present value of family earnings (same as A in the text)
$f(a)$, $g(a)$	functions that determine the effect of altruism on preferences
$\varepsilon_f(a)$, $\varepsilon_g(a)$	elasticities of the f and g functions
$V(c_t, c_{t+1}, a)$	parental preferences as a function of consumption and altruism
$v(a, C)$	reduced form parental preferences as a function of altruism and consumption resources
$\tilde{V}(c_t, c_{t+1}, n_t)$	parental preferences as a function of per capita consumption and fertility
$V(c_t, c_{t+1}, n_t)$	parental preferences as a function of parental consumption, aggregate consumption by children, and fertility
$v(n_t, C)$	reduced form parental preferences as a function of fertility and consumption resources
$f(n)$, $g(n)$	functions that determine the effect of fertility on preferences
$\varepsilon_f(n)$, $\varepsilon_g(n)$	elasticities of the f and g functions

$\tilde{g}(n)$	$ng(n)$
$u(c)$	function determining the effect of consumption on preferences in the case that indifference curves are not L-shaped
$a(q)$	function determining the effect of child-oriented resources on preferences in the case that indifference curves are not L-shaped
$\varepsilon_u(c)$, $\varepsilon_a(q)$	elasticities of the u and a functions
$\eta_u(c)$, $\eta_a(q)$	elasticities of the ε_u and ε_a functions
μ	parameter dictating the relative happiness of child 1 and child 2
$b(q_i)$	function dictating the effect of the promotion of impure altruism on the preferences of donor i
f	a second parameter (in addition to b) dictating a donor's relative preference for pure and impure altruism

REFERENCES

Akerlof, George A. 1983. "Loyalty Filters." *American Economic Review* 73, no. 1 (March): 54–63.

Altonji, Joseph G., Fumio Hayashi, and Larry Kotlikoff. 1992. "Is the Extended Family Altruistically Linked? Direct Tests Using Micro Data." *American Economic Review* 82, no. 5 (December): 1177–98.

American Broadcasting Companies. 1995. "Primetime Live: Who's Saving the Children?" Television Program, December 20.

Andreoni, James. 1988. "Privately Owned Public Goods in a Large Economy: The Limits of Altruism." *Journal of Public Economics* 35, no. 1: 57–73.

———. 1990. "Impure Altruism and Donations to Public Goods: A Theory of Warm Glow Giving." *Economic Journal* 100, no. 401 (June): 464–77.

Atkinson, Anthony B. 1970. "On the Measurement of Inequality." *Journal of Economic Theory* 2: 244–63.

———. 1980/1981. "On Intergenerational Income Mobility in Britain." *Journal of Post Keynesian Economics* 3, no. 2 (Winter): 194–218.

———. 1983. *The Economics of Inequality.* 2d ed. Oxford: Clarendon Press.

Atkinson, Anthony B., A. K. Maynard, and C. G. Trinder. 1983. *Parents and Children: Incomes in Two Generations.* London: Heinemann.

Badcock, Christopher. 1991. *Evolution and Individual Behavior.* Cambridge, MA: Basic Blackwell, Inc.

Barro, Robert J. 1974. "Are Government Bonds Net Wealth?" *Journal of Political Economy* 82, no. 6 (November): 1095–117.

Barro, Robert J., N. Gregory Mankiw, and Xavier Sala-i-Martin. 1995. "Capital Mobility in Neoclassical Models of Growth." *American Economic Review* 85, no. 1 (March): 103–15.

Barro, Robert J., and Chaipat Sahasakul. 1986. "Average Marginal Tax Rates from Social Security and the Individual Income Tax." *Journal of Business* 59, no. 4 (October): 555–66.

Barro, Robert J., and Xavier Sala-i-Martin. 1991. "Convergence Across States and

Regions." *Brookings Papers on Economic Activity.* 1991: vol. 1, April 1991: 107–58.

———. 1992a. "Convergence." *Journal of Political Economy* 100, no. 2 (April): 223–51.

———. 1992b. "Regional Growth and Migration: A Japan-U.S. Comparison." *Journal of Japan and International Economies* 6 (December): 312–46.

———. 1995. *Economic Growth.* New York: McGraw Hill.

Becker, Gary S. 1957. *The Economics of Discrimination.* Chicago: University of Chicago Press.

———. 1965. "A Theory of the Allocation of Time." *Economic Journal* 75, no. 299 (September): 493–517. Reprinted in Gary S. Becker, ed. *The Economic Approach to Human Behavior.* Chicago: University of Chicago Press.

———. 1971. *The Economics of Discrimination.* 2d ed. Chicago: University of Chicago Press.

———. 1974. "A Theory of Social Interactions." *Journal of Political Economy* 82, no. 6 (November): 1063–93.

———. 1975. *Human Capital.* 2d ed. Chicago: University of Chicago Press.

———. 1976. "The Economic Approach to Human Behavior." In Gary S. Becker, ed. *The Economic Approach to Human Behavior,* pp. 3–14. Chicago: University of Chicago Press.

———. 1991. *A Treatise on the Family.* Cambridge, MA: Harvard University Press.

———. 1996. *Accounting for Tastes.* Cambridge, MA: Harvard University Press.

Becker, Gary S., and Robert J. Barro. 1988. "A Reformulation of the Economic Theory of Fertility." *Quarterly Journal of Economics* 103, no. 1 (February): 1–25.

Becker, Gary S., and Casey B. Mulligan. 1997. "The Endogenous Determination of Time Preference." Forthcoming, *Quarterly Journal of Economics.*

Becker, Gary S., and Kevin M. Murphy. 1993. "A Simple Theory of Advertising as a Good or Bad." *Quarterly Journal of Economics* 108, no. 4 (November): 941–64.

Becker, Gary S., and Nigel Tomes. 1979. "An Equilibrium Theory of the Distribution of Income and Intergenerational Mobility." *Journal of Political Economy* 87, no. 6 (December): 1153–89.

———. 1986. "Human Capital and the Rise and Fall of Families." *Journal of Labor Economics* 4, no. 3 (July): S1–S39. Reprinted as the Supplement to Chapter 7 in Gary S. Becker, ed. *A Treatise on the Family.* Cambridge, MA: Harvard University Press, 1991.

Behrman, Jere R. 1987a. "Is Child Schooling a Poor Proxy for Child Quality?" *Demography* 24, no. 3 (August): 341–59.

———. 1987b. "Schooling and Other Human Capital Investments: Can the Effects Be Identified?" *Economics of Education Review* 6, no. 3: 301–5.

Behrman, Jere R., Z. Hrubec, Paul Taubman, and Terence J. Wales. 1980. *Socioeconomic Success: A Study of the Effects of Genetic Endowments, Family Environment, and Schooling.* Amsterdam: North-Holland Pub. Co.

Behrman, Jere R., and Paul Taubman. 1985. "Intergenerational Earnings and Mobility in the United States: Some Estimates and a Test of Becker's Intergenerational Endowments Model." *Review of Economics and Statistics* 67, no. 1 (February): 144–51.

———. 1990. "The Intergenerational Correlation between Children's Adult Income and Their Parent's Income: Results from the Michigan Panel Survey of Income Dynamics." *Review of Income and Wealth* 36, no. 2 (June): 115–27.

Behrman, Jere R., Robert A. Pollak, and Paul Taubman. 1989. "Family Resources, Family Size, and Access to Financing for College Education." *Journal of Political Economy* 97, no. 2 (April): 398–419.

———. 1995. "The Wealth Model: Efficiency and Distribution in the Family." In Jere R. Behrman, Robert A. Pollak, and Paul Taubman, eds. *From Parent to Child,* pp. 113–38. Chicago: University of Chicago Press.

Bénabou, Roland. 1994. "Human Capital, Inequality, and Growth: A Local Perspective." *European Economic Review* 38, nos. 3–4 (April): 817–26.

Bendix, Reinhard, and Seymour Martin Lipset, eds. 1966. *Class, Status, and Power.* 2d ed. New York: Free Press.

Ben Porath, Yoram. 1967. "The Production of Human Capital and the Life Cycle of Earnings." *Journal of Political Economy* 75, no. 4 (August): 352–65.

Bernheim, B. Douglas. 1986. "On the Voluntary and Involuntary Provision of Public Goods." *American Economic Review* 76, no. 4 (September): 789–93.

Bernheim, B. Douglas, and Kyle Bagwell. 1988. *Journal of Political Economy* 96, no. 2 (April): 308–38.

Bernheim, B. Douglas, Andrei Shleifer, and Lawrence H. Summers. 1985. "The Strategic Bequest Motive." *Journal of Political Economy* 93, no. 6 (December): 1045–76.

Björklund, Anders, and Markus Jantti. 1993. "Intergenerational Income Mobility in Sweden Compared to the United States." Working paper, Swedish Institute for Social Research, September.

Blau, Peter M., and Otis D. Duncan. 1967. *The American Occupational Structure.* New York: Wiley.

Blinder, Alan S. 1974. *Toward a Theory of Income Distribution.* Cambridge, MA: The MIT Press.

———. 1980. "The Level and Distribution of Economic Well-Being." In Martin Feldstein, ed. *The American Economy in Transition,* pp. 415–79. Chicago: University of Chicago Press.

Boorman, Scott A., and Paul R. Levitt. 1980. *The Genetics of Altruism.* New York: Academic Press.

Borjas, George J. 1992. "Ethnic Capital and Intergenerational Mobility." *Quarterly Journal of Economics* 107, no. 1 (February): 123–50.

———. 1994. "Long-run Convergence of Ethnic Skill Differentials: The Children and Grandchildren of the Great Migration." *Industrial & Labor Relations Review* 47, no. 4 (July): 553–73.

Brown, Roger. 1986. *Social Psychology.* 2d ed. New York: Free Press, 1986.

Cameron, Stephen V., and James J. Heckman. 1996. "The Dynamics of Educational Attainment for Blacks, Hispanics, and Whites." Working paper, Columbia University, December.

Card, David, and Thomas Lemieux. 1994. "Changing Wage Structure and Black-White Wage Differentials." *American Economic Review* 84, no. 2 (May): 29–33.

Cashin, Paul. 1995. "Government Spending, Taxes, and Economic Growth." *International Monetary Fund Staff Papers* 42, no. 2 (June): 237–69.

Chiswick, Barry R., and Jacob Mincer. 1972. "Time Series Changes in Personal Income Inequality in the United States from 1939, with Projections to 1985." *Journal of Political Economy* 80, no. 3, Part II (May–June): 534–66.

Chu, C. Y. Cyrus. 1991. "Primogeniture." *Journal of Political Economy* 99, no. 1 (February): 78–99.

Clotfelter, Charles T. 1985. *Federal Tax Policy and Charitable Giving.* Chicago: University of Chicago Press for the National Bureau of Economic Research.

Conlisk, John. 1974. "Can Equalization of Opportunity Reduce Social Mobility?" *American Economic Review* 64, no. 1 (March): 80–90.

Cooper, Suzanne J., Steven N. Durlauf, and Paul A. Johnson. 1994. "On the Evolution of Economic Status Across Generations." *American Statistical Association Papers and Proceedings* 1994: 50–58.

Couch, Kenneth A., and Thomas A. Dunn. 1995. "Intergenerational Correlations in Labor Market Status: A Comparison of the United States and Germany." Working paper, Syracuse University, May.

Cox, Donald. 1987. "Motives for Private Income Transfers." *Journal of Political Economy* 95, no. 3 (June): 508–46.

Cox, Donald, and Mark R. Rank. 1992. "Inter-vivos Transfers and Intergenerational Exchange." *Review of Economics and Statistics* 74, no. 2 (May): 305–14.

Crimmins, Eileen M., Richard A. Easterlin, and Yasuhiko Saito. 1991. "Preference Changes among American Youth: Family, Work, and Goods Aspirations, 1976–86." *Population and Development Review* 17, no. 1 (March): 115–33.

Cutler, David M., and Lawrence F. Katz. 1992. "Rising Inequality? Changes in the Distribution of Income and Consumption in the 1980's." *American Economic Review* 82, no. 2 (May): 546–51.

Daly, Martin, and Margo Wilson. 1988. *Homicide.* New York: Aldine de Gruyter.

Debreu, Gerard. 1959. *Theory of Value: An Axiomatic Analysis of Economic Equilibrium.* New Haven: Yale University Press.

Durlauf, Steven N. 1996. "A Theory of Persistent Income Inequality." *Journal of Economic Growth* 1, no. 1 (March): 75–94.

Easterlin, Richard A. 1995. "Preferences and Prices in Choice of Career: The Switch to Business, 1972–87." *Journal of Economic Behavior and Organization* 27, no. 1 (June): 1–34.

Edgeworth, F. Y. 1932 [1881]. *Mathematical Psychics.* London: C. Kegan Paul and Co.

Epstein, Larry G. 1987. "The Global Stability of Efficient Intertemporal Allocations." *Econometrica* 55, no. 2 (March): 329–55.

Featherman, David L., and Robert M. Hauser. 1978. *Opportunity and Change.* New York: Academic Press.

Feldstein, Martin S. 1974. "Social Security, Induced Retirement, and Aggregate Capital Accumulation." *Journal of Political Economy* 82, no. 5 (October): 905–26.

Feldstein, Martin, and Charles Horioka. 1980. "Domestic Saving and International Capital Flows." *Economic Journal* 90, no. 358 (June): 314–29.

Fisher, Irving. 1930. *The Theory of Interest.* New York: Macmillan.
Fox, Thomas, and S. M. Miller. 1965. "Occupational Stratification and Mobility: Intra-country Variations." *Studies in Comparative International Development* 1, no. 1: 3–10. Reprinted in Reinhard Bendix and Seymour Martin Lipset, eds. *Class, Status, and Power.* 2d ed. New York: Free Press, 1966.
Freeman, Richard B. 1981. "Black Economic Progress after 1964: Who Has Gained and Why?" In Sherwin Rosen, ed. *Studies in Labor Markets,* pp. 247–94. Chicago: University of Chicago Press.
Friedman, Milton. 1957. *A Theory of the Consumption Function.* Princeton, NJ: Princeton University Press.
———. 1976. *Price Theory: A Provisional Text.* New York: Aldine de Gruyter.
———. 1992. "Do Old Fallacies Ever Die?" *Journal of Economic Literature* 30, no. 4 (December): 2129–32.
Fudenberg, Drew, and Jean Tirole. 1991. *Game Theory.* Cambridge, MA: The MIT Press.
Gallman, Robert E. 1969. "Trends in the Size Distribution of Wealth in the Nineteenth Century: Some Speculations." In Lee Soltow, ed. *Six Papers on the Size Distribution of Wealth and Income,* pp. 105–52. New York: Columbia University Press for the National Bureau of Economic Research.
Galton, Francis. 1869. *Hereditary Genius: An Inquiry into Its Laws and Consequences.* London: Macmillan.
———. 1889. *Natural Inheritance.* London: Macmillan.
Gintis, Herbert. 1974. "Welfare Criteria with Endogenous Preferences: The Economics of Education." *International Economic Review* 15, no. 2 (June): 415–30.
Glomm, Gerhard, and B. Ravikumar. 1992. "Public vs. Private Investment in Human Capital: Endogenous Growth and Income Inequality." *Journal of Political Economy* 100, no. 4 (August): 818–34.
Goldberger, Arthur S. 1979. "Heritability." *Economica* 46, no. 184: 327–47.
———. 1989. "Economic and Mechanical Models of Intergenerational Transmission." *American Economic Review* 79, no. 3 (June): 504–13.
Goldin, Claudia, and Lawrence F. Katz. 1995. "The Decline of Non-Competing Groups: Changes in the Premium to Education, 1890 to 1940." National Bureau of Economic Research Working Paper No. 5202, August 1995.
Goldin, Claudia, and Robert A. Margo. 1992. "The Great Compression: The Wage Structure in the United States at Mid- Century." *Quarterly Journal of Economics* 107, no. 1 (February): 1–34.
Goode, William J. 1966. "Family and Mobility." In Reinhard Bendix and Seymour Martin Lipset, eds. *Class, Status, and Power,* pp. 582–601. 2d ed. New York: Free Press.
Gould, Stephen Jay. 1977. *Ever Since Darwin.* New York: W. W. Norton and Company.
———. 1992. "The Confusion over Evolution." *New York Review of Books* 39, no. 19 (November 19): 46–53.
Haig, David. 1993. "Genetic Conflicts in Human Pregnancy." *The Quarterly Review of Biology* 68, no. 4 (December): 495–532.
Han, Song, and Casey B. Mulligan. 1997. "Human Capital, Heterogeneity, and

the Estimation of Degrees of Intergenerational Mobility." Discussion Paper no. 97–3. University of Chicago Population Research Center, March.

Hansen, Lars Peter. 1982. "Large Sample Properties of Generalized Method of Moments Estimators." *Econometrica* 50: 1029–54.

Hansson, Ingemar, and Charles Stuart. 1990. "Malthusian Selection of Preferences." *American Economic Review* 80, no. 3 (June): 529–44.

Harbury, C. D., and D. M. W. N. Hitchens. 1979. *Inheritance and Wealth Inequality in Britain.* London: George Allen & Unwin.

Hauser, Robert M., William H. Sewell, and Kenneth G. Lutterman. 1975. "Socioeconomic Background, Ability, and Achievement." In William H. Sewell and Robert M. Hauser, eds. *Education, Occupation, and Earnings.* New York: Academic Press.

Heckman, James J. 1976. "The Common Structure of Statistical Models of Truncation, Sample Selection and Limited Dependent Variables and a Simple Estimator for Such Models." *Annals of Economic and Social Measurement* 5: 475–92.

Hewlett, Barry. 1992. *Father-child Relations: Cultural and Biosocial Contexts.* Hawthorne, NY: Aldine De Gruyter.

Hill, Martha S. 1992. *The Panel Study of Income Dynamics: A User's Guide.* London: Sage Publications.

Hirshleifer, Jack. 1977. "Economics from a Biological Viewpoint." *Journal of Law and Economics* 20, no. 1 (April): 1–52.

Holmstrom, Bengt, and Paul Milgrom. 1994. "The Firm as an Incentive System." *American Economic Review* 84, no. 4 (September): 972–91.

Hoynes, Hilary Williamson. 1995. "Does Welfare Play Any Role in Female Headship Decisions?" National Bureau of Economic Research Working Paper No. 5149, June.

Hume, David. 1878. *A Treatise on Human Nature.* Volume 2. London: Longmans Green and Co.

Isaac, R. Mark, James M. Walker, and Arlington W. Williams. 1994. "Group Size and the Voluntary Provision of Public Goods." *Journal of Public Economics* 54, no. 1 (May): 1–36.

Jensen, Michael C., and Kevin J. Murphy. 1990. "Performance Pay and Top-Management Incentives." *Journal of Political Economy* 98, no. 2 (April): 225–64.

Kearl, James R., and Clayne L. Pope. 1986. "Unobservable Family and Individual Contributions to the Distributions of Income and Wealth." *Journal of Labor Economics* 4, no. 3, Part 2 (July): S48–79.

Kimball, Miles. 1987. "Making Sense of Two-Sided Altruism." *Journal of Monetary Economics* 20, no. 2: 301–26.

Koopmans, Tjalling C. 1960. "Stationary Ordinal Utility and Impatience." *Econometrica* 28: 287–309.

Kotlikoff, Laurence J., and Lawrence H. Summers. 1981. "The Role of Intergenerational Transfers in Aggregate Capital Accumulation." *Journal of Political Economy* 89, no. 4 (August): 706–32.

Kremer, Michael. 1996. "How Much Does Sorting Increase Inequality?" Working paper, Massachusetts Institute of Technology Department of Economics, March.

Laitner, John. 1992. "Random Earnings Differences, Lifetime Liquidity Constraints, and Altruistic Intergenerational Transfers." *Journal of Economic Theory* 58, no. 2 (December): 135–70.

Lam, David, and Robert F. Schoeni. 1993. "Effects of Family Background on Earnings and Returns to Schooling: Evidence from Brazil." *Journal of Political Economy* 101, no. 4 (August): 710–40.

———. 1994. "Family Ties and Labor Markets in the United States and Brazil." *Journal of Human Resources* 29, no. 4 (Fall): 1235–58.

Lancaster, Kelvin J. 1966. "A New Approach to Consumer Theory." *Journal of Political Economy* 74, no. 2 (April): 132–57.

Lazear, Edward P., and Robert T. Michael. 1988. *Allocation of Income within the Household.* Chicago: University of Chicago Press.

Levy, Frank, and Richard J. Murnane. 1992. "U.S. Earnings Levels and Earnings Inequality: A Review of Recent Trends and Proposed Explanations." *Journal of Economic Literature* 30, no. 2 (September): 1333–81.

Lillard, Lee A., and Robert J. Willis. 1994. "Intergenerational Educational Mobility: Effects of Family and State in Malaysia." *Journal of Human Resources* 29, no. 4 (Fall): 1126–66.

Lindert, Peter H. 1977. "Sibling Position and Achievement." *Journal of Human Resources* 12 (Spring): 198–219.

———. 1986. "Unequal English Wealth Since 1670." *Journal of Political Economy* 94, no. 6 (December): 1127–62.

Lipset, Seymour Martin, and Hans L. Zetterberg. 1956. "A Theory of Social Mobility." *Transactions of the Third World Congress of Sociology.* Volume 2, 1956: 155–77. Reprinted in Reinhard Bendix and Seymour Martin Lipset, eds. *Class, Status, and Power.* 2d ed. New York: Free Press, 1966.

Loury, Glenn C. 1981. "Intergenerational Transfers and the Distribution of Earnings." *Econometrica* 49, no. 4 (June): 843–67.

Lucas, Robert E., Jr. 1988. "On the Mechanics of Economic Development." *Journal of Monetary Economics* 22, no. 1 (July): 3–42.

Lucas, Robert E., Jr., and Nancy L. Stokey. 1984. "Optimal Growth with Many Consumers." *Journal of Economic Theory* 32, no. 1 (February): 139–71.

McFadden, Daniel. 1982. "Econometric Models of Probabilistic Choice." In Charles Manski and Daniel McFadden, eds. *Structural Analysis of Discrete Data: With Econometric Applications,* pp. 115–33. Cambridge, MA: The MIT Press.

McNulty, John K. 1994. *Federal Estate and Gift Taxation in a Nutshell.* St. Paul, MN: West Publishing Co.

Mankiw, N. Gregory, David Romer, and David N. Weil. 1992. "A Contribution to the Empirics of Economic Growth." *Quarterly Journal of Economics* 107, no. 2 (May): 407–37.

Margo, Robert A., and George G. Villaflor. 1985. "The Antebellum 'Surge' in Skill Differentials One More Time: New Evidence." National Bureau of Economic Research Working Paper No. 1758, November 1985.

Margolis, Howard. 1982. *Selfishness, Altruism, and Rationality.* Chicago: University of Chicago Press.

Menchik, Paul L. 1979. "Inter-generational Transmission of Inequality: An Empirical Study of Wealth Mobility." *Economica* 46, no. 184 (November): 349–62.

———. 1980. "Primogeniture, Equal Sharing, and the U.S. Distribution of Wealth." *Quarterly Journal of Economics* 94, no. 2 (March): 299–316.

———. 1988. "Unequal Estate Division: Is It Altruism, Reverse Bequest, or Simply Noise?" In Denis Kessler and Andre Masson, eds. *Modelling the Accumulation and Distribution of Wealth,* pp. 105–19. Oxford: Oxford University Press.

Michael, Robert T., Victor R. Fuchs, and Sharon R. Scott. 1980. "Changes in the Propensity to Live Alone: 1950–1976." *Demography* 17, no. 1 (February): 39–56.

Moffitt, Robert. 1994. "Welfare Effects on Female Headship with Area Effects." *Journal of Human Resources* 29, no. 2 (Spring): 621–36.

Mueller, Dennis C. 1989. *Public Choice II.* New York: Cambridge University Press.

Mulligan, Casey B. 1993. "On Intergenerational Altruism, Fertility, and the Persistence of Economic Status." Ph.D. diss., Department of Economics, University of Chicago, August.

———. 1995a. "Pecuniary and Nonpecuniary Incentives to Work in the U.S. during World War II." University of Chicago, Population Research Center Discussion Paper Series #95-3, February.

———. 1995b. "Economic and Biological Approaches to Inheritance: Some Evidence." University of Chicago, Population Research Center Discussion Paper Series #95-14, November.

———. 1996a. "Work Ethic and Family Background." A Report prepared for the Employment Policies Institute. June 1, 1996.

———. 1996b. "Galton vs. the Human Capital Approach to Inheritance: Some Evidence." Working paper, University of Chicago Department of Economics, July.

Navarro-Zermeno, Jesus Ignacio. 1993. "A Model of Bequests and Intergenerational Mobility." Ph.D. diss., Department of Economics, University of Chicago, August.

Neal, Derek A., and William R. Johnson. 1996. "The Role of Premarket Factors in Black-White Wage Differences." *Journal of Political Economy* 104, no. 5 (October): 869–95.

Nelson, Derek. 1995. *The Posters that Won the War.* Osceola, WI: Motorbooks International.

Olneck, Michael. 1977. "On the Use of Sibling Data to Estimate the Effects of Family Background, Cognitive Skills, and Schooling: Results from the Kalamazoo Brothers Study." In Paul Taubman, ed. *Kinometrics: Determinants of Socioeconomic Success within and between Families,* pp. 244–64. Amsterdam: North-Holland Publishing Company.

Peters, H. Elizabeth. 1992. "Patterns of Intergenerational Mobility in Income and Earnings." *Review of Economics and Statistics* 74, no. 3 (August): 456–66.

Pitt, Mark M., and Mark R. Rosenzweig. 1990. "Estimating the Intrahousehold Incidence of Illness: Child Health and Gender-Inequality in the Allocation of Time." *International Economic Review* 31, no. 4 (November): 969–80.

Pollak, Robert A. 1970. "Habit Formation and Dynamic Demand Functions." *Journal of Political Economy* 78, no. 4, Part I (July–August): 745–63.

Rae, John. 1902. "Letters of Rae (1796–1872) to Mill on the Malthusian Doctrine of Population." Reprinted by Charles Whitney Mixter. *Economic Journal* 12 (March).

———. 1905 [1834]. *The Sociological Theory of Capital.* London: Macmillan.

Romer, Paul M. 1986. "Increasing Returns and Long Run Growth." *Journal of Political Economy* 94, no. 5 (October): 1002–37.

———. 1987. "Growth Based on Increasing Returns Due to Specialization." *American Economic Review* 77, no. 2 (May): 56–62.

Rosenzweig, Mark R. 1995. "Welfare, Marital Prospects and Nonmarital Childbearing." Paper presented at a Symposium on the Economic Analysis of Social Behavior, December 1.

Rosenzweig, Mark R., and T. Paul Schultz. 1982. "Market Opportunities, Genetic Endowments, and Intrafamily Resource Distribution: Child Survival in Rural India." *American Economic Review* 72, no. 4 (September): 803–15.

Rotemberg, Julio. 1994. "Human Relations in the Workplace." *Journal of Political Economy* 102, no. 4 (August): 684–717.

Quah, Danny. 1993. "Galton's Fallacy and Tests of the Convergence Hypothesis." *Scandinavian Journal of Economics* 95, no. 4 (December): 427–43.

Sala-i-Martin, Xavier. 1990. "On Growth and States." Ph.D. diss., Department of Economics, Harvard University.

———. 1996. "A Positive Theory of Social Security." *Journal of Economic Growth* 1, no. 2 (June): 277–304.

Sally, David. 1995. "Sympathy and Reason." Ph.D. diss., University of Chicago Graduate School of Business, December.

Schram, A., and F. van Winden. 1991. "Why People Vote: Free Riding and the Production and Consumption of Social Pressure." *Journal of Economic Psychology* 12, no. 4 (December): 575–620.

Schultz, T. Paul. 1982. "Family Composition and Income Inequality." *Population and Development Review* 8, Supplement: 137–50.

———. 1994. "Marital Status and Fertility in the United States." *Journal of Human Resources* 29, no. 2 (Spring): 637–69.

Simon, Julian L. 1974. *The Effects of Income Upon Fertility.* Chapel Hill, NC: Carolina Population Center.

———. 1977. *The Economics of Population Growth.* Princeton, NJ: Princeton University Press.

Skinner, Jonathan. 1987. "A Superior Measure of Consumption from the Panel Study of Income Dynamics." *Economics Letters* 23, no. 2: 213–16.

Slesnick, Daniel T. 1994. "Consumption, Needs and Inequality." *International Economic Review* 35, no. 3 (August): 677–703.

Smith, Adam. 1981 [1776]. *An Inquiry into the Nature and Causes of the Wealth of Nations.* Indianapolis, IN: Liberty Classics.

———. 1982 [1790]. *The Theory of Moral Sentiments.* Indianapolis, IN: Liberty Classics.

Smith, James P., and Finis R. Welch. 1986. "Closing the Gap: Forty Years of Economic Progress for Blacks." Published by Rand, February, 1986.

Solon, Gary. 1992. "Intergenerational Income Mobility in the United States." *American Economic Review* 82, no. 3 (June): 393–408.

Soltow, Lee. 1965. *Toward Income Inequality in Norway.* Madison: University of Wisconsin Press.

———. 1984. "Wealth Inequality in the United States in 1798 and 1860." *Review of Economics and Statistics* 66, no. 3 (August): 444–51.

Spence, Michael, and Richard Zeckhauser. 1971. "Insurance, Information, and Individual Action." *American Economic Review* 61, no. 2 (May): 380–87.

STATA Corporation. 1994. *STATA 3.1 Reference Manual.* Volume 2.

Stigler, George G., and Gary S. Becker. 1977. "De Gustibus Non Est Disputandum." *American Economic Review* 67, no. 2 (March): 76–90.

Stigler, Stephen M. 1986. *The History of Statistics: The Measurement of Uncertainty before 1900.* Cambridge, MA: Harvard University Press.

Stokey, Nancy L., and Robert E. Lucas, Jr. 1989. *Recursive Methods in Economic Dynamics.* Cambridge, MA: Harvard University Press.

Summers, Robert, and Alan Heston. 1991. "The Penn World Table (Mark 5): An Expanded Set of International Comparisons, 1950–1988." *Quarterly Journal of Economics* 106, no. 2 (May): 327–68.

Tamura, Robert. 1991. "Income Convergence in an Endogenous Growth Model." *Journal of Political Economy* 99, no. 3 (June): 522–40.

Tomes, Nigel. 1979. "Uncertain Lifetimes, Imperfect Capital Markets and the Altruistic Motive for Bequests." Research Report No. 7930, Department of Economics, University of Western Ontario, October.

———. 1980. "The Family, Inheritance, and the Intergenerational Transmission of Inequality." University of Western Ontario Research Report No. 8001, January.

———. 1981. "The Family, Inheritance, and the Intergenerational Transmission of Inequality." *Journal of Political Economy* 89, no. 5 (October): 928–58.

United States Council of Economic Advisers. 1992. *Economic Report of the President.* Washington, DC: U.S. Government Printing Office, February.

United States Department of Commerce, Bureau of the Census. 1975. *Historical Statistics of the United States, Colonial Times to 1970.* Bicentennial edition. Washington, DC: U.S. Dept. of Commerce, Bureau of the Census.

United States Department of the Treasury, Internal Revenue Service. 1995a. "Introduction to Estate and Gift Taxes." IRS Publication 950, January 19.

United States Department of the Treasury, Internal Revenue Service. 1995b. *United States Estate (and Generation-Skipping Transfer) Tax Return.* (IRS Form 706 expiring 12-31-95). Washington, DC: Office of Management and Budget.

United States Department of the Treasury, Internal Revenue Service. 1995c. *Instructions for Form 706.* Washington, DC: Office of Management and Budget.

United States House of Representatives, Committee on Ways and Means. 1994. *Background Material and Data on Major Programs within the Jurisdiction of the Committee on Ways and Means.* Washington, DC: Government Printing Office.

United States Social Security Administration. 1995. *Social Security Programs Throughout the World.* Washington, DC: Government Printing Office.

Uzawa, H. 1968. "Time Preference, the Consumption Function, and Optimum Asset Holdings." In J. N. Wolfe, ed. *Value, Capital, and Growth: Papers in Honour of Sir John Hicks.* Edinburgh, Scotland: University of Edinburgh Press.

Wahl, Jenny Bourne. 1985. "Fertility in America: Historical Patterns and Wealth Effects on the Quantity and Quality of Children." Ph.D. diss., Department of Economics, University of Chicago, December.

Weiss, Yoram, and Robert J. Willis. 1985. "Children as Collective Goods and Divorce Settlements." *Journal of Labor Economics* 3, no. 3 (July): 268–92.

Wilhelm, Mark. 1990. "Determinants of Inheritance, Heterogeneous Bequests and Inequality." Ph.D. diss., Department of Economics, New York University.

Williamson, Jeffrey G., and Peter H. Lindert. 1980. *American Inequality: A Macroeconomic History.* New York: Academic Press.

Wolff, Edward N. 1992. "Changing Inequality of Wealth." *American Economic Review* 82, no. 2 (May): 552–58.

Wolff, P. de, and A. R. D. van Slijpe. 1973. "The Relation between Income, Intelligence, Education, and Social Background." *European Economic Review* 4, no. 3: 235–64.

Zimmerman, David J. 1992. "Regression Toward Mediocrity in Economic Stature." *American Economic Review* 82, no. 3 (June): 409–29.

Index

Boldface page citations refer to figures and tables in the text.